Introduction to Distributed-Parameter Networks

With Application to Integrated Circuits

Holt, Rinehart and Winston Series in Electrical Engineering, Electronics, and Systems

CONSULTING EDITORS

Micheal Athans, *Massachusetts Institute of Technology*
Benjamin Leon, *Purdue University*
Robert Pritchard, *Stanford University*

Other Books in the Series:

George R. Cooper and Clare D. McGillem,
Methods of Signal and System Analysis
Samuel Seely, *Electronic Circuits*

Introduction to Distributed-Parameter Networks

With Application to Integrated Circuits

MOHAMMED S. GHAUSI

Professor of Electrical Engineering
New York University

JOHN J. KELLY

Senior Systems Engineer
Norden Division of United Aircraft Corporation

HOLT, RINEHART AND WINSTON, INC.
New York Chicago San Francisco Atlanta
Dallas Montreal Toronto London

Library of Congress Catalog Card Number: 68–13966
2676401
Printed in the United States of America
1 2 3 4 5 6 7 8 9

Preface

This book covers introductory topics in the analysis and synthesis of distributed-parameter networks. These networks include the uniform and nonuniform lossy and lossless transmission lines. Distributed *RC* networks are considered in a greater detail because of their occurrence in the integrated circuit technology. These circuits are exemplified by thin-film or integrated circuits made of *pn* junctions. We have considered carefully and in detail the properties and solutions of distributed *LC* and *RC* networks from the viewpoint of two-port network theory. A full understanding of this material is very helpful in efficient design of linear molecular circuits. The text is written from the circuit theorist viewpoint and in sufficient depth at an intermediate level.

The material presented is illustrated by many examples and accompanied by problems which conclude each chapter. These will help the reader to grasp the subject matter and enable him to apply the theory in practical design problems. The material covered is organized as follows:

The first chapter introduces the reader to distributed-parameter systems—mainly uniform four-parameter *RLCG* transmission lines and passive integrated circuits. The approximation of distributed structures by iterated lumped structures is illustrated. The treatment in the first chapter is somewhat different from the conventional treatment of distributed structures in that the pole-zero approach is emphasized. This approach is further carried over in the succeeding chapters.

Chapter 2 is concerned with a careful treatment of two-port parameters of a nonuniformly distributed network. Nonuniform transmission lines are also covered in some detail in this chapter since the reader is assumed not to be familiar with this topic. Here we have introduced the method of defining the two-port immittances in terms of the basic-set solutions of the transmission-line equations. In particular, we show how to obtain these solutions for tapered networks in infinite series and product forms. We introduce the reader to the Picard-Carson method for series solution and to the Rayleigh principle for finding the poles and zeros of two-port immittance. Many examples illustrating these procedures are given.

Chapter 3 deals with the transient and frequency response of distributed networks. Conventional transform methods for the step response in terms of residues are discussed, as are alternative techniques, such as Elmore's method and the method of excess phase and equivalent dominant pole. Error criteria for the latter method are also established. These methods are shown to be very simple and useful as illustrated in various examples. Some of the results as obtained by the simple methods discussed in this chapter are compared with the exact results.

Chapter 4 is a detailed discussion of closed-form solutions for tapered distributed networks and networks with equivalent electrical characteristics but with different electrical tapers. The reader is introduced to various techniques involving changes of variables in the network differential equation to simplify the solution of the network equation. These methods lead to classes of networks with equivalent characteristics. The final section of the chapter deals with a special type of distributed *RC* structure that approximates rational transfer functions. A number of tables are included, which summarize the immittance parameters of a variety of tapered networks.

In Chapter 5, the analysis is extended to cover combinations of lumped distributed networks. The main topic here is the generalization of the root-locus techniques and stability tests for distributed systems. It is shown how some of the conventional rules are to be modified so that the techniques are also applicable to distributed-parameter systems. The method is illustrated by determining the natural frequencies of distributed-parameter systems as well as systems with both lumped and distributed parameters. Active two-ports are included as well and it is shown how to determine the stability of such systems.

Chapter 6 discusses the synthesis of distributed networks. Since the book is at an intermediate level, no background in lumped synthesis is required. The network synthesis is mainly on distributed *RC* networks, since they are useful in integrated circuits. The realizability and synthesis of two-element lumped networks are first introduced. These are extended to distributed *RC* networks via frequency transformations. Transfer-function synthesis procedures utilizing active device and one-port lumped *RC* networks are first reviewed; they are then extended to the realization of active-distributed *RC* transfer functions. The realization of transfer functions that are quite general in that poles and zeros can lie anywhere in the transformed plane (subject to stability constraint) reduce to those of one-port $\overline{RC}$ synthesis.

In Chapter 7 we consider miscellaneous topics not covered in the other chapters. Some of these topics are somewhat specialized and the problems associated with them are not yet completely solved. They are introduced here merely to familiarize the reader with certain important practical problems. As an example it is shown that distinction should be made between the geometrical and electrical shapes in distributed *RC* networks.

A graphical procedure, based on the method of curvilinear squares, is introduced to show how certain tapered distributed *RC* structures may be realized physically. A section is also included dealing with multilayer $\overline{RC}$ networks.

Brief appendixes are also included, covering such topics as analogous physical systems, the Weierstrass factor theorem, infinite product expansion, summation of infinite series, and the Newton-Raphson iteration method for solving the roots of transcendental equations. Most of this material is found scattered throughout the mathematical literature. A detailed bibliography listing the papers on distributed networks and related topics is also included. In the book we have tried to present these topics at a consistent level so that the material covered is readily comprehended by the reader. The numerous problems at the end of each chapter should help the reader to gain a better understanding of the subject matter discussed in the text.

The book has been designed for seniors and first-year graduate students as well as for self-teaching by practicing research engineers. It has been purposely prepared in a concise form covering a limited number of important topics in order to permit the reader to grasp more readily the principles involved in the analysis and design of distributed-parameter networks.

The authors are indebted to many colleagues who helped make the writing of this book possible. In particular we mention Professors B. J. Leon, D. O. Pederson, C. F. Rehberg, and O. Wing for their comments and reviews. Special thanks are also due to George Hauck for his careful proofreading of the manuscript and compilation of the bibliography, and to Mrs. Kathleen McHugh for her typing of the entire manuscript during her "nonworking" hours. The authors also extend their deepest appreciation to their families for their understanding and for encouragement in this project.

Englewood, New Jersey MOHAMMED S. GHAUSI

Norwalk, Connecticut JOHN J. KELLY

February 1968

Contents

Preface *v*

Chapter 1—Uniformly Distributed Systems and Passive Integrated Circuits *1*

1-1 Introduction
1-2 Electrical Transmission Lines
1-3 Iterative Structure—Lumped-Parameter Approximation
1-4 Passive Linear Integrated Circuits

Chapter 2—Two-Port Parameters of Nonuniformly Distributed Networks *26*

2-1 Introduction
2-2 Nonuniformly Distributed Two-Ports
2-3 Two-Port Parameters of Distributed Networks
2-4 Short-Circuit Admittance Parameters
2-5 Obtaining Basic-Set Solutions
2-6 Product Expansions of the Basic Set
2-7 The Rayleigh Principle

Chapter 3—Transient and Frequency Response of Distributed-Parameter Networks *70*

3-1 Introduction
3-2 Transient Response of a General Uniform Transmission Line
3-3 Lossless Line and *RC* Distributed Network
3-4 Artificial *RC* Line—The Lumped-Parameter Approximation
3-5 Transient Response of a Tapered Distributed *RGC* Network
3-6 Examples of the Application of Elmore's Definitions
3-7 Bandwidth Calculation for Distributed *RC* Networks
3-8 The Equivalent Dominant-Pole and Excess-Phase Approximations
3-9 Examples of the Application of Equivalent Dominant-Pole and Excess-Phase Approximations
3-10 Numerical Inversion of the Laplace Transform

Chapter 4—Closed-Form Solutions and Equivalent Tapered Distributed Networks *114*

4-1 Introduction
4-2 Immittance Parameters of Some Tapered Distributed Networks
4-3 Equivalent Tapered Networks
4-4 Determination of Network Taper Functions
4-5 Distributed RC Networks with Rational Immittances

Chapter 5—The Root-Locus Technique and Stability of Active Lumped Distributed Networks *145*

5-1 Introduction
5-2 Natural Frequencies
5-3 Root-Locus Construction for Distributed-Parameter Networks
5-4 Representative Examples
5-5 Stability of Lumped Distributed Active Networks

Chapter 6—Synthesis of Distributed Networks *184*

6-1 Introduction
6-2 Realizability of Lumped Passive Driving-Point Functions

6-3 Synthesis of Two-Element One-Port Lumped Networks
6-4 Driving-Point Synthesis of Resistive Uniform-Transmission-Line Networks
6-5 Synthesis of Uniformly Distributed *RC* Driving-Point Functions
6-6 Cascade Synthesis of Uniformly Distributed *RC* Networks
6-7 Driving-Point Synthesis of Distributed *RC* Networks Based On O'Shea's Transformation
6-8 Transfer-Function Synthesis
6-9 Transfer Function Synthesis Using NIC and One-Port $\overline{RC}$ Networks
6-10 Transfer-Function Synthesis Using Two Grounded Voltage Amplifiers and One-Port $\overline{RC}$ Networks
6-11 Critique and the Approximation Problem

Chapter 7—Miscellaneous Topics *238*
7-1 Introduction
7-2 Boundary Effects in Distributed *RC* Structures
7-3 Approximation of Electrical Taper by a Geometric Shape
7-4 Multilayer Distributed *RC* Networks
7-5 Design Considerations for *RC* Networks

Appendix A—Analogous Physical Systems *283*

Appendix B—Factor Theorem of Weierstrass *287*

Appendix C—Some Useful Infinite-Product Expansions *291*

Appendix D—Summation of Infinite Series *294*

Appendix E—Finding the Roots of Transcendental Equations *302*

Bibliography *313*

Index *327*

Introduction to Distributed-Parameter Networks

With Application to Integrated Circuits

CHAPTER

1

Uniformly Distributed Systems and Passive Integrated Circuits

1-1 Introduction

A comprehensive theory for linear time-invariant lumped-parameter systems has been developed in many books. When transform methods are used, the problems of calculating the frequency and the transient responses, and the problem of determining the stability of the lumped time-invariant system reduce to the problem of solving a system of algebraic equations.

For a lumped element, the dimensions of the circuit are small compared to the wavelength associated with the highest frequency. A single lumped element with two terminals can be specified by a single spatially independent parameter. In an electric circuit, typical passive lumped elements are resistors, capacitors, inductors, transformers, and ideal gyrators. In a mechanical system, they are friction coefficient, stiffness, and mass. In a thermal system, they are thermal capacitance and thermal resistance.

The equilibrium equations of the lumped-parameter systems can be represented by ordinary linear differential equations. However, all physical components cannot be treated as lumped. Systems such as electrical transmission lines, and some integrated circuits and processes such as thermal conduction in a rod, carrier motion in transistors, vibration of strings, and so on, are characterized by partial differential equations and distributed parameters are needed to describe mathematically their physical behavior. In such systems the spatial configuration plays an important role. The equilibrium equations of these systems are represented by partial differential equations.

In general, the solution of partial differential equations is inherently more difficult than the solution of ordinary differential equations with constant coefficients. This is one of the reasons a compact comprehensive theory is not available for distributed systems as it is for lumped-parameter time-invariant systems.

This book will not attempt such an ambitious venture as the development of a compact comprehensive theory for all types of distributed systems. In other words, we shall not concern ourselves with the solution of various types of linear partial differential equations in three dimensions. Instead, we will confine our discussion only to those systems where a one-dimensional spatial variation assumption is valid. Thus the independent variables in the partial differential equations that we shall consider are time and distance. (Fortunately a good number of physical systems belong to or can be adequately described by such partial differential equations.) Even for such systems, we do not plan to go into an exhaustive study but rather we shall develop basic techniques that are very useful in the analysis and design of distributed-parameter systems. We shall concern ourselves mainly with the finite distributed electrical systems such as distributed *LC* and distributed *RC* networks; however, the methods and techniques are applicable to other analogous physical systems. Some of these analogies are pointed out in Appendix A.

It should be emphasized at the outset that we shall often attempt to obtain approximate, simple, and practical methods of solution of the problems. As an example, for calculating frequency and transient response of some distributed circuits, methods are developed that can be performed by slide-rule manipulation and that are sufficiently accurate for most engineering purposes. Iterative methods of solution, suitable for machine computation, are also developed. Unlike the conventional approach to distributed-parameter systems, the techniques employed here make liberal use of poles and zeros of network functions which are familiar to students of lumped-parameter systems. Although the number of singularities of distributed systems is countably infinite, we develop methods that simplify the analysis and design by using the knowledge of pole-zero locations of the network function.

1-2 Electrical Transmission Lines

The electrical transmission line has been discussed thoroughly in the literature. Most electrical engineers are familiar with many of its properties, and thus it provides a good starting point for our study. Since the discussion of this section follows the standard approach found in most textbooks dealing with this topic,[1] we shall be brief in our exposition. Furthermore, the differential equations of a transmission line are analogous to those of many other physical systems, and therefore we shall derive the partial differential equations for the voltage and the current along a general finite transmission line.

Consider the network representation of a section of transmission line of length Δx, as shown in Figure 1-1. The incremental network representation is an approximation that becomes more accurate as $\Delta x \to 0$. The four distributed parameters characterizing the transmission line are the resistance, inductance, conductance, and capacitance, all given in per-unit-length form. When all of these parameters are constants the line is called a uniform transmission line or *RLCG* line. The dimensions of these parameters are as follows: r [ohms/meter], l [henries/meter], g [mhos/meter] and c [farads/meter]. We neglect here the higher-order effects of propagation through the system. In other words, we assume that the transmission system under consideration has a transmission line model. We have decided to concentrate on the fundamentals of distributed parameter systems for which the transmission line model

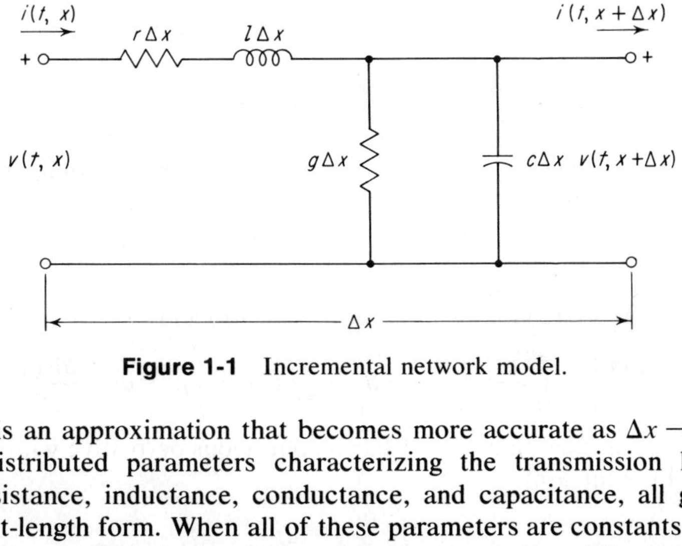

Figure 1-1 Incremental network model.

[1] See, for example, E. Weber, *Linear Transient Analysis* (New York, Wiley, 1956), Vol. 2.

is an adequate representation and does agree with experimental observations. We demonstrate the application of the pole-zero approach with analysis and synthesis of distributed networks. It should also be mentioned that the frequency range of interest in this book is under the microwave region, although the techniques described could be applied to microwave networks.

The equilibrium equations of the circuit, by Kirchhoff's voltage and current laws, are

$$v(t, x + \Delta x) - v(t, x) \approx -\Delta x \left[l \frac{\partial i(t, x)}{\partial t} + ri(t, x) \right] \tag{1-1a}$$

$$i(t, x + \Delta x) - i(t, x) \approx -\Delta x \left[c \frac{\partial v(t, x + \Delta x)}{\partial t} + gv(t, x + \Delta x) \right] \tag{1-1b}$$

By dividing (1-1) by Δx and taking the limit as $\Delta x \to 0$, we obtain the following partial differential equations:

$$\frac{\partial v(t, x)}{\partial x} = -l \frac{\partial i(t, x)}{\partial t} - ri(t, x) \tag{1-2a}$$

$$\frac{\partial i(t, x)}{\partial x} = -c \frac{\partial v(t, x)}{\partial t} - gv(t, x) \tag{1-2b}$$

Assuming that $v(t, x)$ and $i(t, x)$ possess a Laplace transform with respect to time, that is,[2]

$$V(s, x) = \mathscr{L}[v(t, x)] = \int_0^\infty v(t, x) \epsilon^{-st}\, dt \tag{1-3}$$

we can differentiate (1-3) with respect to x, to yield

$$\mathscr{L}\left[\frac{\partial v(t, x)}{\partial x}\right] = \int_0^\infty \frac{\partial v(t, x)}{\partial x} \epsilon^{-st}\, dt = \frac{\partial}{\partial x} \int_0^\infty v(t, x) \epsilon^{-st}\, dt = \frac{\partial V(s, x)}{\partial x} \tag{1-4}$$

where it is assumed that $v(t, x)$ has a continuous derivative with respect to x, and the integral

$$\int_0^\infty \frac{\partial v}{\partial x} \epsilon^{-st}\, dt$$

is uniformly convergent with respect to x. Known conditions at specific values of x are called *boundary conditions* and those with respect to t are referred to as *initial conditions*. If the initial conditions are assumed, for convenience, to be zero, the transform equation corresponding to (1-2a) is

$$\frac{\partial V(s, x)}{\partial x} = -(ls + r) I(s, x) \tag{1-5}$$

[2] G. Doetsch, *Guide to the Applications of Laplace Transform* (Princeton, N.J., Van Nostrand, 1961), Chap. 5.

Note further that since the derivative with respect to s does not appear in (1-5), this equation may be written as an ordinary differential equation:

$$\frac{d}{dx} V(s,x) = -(ls + r) I(s,x) \tag{1-6}$$

In an identical manner the current equation is obtained as

$$\frac{d}{dx} I(s,x) = -(cs + g) V(s,x) \tag{1-7}$$

Differentiating (1-6) with respect to x, when r, l, c, and g are not functions of x, gives

$$\frac{d^2}{dx^2} V(s,x) = -(ls + r) \frac{d}{dx} I(s,x) \tag{1-8}$$

For the uniform transmission line, substitution of (1-7) into (1-8) yields

$$\frac{d^2}{dx^2} V - (ls + r)(cs + g) V = 0 \tag{1-9a}$$

Similarly,

$$\frac{d^2 I}{dx^2} - (ls + r)(cs + g) I = 0 \tag{1-9b}$$

The solutions of the second-order, linear, homogeneous differential equations, (1-9a) and (1-9b), are known to be

$$V(s,x) = A_1 \cosh \Gamma x + A_2 \sinh \Gamma x \tag{1-10a}$$

$$I(s,x) = B_1 \cosh \Gamma x + B_2 \sinh \Gamma x \tag{1-10b}$$

where

$$\Gamma = \sqrt{(ls + r)(cs + g)} \tag{1-11}$$

Γ is usually referred to as the propagation function. The terms A_1, A_2, B_1, and B_2 are not functions of x and are determined from the boundary conditions. For a transmission line of finite length d, viewed as a two-port network, the boundary conditions at the input are $V(s,0)$, $I(s,0)$ and at the output are $V(s,d)$ and $I(s,d)$.[3]

---

[3] For an infinitely long line the traveling-wave solution is more appropriate than the standing-wave solution. The latter approach is usually used for a finite line and we use it in this book. For an infinitely long line the solution of $d^2V/dx^2 - \Gamma^2 V = 0$ is $V(s,x) = c_1\epsilon^{-\Gamma x} + c_2\epsilon^{\Gamma x}$. Since in an infinite line the propagation is in one direction only, the constant c_2 must be equal to zero. Thus $V(s,x) = V(s,0)\epsilon^{-\Gamma x}$ for infinite lines. Similarly, $I(s,x) = I(s,0)\epsilon^{-\Gamma x}$. The ratio $V(s,x)/I(s,x)$ is independent of the position and is a property of the transmission line. This ratio is found to be $\sqrt{(ls + r)/(cs + g)}$ and is called the characteristic impedance Z_0 of the uniform transmission line.

For nonuniform and finite transmission lines, the ratio $V(s,x)/I(s,x)$ is generally not a constant quantity. It is a function of position on the line and in this case a better nomenclature may be the "wave impedance."

From Equation (1-10), at $x = 0$,

$$A_1 = V(s, 0) \qquad B_1 = I(s, 0) \tag{1-12}$$

Differentiating (1-10a) and (1-10b) with respect to x, and employing (1-6) and (1-7), setting $x = 0$, we obtain

$$\begin{aligned} A_2 &= -\sqrt{\frac{ls + r}{cs + g}}\, I(s, 0) \qquad & B_2 &= -\sqrt{\frac{cs + g}{ls + r}}\, V(s, 0) \\ &= -Z_0 I(s, 0) & &= -\frac{V(s, 0)}{Z_0} \end{aligned} \tag{1-13}$$

where Z_0 is the characteristic impedance of the uniform line. Thus the input-output two-port description of the RLCG line is obtained from Equations (1-10), (1-12), and (1-13). Figure 1-2 shows a linear two-port

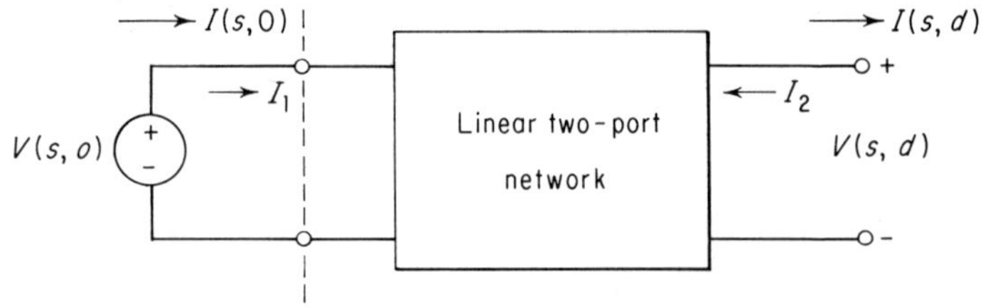

Figure 1-2

network with the standard two-port sign convention. For this case $V(s, 0)$ and $I(s, 0)$ correspond to the voltage and current, respectively, at port 1 (usually written as V_1, I_1); $V(s, d)$, $I(s, d)$ correspond to the voltage and current at port 2 (usually written as $V_2, -I_2$). For cascaded networks the $ABCD$ parameters are preferable. These parameters are defined by the matrix equation

$$\begin{bmatrix} V_1 \\ I_1 \end{bmatrix} = \begin{bmatrix} A & B \\ C & D \end{bmatrix} \begin{bmatrix} V_2 \\ -I_2 \end{bmatrix} \tag{1-14}$$

Note the negative sign in the definition of (1-14); see also Figure 1-2. Thus if two networks are cascaded as shown in Figure 1-3, the over-all $ABCD$ description is given by

$$\begin{bmatrix} V_1 \\ I_1 \end{bmatrix} = \begin{bmatrix} A^a & B^a \\ C^a & D^a \end{bmatrix} \begin{bmatrix} A^b & B^b \\ C^b & D^b \end{bmatrix} \begin{bmatrix} V_2 \\ -I_2 \end{bmatrix} = \begin{bmatrix} A & B \\ C & D \end{bmatrix} \begin{bmatrix} V_2 \\ -I_2 \end{bmatrix} \tag{1-15}$$

where

$$\begin{aligned} A &= A^a A^b + B^a C^b \qquad & B &= A^a B^b + B^a D^b \\ C &= C^a A^b + D^a C^b & D &= C^a B^b + D^a D^b \end{aligned}$$

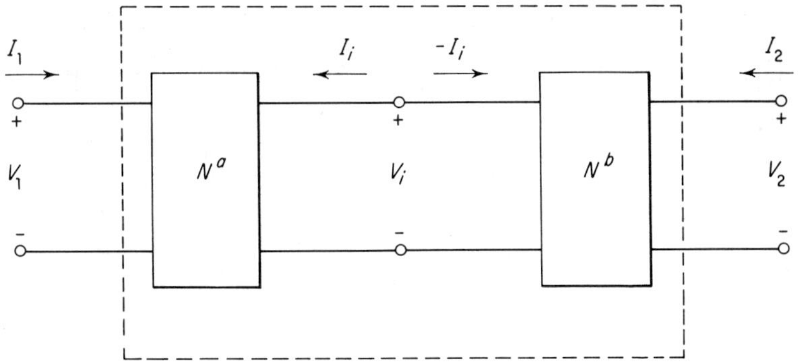

Figure 1-3

The chain parameters *ABCD* are defined in Table 1-1. Substituting Equations (1-12) and (1-13) into (1-10) immediately yields the $\mathscr{ABCD}$ parameters:

$$\begin{bmatrix} V(s,d) \\ -I(s,d) \end{bmatrix} = \begin{bmatrix} \cosh \Gamma d & Z_0 \sinh \Gamma d \\ \dfrac{\sinh \Gamma d}{Z_0} & \cosh \Gamma d \end{bmatrix} \begin{bmatrix} V(s,0) \\ -I(s,0) \end{bmatrix} \tag{1-16}$$

Once the $\mathscr{ABCD}$ parameters are known, as in (1-16), conversion to the open-circuit impedance parameters z_{ij}, short-circuit admittance parameters y_{ij}, and the mixed hybrid parameters g_{ij} and h_{ij} is very simple and straightforward.[4]

For convenience some of the two-port conversion formulas are given in Table 1-1.

The open-circuit and short-circuit two-port parameters of the uniform *RLCG* line are

$$[z_{ij}] = Z_0 \begin{bmatrix} \coth \Gamma d & \operatorname{csch} \Gamma d \\ \operatorname{csch} \Gamma d & \coth \Gamma d \end{bmatrix} \tag{1-17}$$

$$[y_{ij}] = \frac{1}{Z_0} \begin{bmatrix} \coth \Gamma d & -\operatorname{csch} \Gamma d \\ -\operatorname{csch} \Gamma d & \coth \Gamma d \end{bmatrix} \tag{1-18}$$

The pole-zero locations of the two-port parameters of the line may be placed into evidence by expanding the transcendental functions directly into the product form. This is permissible by the Weierstrass factor theorem (Appendix B). For convenience, a list of product expansions are also included in Appendix C; thus,

[4] M. S. Ghausi, *Principles and Design of Linear Active Circuits* (New York, McGraw-Hill, 1965), Chap. 3.

Table 1-1 CONVERSION OF TWO-PORT MATRIX PARAMETERS*

	$\begin{bmatrix} V_1 \\ V_2 \end{bmatrix} = \begin{bmatrix} z_{11} & z_{12} \\ z_{21} & z_{22} \end{bmatrix} \begin{bmatrix} I_1 \\ I_2 \end{bmatrix}$		$\begin{bmatrix} I_1 \\ I_2 \end{bmatrix} = \begin{bmatrix} y_{11} & y_{12} \\ y_{21} & y_{22} \end{bmatrix} \begin{bmatrix} V_1 \\ V_2 \end{bmatrix}$		$\begin{bmatrix} V_1 \\ I_1 \end{bmatrix} = \begin{bmatrix} A & B \\ C & D \end{bmatrix} \begin{bmatrix} V_2 \\ -I_2 \end{bmatrix}$		$\begin{bmatrix} V_2 \\ I_2 \end{bmatrix} = \begin{bmatrix} \mathcal{A} & \mathcal{B} \\ \mathcal{C} & \mathcal{D} \end{bmatrix} \begin{bmatrix} V_1 \\ -I_1 \end{bmatrix}$	
$[z_{ij}]$	z_{11}	z_{12}	$\frac{y_{22}}{\Delta_y}$	$-\frac{y_{12}}{\Delta_y}$	$\frac{A}{C}$	$\frac{\Delta_A}{C}$	$\frac{\mathcal{D}}{\mathcal{C}}$	$\frac{1}{\mathcal{C}}$
	z_{21}	z_{22}	$-\frac{y_{21}}{\Delta_y}$	$\frac{y_{11}}{\Delta_y}$	$\frac{1}{C}$	$\frac{D}{C}$	$\frac{\Delta_{\mathcal{A}}}{\mathcal{C}}$	$\frac{\mathcal{A}}{\mathcal{C}}$
$[y_{ij}]$	$\frac{z_{22}}{\Delta_z}$	$-\frac{z_{12}}{\Delta_z}$	y_{11}	y_{12}	$\frac{D}{B}$	$-\frac{\Delta_A}{B}$	$\frac{\mathcal{A}}{\mathcal{B}}$	$-\frac{1}{\mathcal{B}}$
	$-\frac{z_{21}}{\Delta_z}$	$\frac{z_{11}}{\Delta_z}$	y_{21}	y_{22}	$-\frac{1}{B}$	$\frac{A}{B}$	$-\frac{\Delta_{\mathcal{A}}}{\mathcal{B}}$	$\frac{\mathcal{D}}{\mathcal{B}}$
$\begin{bmatrix} A & B \\ C & D \end{bmatrix}$	$\frac{z_{11}}{z_{21}}$	$\frac{\Delta_z}{z_{21}}$	$-\frac{y_{22}}{y_{21}}$	$-\frac{1}{y_{21}}$	A	B	$\frac{\mathcal{D}}{\Delta_{\mathcal{A}}}$	$\frac{\mathcal{B}}{\Delta_{\mathcal{A}}}$
	$\frac{1}{z_{21}}$	$\frac{z_{22}}{z_{21}}$	$-\frac{\Delta_y}{y_{21}}$	$-\frac{y_{11}}{y_{21}}$	C	D	$\frac{\mathcal{C}}{\Delta_{\mathcal{A}}}$	$\frac{\mathcal{A}}{\Delta_{\mathcal{A}}}$
$\begin{bmatrix} \mathcal{A} & \mathcal{B} \\ \mathcal{C} & \mathcal{D} \end{bmatrix}$	$\frac{z_{22}}{z_{12}}$	$\frac{\Delta_z}{z_{12}}$	$-\frac{y_{11}}{y_{12}}$	$-\frac{1}{y_{12}}$	$\frac{D}{\Delta_A}$	$\frac{B}{\Delta_A}$	$\mathcal{A}$	$\mathcal{B}$
	$\frac{1}{z_{12}}$	$\frac{z_{11}}{z_{12}}$	$-\frac{\Delta_y}{y_{12}}$	$-\frac{y_{22}}{y_{12}}$	$\frac{C}{\Delta_A}$	$\frac{A}{\Delta_A}$	$\mathcal{C}$	$\mathcal{D}$

* All matrices appearing in the same row in the table are equivalent; for example, $z_{11} = A/C$. Δ is the matrix determinant; for example, $\Delta_z = z_{11}z_{22} - z_{12}z_{21}$. For a reciprocal network, $z_{12} = z_{21}$, and so forth. For a symmetrical network, $z_{11} = z_{22}$, and so forth.

$$\frac{\sinh \theta}{\theta} = \prod_{n=1}^{\infty} \left(1 + \frac{\theta^2}{n^2\pi^2}\right) \tag{1-19a}$$

$$\cosh \theta = \prod_{n=1}^{\infty} \left[1 + \frac{4\theta^2}{(2n-1)^2\pi^2}\right] \tag{1-19b}$$

Two special cases are of interest. If $r = 0$ and $g = 0$, the line is called a lossless transmission line or LC line. For convenience we shall sometimes write $\overline{ULC}$, which will designate a uniformly distributed LC network. For this case the short-circuit admittance parameters are

$$y_{11} = y_{22} = \sqrt{\frac{c}{l}} \coth sd\sqrt{lc} = \frac{1}{lds} \prod_{n=1}^{\infty} \frac{1 + \dfrac{4lcd^2s^2}{(2n-1)^2\pi^2}}{1 + \dfrac{lcd^2s^2}{n^2\pi^2}} \tag{1-20a}$$

$$y_{12} = y_{21} = -\sqrt{\frac{c}{l}}\,\text{csch}\, sd\sqrt{lc} = -\frac{1}{lds}\prod_{n=1}^{\infty}\frac{1}{1+\dfrac{lcd^2s^2}{n^2\pi^2}} \tag{1-20b}$$

If $l = 0$ and $g = 0$, the line is called a distributed RC network or simply an RC line. For convenience, we shall often write $\overline{URC}$, which designates a uniformly distributed RC network. The short-circuit admittance parameters for this case are

$$\begin{aligned} y_{11} = y_{22} &= \sqrt{\frac{sc}{r}}\,\coth d\sqrt{scr} \\ &= \frac{1}{rd}\prod_{n=1}^{\infty}\frac{1+\dfrac{4rcd^2s}{(2n-1)^2\pi^2}}{1+\dfrac{rcd^2s}{n^2\pi^2}} \end{aligned} \tag{1-21a}$$

$$\begin{aligned} y_{12} = y_{21} &= -\sqrt{\frac{sc}{r}}\,\text{csch}\, d\sqrt{scr} \\ &= -\frac{1}{rd}\prod_{n=1}^{\infty}\frac{1}{1+\dfrac{rcd^2s}{n^2\pi^2}} \end{aligned} \tag{1-21b}$$

From Equation (1-20a), the poles and zeros of the short-circuit driving-point admittance of the LC line are readily found. Thus,

$$p_0 = 0 \qquad p_n = \pm j\,\frac{n\pi}{d\sqrt{lc}} \tag{1-22a}$$

$$z_n = \pm j\,\frac{(2n-1)\pi}{2d\sqrt{lc}} \qquad n = 1, 2, 3, \ldots \tag{1-22b}$$

where p_n is the nth pole and z_n the nth zero of (1-20a). Note that the poles and zeros alternate on the imaginary axis. Similarly, the short-circuit driving-point admittance of the RC line has poles and zeros at

$$p_n = -\left(\frac{n\pi}{d\sqrt{rc}}\right)^2, \qquad z_n = -\left[\frac{(2n-1)\pi}{2d\sqrt{rc}}\right]^2 \tag{1-23}$$

$$n = 1, 2, 3, \ldots$$

In this case, the poles and zeros alternate along the negative real axis.

The pole-zero patterns for the lossless and lossy lines are shown in Figure 1-4. Note that the number of poles and zeros is infinite. Just as in the case of the lumped network, Bode plots[5] (frequency-response

[5] See H. W. Bode, *Network Analysis and Feedback Amplifier Design* (Princeton, N.J., Van Nostrand, 1945).

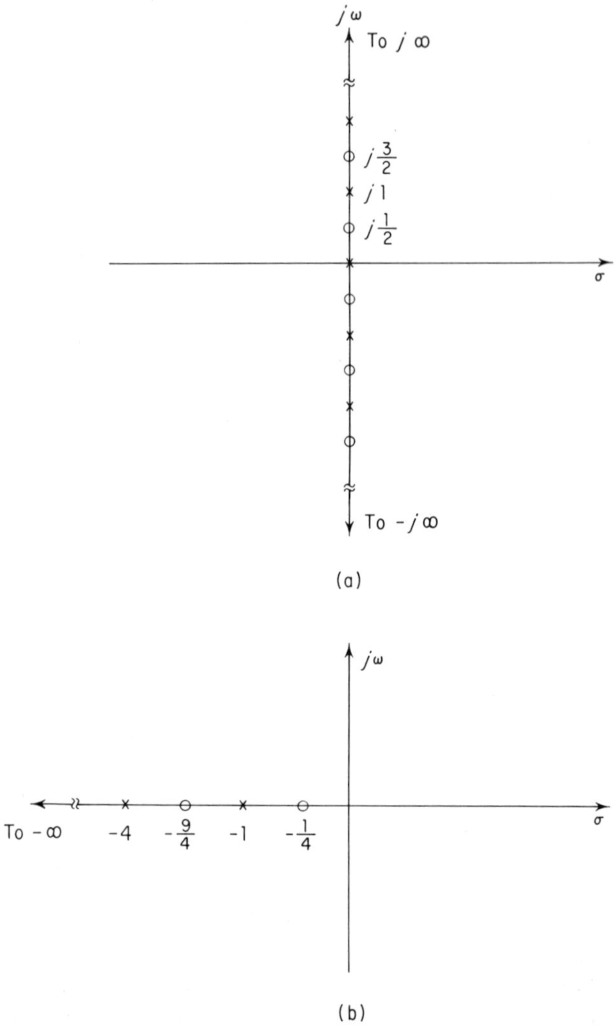

Figure 1-4 Pole zeros of y_{11}. **(a)** lossless uniform line (normalized to $\pi/d\sqrt{lc}$). **(b)** $\overline{RC}$ network (normalized to π^2/d^2rc).

plots) can be constructed for the distributed-parameter network. For example, the Bode plot of the short-circuit input admittance of the *RC* line is shown in Figure 1-5, from which it can be seen that the network input admittance is a monotonic, increasing function of frequency. Note that the asymptotic slope is +3 dB per octave, which is different from that of the lumped passive network. For the latter, the asymptotic slope of driving-point immittance is ±6 dB per octave. Further discussion of the

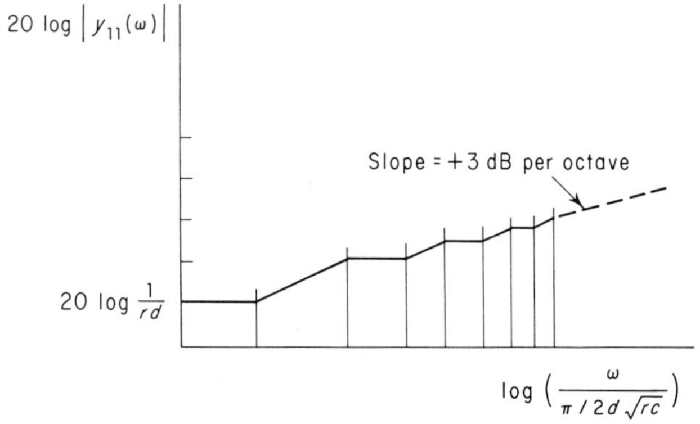

Figure 1-5 Bode plot of $|Y_{11}(\omega)|$ for uniform $\overline{RC}$ network.

frequency and transient response of the distributed network in exact form and approximate form, from the pole-zero viewpoint, is reserved for Chapter 3.

In the next section, we shall examine iterative lumped-parameter networks and will show how they approximate distributed structures.

1-3 Iterative Structure—Lumped-Parameter Approximation

For iterative structures with a large number of identical sections (Figure 1-6) the difference equation[6] plays an important role. The iterated lumped structure approximates the distributed structure when the individual sections are small and there are many per unit of length. The number of lumped sections that adequately describe a distributed network depends on the desired degree of accuracy and the frequency range of interest in terms of the time constant of the line (Problem 1-5). In this section we take this approach and show that similar results are obtained for the uniformly distributed structure to those obtained in Section 1-1. In other words, we shall show that the uniform transmission-line parameters can be obtained without solving partial differential equations. The technique used is to allow the number of sections of the iterative structure to approach infinity as a limit.

A symmetrical uniform transmission line of finite length may be approximated by the lumped iterative two-port structure shown in Figure 1-6. A typical T structure for a section of the line is shown for

[6] P. M. DeRusso, R. J. Roy, and C. M. Close, *State Variables for Engineers* (New York, Wiley, 1965), Chap. 2.

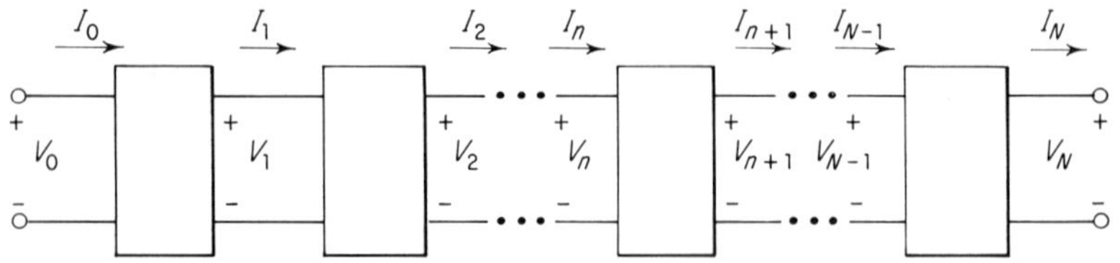

Figure 1-6 Iterative two-port network model.

convenience in Figure 1-7.[7] Initial conditions are assumed to be zero. The mesh transform equations of the circuit are

$$\begin{aligned}(Z_1 + Z_2)I_n - Z_2 I_{n+1} &= V_n \\ Z_2 I_n - (Z_1 + Z_2)I_{n+1} &= V_{n+1} \qquad n = 0, \ldots, N-1\end{aligned} \tag{1-24}$$

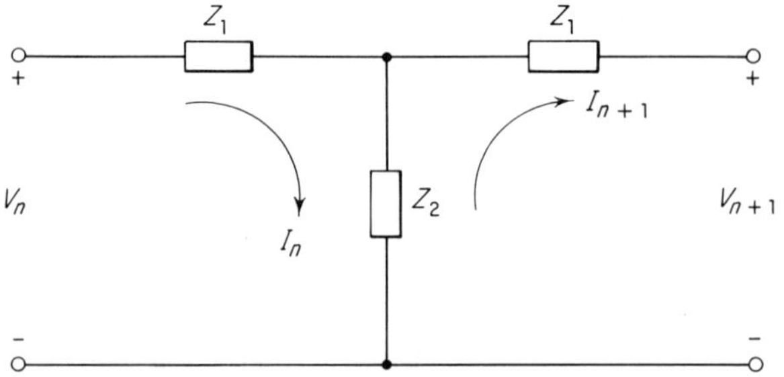

Figure 1-7 T-network representation.

Equation (1-24) may be rearranged in the following recurrence form:

$$\begin{bmatrix} V_{n+1} \\ I_{n+1} \end{bmatrix} = \begin{bmatrix} 1 + \dfrac{Z_1}{Z_2} & -\left(\dfrac{Z_1^{\,2}}{Z_2} + 2Z_1\right) \\ -\dfrac{1}{Z_2} & 1 + \dfrac{Z_1}{Z_2} \end{bmatrix} \begin{bmatrix} V_n \\ I_n \end{bmatrix} \tag{1-25}$$

In the difference equations (1-24) one boundary value must be given for each unknown: these boundary values are V_o, I_o.

Equation (1-25) may be written in matrix form as

$$[x_{n+1}] = [M][x_n] \tag{1-26}$$

where

$$[M] = \begin{bmatrix} 1 + \dfrac{Z_1}{Z_2} & -\left(\dfrac{Z_1^{\,2}}{Z_2} + 2Z_1\right) \\ -\dfrac{1}{Z_2} & 1 + \dfrac{Z_1}{Z_2} \end{bmatrix} \tag{1-27a}$$

[7] A π section can also be used. For a detailed treatment of artificial transmission lines see Weber (Ref. 1), Chap. 1.

$$[x_{n+1}] = \begin{bmatrix} V_{n+1} \\ I_{n+1} \end{bmatrix} \quad \text{and} \quad [x_n] = \begin{bmatrix} V_n \\ I_n \end{bmatrix} \tag{1-27b}$$

From (1-26) it is clear that

$$[x_n] = [M]^n [x_o] \tag{1-28}$$

Thus, to determine $[M]^n$ we find the eigenvalues of $[M]$. The eigenvalues are the roots of the characteristic equation,[8] that is,

$$\det |[M] - \lambda [I]| = \lambda^2 - 2\lambda \left(\frac{Z_1}{Z_2} + 1\right) + 1 = 0 \tag{1-29}$$

where $[I]$ is the identity or unit matrix. The two eigenvalues, from Equation (1-29), are related by

$$\lambda_1 \lambda_2 = 1 \tag{1-30a}$$

$$\lambda_1 + \lambda_2 = 2\left(\frac{Z_1}{Z_2} + 1\right) \tag{1-30b}$$

For convenience, let $\lambda_1 = e^{\tau}$; then from (1-30a), $\lambda_2 = e^{-\tau}$. From (1-30b), $\cosh \tau = (Z_1/Z_2) + 1$. Now to find $[M]^n$ we invoke the Cayley-Hamilton theorem and put

$$[M]^n = C_o[I] + C_1[M] \tag{1-31}$$

We must have

$$(e^{\tau})^n = C_0 + C_1(e^{\tau}) \tag{1-32a}$$

$$(e^{-\tau})^n = C_0 + C_1(e^{-\tau}) \tag{1-32b}$$

The solution of (1-32) is

$$C_0 = -\frac{\sinh (n-1)\tau}{\sinh \tau} \qquad C_1 = \frac{\sinh n\tau}{\sinh \tau}$$

$$[M]^n = \begin{bmatrix} -\dfrac{\sinh (n-1)\tau}{\sinh \tau} + \dfrac{\sinh n\tau \cosh \tau}{\sinh \tau} & -\left(\dfrac{Z_1^2}{Z_2} + 2Z_1\right)\dfrac{\sinh n\tau}{\sinh \tau} \\ -\dfrac{1}{Z_2}\dfrac{\sinh n\tau}{\sinh \tau} & -\dfrac{\sinh (n-1)\tau}{\sinh \tau} + \dfrac{\sinh n\tau \cosh \tau}{\sinh \tau} \end{bmatrix} \tag{1-33}$$

Equation (1-33) can be simplified if use is made of the following identities:

$$-\sinh (n-1)\tau = -\sinh n\tau \cosh \tau + \cosh n\tau \sinh \tau \tag{1-34}$$

[8] For a good discussion of matrix theory and linear algebra see G. E. Shilov, *An Introduction to the Theory of Linear Spaces* (Englewood Cliffs, N.J., Prentice-Hall, 1961). For a very brief discussion see also Ghausi (Ref. 4), Appendix A.

and

$$-\left(\frac{Z_1^2}{Z_2} + 2Z_1\right) = Z_2 - Z_2\left(\frac{Z_1 + Z_2}{Z_2}\right)^2 = Z_2(1 - \cosh^2 \tau) = -Z_2 \sinh^2 \tau \tag{1-35}$$

The use of these identities in Equation (1-33) gives the final result[9]

$$\begin{bmatrix} V_n \\ I_n \end{bmatrix} = \begin{bmatrix} \cosh n\tau & -Z_2 \sinh \tau \sinh n\tau \\ -\dfrac{\sinh n\tau}{Z_2 \sinh \tau} & \cosh n\tau \end{bmatrix} \begin{bmatrix} V_0 \\ I_0 \end{bmatrix} \tag{1-36}$$

The voltage and current in the nth section for the special terminations of open circuit and short circuit are found immediately. For the output short-circuit case, $V_N = 0$. From the first of the equations in (1-36) and substituting N for n we obtain

$$I_0 = \frac{\cosh N\tau}{Z_2 \sinh \tau \sinh N\tau} V_0 \tag{1-37}$$

From (1-36) and (1-37) the current and the voltage in the nth section are given by

$$I_n = \frac{\cosh (N - n)\tau}{Z_2 \sinh \tau \sinh N\tau} V_0 \tag{1-38}$$

$$V_n = \frac{\sinh (N - n)\tau}{\sinh N\tau} V_0 \tag{1-39}$$

Similarly, for the output open-circuit case $I_N = 0$. From the second of the equations in (1-36),

$$I_0 = \frac{\sinh N\tau}{Z_2 \sinh \tau \cosh N\tau} V_0 \tag{1-40}$$

The corresponding current and voltage for the nth sections are

$$I_n = \frac{\sinh (N - n)\tau}{Z_2 \sinh \tau \cosh N\tau} V_o \tag{1-41}$$

$$V_n = \frac{\cosh (N - n)\tau}{\cosh N\tau} V_0 \tag{1-42}$$

---

[9] Alternatively, (1-27a) can be rewritten as

$$[M] = \begin{bmatrix} \cosh \tau & -Z_2 \sinh^2 \tau \\ -\dfrac{1}{Z_2} & \cosh \tau \end{bmatrix}$$

and $[M]^n$ is obtained directly as

$$[M]^n = \begin{bmatrix} \cosh n\tau & -Z_2 \sinh \tau \sinh n\tau \\ -\dfrac{\sinh n\tau}{Z_2 \sinh \tau} & \cosh n\tau \end{bmatrix}$$

Note that $Z_2 \sinh \tau$ has physical significance as characteristic impedance.

[Compare Equations (1-38), (1-39), (1-41), and (1-42) with the results of Problem (1-1).] It should be noted that in (1-36) the matrix elements are nothing but the $\mathcal{ABCD}$ parameters of the linear two-port network. The over-all two-port $\mathcal{ABCD}$ parameters of the N cascaded sections of the network as shown in Figure 1-7 are then given by Equation (1-36), with n replaced by N and the appropriate signs changed in order to conform to the two-port sign convention of Figure 1-2. This yields

$$\begin{bmatrix} V_N \\ -I_N \end{bmatrix} = \begin{bmatrix} \cosh N\tau & Z_2 \sinh \tau \sinh N\tau \\ \dfrac{\sinh N\tau}{Z_2 \sinh \tau} & \cosh N\tau \end{bmatrix} \begin{bmatrix} V_0 \\ -I_0 \end{bmatrix} \tag{1-43}$$

The short-circuit admittance parameters can be obtained from Equation (1-43) and Table 1-1. They are

$$y_{11} = y_{22} = \frac{\cosh N\tau}{Z_2 \sinh \tau \sinh N\tau} = \frac{1}{Z_2 \sinh \tau} \coth N\tau \tag{1-44}$$

$$y_{12} = y_{21} = \frac{-1}{Z_2 \sinh \tau \sinh N\tau} = -\frac{1}{Z_2 \sinh \tau} \operatorname{csch} N\tau \tag{1-45}$$

It is noted that these equations are quite similar to (1-18), for the distributed network, since $Z_2 \sinh \tau$ is the characteristic impedance of the line. By using the identities[10]

$$\cosh N\tau = 2^{N-1} \prod_{n=1}^{N} \left[\cosh \tau - \cos \frac{(2n-1)\pi}{2N} \right] \tag{1-46}$$

$$\sinh N\tau = 2^{N-1} \sinh \tau \prod_{n=1}^{N-1} \left[\cosh \tau - \cos \frac{n\pi}{N} \right] \tag{1-47}$$

we can put these general relationships in factored form—a desirable form when the pole-zero approach is used. Thus,

$$y_{11} = y_{22} = \frac{2^{N-1} \prod_{n=1}^{N} \left[\cosh \tau - \cos \dfrac{(2n-1)\pi}{2N} \right]}{Z_2 2^{N-1} \sinh^2 \tau \prod_{n=1}^{N-1} \left[\cosh \tau - \cos \dfrac{n\pi}{N} \right]} \tag{1-48}$$

which can be simplified to read

$$y_{11} = y_{22} = \frac{\prod_{n=1}^{N} \left[\cosh \tau - \cos \dfrac{(2n-1)\pi}{2n} \right]}{Z_2[\cosh^2 \tau - 1] \prod_{n=1}^{N-1} \left[\cosh \tau - \cos \dfrac{n\pi}{N} \right]} \tag{1-49}$$

Further,

[10] See G. Chrystal, *Textbook of Algebra* (New York, Chelsea), Vol. 2, pp. 348 and 353.

$$y_{12} = y_{21} = \frac{-1}{Z_2 2^{N-1}[\cosh^2 \tau - 1] \prod_{n=1}^{N-1} \left[\cosh \tau - \cos \frac{n\pi}{N} \right]} \tag{1-50}$$

Since $\cosh \tau = (1 + Z_1/Z_2)$, the short-circuit admittance parameters are generally written in the form

$$y_{11} = y_{22} = \frac{1}{Z_2} \frac{\prod_{n=1}^{N} \left[1 + \frac{Z_1}{Z_2} - \cos \frac{(2n-1)\pi}{2N} \right]}{\left[\left(1 + \frac{Z_1}{Z_2}\right)^2 - 1 \right] \prod_{n=1}^{N-1} \left[\left(1 + \frac{Z_1}{Z_2}\right) - \cos \frac{n\pi}{N} \right]} \tag{1-51}$$

and

$$y_{12} = y_{21} = \frac{-1}{Z_2 2^{N-1} \left[\left(1 + \frac{Z_1}{Z_2}\right)^2 - 1 \right] \prod_{n=1}^{N-1} \left[\left(1 + \frac{Z_1}{Z_2}\right) - \cos \frac{n\pi}{N} \right]} \tag{1-52}$$

It is noted that the y_{ij} are rational functions of s for rational Z_1 and Z_2 and that there are N factors in the numerator and denominator of y_{11} and y_{22}.

For the lossless transmission line, with $Z_1 = sL/2$, $Z_2 = 1/sC$ then $Z_1/Z_2 = s^2LC/2$, and

$$y_{11} = y_{22} = \frac{sC \prod_{n=1}^{N} \left\{ \left[1 - \cos \frac{(2n-1)\pi}{2N} \right] + \frac{s^2LC}{2} \right\}}{\left[\left(1 + \frac{s^2LC}{2}\right)^2 - 1 \right] \prod_{n=1}^{N-1} \left[\left(1 - \cos \frac{n\pi}{N}\right) + \frac{s^2LC}{2} \right]} \tag{1-53}$$

Also,

$$y_{12} = y_{21} = \frac{-sC}{2^{N-1} \left[\left(1 + \frac{s^2LC}{2}\right)^2 - 1 \right] \prod_{n=1}^{N-1} \left[\left(1 - \cos \frac{n\pi}{N}\right) + \frac{s^2LC}{2} \right]} \tag{1-54}$$

It is noted that the poles and zeros of y_{11} and y_{22} lie on the $j\omega$ axis and are simple, as expected.

For the RC line with $Z_1 = R/2$, $Z_2 = 1/sC$, $Z_1/Z_2 = RCs/2$, and

$$y_{11} = y_{22} = \frac{sC \prod_{n=1}^{N} \left\{ \left[1 - \cos \frac{(2n-1)\pi}{2N} \right] + \frac{sRC}{2} \right\}}{\left[\left(1 + \frac{sRC}{2}\right)^2 - 1 \right] \prod_{n=1}^{N-1} \left[\left(1 - \cos \frac{n\pi}{N}\right) + \frac{sRC}{2} \right]} \tag{1-55}$$

Also,

$$y_{12} = y_{21} = \frac{-sC}{2^{N-1}\left[\left(1+\frac{sRC}{2}\right)^2 - 1\right] \prod_{n=1}^{N-1} \left[\left(1-\cos\frac{n\pi}{N}\right) + \frac{sRC}{2}\right]} \tag{1-56}$$

with simple poles on the negative real axis at

$$s = -\frac{2}{RC}\left[1 - \cos\frac{n\pi}{N}\right] \qquad n = 0, 1, \ldots, N \tag{1-57}$$

For a two-element network one need only study one type, such as the *RC* network, and the results for the *RL* or *LC* can be obtained by a simple frequency transformation. The frequency transformation is obtained as follows:

For an *RC* network the impedance of a branch may be written as

$$Z_{ij}\Big|_{RC} = R_{ij} + \frac{1}{C_{ij}s} \tag{1-58}$$

If we make the frequency transformation $s = p^2$, Equation (1-58) can be written as

$$Z_{ij}\Big|_{RC} = R_{ij} + \frac{1}{C_{ij}p^2} = \frac{1}{p}\left(pR_{ij} + \frac{1}{C_{ij}p}\right) \tag{1-59}$$

For an *LC* network, however, the impedance of a branch is

$$Z_{ij}\Big|_{LC} = sL_{ij} + \frac{1}{sC_{ij}} \tag{1-60}$$

Thus from Equations (1-59) and (1-60) it is evident that

$$Z_{RC}(s) = Z_{RC}(p^2) = \frac{1}{p}Z_{LC}(p) \tag{1-61}$$

On an admittance basis, the transformation is

$$Y_{RC}(s) = pY_{LC}(p) \tag{1-62}$$

as may be verified easily by carrying out the necessary steps. Similarly, for a transformation from an *RL* to an *LC* network,

$$Z_{RL}(s) = pZ_{LC}(p) \qquad Y_{RL}(s) = \frac{1}{p}Y_{LC}(p) \tag{1-63}$$

These transformations are useful in lumped-network synthesis procedures.

In order to utilize lumped-network synthesis techniques in the synthesis of resistor lossless transmission lines and of distributed *RC* networks, a transformation from a transcendental equation to an algebraic equation is needed. The transformations and the synthesis procedures are discussed in Chapter 6.

1-4 Passive Linear Integrated Circuits

In this section, we discuss the passive integrated circuit[11] and show its relationship to distributed *RC* networks. A two-port passive integrated circuit structure is shown in Figure 1-8. It is made up of a uniform resistive sheet, a uniform dielectric sheet, and a conducting sheet. The

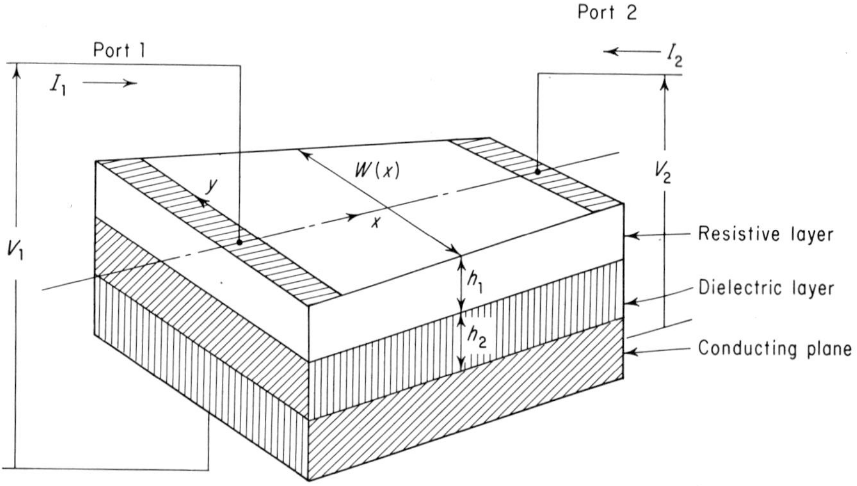

Figure 1-8 A tapered two-port distributed *RC* structure.

dimensions are exaggerated for the sake of illustration. The sheet thicknesses are typically of the order of 10^{-5} inch. Two of the structures used in passive microcircuits are the thin-film structure and the monolithic structure.

The thin-film structure consists of layers or strata of various materials deposited on a suitable supporting medium or substrate. As an example, the wafer of the dielectric material may be titanate with a thin nichrome resistive film deposited on top and a conductive copper-film plate on the bottom. Fabrication involves deposition of the resistive material on the passive substrate by vaporization or an electrochemical technique.

The monolithic structure consists of layers of semiconductor materials formed in a small block. Distributed resistance is obtained from a lightly doped semiconductor. Distributed capacitance is obtained from a p-n junction with reverse bias potential applied.

[11] Integrated circuit is defined as a combination of interconnected circuit elements inseparably associated on or within a continuous substrate. (See *IEEE Standard Definitions of Terms for Integrated Electronics;* also *1967 International Solid-State Circuits Conference Digest of Papers,* p. 131.)

At the present time microcircuits are limited primarily to distributed *RC* active networks, and no practical method of producing large values of inductance usable in the audio and video frequency range has been developed. The electrical performance of the structure depends on the characteristics of the materials and their geometry. The process used to fabricate the structure also imposes limitations on their size and performance characteristics.[12] The structure of a typical integrated *RC* circuit is shown in Figure 1-9(a) and its circuit symbol is shown in Figure 1-9(b).

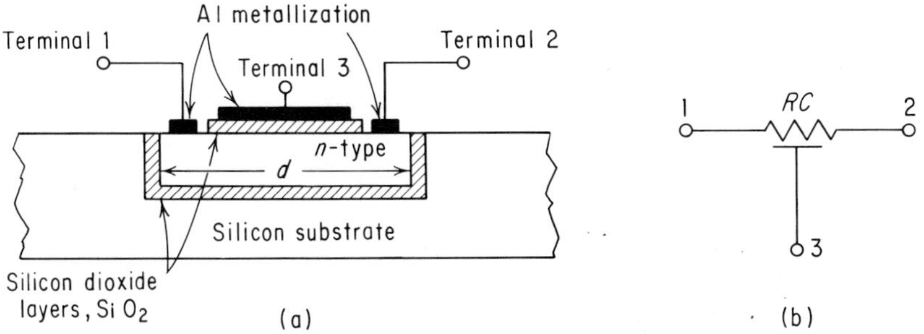

Figure 1-9 **(a)** An integrated passive *RC* circuit. **(b)** Circuit symbol.

We shall now develop the network relations for typical distributed *RC* structures. We shall assume that the geometry of the structure is such that one-dimensional current flow occurs.[13] Referring back to Figure 1-8, we see that the typical two-port distributed *RC* structure is made up of a resistive sheet, a dielectric sheet, and a conducting sheet.[14] Under conditions of one dimensional current flow, the network can be divided into incremental sections of length Δx, as shown in Figure 1-10. The resistance of each series element is a function of the sheet resistivity and the dimensions of the element. The series resistance of the element, $r(x)\,\Delta x$, is given by

[12] R. Warner and J. Fordemwalt, *Integrated Circuits, Design Principles and Fabrication* (New York, McGraw-Hill, 1965).

[13] The conditions for one-dimensional current flow are considered in detail in Chapter 7.

[14] For quick and simple experimental studies the reader can make up a distributed network of convenient geometry by using Teledeltos paper as a resistive sheet. The resistivity is about 2 kilohms/square and the thickness is approximately 0.004 in. For the dielectric sheet DuPont Mylar polyester film can be used. A Mylar sheet approximately 0.0006 inch thick is suitable. It has a relative dielectric constant $\epsilon = 3.12$ (at 1 KHz and 20°C). For the conductive film, copper or aluminum foil can be used. Equipotential boundaries at input and output ports may be obtained by using Hanovia No. 13 flexible silver paint. Alternatively, a thick-film technique using conductive inks and simple equipment with inexpensive materials can also be employed. For details, see L. I. deGennaro, *Electron. Design* (Sept. 13, 1966), 52–55.

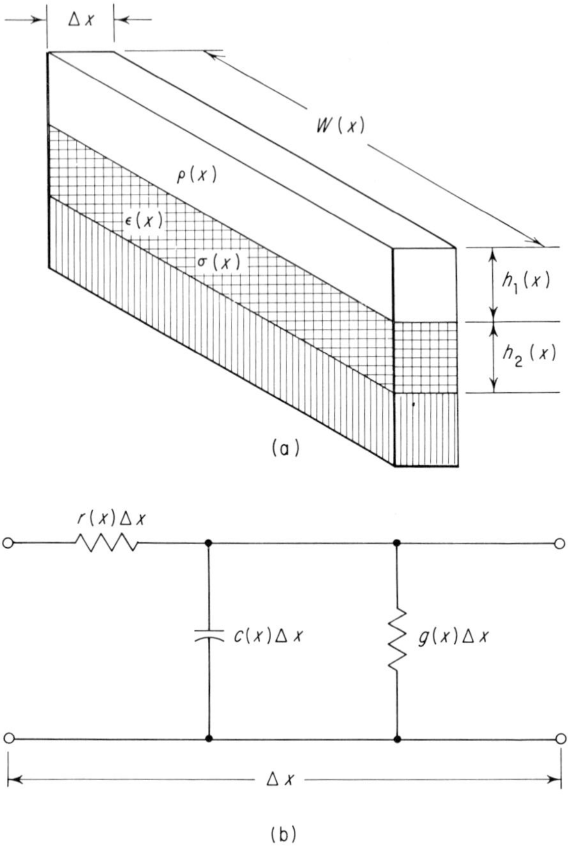

Figure 1-10 **(a)** Incremental passive integrated $\overline{RC}$ structure. **(b)** Incremental network representation.

$$r(x)\ \Delta x = \frac{\rho \Delta x}{W h_1} \tag{1-64}$$

where ρ and h_1 are the resistivity and the thickness, respectively, of the resistive sheet at x, and W is the width of the element at x.

The shunt admittance of the element can be found in a similar fashion. It is composed of a capacitance and conductance of the dielectric sheet (assumed lossy here) of the element. These are

$$c(x)\ \Delta x = \frac{\epsilon W \Delta x}{h_2} \qquad \text{and} \qquad g(x)\ \Delta x = \frac{\sigma W \Delta x}{h_2} \tag{1-65}$$

where ϵ and σ are the permittivity and the conductivity, respectively, of the dielectric sheet, and h_2 is the thickness of the dielectric layer at x.

Letting Δx approach zero as a limit, the resistance, capacitance, and conductance per unit length are

$$r(x) = \frac{\rho}{Wh_1}$$
$$c(x) = \frac{\epsilon W}{h_2} \qquad \text{(1-66)}$$
$$g(x) = \frac{\sigma W}{h_2}$$

The values of $r(x)$, $c(x)$, and $g(x)$ are always real, positive, and finite. These restrictions are important in determining the nature of the solutions for the differential equations that describe the network. Often the leakage conductance $g(x)$ is negligible.

The two-port model for the uniform distributed RC network, where the dielectric loss is negligible, is identical to the one in Figure 1-1 except that the inductance and conductance are negligible (that is, $l = g = 0$). Symbolically, the network for a nonuniform distributed RC network is represented by Figure 1-11(a) where the curved line indicates a general

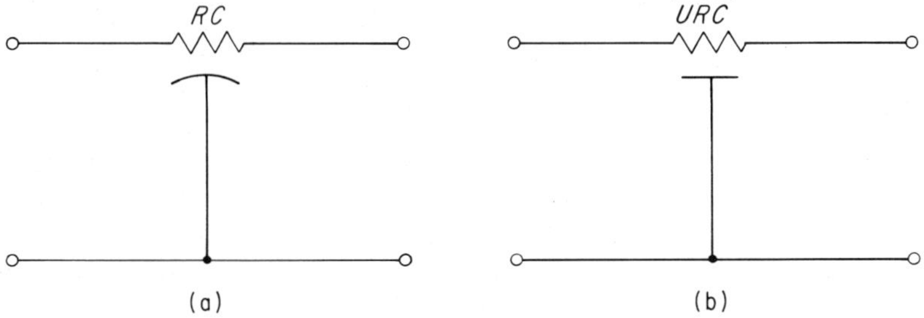

Figure 1-11 Symbolic representation of $\overline{URC}$.

nonuniform distributed RC network. If the curve under R is a straight line it indicates a uniform distributed network. We have already discussed the uniform case and now briefly examine the nonuniform distributed RC case.

The transform voltage-current relationship for a nonuniform case is immediately written from Equations (1-6) and (1-7) as

$$\frac{dV(s, x)}{dx} = -r(x)I(s, x) \qquad \text{(1-67a)}$$

$$\frac{dI(s, x)}{dx} = -[sc(x)]V(s, x) \qquad \text{(1-67b)}$$

In Equation (1-67) the network is assumed to be initially relaxed. Differentiating (1-67) with respect to x and rearranging the terms produces a pair of second-order, linear, homogeneous, ordinary differential equations, one for voltage and the other for current. The resulting equations are

$$V'' - \frac{r'V'}{r} - r\,sc\,V = 0 \tag{1-68a}$$

$$I'' - \frac{c'}{c}I' - r\,sc\,I = 0 \tag{1-68b}$$

where the prime represents differentiation with respect to x. We assume that $r(x)$ and $c(x)$ are continuous functions of x. Equations (1-68) are Sturm-Liouville equations. The properties of their solution were first studied in detail by Sturm in 1836.[15] Equation (1-68a) can also be written as

$$\frac{d}{dx}\left[\frac{1}{r(x)}\frac{dV}{dx}\right] - sc(x)V = 0 \tag{1-69a}$$

and

$$\frac{d}{dx}\left[\frac{1}{sc(x)}\frac{dI}{dx}\right] - r(x)I = 0 \tag{1-69b}$$

Note that if $sl(x)$ is substituted for $r(x)$ in (1-69a), the differential equation is that of a tapered, lossless, distributed *LC* network, as follows:

$$\frac{d}{dx}\left[\frac{1}{l(x)}\frac{dV}{dx}\right] - s^2c(x)V = 0 \tag{1-70}$$

Thus the results for distributed *RC* networks can also be interpreted for a distributed *LC* network, using the appropriate transformation.

The voltage and current relationship for the distributed *RC* network given in (1-69) may also be transformed into a first-order nonlinear differential equation of the Riccati type[16] by a change of the dependent variable. Sometimes this procedure facilitates the determination of the immittance parameters. If we let

$$U(x) = -\frac{1}{r(x)V(x)}\frac{dV(x)}{dx} \tag{1-71}$$

then

$$\frac{dV}{dx} = -UrV \tag{1-72}$$

and

$$\frac{d^2V}{dx^2} = -(V'Ur + rU'V + r'UV) \tag{1-73}$$

Substituting (1-72) and (1-73) into (1-69a) and rearranging terms, we get

$$\frac{dU(x)}{dx} = r(x)U(x) - [sc(x)] \tag{1-74}$$

[15] See, for example, E. L. Ince, *Ordinary Differential Equations* (New York, Dover reprint, 1956).

[16] See Ince (Ref. 15), Chap. 1.

Thus we have a first-order nonlinear differential equation in the variable $U(s, x)$. Solutions of the nonlinear first-order differential equation of the form given in Equation (1-74) were first published by Jacopo Riccati in 1712. The Riccati equation, its solutions, and its application to transmission lines have also been studied by various investigators,[17,18] and will not be discussed at this point. The method of change of variables is covered in Chapter 4.

PROBLEMS

1-1 **a.** For a uniform *RLCG* line of length d show that the transform of the voltage and current as a function of position x is given by

$$V(s,x) = V(s,d)\cosh\Gamma(d-x) + I(s,d)Z_0\sinh\Gamma(d-x)$$

$$I(s,x) = I(s,d)\cosh\Gamma(d-x) + \frac{V(s,d)}{Z_0}\sinh\Gamma(d-x)$$

where $$Z_0 = \sqrt{\frac{ls+r}{cs+g}} \qquad \Gamma = \sqrt{(ls+r)(cs+g)}$$

b. If the output is short-circuited, and $V(s,0)$ is given, show that

$$V(s,x) = \frac{V(s,0)\sinh\Gamma(d-x)}{\sinh\Gamma d}$$

$$I(s,x) = \frac{V(s,0)\cosh\Gamma(d-x)}{Z_0\sinh\Gamma d}$$

c. If the output is open-circuited and $V(s,0)$ is given, show that

$$V(s,x) = \frac{V(s,0)\cosh\Gamma(d-x)}{\cosh\Gamma d}$$

$$I(s,x) = \frac{V(s,0)\sinh\Gamma(d-x)}{Z_0\cosh\Gamma d}$$

1-2 A voltage source with an impedance Z_s is applied at the input of a finite *RLCG* line of length d and the output is terminated in a load Z_L. Show that

a. $$I(s,x) = V(s,0)\,\frac{Z_0\cosh\Gamma(d-x) + Z_L\sinh\Gamma(d-x)}{(Z_L+Z_s)Z_0\cosh\Gamma d + (Z_L Z_s + Z_0{}^2)\sinh\Gamma}$$

---

[17] J. R. Pierce, *Bell System Tech. J.*, **22** (1943), 263–265.

[18] L. A. Pipes, *Trans. AIEE,* **75** (1956), pt. 1, 551–554.

$$V(s, x) = V(s, 0)Z_0 \frac{Z_L \cosh \Gamma(d-x) + Z_0 \sinh \Gamma(d-x)}{(Z_L + Z_s)Z_0 \cosh \Gamma d + (Z_L Z_s + Z_0^2) \sinh \Gamma d}$$

The input impedance of the line is given by

b. $$Z_{\text{in}} = Z_0 \frac{Z_L \cosh \Gamma L + Z_0 \sinh \Gamma L}{Z_0 \cosh \Gamma L + Z_L \sinh \Gamma L}$$

1-3 Determine the two-port open-circuit impedance parameters of a distortionless *RLCG* line. (A distortionless *RLCG* line implies that $r/l = c/g$.) Plot the pole-zero locations.

1-4 Show that in the limit as $\Delta x \to 0$ or $N \to \infty$ (in other words, keeping the total length fixed), the admittance parameters of the iterated structure [Equations (1-44) and (1-45)] approach those of the distributed network [Equation (1-18)].

1-5 Determine the minimum number of T sections if an iterated structure is to approximate within 5 percent the voltage transfer function of a uniform *RC* line within a frequency range $\omega \leqslant 5\omega_0$, where $\omega_0 = 1/r_0 c_0 d^2 = 1/RC$.

1-6 Two uniformly distributed *RC* networks are cascaded as shown. The two networks are made up of the same material, which has resistance of r_0 per square and a capacitance of c_0 per unit area. Assume $d_1 = 2d_2$.

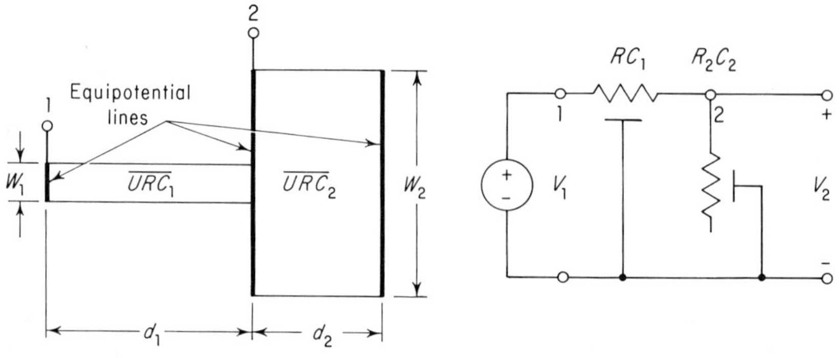

(a) (b)

a. Determine the voltage transfer function in a closed form.
b. If $W_1/W_2 = 0.1$, express the result of part (a) in the form of

$$T_V(s) = \frac{1}{a_0 + a_1 s_n + a_2 s_n^2 + a_3 s_n^3 + \ldots}$$

and determine a_0, a_1, a_2, and a_3. Note that $s_n = sr_0c_0d^2$.

1-7 For the structure shown, use the iterated lumped approach with each network approximated by three sections.

a. Determine $[M]^3$ for the network.

b. Determine the voltage transfer function $V_0/V_i(s)$.

1-8 If a distributed *RC* network is approximated by an iterated structure, determine the pole-zero locations of the approximating lumped network

a. if two sections are used.

b. if three sections are used.

c. Compare (a) and (b) with the lowest critical frequencies of the actual distributed network.

1-9 Repeat Problem 1-8 for a distributed *LC* network.

CHAPTER

2

Two-Port Parameters of Nonuniformly Distributed Networks

2-1 Introduction

In the first chapter, we discussed in some detail the uniform distributed two-port network and its approximation by iterated lumped-element networks. We introduced the nonuniform case in Section 1-4. The general case, in which the per-unit-length series impedance and shunt admittance vary along the length of the network, is considered in detail in this chapter. The general nonuniformly distributed two-port is more difficult to treat than the uniform network to say the least. However, we shall develop procedures for producing a set of equations that are simple to interpret and to apply to nonuniformly distributed two-port networks.

The pole-zero approach will be emphasized in our analysis of nonuniform finite networks because it provides a direct connection between lumped- and distributed-parameter systems. We shall also show the similarities between lumped- and distributed-parameter systems so that many techniques for the analysis of lumped-constant circuit theory can be translated directly into the study of distributed systems.

2-2 Nonuniformly Distributed Two-Ports

A nonuniformly distributed two-port is a network in which the per-unit-length series impedance $Z(s, x)$ and shunt admittance $Y(s, x)$ are variables; that is, $Z(s, x)$ and $Y(s, x)$ are functions of s as well as x. Such a network and the equivalent circuit of an elemental portion of the network are shown in Figure 2-1.

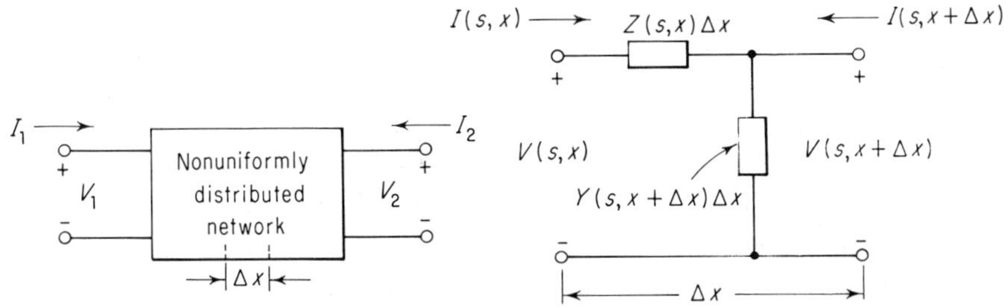

Figure 2-1 Nonuniform network and model of elemental length.

The incremental model can be described conveniently by a pair of first-order linear differential equations. For simplicity, we shall assume that the network is initially relaxed—that is, that there is zero initial current in all inductive elements and zero initial charge on all capacitive elements. We shall further restrict ourselves to linear networks—that is, networks in which $Z(s, x)$ and $Y(s, x)$ do not change when the voltage or current levels are changed. To a first order of approximation, nonlinear distributed two-ports such as junction diodes and field effect transistors can be represented by linear distributed models.

The equations of the nonuniform network based on the incremental model, which assumes one-dimensional spatial variation for the voltage and current, are

$$\frac{dV(s, x)}{dx} = -Z(s, x)I(s, x) \tag{2-1a}$$

$$\frac{dI(s, x)}{dx} = -Y(s, x)V(s, x) \tag{2-1b}$$

The case of two-dimensional spatial variation of the voltage and current is treated in Chapter 7. By differentiating (2-1) with respect to x,[1] assuming that the derivatives exist, we obtain

$$\frac{d^2V(s, x)}{dx^2} = -Z(s, x)\frac{dI(s, x)}{dx} - I(s, x)\frac{dZ(s, x)}{dx} \tag{2-2a}$$

[1] Note that $dZ(s, x)/dx$ and $dY(s, x)/dx$ are zero for the uniform network.

$$\frac{d^2I(s,x)}{dx^2} = -Y(s,x)\,\frac{dV(s,x)}{dx} - V(s,x)\,\frac{dY(s,x)}{dx} \tag{2-2b}$$

Upon substitution of (2-1) into (2-2), we obtain the following pair of differential equations relating the voltage and current at any point x in the nonuniform network.

$$\frac{d^2V(s,x)}{dx^2} - \left[\frac{1}{Z(s,x)}\,\frac{dZ(s,x)}{dx}\right]\frac{dV(s,x)}{dx} - Y(s,x)Z(s,x)V(s,x) = 0 \tag{2-3a}$$

$$\frac{d^2I(s,x)}{dx^2} - \left[\frac{1}{Y(s,x)}\,\frac{dY(s,x)}{dx}\right]\frac{dI(s,x)}{dx} - Y(s,x)Z(s,x)I(s,x) = 0 \tag{2-3b}$$

When $Z(s,x)$ and $Y(s,x)$ are nonzero and finite, and when their derivatives with respect to x exist, Equations (2-3a) and (2-3b) are a pair of second-order, homogeneous, linear differential equations. Further, V and I have two linearly independent solutions, which are analytic in s and x if $Z(s,x)$ and $Y(s,x)$ are analytic in s and x.

For instance, let $Z(s,x)$ and $Y(s,x)$ be given by

$$Z(s,x) = Z(s)f_1(x) \qquad Y(s,x) = Y(s)f_2(x) \tag{2-4}$$

Then V and I are analytic in x and s provided that $Z(s)$ and $Y(s)$ are analytic in s, and $f_1(x)$ and $f_2(x)$ are analytic in x over the interval $0 \leqslant x \leqslant d$, where d is the network length. This is equivalent to saying that V and I have analytic solutions when the per-unit-length series impedance and shunt admittance are finite, and continuous over the network length. It is a characteristic of physical networks that the series resistance per unit length $r(x)$, the series inductance per unit length $l(x)$, the per-unit-length shunt conductance $g(x)$, and the per-unit-length shunt capacitance $c(x)$ are all positive and bounded. Recall that $Z(s)$ and $Y(s)$ are the series impedance and shunt admittance of the line and, for the most general case considered here,

$$Z(s) = r(x) + sl(x) \quad \text{and} \quad Y(s) = g(x) + sc(x)$$

We may write these in the form of Equation (2-4) as $Z(s,x) = (r_o + sl_0)f_1(x)$ and $Y(s,x) = (g_0 + sc_0)f_2(x)$. Under this form Equation (2-3) becomes

$$\frac{d^2V}{dx^2} - \left[\frac{1}{\not{Z}(s)f_1(x)}\,\not{Z}(s)\,\frac{df_1(x)}{dx}\right]\frac{dV}{dx} - Y(s)Z(s)f_1(x)f_2(x)V = 0$$

Note that in this equation we require only a finite nonzero $f_1(x)$, having a first derivative. Hence, except possibly at points of discontinuity resulting from geometry, the distributed networks we speak about all have analytic solutions in V and I. In the case where a discontinuity arises, the network may be divided into sections at the points of the discontinuity, and each section analyzed separately.

In this text, we assume that $Z(s, x)$ and $Y(s, x)$ satisfy the conditions of Equation (2-4) that give analytic solutions for V and I, and we will confine our discussion henceforth to these cases. In other words, we consider $Z(s, x) = Z(s) f_1(x)$ in which $f_1(x)$ is not zero and $Z(s)$ is a function of s independent of x. We then have, as solutions to (2-3),

$$V(s, x) = aV_a(s, x) + bV_b(s, x) \tag{2-5a}$$

and since

$$I(s, x) = \frac{-1}{Z(s, x)} \frac{dV(s, x)}{dx}$$

we also have

$$I(s, x) = \frac{-1}{Z(s, x)} \left[a \frac{dV_a(s, x)}{dx} + b \frac{dV_b(s, x)}{dx} \right] \tag{2-5b}$$

where a and b are constants determined by the boundary conditions on the network, and V_a and V_b are any two linearly independent solutions of (2-3a). We see immediately from (2-5) that $I(s, x)$ is determined uniquely when V is known. For convenience, we rewrite Equation (2-3a) as

$$\frac{d^2V}{dx^2} - \frac{1}{Z} \frac{dZ}{dx} \frac{dV}{dx} - YZV = 0 \tag{2-6a}$$

Equation (2-6a) may be written in an alternate form, which is useful in simplifying the mathematical treatment of the general distributed two-port. The alternate form is

$$Z\left[\frac{d}{dx} \left(\frac{1}{Z} \frac{dV}{dx} \right) - YV \right] = 0 \tag{2-6b}$$

Similarly, the current equation (2-3b) can be written in the simplified form

$$Y\left[\frac{d}{dx} \left(\frac{1}{Y} \frac{dI}{dx} \right) - ZI \right] = 0 \tag{2-6c}$$

For such self-adjoint[2] second-order systems, with two linearly independent solutions (V_a, V_b), Abel's identity[3] holds; that is,

$$\frac{1}{Z(s, x)} [V_a V_b' - V_b V_a'] \equiv k$$

[2] B. Friedman, *Principles and Techniques of Applied Mathematics* (New York, Wiley, 1956).

[3] E. L. Ince, *Ordinary Differential Equations* (New York, Dover reprint, 1956).

for all values of x over the interval $0 \leqslant x \leqslant d$, where d is the network length. Note that $V_a V_b' - V_b V_a'$ is called the Wronskian of the system.

These properties will be of prime importance in obtaining simple expressions for the distributed-network two-port parameters. Equations (2-6) are known as Sturm equations, and the two linearly independent solutions are orthogonal. These equations are treated in more detail in the next section.

2-3 Two-Port Parameters of Distributed Networks

The preceding section has described certain standard forms of the differential equation describing the general distributed two-port structure. In this section we consider the Sturm equation in detail from the two-port circuit viewpoint. Certain properties of the solutions of the Sturm equation lend themselves readily to the evaluation of the two-port parameters of the distributed two-port network.

In terms of the solution $V(s, x)$ of the voltage equation (2-6a) for the two-port network of length d shown in Figure 2-1(a) we have, from (2-1),

$$V_1 = V(s, 0) \qquad V_2 = V(s, d) \tag{2-7a}$$

Also

$$I_1 = \frac{-1}{Z(s, 0)} V'(s, 0) \qquad I_2 = \frac{+1}{Z(s, d)} V'(s, d) \tag{2-7b}$$

where the prime represents differentiation with respect to x. From (2-7) and the definition of short-circuit admittance parameters we have, with the complex frequency parameter s dependence understood,

$$y_{11} = \left.\frac{I_1}{V_1}\right|_{V_2 = 0} = \frac{-1}{Z(0)} \frac{V'(0)}{V(0)} \qquad y_{12} = \left.\frac{I_1}{V_2}\right|_{V_1 = 0} = \frac{-1}{Z(0)} \frac{V'(0)}{V(d)} \tag{2-8a}$$

$$y_{21} = \left.\frac{I_2}{V_1}\right|_{V_2 = 0} = \frac{+1}{Z(d)} \frac{V'(d)}{V(0)} \qquad y_{22} = \left.\frac{I_2}{V_2}\right|_{V_1 = 0} = \frac{+1}{Z(d)} \frac{V'(d)}{V(d)} \tag{2-8b}$$

Note that $y_{12} = y_{21}$, as will be shown later in Section 2-4. As shown by (2-8), the short-circuit admittance parameters are easily evaluated for a given network once the solution of the voltage equation is known.

For the distributed two-port network with variable $Z(s, x)$ and $Y(s, x)$, the voltage solution of (2-6a) is generally a transcendental function in the variables s and x. Further, these transcendental functions are often not expressible in closed forms. Some exceptions are the uniform, exponentially tapered, square-law, and trigonometric tapered networks whose solutions are hyperbolic functions.[4] Another exception is the class of Bessel networks, where Z and Y vary as $(l + kx)^a$. The

[4] J. J. Kelly and M. S. Ghausi, *IEEE Trans. Circuit Theory*, **CT-12** (1965), 554–558.

solutions for the Bessel networks are modified Bessel functions. These are discussed in Chapter 4.

Solutions for the networks with $Z(s, x)$ and $Y(s, x)$ expressible as arbitrary power series in x do not exist in closed form but are obtainable as infinite series in powers of s or x. These cases usually employ the Picard-Carson method, which will be treated later.

To simplify the calculation of the immittance parameters from solutions of the voltage equation it is expedient to solve this equation by means of the simplest approach. In this way, the immittance parameters of the two-port distributed network can be written in a concise and useful form.

It is known from the theory of differential equations that a second-order differential equation has two linearly independent solutions. The complete solution is a linear combination of the two separate orthogonal solutions and is written as

$$V(s, x) = aV_{\text{I}}(s, x) + bV_{\text{II}}(s, x) \tag{2-9}$$

where a and b are determined by the network boundary conditions and V_{I} and V_{II} are the linearly independent solutions.

A proper choice of V_{I} and V_{II}, as given in Equation (2-9), can materially reduce the labor of the calculation of the immittance parameters. A form particularly suited to the evaluation of the two-port parameters is the *basic set*, defined by Morse and Feshbach.[5]

In the basic-set notation for identifying the two linearly independent solutions for V, V_{I} and V_{II} are normalized as follows:

$$V_{\text{I}} = 1 \qquad V_{\text{I}}' = 0 \qquad \text{at} \qquad x = 0 \tag{2-10a}$$

$$V_{\text{II}} = 0 \qquad V_{\text{II}}' = 1 \qquad \text{at} \qquad x = 0 \tag{2-10b}$$

Using this definition, V_{I} is determined by the value of the voltage at $x = 0$, while V_{II} is determined by the value of the first derivative of the voltage with respect to x at $x = 0$. The normalization constants are included in the terms a and b of the complete solution in (2-9), and have the dimensions of voltage.

It is noted that V_{I} represents the normalized voltage at port 1 of the network while V_{II} represents the normalized current at port 1. This property of the basic set simplifies the determination of the network immittance parameters.

As noted before, a useful property of linearly independent solutions of the voltage equation is that the *Wronskian* does not vanish in the interval $0 \leq x \leq d$; that is, for V_{I} and V_{II},

$$[V_{\text{I}}V_{\text{II}}' - V_{\text{I}}'V_{\text{II}}] \neq 0 \qquad 0 \leq x \leq d \tag{2-11}$$

[5] See P. Morse and H. Feshbach, *Methods of Theoretical Physics* (New York, McGraw-Hill, 1953), Vol. 1, p. 531.

where the prime represents differentiation with respect to x. Since V_{I} and V_{II} are functions of both s and x, Equation (2-11) states that for no value of s or x can both solutions be zero simultaneously.

Another useful property of linearly independent solutions of the distributed-network voltage equation stems from the fact that it is a solution of the Sturm equation. The Sturm equation is self-adjoint, as mentioned in Section 2-2. For self-adjoint equations, Abel's identity[3] holds; that is, in the interval $0 \leqslant x \leqslant d$,

$$\frac{1}{Z(s,x)}\,[V_{\mathrm{I}}V_{\mathrm{II}}' - V_{\mathrm{I}}'V_{\mathrm{II}}] = \text{a constant independent of } x \tag{2-12}$$

where $Z(s,x)$ represents the impedance function $Z(s)f(x)$.

The constant in (2-12) can be found by evaluating the equation at $x = 0$. From the definition of the basic set, at $x = 0$, we have

$$\frac{1}{Z(s,0)}\,[1-0] = \frac{1}{Z(s,0)} \tag{2-13}$$

for all values of s; hence,

$$\frac{1}{Z(s,x)}\,[V_{\mathrm{I}}V_{\mathrm{II}}' - V_{\mathrm{I}}'V_{\mathrm{II}}] = \frac{1}{Z(s,0)} \tag{2-14}$$

This relation holds at any point in the interval $0 \leqslant x \leqslant d$ and for all values of s.

2-4 Short-Circuit Admittance Parameters

Using the basic-set solutions of Equation (2-6a) $[V_{\mathrm{I}}(s,x),\ V_{\mathrm{II}}(s,x)]$, and recognizing that Abel's identity holds, we now are able to obtain the short-circuit admittance parameters in a simple form. The voltage solution for the network in terms of the basic set is

$$V(s,x) = aV_{\mathrm{I}}(s,x) + bV_{\mathrm{II}}(s,x) \tag{2-15a}$$

The solution for the current is

$$I(s,x) = \frac{-1}{Z(s,x)}\,[aV_{\mathrm{I}}'(s,x) + bV_{\mathrm{II}}'(s,x)] \tag{2-15b}$$

where a and b are constants with respect to x and are determined by the boundary conditions imposed on the network. From these solutions, the two-port voltages and currents are found as follows. At the input, port 1, we have for the voltage

$$\begin{aligned} V_1 &= aV_{\mathrm{I}}(s,0) + bV_{\mathrm{II}}(s,0) \\ &= a(1) + b(0) = a \end{aligned} \tag{2-16a}$$

At the output, port 2, we have

$$V_2 = aV_{\rm I}(s, d) + bV_{\rm II}(s, d) \tag{2-16b}$$

Also, at these ports, we have for the currents

$$\begin{aligned} I_1 &= -\frac{1}{Z(s,0)}\left[aV_{\rm I}'(s,0) + bV_{\rm II}'(s,0)\right] \\ &= -\frac{1}{Z(s,0)}\left[a(0) + b(1)\right] = -\frac{b}{Z(s,0)} \end{aligned} \tag{2-17a}$$

and

$$I_2 = +\frac{1}{Z(s,d)}\left[aV_{\rm I}'(s,d) + bV_{\rm II}'(s,d)\right] \tag{2-17b}$$

From Equations (2-14), (2-16), and (2-17), and from the definition of the short-circuit admittance parameters (2-8), we get

$$y_{11} = \frac{1}{Z(s,0)}\frac{V_{\rm I}(s,d)}{V_{\rm II}(s,d)} \qquad y_{12} = \frac{-1}{Z(s,0)}\frac{1}{V_{\rm II}(s,d)} \tag{2-18a}$$

$$y_{21} = \frac{-1}{Z(s,0)}\frac{1}{V_{\rm II}(s,d)} \qquad y_{22} = \frac{1}{Z(s,d)}\frac{V_{\rm II}'(s,d)}{V_{\rm II}(s,d)} \tag{2-18b}$$

It is noted that the representation of the distributed two-port short-circuit admittance parameters $[y_{ij}]$ in basic-set notation is a relatively simple set of relationships. [Compare (2-18) with the result in Problem 2-7.] The expressions in (2-18) lend themselves readily to pole-zero expansion since only a single transcendental function appears in either numerator or denominator.

So far, we have been concerned only with the general distributed-parameter two-port. Let us now choose the distributed *RC* network for some specific examples of the results to this point.

A number of interesting conclusions can be drawn about the behavior of distributed *RC* networks with $r(x)$, $r'(x)$, $c(x)$, and $g(x)$ continuous and bounded in the interval $0 \leq x \leq d$.

First, since $V_{\rm I}(s, d)$ and $V_{\rm II}(s, d)$ are analytic in s over the interval $0 \leq x \leq d$, they are analytic functions at d for all finite s.[6] Hence, the poles of $[y_{ij}]$ are determined only by the zeros of $V_{\rm II}(s, d)$.

Second, since the Wronskian of the system is never zero in the interval $0 \leq x \leq d$, the zeros of $V_{\rm I}(s, d)$ and $V_{\rm II}'(s, d)$ do not coincide with the zeros of $V_{\rm II}(s, d)$. Therefore, the zeros of y_{11} and of y_{22} are determined only by the zeros of $V_{\rm I}(s, d)$ and $V_{\rm II}'(s, d)$, respectively, since there is no cancellation of common factors in numerator and denominator.

[6] When $r(x)$, $c(x)$, and $g(x)$ are analytic in x, then $V_{\rm I}(s, x)$ and $V_{\rm II}(s, x)$ are also analytic functions of s as well as x.

Third, distributed *RC* networks are reciprocal; that is, $y_{12} = y_{21}$. The general distributed passive two-port is also reciprocal, as is true in general for the passive *RLC* lumped-parameter two-port. It is noted that $V_I(s, d)$ and $V_{II}(s, d)$ are analytic functions and thus can be represented by Taylor series in s. Hence, they are entire functions. Further, from the theory of Sturm equations, the zeros of $V_I(s, d)$ and $V_{II}(s, d)$ lie on the negative real axis and are simple, and have no accumulation point[7] in the finite plane. Therefore, the short-circuit admittance parameters are meromorphic functions of s. A meromorphic function has only poles as singularities, but these may be infinite in number and are isolated.

Other important network characteristics can be deduced from the properties of the Sturm equation as applied to the distributed *RC* network. The poles and zeros of the driving-point functions of the short-circuited network are really the eigenvalues of the solutions of the Sturm equation when the appropriate boundary values are specified. Determination of the admittance parameters at port 1 requires that $V(d) = 0$. In addition, the basic-set condition for V_I is that $V_I'(0) = 0$, and for V_{II} is that $V_{II}(0) = 0$. A study of the eigenvalues of the distributed *RC* network shows the following properties:

1. The zeros of $V_I(s, d)$, $V_{II}(s, d)$, $V_{II}'(s, d)$ are real, and negative in the s-plane.
2. The zeros are simple.
3. The zeros are infinite in number with an accumulation point at $-\infty$.
4. The zeros of V_I and V_{II} interlace on the negative real axis.
5. The first zero of V_I occurs closer to the origin than the first zero of V_{II}.
6. The first zero of $V_{II}'(s, d)$ occurs closer to the origin than the first zero of $V_{II}(s, d)$.

These properties are readily demonstrated for the uniform *RC* two-port, where

$$V_I(s, d) = \cosh d\sqrt{src}$$

$$V_{II}(s, d) = \frac{\sinh d\sqrt{src}}{\sqrt{src}}$$

$$V_{II}'(s, d) = \cosh d\sqrt{src}$$

Hence the zeros of $V_I(s, d)$ and $V_{II}'(s, d)$ lie at

[7] An accumulation point of zeros is a point in the s plane at which the number of zeros becomes infinite. For example, the function sin $[1/(s + a)]$ has an accumulation point of zeros at $s = -a$.

$$s = -\frac{1}{d^2rc}\,\frac{(2n-1)^2\pi^2}{4}$$

and the zeros of $V_{\text{II}}(s, d)$ lie at

$$s = \frac{-1}{d^2rc}\,n^2\pi^2 \qquad n = 1, 2, 3, \ldots$$

For a nonuniform RC network these properties follow from the Sturm theory.[8]

The conclusion is that the distributed RC network with continuous and bounded $r(x)$, $r'(x)$, $c(x)$, and $g(x)$ exhibits the same general properties as a lumped RC ladder network, except that the number of network critical frequencies is infinite in number.

It is noted that if the basic-set form of solution is not used for the RC network, but instead any pair of linearly independent solutions of the voltage equation, say $V_a(s, x)$ and $V_b(s, x)$, is used, then the expression for y_{11} becomes

$$y_{11} = \frac{-1}{r(0)}\,\frac{V_a'(s,0)V_b(s,d) - V_a(s,d)V_b'(s,0)}{V_a(s,0)V_b(s,d) - V_a(s,d)V_b(s,0)} \tag{2-19}$$

as may be demonstrated from the solution of Problem 2-7.

The other admittance parameters are given by similarly cumbersome expressions. Remembering that V_a and V_b are transcendental functions, which appear many times in (2-19), the difficulty of drawing any conclusions about the characteristics of y_{11} from (2-19) are immediately apparent. For all practical purposes, Equation (2-19) is an undesirable form for determining the poles and zeros of y_{11}. The basic-set approach is a much more desirable technique for the description of distributed network two-port parameters. Let us now determine some of the other two-port parameters of a distributed two-port.

Using the basic set we next obtain the open-circuit impedance parameters of a general two-port distributed network. From the definition of the open-circuit impedance parameters we have

$$z_{11} = \left.\frac{V_1}{I_1}\right|_{I_2=0} = Z(s,0)\,\frac{V_{\text{II}}'(s,d)}{V_{\text{I}}'(s,d)} \tag{2-20a}$$

$$z_{21} = \left.\frac{V_2}{I_1}\right|_{I_2=0} = \frac{Z(s,d)}{V_{\text{I}}'(s,d)} \tag{2-20b}$$

$$z_{12} = \left.\frac{V_1}{I_2}\right|_{I_1=0} = \frac{Z(s,d)}{V_{\text{I}}'(s,d)} \tag{2-20c}$$

[8] See Ince (Ref. 3), Chap. 11.

$$z_{22} = \frac{V_2}{I_2}\bigg|_{I_1=0} = Z(s,d)\,\frac{V_{\mathrm{I}}(s,d)}{V_{\mathrm{I}}'(s,d)} \tag{2-20d}$$

These equations can also be obtained by using Table 1-1 and the $[y_{ij}]$ parameters of (2-18).

Similar conclusions about the pole-zero locations of $[z_{ij}]$ for the distributed RC two-port can be reached. Of course there are an infinite number of critical frequencies for the distributed network. The conclusions are briefly as follows: The poles and zeros of $[z_{ij}]$ for the distributed RC two-port are simple, real, and on the negative real axis. The zeros of z_{12} are all at infinity. The lowest critical frequency of the driving functions is a pole, and the poles and zeros alternate.

From the immittance parameters, one can easily obtain the other two-port parameters. Since the method is straightforward and well known, we shall only give the results in Table 2-1 in terms of the basic-set solutions of the voltage equation.

It is noted that in all cases the zeros and poles of the network two-port parameters, as listed in Table 2-1, are located at the zeros of the basic set (or its derivative evaluated at $x = d$). From the theory of Sturm equations, they are infinite in number and have no accumulation point in the finite s plane.

Table 2-1 THE TWO-PORT PARAMETERS OF THE GENERAL DISTRIBUTED NETWORK IN TERMS OF THE BASIC SET

$z_{11} = Z(s,0)\dfrac{V_{\mathrm{II}}'}{V_{\mathrm{I}}'}$	$z_{21} = \dfrac{Z(s,d)}{V_{\mathrm{I}}'}$	$y_{11} = \dfrac{1}{Z(s,0)}\dfrac{V_{\mathrm{I}}}{V_{\mathrm{II}}}$	$y_{21} = \dfrac{-1}{Z(s,0)V_{\mathrm{II}}}$
$z_{12} = \dfrac{Z(s,d)}{V_{\mathrm{I}}'}$	$z_{22} = \dfrac{Z(s,d)V_{\mathrm{I}}}{V_{\mathrm{I}}'}$	$y_{12} = \dfrac{-1}{Z(s,0)V_{\mathrm{II}}}$	$y_{22} = \dfrac{V_{\mathrm{II}}'}{Z(s,d)V_{\mathrm{II}}}$
$h_{11} = Z(s,0)\dfrac{V_{\mathrm{II}}}{V_{\mathrm{I}}}$	$h_{21} = \dfrac{-1}{V_{\mathrm{I}}}$	$g_{11} = \dfrac{V_{\mathrm{I}}'}{Z(s,0)V_{\mathrm{II}}'}$	$g_{21} = \dfrac{Z(s,d)}{Z(s,0)}\dfrac{1}{V_{\mathrm{II}}'}$
$h_{12} = \dfrac{1}{V_{\mathrm{I}}}$	$h_{22} = \dfrac{V_{\mathrm{I}}'}{Z(s,d)V_{\mathrm{I}}}$	$g_{12} = -\dfrac{Z(s,d)}{Z(s,0)}\dfrac{1}{V_{\mathrm{II}}'}$	$g_{22} = Z(s,d)\dfrac{V_{\mathrm{II}}}{V_{\mathrm{II}}'}$
$A = \dfrac{Z(s,0)}{Z(s,d)}V_{\mathrm{II}}'$	$B = Z(s,0)V_{\mathrm{II}}$	$\mathscr{A} = V_{\mathrm{I}}$	$\mathscr{B} = Z(s,0)V_{\mathrm{II}}$
$C = \dfrac{V_{\mathrm{I}}'}{Z(s,d)}$	$D = V_{\mathrm{I}}$	$\mathscr{C} = \dfrac{V_{\mathrm{I}}'}{Z(s,d)}$	$\mathscr{D} = \dfrac{Z(s,0)}{Z(s,d)}V_{\mathrm{II}}'$
$\Delta_z = Z(s,0)Z(s,d)\dfrac{V_{\mathrm{II}}}{V_{\mathrm{I}}'}$		$\Delta_y = \dfrac{V_{\mathrm{I}}'}{Z(s,0)Z(s,d)V_{\mathrm{II}}}$	

2-5 Obtaining Basic-Set Solutions

In the preceding section we saw how the two-port parameters of the distributed network can be written as simple relations containing ratios of basic-set solutions of the network voltage (or current). Now we shall investigate some ways of obtaining the basic-set solutions. These are the expansion of the basic-set solutions as power series in the complex frequency variable s, and as infinite product expansions. First, let us turn our attention to power-series solutions for the basic set.

Power-series solutions for the basic set are obtained by solving Equation (2-1) by Picard's method.[9] Note that (2-1) is a pair of first-order linear differential equations in the variable x with the complex variable s as a parameter. The solutions may be obtained in a number of different forms. Because the network parameters $Z(s,x)$ and $Y(s,x)$ are fairly arbitrary functions of x, in the general case there is no closed-form solution for the basic set.

The fact that V_{I} and V_{II} are not generally available in closed form, at first may seem to place a severe restriction on the information that can be obtained about the distributed network from the basic-set V_{I} and V_{II}. However, infinite power series and infinite product-form solutions are often preferable for the distributed networks from the pole-zero viewpoint. Even the closed form solutions, when available, have to be put in the series form or in the product form to expose the network pole-zero pattern.

It will be shown in Chapter 3 that under certain conditions the transient behavior of the distributed network is determined principally by the first few terms of the series or product solution of the *basic set*. It will also be shown that the dominant poles and zeros of the distributed RC network can be obtained efficiently when the series or product solution is set up properly.

Picard-Carson method. A powerful method for describing the behavior of distributed networks was presented by Carson in 1921.[10] Carson's method is based on the solution of the transmission-line equations

$$\frac{dV(s,x)}{dx} = -Z(s,x)I \qquad \frac{dI(s,x)}{dx} = -Y(s,x)V \tag{2-21}$$

[9] Picard's method is a standard method of solving numerically for the power-series representation of a differential equation, or a set of differential equations. See, for example, E. Goursat, *A Course in Mathematical Analysis* (New York, Dover, 1945), Vol. 2, Pt. 2, pp. 61–64.

[10] See J. R. Carson, *London Electrician*, **86** (March 4, 1921), 272–273.

employing Picard's method of approximation. Using this method, a uniformly convergent sequence of approximate solutions is obtained to the pair of equations

$$V_x = V_1 - \int_0^x ZI\, dx \qquad I_x = I_1 - \int_0^x YV\, dx \tag{2-22}$$

where Z is the series impedance per unit length of the distributed network and Y is the shunt admittance per unit length of the distributed network. Following Carson, we show the solution in the form of two-port $\mathcal{ABCD}$ parameters, with

$$V_x = V_1 \sum \zeta_{2n} - I_1 \sum \zeta_{2n-1} \tag{2-23a}$$

$$I_x = I_1 \sum \psi_{2n} - V_1 \sum \psi_{2n-1} \tag{2-23b}$$

where V_x and I_x are the voltage and current transforms at point x, and V and I are the voltage and current transforms at the input port, as shown in Figure 2-2. The terms in the four summations of (2-23) are

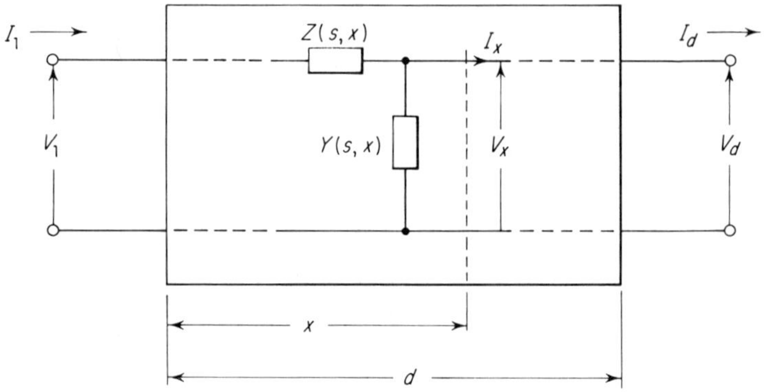

Figure 2-2 Convention for Picard-Carson method.

found by evaluating the following integrals iteratively:

$$\zeta_0 = 1 \qquad \psi_0 = 1 \tag{2-24a}$$

$$\zeta_n = \int_0^x Z\psi_{n-1}\, dx \qquad \psi_n = \int_0^x Y\zeta_{n-1}\, dx \tag{2-24b}$$

An example illustrating this method is worked out later in this section. These equations are very general and apply to all distributed-parameter two-port networks where $Z(s, x)$ and $Y(s, x)$ are integrable—that is, where Z and Y are piecewise continuous and bounded functions of x for all finite values of s.

Thus, Equation (2-24) can be used to obtain solutions for the distributed two-port network parameters for rather arbitrary $Z(x)$ and $Y(x)$ provided that Z and Y are piecewise continuous and bounded. From Equation (2-23), we at once see that these are the $\mathcal{A}\mathcal{B}\mathcal{C}\mathcal{D}$ parameters (if we write using the two-port convention)

$$\begin{bmatrix} V_x \\ -I_x \end{bmatrix} = \begin{bmatrix} \sum \zeta_{2n} & \sum \zeta_{2n-1} \\ \sum \psi_{2n-1} & \sum \psi_{2n} \end{bmatrix} \begin{bmatrix} V_1 \\ -I_1 \end{bmatrix} \tag{2-25}$$

From Equation (2-25) and Table 1-1, the $ABCD$ parameters are

$$A = \sum \psi_{2n} \qquad B = \sum \zeta_{2n-1}$$
$$C = \sum \psi_{2n-1} \qquad D = \sum \zeta_{2n} \tag{2-26}$$

Note that for the nonuniform distributed RC networks, from Equations (2-24) and (2-26) the first coefficient of $B(s)$, when expressed in the form of an infinite series in s, is the total resistance of the network, whereas the first coefficient of $C(s)$ is the total capacitance of the distributed network.

Similarly, the short-circuit admittance parameters are

$$y_{11} = \frac{\sum \zeta_{2n}(d)}{\sum \zeta_{2n-1}(d)} \qquad y_{22} = \frac{\sum \psi_{2n}(d)}{\sum \zeta_{2n-1}(d)}$$
$$y_{12} = y_{21} = \frac{-1}{\sum \zeta_{2n-1}(d)} \tag{2-27}$$

where d is the network length; that is, the integrals in Equation (2-24) are taken from the limits 0 to d.

The $ABCD$ parameters may be expressed in terms of the basic set or vice versa. The result for distributed RC two-ports using Table 2-1 and noting that $Z(s, 0) = r(0)$ and $Z(s, d) = r(d)$ is

$$A = \sum \psi_{2n} = \frac{r(0)}{r(d)} V'_{\text{II}}(s, d) \qquad B = \sum \zeta_{2n-1} = r(0) V_{\text{II}}(s, d)$$
$$C = \sum \psi_{2n-1} = \frac{V'_{\text{I}}(s, d)}{r(d)} \qquad D = \sum \zeta_{2n} = V_{\text{I}}(s, d) \tag{2-28}$$

Hence the series forms of V_{I} and V_{II} may be obtained from (2-28). The Picard-Carson method of determining the parameters of the general distributed-parameter two-port is a practical method for obtaining the two-port parameters of nonuniformly distributed networks.

To illustrate with an example, consider the exponentially tapered[11] distributed RC network, which includes the leakage conductance $g(x)$, as follows:

$$Z(s, x) = r(x) = r_0\epsilon^{2kx}$$

$$Y(s, x) = g(x) + sc(x) = c_0(s + \Omega)\epsilon^{-2kx}$$

Let $S = s + \Omega$, $\Omega = g(x)/c(x) =$ a constant, and $r_0c_0 = \tau$; then

$$Z(s, x) = r(x) = r_0\epsilon^{2kx} \qquad Y(s, x) = Sc(x) = Sc_0\epsilon^{-2kx} \tag{2-29}$$

From the definitions of the coefficients, we write

$$\zeta_0 = 1 \qquad \psi_0 = 1$$

Next, from Equation (2-24), we have

$$\zeta_1(x) = \int_0^x Z(s, x)\psi_0 \, dx = \int_0^x r_0\epsilon^{2kx} \, dx = r_0\left[\frac{\epsilon^{2kx} - 1}{2k}\right]$$

$$\psi_1(x) = \int_0^x Y(s, x)\zeta_0 \, dx = \int_0^x Sc_0\epsilon^{-2kx} \, dx = -Sc_0\left[\frac{\epsilon^{-2kx} - 1}{2k}\right]$$

Using $\zeta_1(x)$ and $\psi_1(x)$ to obtain $\zeta_2(x)$ and $\psi_2(x)$, we find

$$\zeta_2(x) = \int_0^x Z(s, x)\psi_1 \, dx = -\int_0^x r_0\epsilon^{2kx}\left[Sc_0\,\frac{\epsilon^{-2kx} - 1}{2k}\right] dx$$

$$= \frac{-S\tau}{2k}\int_0^x (1 - \epsilon^{2kx}) \, dx = \frac{+S\tau}{(2k)^2}\,(\epsilon^{2kx} - 2kx - 1)$$

$$\psi_2(x) = \int_0^x Y(S, x)\zeta_1(x) \, dx = \int_0^x Sc_0\epsilon^{-2kx}r_0\left(\frac{\epsilon^{2kx} - 1}{2k}\right) dx$$

$$= \frac{S\tau}{2k}\int_0^x (1 - \epsilon^{-2kx}) \, dx = \frac{S\tau}{(2k)^2}\,(\epsilon^{-2kx} + 2kx - 1)$$

Proceeding to the next step in the process gives $\zeta_3(x)$ and $\psi_3(x)$ as

$$\zeta_3(x) = \frac{S\tau r_0}{(2k)^2}\int_0^x (1 + 2kx\epsilon^{2kx} - \epsilon^{2kx}) \, dx$$

$$= \frac{S\tau r_0}{(2k)^3}\,[2 + 2kx - \epsilon^{2kx}(2 - 2kx)]$$

$$\psi_3(x) = \frac{-S^2\tau c_0}{(2k)^2}\int_0^x [2kx\epsilon^{-2kx} + \epsilon^{-2kx} - 1] \, dx$$

$$= \frac{+S^2\tau c_0}{(2k)^3}\,[2kx - 2 + \epsilon^{-2kx}(2kx + 2)]$$

[11] It should be noted that by taper we mean electrical taper and not geometric taper. The physical shape in general is not the same as the electrical shape. This topic is discussed in Chapter 7.

Further iteration of the procedure gives more terms in the series. Thus, ζ_4 is found to be

$$\zeta_4(x) = \frac{+S^2\tau^2}{(2k)^3} \int_0^x [\epsilon^{2kx}(2kx - 2) + (2kx + 2)]\, dx$$

$$= \frac{+S^2\tau^2}{(2k)^4} \left[(2kx - 3)\,\epsilon^{2kx} + 3 + 2(2kx) + \frac{(2kx)^2}{2!} \right]$$

and additional terms are found in a routine fashion. It is noted that each step in the procedure produces more involved integral expressions. This is the chief difficulty in the application of Picard-Carson method for obtaining the two-port parameters of nonuniformly distributed networks. However, the method makes it possible, in the limit, to obtain complete series solutions for the two-port parameters of all types of distributed-parameter two-ports in which $Z(s, x)$ and $Y(s, x)$ are integrable functions. In practical applications, only the first few terms of the series are easily obtained. A resort to iterative techniques suitable to digital computers is necessary when a substantial number of terms in the power-series expansions is desired. This approach has been taken by some authors.[12] This is no real impediment to the method, as applied in practical situations.

In Chapter 3, we shall see how only the first few terms in the power-series expansion, in certain cases, can be used to give a great deal of information about the network behavior. For this reason, the limitation mentioned earlier is not serious. The method gives an exact solution when carried out to the full infinite number of terms. Truncated series solutions provide the information required to describe approximately the key features of network behavior. The Picard-Carson method provides a straightforward method of evaluating the principal or dominant terms in the series solutions and hence can be used to describe the dominant network characteristics to any desired degree of accuracy.

From Equation (2-28) and the result of this illustrative example, we find V_{I} and V_{II} as

$$V_{\text{I}}(s, d) = \sum \zeta_{2n}(d) = 1 + \zeta_2(d) + \zeta_4(d) + \cdots$$

$$= 1 + \frac{S\tau}{(2k)^2} (\epsilon^{2kd} - 2kd - 1)$$

$$+ \frac{(S\tau)^2}{(2k)^4} \left[(2kd - 3)\epsilon^{2kd} + 3 + 2(2kd) + \frac{(2kd)^3}{2!} \right] + \cdots \quad \textbf{(2-30)}$$

$$V_{\text{II}}(s, d) = \frac{1}{r(0)} \sum \zeta_{2n-1} = \frac{1}{r(0)} [\zeta_1 + \zeta_3 + \zeta_5 + \cdots] \quad \textbf{(2-31a)}$$

[12] E. C. Bertnolli, Doctoral Dissertation, Spec. Rept. 57, Kansas Engineering Experiment Station, Manhattan, Kans., Sept. 1965.

$$= \frac{\epsilon^{2kx} - 1}{2k} + \frac{S\tau r_0}{(2k)^3} [2 + 2kx - \epsilon^{2kx}(2 - 2kx)] + \cdots \tag{2-31b}$$

The complete solution for the voltage at the output is written from Equation (2-15a) with appropriate boundary conditions imposed on the network.

For a second example of this method, let us find the power series expansion for the *ABCD* parameters of a uniformly distributed *LC* network (lossless transmission line). Here, an exact solution, in terms of tabulated functions, is readily obtained. In this case, we have

$$Z(s, x) = sl \qquad Y(s, x) = sc \tag{2-32}$$

where l and c are the inductance and capacitance per unit length, respectively. Again,

$$\zeta_0 = 1 \qquad \psi_0 = 1$$

From Equation (2-24) we have

$$\zeta_1(x) = \int_0^x Z(s, x)\psi_0 \, dx = slx$$

$$\psi_1(x) = \int_0^x Y(s, x)\zeta_0 \, dx = scx$$

Next, we obtain

$$\zeta_2(x) = \int_0^x Z(s, x)\psi_1 \, dx = \frac{s^2lcx^2}{2!}$$

$$\psi_2(x) = \int_0^x Y(s, x)\zeta_1 \, dx = \frac{s^2lcx^2}{2!}$$

At this point, the general solutions are obvious and, from Equation (2-26) and the fact that the network is symmetric, we can write immediately that

$$A = D = \sum_{n=0}^{\infty} \zeta_{2n} = \sum_{n=0}^{\infty} \psi_{2n} = 1 + \frac{(sx\sqrt{lc})^2}{2!} + \frac{(sx\sqrt{lc})^4}{4!} + \cdots$$
$$= \cosh sx\sqrt{lc} \tag{2-33a}$$

$$B = \sum_{n=1}^{\infty} \zeta_{2n-1} = \sqrt{\frac{l}{c}} \left[sx\sqrt{lc} + \frac{(sx\sqrt{lc})^3}{3!} + \cdots \right]$$
$$= \sqrt{\frac{l}{c}} \sinh sx\sqrt{lc} \tag{2-33b}$$

$$C = \sum_{n=1}^{\infty} \psi_{2n-1} = \sqrt{\frac{c}{l}} \left[sx\sqrt{lc} + \frac{(sx\sqrt{lc})^3}{3!} + \cdots \right]$$
$$= \sqrt{\frac{c}{l}} \sinh sx\sqrt{lc} \tag{2-33c}$$

Note that $AD - BC = \cosh^2 sx\sqrt{lc} - \sinh^2 sx\sqrt{lc} \equiv 1$, which we know to be true for a reciprocal network. Compare Equation (2-33) with the $\mathcal{ABCD}$ parameters as obtained from Equation (1-20) and Table 1-1, where d is the network length. The results are as expected.

Frobenius' method of undetermined coefficients. The method of Frobenius[13] is a classical method of determining infinite-series solutions of differential equations and is readily adapted to the basic-set description of tapered distributed parameter networks. However, its use must be confined to those networks where the per-unit-length series impedance and shunt admittance can be expressed as convergent power-series expansions in x. For the general $\overline{RLCG}$ two-port, we have the second-order homogeneous differential equation

$$V'' - \left[\frac{1}{Z(s,x)}\frac{dZ(s,x)}{dx}\right]V' - Z(s,x)Y(s,x)V = 0 \qquad \text{(2-34a)}$$

which may, for many types of tapered networks, be written as[14]

$$V'' + F_1(s)P(x)V' + F_2(s)Q(x)V = 0 \qquad \text{(2-34b)}$$

where

$$F_1(s)\,P(x) = -\frac{1}{Z(s,x)}\frac{dZ(s,x)}{dx}$$

$$F_2(x)\,Q(x) = -Z(s,x)\,Y(s,x)$$

The method is applicable to basic-set treatment when $P(x)$ and $Q(x)$ can be expressed as Taylor series in x. We then have

$$P(x) = \sum_{j=0}^{\infty} p_j x^j \qquad \text{(2-35)}$$

$$Q(x) = \sum_{j=0}^{\infty} q_j x^j \qquad \text{(2-36)}$$

over the interval $0 \leqslant x \leqslant d$. In general, it is required that there be no discontinuities in the distributed parameter network. For example, the method of Frobenius is applicable to the uniform $RLCG$ network, where $Z(s,x) = r + sl$, $Y(s,x) = g + sc$, and

$$V'' - (r + sl)(g + sc)V = 0 \qquad \text{(2-37a)}$$

[13] G. Birkhoff and G. Rota, *Ordinary Differential Equations* (Boston, Ginn, 1962), pp. 50–53.

[14] The method is readily extended to more complicated immittance functions such as

$$-\frac{1}{Z(s,x)}\frac{dZ(s,x)}{dx} = F_{11}(s)P_1(x) + F_{12}(s)P_2(x) + \cdots$$

$$Z(s,x)Y(s,x) = F_{21}(s)Q_1(x) + F_{22}(s)Q_2(x) + \cdots$$

with $P(x) = 0$, $Q(x) = 1$, and $F_2(s) = -(r + sl)\,(g + sc)$. Another example is the exponentially tapered network, where $Z(s, x) = (r + sl)\epsilon^{-2kx}$ $Y(s, x) = (g + sc)\epsilon^{2kx}$, and

$$V'' - 2kV' - (r + sl)\,(g + sc)V = 0 \tag{2-37b}$$

with $P(x) = 2k$, $Q(x) = 1$, $F_1(s) = -1$, $F_2(s) = -(r + sl)(g + sc)$.

In general, the basic-set solutions are found by assuming power-series solutions for V_I and V_{II} that are consistent with Equation (2-10); that is,

$$V_{\mathrm{I}}(s, x) = \sum_{n=0}^{\infty} a_n x^n \qquad a_0 = 1 \qquad a_1 = 0 \tag{2-38a}$$

and

$$V_{\mathrm{II}}(s, x) = \sum_{n=0}^{\infty} b_n x^n \qquad b_0 = 0 \qquad b_1 = 1 \tag{2-38b}$$

The assumed solutions, (2-38a) and (2-38b), are substituted in turn into (2-34b), giving V_{I} and V_{II} as power series in x. Coefficients of like powers of x are set equal to zero to satisfy the differential equation, and thus the coefficients a_n and b_n are determined. For example, the basic-set solution V_{I} is found as follows. From Equation (2-38a),

$$V_{\mathrm{I}} = \sum_{n=0}^{\infty} a_n x^n$$

The differentiation yields

$$V_{\mathrm{I}}' = \sum_{n=1}^{\infty} n a_n x^{n-1} \tag{2-39}$$

and

$$V_{\mathrm{I}}'' = \sum_{n=2}^{\infty} n(n-1)\, a_n x^{n-2}$$

Substitution of Equation (2-39) in (2-34b) yields

$$V_{\mathrm{I}}'' + F_1 P V_{\mathrm{I}}' + F_2 Q V_{\mathrm{I}} = 0 \tag{2-40a}$$

From Equations (2-40a), (2-35), and (2-36),

$$\sum_{n=2}^{\infty} n(n-1) a_n x^{n-2} + F_1 \sum_{n=1}^{\infty} n a_n x^{n-1} \sum_{n=0}^{\infty} p_j x^j + F_2 \sum_{n=0}^{\infty} a_n x^n \sum_{j=0}^{\infty} q_j x^j = 0 \tag{2-40b}$$

The terms in Equation (2-40b) are rearranged so that coefficients of like powers of x are grouped together. Thus, from Equation (2-40b) and upon carrying the multiplications and summing terms, we have

$$\sum_{n=2}^{\infty} n(n-1) a_n x^{n-2} = 2a_2 + 6a_3 x + 12 a_4 x^2 \cdots \tag{2-41a}$$

$$\sum_{n=1}^{\infty} na_n x^{n-1} \sum_{j=0}^{\infty} p_j x^j = a_1 p_0 + (2a_2 p_0 + a_1 p_1)x + (3a_3 p_0 + 2a_2 p_1 + a_1 p_2)x^2 + \cdots$$

$$= \sum_{n=2}^{\infty} \left[x^{n-2} \sum_{j=0}^{n-2} (j+1) a_{j+1} p_{n-2-j} \right] \tag{2-41b}$$

and

$$\sum_{n=0}^{\infty} a_n x^n \sum_{j=0}^{\infty} q_j x^j = a_0 q_0 + (a_1 q_0 + a_0 q_1)x + (a_2 q_0 + a_1 q_1 + a_0 q_2)x^2 + \cdots$$

$$= \sum_{n=2}^{\infty} \left(x^{n-2} \sum_{j=0}^{n-2} a_j q_{n-2-j} \right) \tag{2-41c}$$

In power-series form, Equation (2-34b) becomes

$$\sum_{n=2}^{\infty} x^{n-2} \left[n(n-1)a_n + F_1 \sum_{j=0}^{n-2} (j+1) a_{j+1} p_{n-2-j} + F_2 \sum_{j=0}^{n-2} a_j q_{n-2-j} \right] = 0 \tag{2-42}$$

Since each coefficient in the series must be zero, we have

$$a_n = \frac{F_1 \sum_{j=0}^{n-2} (j+1) a_{j+1} p_{n-2-j} + F_2 \sum_{j=0}^{n-2} a_j q_{n-2-j}}{-n(n-1)} \qquad n \geqslant 2 \tag{2-43}$$

We recall that in the power-series expansion for V_{I}, $a_0 = 1$ and $a_1 = 0$. These values uniquely determine the remaining coefficients a_i. Thus, from Equation (2-43), with $a_0 = 1$ and $a_1 = 0$,

$$a_2 = -\frac{F_2 a_0 q_0}{2} = -\frac{F_2 q_0}{2} \tag{2-44a}$$

$$a_3 = \frac{F_1(2a_2 p_0) + F_2 a_0 q_1}{-6} = \frac{2F_1 p_0 + F_2 q_1}{-6} \tag{2-44b}$$

and so forth.

Using similar methods of analysis, the coefficients of the power series in x for V_{II} can be determined. The general term is

$$b_n = \frac{F_1 \sum_{j=1}^{n-2} (j+1) b_{j+1} p_{n-2-j} + F_2 \sum_{j=0}^{n-2} b_j q_{n-2-j}}{-n(n-1)} \qquad n \geqslant 2 \tag{2-45}$$

where $b_0 = 0$ and $b_1 = 1$ for V_{II}.

The method of undetermined coefficients provides a means of determining series solutions in x for the basic set when $P(x)$ and $Q(x)$ are analytic functions of x. Equations (2-43) and (2-45) for the coefficients a_n and b_n are easy to evaluate when $P(x)$ and $Q(x)$ are simple functions with few terms in their Taylor expansions.

The basic set is obtained by setting $x = d$. It is noted that the power-series solutions for V_{I} and V_{II} are analytic in d and may be differentiated with respect to d to obtain V_{I} and V_{II}. They are also analytic in s for analytic $F_1(s)$ and $F_2(s)$. This may be seen from Equations (2-43) and (2-45), where F_1 and F_2 occur only in positive, integral powers. Hence the solutions V_{I}, V_{I}', V_{II}, and V_{II}' are analytic functions of two variables, d and s.

The power-series solutions in d are absolutely convergent over the interval $0 \leqslant x \leqslant d$, since $P(x)$ and $Q(x)$ must be analytic if the method is to be used. Therefore, the terms of the power series can be rearranged[15] without affecting convergence. In particular, the series can be rearranged with coefficients that are functions of d multiplying ascending powers of s. Essentially, this provides a means to obtain a power series in s for V_{I}, V_{I}', V_{II}, and V_{II}'. From complex-function theory, this is the Taylor expansion in s of V_{I}, V_{I}', V_{II}, and V_{II}'.

As an illustration of the method of Frobenius, consider the exponentially tapered $\overline{RLCG}$ network. For this example,

$$Z(s, x) = (r_0 + sl_0)\,\epsilon^{2kx} \qquad Y(s, x) = (g_0 + sc_0)\,\epsilon^{-2kx}$$

From this, $P(x) = p_0 = 2k$, $F_1(s) = -1$, $Q(x) = q_0 = 1$, and $F_2(s) = -(r_0 + sl_0)(g_0 + sc_0)$. Using Equation (2-43),

$$a_n = \frac{2k(n-1)a_{n-1} + (r_0 + sl_0)(g_0 + sc_0)a_{n-2}}{n(n+1)} \qquad n \geqslant 2 \tag{2-46}$$

and the first few coefficients of V_{I} are

$$a_0 = 1 \qquad a_1 = 0 \qquad a_2 = \frac{(r_0 + sl_0)(g_0 + sc_0)}{2 \cdot 1}$$

$$a_3 = \frac{2k(r_0 + sl_0)(g_0 + sc_0)}{3 \cdot 2}$$

$$a_4 = \frac{(r_0 + sl_0)^2(g_0 + sc_0)^2 + (2k)^2(r_0 + sl_0)(g_0 + sc_0)}{4 \cdot 3 \cdot 2}$$

and so on.

The power-series expansion in d for $V_{\text{I}}(s, d)$ is simply

$$V_{\text{I}}(s, d) = 1 + a_2 d^2 + a_3 d^3 + \ldots \tag{2-47}$$

[15] P. Dienes, *The Taylor Series* (New York, Dover, 1957), pp. 145–146.

By expanding the coefficients in terms of like powers of s, a series of the form

$$V_{\mathrm{I}}(s, d) = \alpha_0 + \alpha_1 s + \alpha_2 s^2 + \alpha_3 s^3 + \cdots \tag{2-48}$$

can be obtained. For the exponentially tapered $\overline{RLCG}$ network, the coefficients of s are

$$\alpha_0 = 1 + \frac{r_0 g_0 d^2}{2!} + \frac{(2kd) r_0 g_0 d^2}{3!} + \cdots \tag{2-49a}$$

$$\alpha_1 = \frac{(g_0 l_0 + r_0 c_0) d^2}{2!} + \frac{(2kd)(g_0 l_0 + r_0 c_0) d^2}{3!} + \cdots \tag{2-49b}$$

$$\alpha_2 = \frac{l_0 c_0 d^2}{2!} + \frac{(2kd) l_0 c_0 d^2}{3!} + \cdots \tag{2-49c}$$

and so on.

For the special case of the exponentially tapered $\overline{RC}$ network (that is, $g_0 = l_0 = 0$) the coefficients α_i in (2-49) are

$$\alpha_1 = r_0 c_0 d^2 \left[\frac{1}{2!} + \frac{(2k)d}{3!} + \frac{(2k)^2 d^2}{4!} + \cdots\right] \tag{2-50a}$$

$$\alpha_2 = (r_0 c_0 d^2)^2 \left[\frac{1}{4!} + \frac{2(2k)d}{5!} + \frac{3(2k)^2 d^2}{6!} + \cdots\right] \tag{2-50b}$$

$$\alpha_3 = (r_0 c_0 d^2)^3 \left[\frac{1}{6!} + \frac{3(2k)d}{7!} + \frac{6(2k)^2 d^2}{8!} + \cdots\right] \tag{2-50c}$$

With some manipulation, the coefficients α_i may be recognized as closed-form expressions; thus,

$$\alpha_1 = \left(\frac{1}{2kd}\right)^2 (\epsilon^{2kd} - 2kd - 1)\tau \tag{2-50d}$$

$$\alpha_2 = \left(\frac{1}{2kd}\right)^4 \left[\epsilon^{2kd}(2kd - 3) + 3 + 2skd + \frac{(2kd)^2}{2!}\right]\tau^2 \tag{2-50e}$$

and so on. Note that $\tau = r_0 c_0 d^2$.

It is by no means obvious that

$$V_{\mathrm{I}} = \cosh d\sqrt{s\tau + k^2} - \frac{k \sinh d\sqrt{s\tau + k^2}}{\sqrt{s\tau + k^2}} \tag{2-51}$$

which is the closed-form solution of Equation (2-34) for the $\overline{ERC}$ network, obtained by other methods (see Chapter 4).

A solution for V_{II} using the method of undetermined coefficients also produces unwieldy expressions for the coefficients of s (Problem 2-5).

The chief disadvantage in applying the method of undetermined coefficients to tapered distributed-parameter networks is the difficulty of rearranging the terms of the power series from a Taylor expansion in d to a Taylor expansion in s so that the network behavior in the complex-frequency plane can be evaluated. However, the method of undetermined coefficients shows that Taylor expansions in $s\tau$ exist for the basic set when $P(x)$ and $Q(x)$ are analytic on the interval $0 \leqslant x \leqslant d$, provided $F_1(s)$ and $F_2(s)$ are analytic.

2-6 Product Expansions of the Basic Set

In this section, we shall discuss product solutions of the distributed-parameter two-port voltage and current relations. The methods of product solution, and infinite products in general, are not as familiar to many electrical engineers as are the methods of infinite-series solutions. Therefore, we shall first show how product expansions are used to describe network functions. The infinite product is usually very similar to the factored form of a polynomial network function. To illustrate the concept of the infinite product expansion, we consider the familiar and simple cases of the uniformly distributed LC and RC networks. Methods of obtaining the product solutions for the general nonuniform case are treated in the next two sections.

The product expansion of a basic-set solution, say $V_\text{I}(s, d)$, is written in the form

$$V_\text{I}(s, d) = V_\text{I}(0, d) \prod_{n=1}^{\infty} \left(1 + \frac{s}{z_n}\right) \tag{2-52}$$

where $V_\text{I}(0, d)$ is the dc (zero-frequency) value of V_I, and z_n is the nth zero of $V_\text{I}(s, d)$.

For example, for the uniform lossless distributed lc (abbreviated as $\overline{ULC}$) two-port, where $V_\text{I} = \cosh sd\sqrt{lc}$, the product expansion for V_I is

$$V_\text{I}(s, d) = \cosh sd\sqrt{lc} = \prod_{n=1}^{\infty} \left[1 + \frac{4s^2d^2lc}{(2n-1)^2\pi^2}\right] \tag{2-53}$$

Also, for the lossless $\overline{ULC}$ two-port,

$$V_\text{II} = \frac{\sinh sd\sqrt{lc}}{s\sqrt{lc}}$$

and the product expansion for V_II is

$$V_\text{II}(s, d) = \frac{\sinh sd\sqrt{lc}}{s\sqrt{lc}} = d \prod_{n=1}^{\infty} \left(1 + \frac{s^2d^2lc}{n^2\pi^2}\right) \tag{2-54}$$

Using Equations (2-53) and (2-54), we obtain the short-circuit driving-point admittance of the $\overline{ULC}$ two-port of length d as

$$y_{11} = \frac{1}{sl}\frac{V_{\text{I}}}{V_{\text{II}}} = \frac{1}{sld}\prod_{n=1}^{\infty}\frac{\left[1+\dfrac{4s^2d^2lc}{(2n-1)^2\pi^2}\right]}{\left[1+\dfrac{s^2d^2lc}{n^2\pi^2}\right]} \tag{2-55}$$

The lossless distributed lc two-port is shown schematically in Figure 2-3(a), and the pole-zero pattern from (2-55) is shown in Figure 2-3(b).

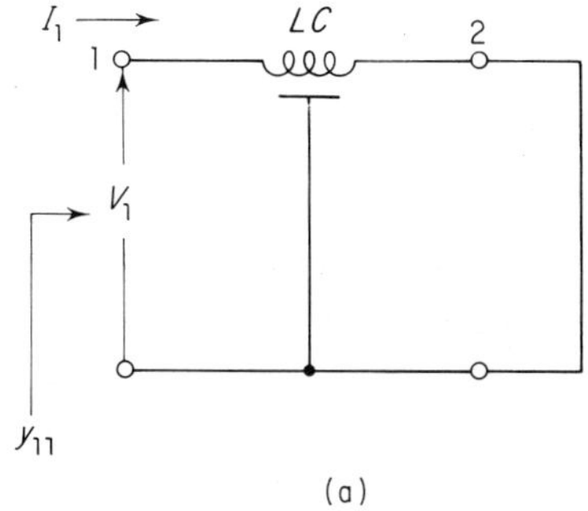

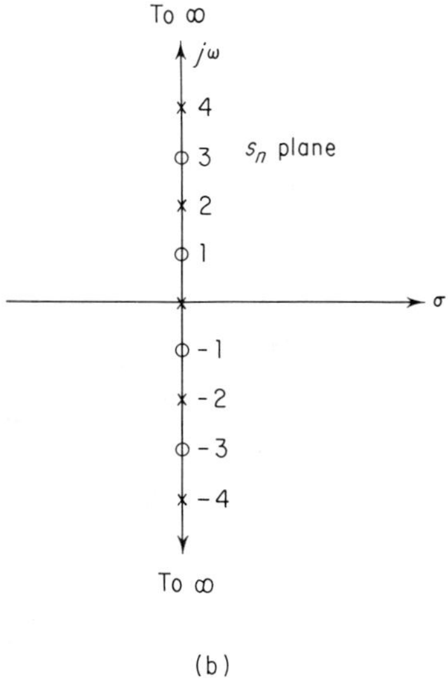

Figure 2-3 (**a**) Lossless lc two-port $(\overline{ULC})$. (**b**) Pole-zero pattern of y_{11} (normalized to $2d\sqrt{lc}/\pi$).

As shown by Equation (2-55) and in Figure 2-3(b), the poles and zeros of y_{11} interlace on the imaginary axis, and the first critical frequency is a pole at $\omega = 0$. From Equation (2-55) it is obvious that y_{11} is infinite at zero frequency, thus giving the pole at $\omega = 0$. Furthermore, the driving-point admittance of the short-circuited $\overline{ULC}$ network has a pole-zero pattern that interlaces, which is similar to the pole-zero characteristic of driving-point admittance of lumped LC networks. The short-circuit driving-point admittance of a finite lumped-constant LC network can be written (see Chapter 6) in factored form as

$$y_{11} = \frac{y_{11}(0)}{s}\left[\frac{\left(1+\dfrac{s^2}{\omega_0{}^2}\right)\left(1+\dfrac{s^2}{\omega_2{}^2}\right)\left(1+\dfrac{s^2}{\omega_4{}^2}\right)\cdots\left(1+\dfrac{s^2}{\omega_{2N}{}^2}\right)}{\left(1+\dfrac{s^2}{\omega_1{}^2}\right)\left(1+\dfrac{s^2}{\omega_3{}^2}\right)\left(1+\dfrac{s^2}{\omega_5{}^2}\right)\cdots\left(1+\dfrac{s^2}{\omega_{2N+1}{}^2}\right)}\right]$$

where $\omega_0 < \omega_1 < \omega_2 < \cdots < \omega_{2n-1} < \omega_{2N} < \omega_{2N+1}$. However, there are an infinite number of critical frequencies for the distributed two-port.

Thus, product expansions of the basic set contain a great deal of useful information about the network characteristics.

As further illustration of the usefulness of the product expansion as a source of information about distributed-network behavior, consider the uniform RC distributed network ($\overline{URC}$). For this network, V_{I} and V_{II} in product form are given by

$$V_{\text{I}}(s, d) = \cosh d\sqrt{src} = \prod_{n=1}^{\infty} \left[1 + \frac{4srcd^2}{(2n-1)^2\pi^2}\right] \tag{2-56a}$$

and

$$V_{\text{II}}(s, d) = \frac{\sinh d\sqrt{src}}{\sqrt{src}} = d\prod_{n=1}^{\infty} \left(1 + \frac{srcd^2}{n^2\pi^2}\right) \tag{2-56b}$$

The roots of V_{I} and V_{II} for the $\overline{URC}$ two-port lie on the negative real axis. The short-circuit driving-point admittance in product form is

$$y_{11} = \frac{1}{r}\frac{V_{\text{I}}(s, d)}{V_{\text{II}}(s, d)} = \frac{1}{rd}\prod_{n=1}^{\infty} \frac{\left[1 + \dfrac{4srcd^2}{(2n-1)^2\pi^2}\right]}{\left[1 + \dfrac{srcd^2}{n^2\pi^2}\right]} \tag{2-57}$$

Circuit representations of the $\overline{URC}$ two-port and the pole-zero patterns of y_{11} are shown in Figure 2-4(a) and (b), respectively.

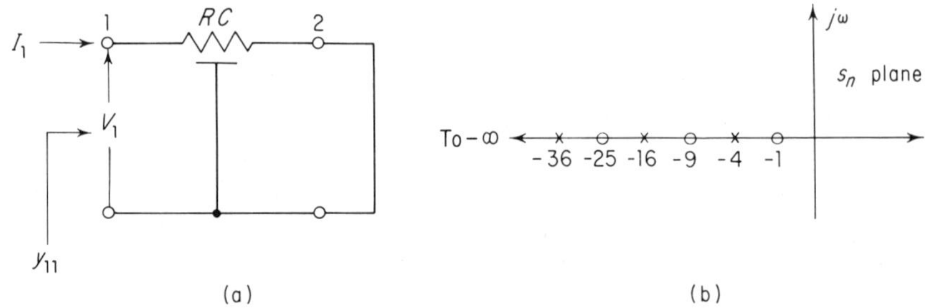

Figure 2-4 (**a**) RC two-port ($\overline{URC}$) with output short-circuited. (**b**) Pole-zero pattern of y_{11} (normalized to $4rcd^2/\pi^2$).

As in the previous example for the uniformly distributed lc ($\overline{ULC}$) two-port, the product expansion of y_{11} for the uniform rc two-port provides useful information about the network behavior. It can be seen from Figure 2-4(b) that the poles and zeros of y_{11} alternate on the negative real axis, as they do for lumped RC two-ports. Further, the dc (zero-frequency) value of y_{11} is nonzero, and $y_{11}(0) = (rd)^{-1}$, which is the reciprocal of the series resistance of the RC network.

The product expansion of basic-set functions also makes it possible to construct frequency-domain plots of network functions in a relatively simple manner. Using the short-circuit driving-point admittance of the $\overline{URC}$ network as an example, we can readily obtain the driving-point admittance in the frequency domain from Equation (2-57) as

$$y_{11}(j\omega) = \frac{1}{rd}\prod_{n=1}^{\infty}\frac{\left[1 + j\dfrac{4\omega rcd^2}{(2n-1)^2\pi^2}\right]}{\left[1 + j\dfrac{\omega rcd^2}{n^2\pi^2}\right]} \tag{2-58}$$

$$= |y_{11}(j\omega)|\epsilon^{j\phi(j\omega)}$$

where $|y_{11}(j\omega)|$ is the magnitude of y_{11} and $\phi(j\omega)$ is the phase function. These are found from

$$|y_{11}(j\omega)|^2 = \left(\frac{1}{rd}\right)^2\prod_{n=1}^{\infty}\frac{\left[1 + \dfrac{16\omega^2r^2c^2d^4}{(2n-1)^4\pi^4}\right]}{\left[1 + \dfrac{\omega^2r^2c^2d^4}{n^4\pi^4}\right]} \tag{2-59a}$$

$$\phi(j\omega) = \sum_{n=1}^{\infty}\left[\tan^{-1}\frac{4\omega rcd^2}{(2n-1)^2\pi^2} - \tan^{-1}\frac{\omega rcd^2}{n^2\pi^2}\right] \tag{2-59b}$$

A simple way of estimating graphically the magnitude and phase functions is to use the Bode plot, which shows a positive slope in the magnitude function of 6 dB per octave (20 dB per decade) at each radian frequency numerically equal to a simple real zero, and a slope of -6 dB per octave at each radian frequency numerically equal to a simple pole. The phase function is sketched by summing up, assigning phase lead or lag angle of 45 degrees at each zero or pole, and assigning 0° to the phase contributions one decade in frequency below the zero or pole and ±90° to the contributions one decade in frequency above the zero of pole. Linear interpolation on semilog paper is used to estimate phase contributions in the intermediate regions. The Bode plot in general does not provide a good approximation at or near the break frequencies.

A Bode plot of $y_{11}(j\omega)$, magnitude and phase, for the uniform RC two-port is shown in Figure 2-5. The true values are shown for comparison. Note that the magnitude slope asymptotically approaches +3 dB per octave, whereas the phase asymptotically approaches +45°. From this example, it is evident that the product expansion of basic-set solutions provides a simple method to sketch Bode plots. From these plots,

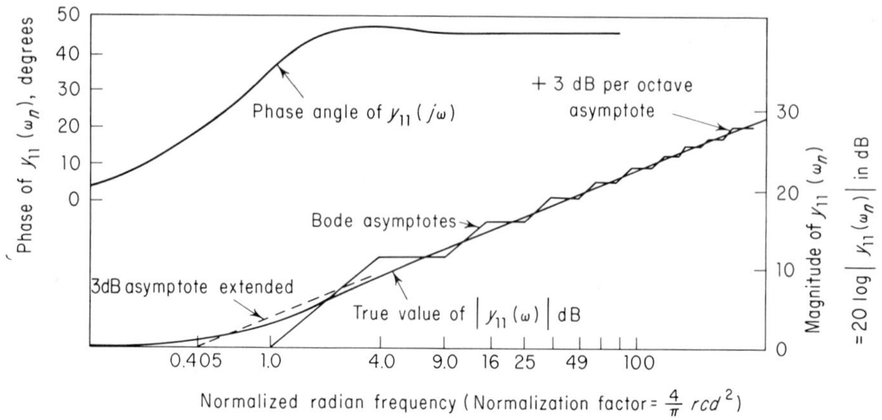

Figure 2-5 Bode plot of $y_{11}(j\omega)$ for $\overline{URC}$. Magnitude and phase of $y_{11}(j\omega)$ for the uniform rc two-port.

the network behavior in the frequency domain can be estimated quickly and to an adequate degree of precision for most engineering purposes.

Unlike the technique for series solution of distributed network two-port parameters given in Section 2-4, which presents explicit expressions for the coefficients in the series, there is no general method for obtaining explicit values for the roots of the basic set for the nonuniformly distributed two-port. The reason is that the roots of the immittance parameters are roots of transcendental equations and cannot in general be written exactly. However, it is possible to find the roots of the basic set to an arbitrary degree of precision. The procedures employed are numerical. We shall limit our discussion here to two general approaches for finding the roots of the basic set.[16] The first is based on a method developed by Lagrange in which the distributed system is approximated by a sequence of lumped-element networks in cascade. This approach is somewhat similar to the iterated structure approach of Chapter 1 with which the reader has some familiarity. The second approach is based on the Rayleigh principle, by which estimates of the roots of the basic-set solutions—and more important, bounds on the errors in determining the roots—can be made. We shall first discuss the method developed by Lagrange.

Lagrange's method. The method to be discussed in the following section is referred to by Kopal[17] as the Lagrangian three-point formula. It is basically an application of difference equations. As before, the basic

[16] For a comprehensive treatment of the method, see L. Collatz, *The Numerical Treatment of Differential Equations* (Berlin, Springer, 1960). Also, L. Collatz, *Eigenwertprobleme und ihre Numerische Behandlung* (New York, Chelsea reprint).

[17] Z. Kopal, *Numerical Analysis* (New York, Wiley, 1961), pp. 299–319.

set is used to describe the distributed network two-port parameters, and the Lagrangian three-point formula is used to obtain estimates of the zeros of these functions.

The method is applicable to the solution of differential equations of many types, particularly when boundary values are important, as is the case for basic set solutions. Consider the voltage equation for the distributed *RLCG* two-port:

$$V'' - \frac{Z'(s,x)}{Z(s,x)} V' - Z(s,x)Y(s,x)V = 0 \tag{2-60}$$

As shown in Section 2-5, Equation (2-60) has Taylor-series solutions as power series in x when the coefficients of V' and V can be written as Taylor expansions in x; that is, at any point in the network, with $0 \leqslant a \leqslant d$, we can write the voltage as

$$V(a \pm h) = V(a) \pm hV'(a) + \frac{h^2 V''(a)}{2!} + \cdots \tag{2-61}$$

From Equation (2-61) we can estimate $V'(a)$ and $V''(a)$ from the values taken by $V(x)$ at three points: $x = a - h$, $x = a$, and $x = a + h$. Thus, by subtraction and addition, respectively, in Equation (2-61),

$$V'(a) \approx \frac{V(a+h) - V(a-h)}{2h} \tag{2-62a}$$

$$V''(a) \approx \frac{V(a+h) + V(a-h) - 2V(a)}{h^2} \tag{2-62b}$$

The truncation error is of the order of $(2h^3/3!)V^{\text{III}}(a)$ for Equation (2-62a) and of the order of $(2h^4/4!)V^{\text{IV}}(a)$ for Equation (2-62b). For small increments, these become negligible. Upon substitution of (2-62) into the voltage equation (2-60), we find after clearing fractions that the differential equation is approximated by

$$\left[\frac{1}{hZ(a)} + \frac{Z'(a)}{2Z^2(a)}\right] V(a-h) - \left[hY(a) + \frac{2}{hZ(a)}\right] V(a) + \left[\frac{1}{hZ(a)} - \frac{Z'(a)}{2Z^2(a)}\right] V(a+h) = 0 \tag{2-63a}$$

or by the equivalent alternate form more suited to direct substitution for purposes of calculation

$$\left(2 - \frac{Z'}{Z}h\right) V(a+h) - (4 + 2h^2 ZY)V(a) + \left(2 + \frac{Z'}{Z}h\right) V(a-h) = 0 \tag{2-63b}$$

where $Z(a)$ and $Y(a)$ are the per-unit length series impedance and shunt conductance at $x = a$, and h is an incremental length of network. Equation (2-63) can be interpreted by a network model, as shown in Figure 2-6.

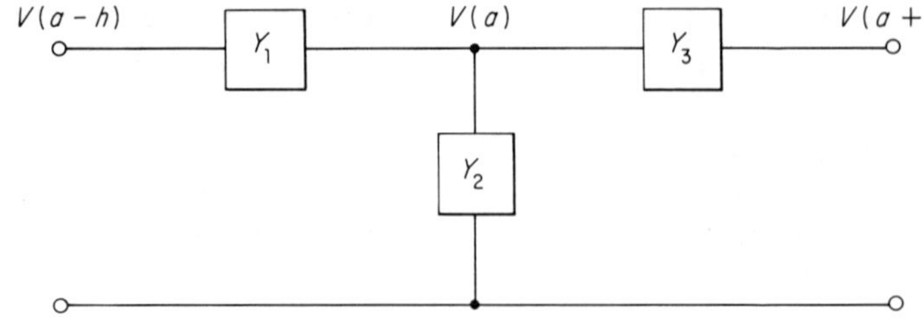

$$Y_1 = \frac{1}{hZ(a)} + \frac{Z'(a)}{2Z^2(a)} \approx \frac{1}{h\left[Z(a) - \frac{hZ'(a)}{2}\right]} \approx \frac{1}{hZ_1}$$

$$Y_2 = hY(a)$$

$$Y_3 = \frac{1}{hZ(a)} - \frac{Z'(a)}{2Z^2(a)} \approx \frac{1}{h\left[Z(a) + \frac{hZ'(a)}{2}\right]} = \frac{1}{hZ_3}$$

Figure 2-6 Network representation of Lagrange three-point formula.

The T network shown has an admittance Y_1 between points $x = a - h$ and $x = a$. The value of the admittance is simply the reciprocal of the average per-unit-length series impedance between points $(a - h)$ and a, multiplied by h. The admittance Y_2 is the average per unit-length shunt admittance between points $(a - h/2)$ and $(a + h/2)$ multiplied by h. The admittance Y_3 is the reciprocal of the average per-unit-length series impedance between points a and $(a + h)$, multiplied by h. The Lagrangian three-point formula can be regarded as a method to replace a distributed structure by a lumped structure.

To apply the Lagrangian three-point formula, divide the network into a number of T sections, each of length h. The network equation (2-63) is then written for each T section. For example, suppose the network is divided into two parts. Then $h = d/2$, and $a = d/2$ and we have one T section. The network equation is

$$\left[\frac{2}{dZ(d/2)} + \frac{Z'(d/2)}{2Z^2(d/2)}\right] V(0) - \left[(d/2)Y(d/2) + \frac{4}{dZ(d/2)}\right] V(d/2)$$
$$+ \left[\frac{2}{dZ(d/2)} - \frac{Z'(d/2)}{2Z^2(d/2)}\right] V(d) = 0 \qquad \textbf{(2-64)}$$

For $h = d/3$, $a_1 = d/3$, and $a_2 = 2d/3$, we have two T sections and the system of equations

$$y_{12}V(0) - y_{22}V(d/3) + y_{32}V(2d/3) = 0$$
$$y_{23}V(d/3) - y_{33}V(2d/3) + y_{43}V(d) = 0 \qquad \textbf{(2-65)}$$

where y_{ij} are the admittances defined by Equation (2-63). The approximate values of the zeros of V_{I} and V_{II} are found by setting the determinant of the coefficients of V equal to zero after applying the appropriate boundary conditions. For example, the zeros of V_{I} are found approximately using the boundary conditions $V'(0) = 0$, $V(d) = 0$; the boundary conditions appropriate for V_{II} are $V(0) = V(d) = 0$. To show the application of the Lagrangian three-point formula, it is best to give an example.

Consider the exponentially tapered RC network ($\overline{ERC}$ network) with $r(x) = r_0\epsilon^{2kx}$, $c(x) = c_0\epsilon^{-2kx}$. For convenience, normalize the network to unit length; that is, set $d = 1$. For this example let $h = 1/2$, in which case the network is divided into two parts. Then $a = 1/2$, and $Z'/Z = +2k$. From Equation (2-63b)

$$(1 + k/2)V(0) - (2 + \lambda/4)V(1/2) + (1 - k/2)V(1) = 0 \tag{2-66}$$

where $\lambda = sr_0c_0d^2 = s\tau$. If an approximation to the zeros of V_{II} is sought, it is noted from the boundary conditions on V_{II} that Equation (2-66) reduces to

$$(2 + \lambda/4)V_{\mathrm{II}}(1/2) = 0 \tag{2-67}$$

since $V_{\mathrm{II}}(0) = V_{\mathrm{II}}(1) = 0$. From Equation (2-67) $\lambda = -8$, from which the dominant root of V_{II}, $s_1 \simeq -8/\tau$. The true value of s_1 is $-(1/\tau)$, $[\pi^2 + k^2]$ – that is, $s_1 = -(1/\tau)\ [9.87 + k^2]$ – and the approximation to s_1 is too low by 19 percent for $k = 0$. To obtain better accuracy on the values of the roots, the network must be divided into a greater number of sections.

Next, consider the network divided into three parts, with $h = 1/3$, $a_1 = 1/3$, $a_2 = 2/3$. Substituting these values into Equation (2-63) produces the pair of equations

$$(1 - k/3)V(2/3) + (1 + k/3)V(0) - (2 + \lambda/9)V(1/3) = 0 \tag{2-68a}$$

$$(1 - k/3)V(1) - (2 + \lambda/9)V(2/3) + (1 + k/3)V(1/3) = 0 \tag{2-68b}$$

The pair of equations has a nontrivial solution only if the determinant of the coefficients vanishes. Note that when solving for V_{II}, boundary conditions require that $V(0) = 0$. The system of equations then becomes

$$(1 - k/3)V_{\mathrm{II}}(2/3) - (2 + \lambda/9)V_{\mathrm{II}}(1/3) = 0 \tag{2-69a}$$

and

$$-(2 + \lambda/9)V_{\mathrm{II}}(2/3) + (1 + k/3)V_{\mathrm{II}}(1/3) = 0 \tag{2-69b}$$

from which V_{II} has a nontrivial solution if λ satisfies the equation

$$\lambda^2 + 36\lambda + (243 + 9k^2) = 0 \tag{2-70a}$$

giving

$$\lambda = -9\ [2 \pm \sqrt{1 - (k/3)^2}] \tag{2-70b}$$

For small k, the square root may be approximated by $1 - k^2/18$, in which case

$$s_1 \simeq -\frac{1}{\tau}[9 + k^2/2] \tag{2-71a}$$

$$s_2 \simeq -\frac{1}{\tau}[27 - k^2/2] \tag{2-71b}$$

The true solutions are

$$s_1 = -\frac{1}{\tau}[\pi^2 + k^2] \qquad s_2 = -\frac{1}{\tau}[4\pi^2 + k^2]$$

and the approximate values are too low by 8.8 percent and 32 percent respectively for $k = 0$. It is noted, however, that the approximation to the first root using three intervals is better than the approximation using two intervals, and that in each case the approximate value is smaller than the true value.

For a second example, consider the zeros of V_{I} of the $\overline{ERC}$ network. From the boundary conditions on V_{I}—that is, $V_{\mathrm{I}}'(0) = V_{\mathrm{I}}(1) = 0$—it is seen from Equation (2-62a) that

$$V_{\mathrm{I}}(h) = V_{\mathrm{I}}(-h) \qquad V_{\mathrm{I}}(1) = 0 \tag{2-72}$$

For the first step in this example, let $h = 1/2$, $a_1 = 0$, $a_2 = 1/2$. Then,

$$(1 - k/2)\, V_{\mathrm{I}}(1/2) + (1 + k/2) V_{\mathrm{I}}(-1/2) - (\lambda/4 + 2) V_{\mathrm{I}}(0) = 0 \tag{2-73a}$$

and $$(1 - k/2) V_{\mathrm{I}}(1) + (1 + k/2) V_{\mathrm{I}}(0) - (\lambda/4 + 2) V_{\mathrm{I}}(1/2) = 0 \tag{2-73b}$$

and, upon insertion of the boundary conditions, this becomes

$$2V_{\mathrm{I}}(1/2) - (\lambda/4 + 2) V_{\mathrm{I}}(0) = 0 \tag{2-74a}$$

$$-(\lambda/4 + 2) V_{\mathrm{I}}(1/2) + (1 + k/2) V_{\mathrm{I}}(0) = 0 \tag{2-74b}$$

For a nontrivial solution of Equation (2-74) to exist, the determinant of the coefficients must equal zero, from which we find that λ must satisfy

$$\lambda^2 + 16\lambda + (32 - 16k) = 0 \tag{2-75}$$

with solutions

$$\lambda = -8 \pm 5.6568\sqrt{1 + k/2} \tag{2-76}$$

giving, for $k = 0$,

$$s_1 \simeq -\frac{1}{\tau}[2.3432] \qquad s_2 \simeq -\frac{1}{\tau}[13.6568] \tag{2-77}$$

The approximate values s_1 and s_2 are too low by 5 percent and 38 percent, respectively, for $k = 0$.

A better approximation to the zeros of V_{I} can be obtained if the origin is not a point in the equations. Taking $h = 2/5$ and $a_1 = 1/5$, $a_2 = 3/5$, substitution into (2-63) gives the following pair of equations:

$$\left(1 - \frac{2k}{5}\right)V\left(\frac{3}{5}\right) + \left(1 + \frac{2k}{5}\right)V\left(-\frac{1}{5}\right) - \left(\frac{4\lambda}{25} + 2\right)V\left(\frac{1}{5}\right) = 0 \quad \textbf{(2-78a)}$$

$$\left(1 - \frac{2k}{5}\right)V(1) + \left(1 + \frac{2k}{5}\right)V\left(\frac{1}{5}\right) - \left(\frac{4\lambda}{25} + 2\right)V\left(\frac{3}{5}\right) = 0 \quad \textbf{(2-78b)}$$

Using the boundary conditions stated in Equation (2-72), the equations for V_{I} reduce to

$$\left(1 - \frac{2k}{5}\right)V_{\mathrm{I}}\left(\frac{3}{5}\right) - \left(\frac{4\lambda}{25} - \frac{2k}{5} + 1\right)V_{\mathrm{I}}\left(\frac{1}{5}\right) = 0 \quad \textbf{(2-79a)}$$

$$-\left(\frac{4\lambda}{25} + 2\right)V_{\mathrm{I}}\left(\frac{3}{5}\right) + \left(1 + \frac{2k}{5}\right)V_{\mathrm{I}}\left(\frac{1}{5}\right) = 0 \quad \textbf{(2-79b)}$$

For a nontrivial voltage solution to exist, the determinant of the coefficients of V_{I} must equal zero, from which we get

$$16\lambda^2 + (300 - 40k)\lambda + (25 - 10k)^2 = 0 \quad \textbf{(2-80a)}$$

with the solutions

$$\lambda = -\left[\frac{(300 - 40k) \pm 223.60\sqrt{1 + 0.160k - 0.0960k^2}}{32}\right] \quad \textbf{(2-80b)}$$

The approximations to the first two zeros of V_{I} with $k = 0$ are

$$s_1 \simeq -\frac{1}{\tau}[2.3875] \qquad s_2 \simeq -\frac{1}{\tau}[16.331] \quad \textbf{(2-81)}$$

which are 3.6 percent and 26.1 percent lower than the true values

$$s_1 = -\frac{1}{\tau}\left(\frac{\pi^2}{4}\right) \qquad s_2 = -\frac{1}{\tau}9\left(\frac{\pi^2}{4}\right) \qquad \text{for } k = 0$$

The examples given in this section demonstrate that reasonably good approximations to the first zeros of V_{I} and V_{II}, which are usually dominant, can be obtained with simple numerical techniques. In these examples the solution of simple systems of algebraic equations is required. Taking more intervals will increase the number of network zeros found and will also improve the accuracy of the approximations. The price to be paid for the greater accuracy and the greater number of network zeros is the greater amount of work required to find the roots of the polynomial that determine the network zeros; that is, a third-order polynomial must be factored to get the first three zeros, and an nth order polynomial for the first n zeros.

If only the first few network zeros are needed, and values to an accuracy of approximately 1 percent are good enough, then Richardson's extrapolation procedure[18] may be applied to the information obtained by the Lagrangian three-point formula. This procedure is described briefly in the following section.

Richardson's extrapolation procedure. When applied in conjunction with the Lagrange three-point formula, Richardson's extrapolation procedure yields the eigenvalues of the distributed system with very small errors. It assumes that the eigenvalues are even functions of h, the interval chosen in the Lagrangian formula; that is, it assumes that the sign of h does not affect the magnitude of the error. Under this assumption the eigenvalue can be expressed by the power-series expansion in h as

$$\lambda_h = \lambda_0 + h^2\lambda_2 + h^4\lambda_4 + \cdots + h^{2n}\lambda_{2n} + \cdots \tag{2-82}$$

where λ_h is the approximate eigenvalue found by the Lagrangian formula, h is the interval used to obtain λ_h, λ_0 is the true value of the eigenvalue, and λ_2, λ_4, and λ_{2n} are numbers independent of h.

If two separate intervals, h_1 and h_2, have been used to obtain two approximate values of the eigenvalue, λ_{h1} and λ_{h2}, a truncation of Equation (2-82) at the h^2 term permits approximate solution of (2-82) for λ_0 as a weighted mean of λ_{h1} and λ_{h2}. Thus, using a two-point extrapolation formula, and inserting h_1 and h_2 in (2-82) and solving for λ_0, we get

$$\lambda_0 = \frac{h_2^2}{h_2^2 - h_1^2}\lambda_{h1} + \frac{h_1^2}{h_1^2 - h_2^2}\lambda_{h2} \tag{2-83}$$

and a better approximation is obtained for the eigenvalue. If we use the values of the zeros of V_{II}, as obtained in the previous example for the $\overline{ERC}$ network, the weighted mean for the first, or dominant, zero of V_{II}, with $k = 0$, is

$$\begin{aligned}\lambda_0 &= \frac{-1/9\, d^2}{1/9\, d^2 - 1/4\, d^2}\left(\frac{8}{\tau d^2}\right) - \frac{1/4\, d}{1/4\, d^2 - 1/9\, d^2}\left(\frac{9}{\tau d^2}\right)\\ &= \frac{-9.80}{\tau d^2}\end{aligned} \tag{2-84}$$

This value is too low by 0.7 percent, but is an improved approximation to the dominant zero of $V_{\mathrm{II}}(s, d)$.

An important drawback of Richardson's extrapolation is the proneness of the extrapolant to oscillate. The magnitude of the oscillations around the eigenvalue may diminish slowly with increasing the degree of the extrapolation.

Some of the more elaborate procedures available produce more accurate results, but for simplicity and ease of manipulation, the Lagrangian

---

[18] See Kopal (Ref. 17), pp. 250–255.

three-point formula combined with Richardson's extrapolation procedure usually produces results that are adequate for practical purposes.

2-7 The Rayleigh Principle

Through use of the Rayleigh principle,[19] close estimates may be obtained of the zeros of solutions of differential equations when boundary values are prescribed. Hence, this principle may be used to find the zeros of the basic set and thereby determine the poles and zeros of distributed-parameter networks. It is used extensively in vibration analysis and is readily applied to distributed-parameter network analysis. For example, for the distributed network in which $Z(s,x) = Z(s)/f(x)$ and $Y(s,x) = Y(s)g(x)$, the network differential equation can be written in the form

$$\frac{d}{dx}\left[f(x)\,\frac{dV}{dx}\right] - \lambda g(x) V = 0 \tag{2-85}$$

where $\lambda = -Z(s)Y(s)$. For the $\overline{RC}$ network, $\lambda = -sr_0c_0$; for the $\overline{LC}$ network, $\lambda = -s^2 l_0c_0$. The basic-set solutions for Equation (2-85) are $V_{\text{I}}(\lambda, x)$ and $V_{\text{II}}(\lambda, x)$; to determine the poles and zeros of the short-circuit admittance parameters $[y_{ij}]$, we really need to determine the zeros of $V_{\text{I}}(\lambda, d)$ and $V_{\text{II}}(\lambda, d)$, where d is the network length.

The Rayleigh principle is a direct means for estimating these zeros, or eigenvalues. In general, there are an infinite number of zeros for distributed-network functions, and the nth zero is λ_n. For the $\overline{RC}$ network, the nth s-plane zero is $s_n = -\lambda_n/r_0c_0d^2$ while for the $\overline{LC}$ network the nth pair of zeros is

$$s_n,\ s_n^* = \pm jd\sqrt{\frac{\lambda_n}{l_0c_0}}$$

The Rayleigh principle states that if $u(x)$ is an approximate solution $[u(x) \approx V(x)]$ to Equation (2-85), satisfying the boundary conditions on $V(x)$ at $x = 0$, $x = d$, then the first zero, or eigenvalue, of $V_{\text{I}}(\lambda, d)$ or $V_{\text{II}}(\lambda, d)$ is bounded from above by

$$\lambda_1 \leqslant \frac{\displaystyle\int_0^d f(x)\left(\frac{du}{dx}\right)^2 dx}{\displaystyle\int_0^d g(x)u^2\,dx} \tag{2-86}$$

where u is the function that approximates $V(x)$ on the boundaries. Since Equation (2-86) yields only upper limits, a number of approximating

[19] Lord Rayleigh, *The Theory of Sound* (New York, Dover reprint, 1945), Vol I, Sect. 207.

functions must be tried to form a good estimate of λ_1, inasmuch as the lowest value obtained lies closest to the true value. Many iterative procedures[20] that converge to the lowest eigenvalue have been developed. In one such procedure, attributed to Schwarz, a function $u_0(x)$ is chosen to satisfy the required boundary values on $V(x)$ at $x = 0$ and $x = d$, and Equation (2-86) is evaluated. Next, a new approximating function $u_1(x)$ is obtained from $u_0(x)$ by solving the differential equation

$$\frac{d}{dx}\left[f(x)\,\frac{du_1}{dx}\right] = -u_0 g(x) \tag{2-87}$$

with appropriate boundary conditions on u_1. The process is repeated until an estimate to λ_1 is obtained to the desired accuracy. In the nth step,

$$\frac{d}{dx}\left[f(x)\,\frac{du_n}{dx}\right] = -u_{n-1} g(x) \tag{2-88}$$

In the iterative procedure developed by Schwarz,[21] the following definitions are used:

$$a_0 = \int_0^d (u_0')^2\,dx \qquad a_1 = \int_0^d (u_0)^2\,dx \tag{2-89a}$$

$$a_2 = \int_0^d (u_1')^2\,dx \qquad a_3 = \int_0^d (u_1)^2\,dx \tag{2-89b}$$

and, in general,

$$a_{2n} = \int_0^d (u_n')^2\,dx \qquad a_{2n+1} = \int_0^d (u_n)^2\,dx \tag{2-89c}$$

and the estimates for the first eigenvalue λ_1 are

$$\lambda_{1,1} = \frac{a_0}{a_1} \qquad \lambda_{1,2} = \frac{a_1}{a_2} \qquad \lambda_{1,n+1} = \frac{a_n}{a_{n+1}} \tag{2-90}$$

Let us illustrate the iterative procedure by determining λ_1 for the basic-set solution $V_{\rm I}(\lambda, d)$, which defines the first zero of y_{11} for the distributed two-port. The boundary conditions on $V_{\rm I}(\lambda, x)$ are that $V_{\rm I}'(\lambda, 0) = V_{\rm I}(\lambda, d) = 0$. We approximate $V_{\rm I}(\lambda, x)$ by a function $u_0(x)$ that satisfies the boundary conditions. The simplest polynomial approximating function $u_0(x)$ that satisfies the boundary conditions is

$$u_0(x) = 1 - \left(\frac{x}{d}\right)^2$$

---

[20] See Kopal (Ref. 17), Chap. 6.

[21] See Kopal (Ref. 17), pp. 322–331.

Let us start with this $u_0(x)$ and find the first eigenvalue of $V_I(\lambda, d)$ for the uniformly distributed RC two-port. For this network, $f(x) = g(x) = 1$. We also simplify the algebra by normalizing x to d, so that $x/d = 1$. This step is equivalent to multiplying λ by d^2. Using the normalized expressions and $u_0 = 1 - x^2$, from Equation (2-89) we find

$$a_0 = \int_0^1 4(x^2)\, dx = \frac{4}{3} \tag{2-91a}$$

$$a_1 = \int_0^1 [1 - 2x^2 + x^4]\, dx = \frac{8}{15} \tag{2-91b}$$

and

$$d^2\lambda_{1,1} = \frac{a_0}{a_1} = 2.5000 \tag{2-91c}$$

From Equation (2-87), we find $u_1(x)$, the next approximating function, for the uniform network by solving

$$u_1'' = -(1 - x^2) \tag{2-92}$$

with the boundary conditions $u_1'(0) = u_1(1) = 0$. The solution is

$$u_1 = \frac{1}{12}[5 - 6x^2 + x^4]$$

From Equation (2-89),

$$a_2 = \int_0^1 \left(-x + \frac{x^3}{3}\right)^2 dx = \int_0^1 \left(x^2 - \frac{2}{3}x^4 + \frac{x^6}{9}\right) dx = \frac{68}{315} \tag{2-93a}$$

$$a_3 = \int_0^1 \frac{1}{144}[25 - 60x^2 + 46x^4 - 12x^6 + x^8]\, dx = \frac{248}{2835} \tag{2-93b}$$

giving $d^2\lambda_{1,2} = \dfrac{a_1}{a_2} = \dfrac{8}{15} \div \dfrac{68}{315} = 2.47058$ (2-93c)

and $d^2\lambda_{1,3} = \dfrac{a_2}{a_3} = \dfrac{68}{315} \div \dfrac{248}{2835} = 2.46774$ (2-93d)

Note that each iteration produces a lower estimate of λ_1. We know that $d^2\lambda_1$ for the uniform network is $\pi^2/4 = 2.46740$, and hence that Equation (2-93d) is in error by about four parts in twenty-five thousand. In the general case, however, we have no advanced information on the true value of $d^2\lambda_1$ and must use other means to estimate accuracy.

Fortunately, a reliable means exists by which the accuracy of the estimate to λ_1 can be established at each step in the iteration. Temple[22] has shown that upper and lower bounds for λ_1 can be established in terms of the successive approximate values, $\lambda_{1,n}$ and $\lambda_{1,n+1}$. We omit details

[22] G. Temple and W. Bickley, *Rayleigh's Principle* (New York, Dover, 1956), Chap. 1. See also Kopal (Ref. 17), pp. 333–335.

of proof and state the result; that is,

$$\lambda_{1,n+1} > \lambda_1 > \lambda_{1,n+1} - \frac{\lambda_{1,n} - \lambda_{1,n+1}}{\dfrac{\lambda_2}{\lambda_{1,n+1}} - 1} \tag{2-94}$$

where λ_2 is the second lowest eigenvalue of the basic-set solution such that $\lambda_2 > \lambda_1$.

In general,

$$\frac{\lambda_2}{\lambda_{1,n+1}} - 1 > 1$$

and, since we have no estimate for λ_2 at present, the error bounds on λ_1 are written simply as

$$\lambda_{1,n+1} > \lambda_1 > 2\lambda_{1,n+1} - \lambda_{1,n} \tag{2-95}$$

Using Equation (2-95), and with no knowledge of the true value of λ_2, we find from (2-93c) and (2-93d) that

$$2.46774 > d^2\lambda_1 > 2.46490 \tag{2-96}$$

and that (2-93d) is accurate to at least three parts in twenty-five hundred. Having determined this, we then can decide if further iteration is required for additional accuracy.

The steps in the iterative procedure to find the first eigenvalues of $V_{\text{I}}(\lambda, d)$ and $V_{\text{II}}(\lambda, d)$ for the uniform network are shown in Table 2-2. Using Temple's criterion, the first eigenvalue of $V_{\text{II}}(\lambda, d)$ is bounded by

$$9.87096 > d^2\lambda_1 > 9.86169 \tag{2-97}$$

which represents a maximum error of one part in a thousand. (The true value of $d^2\lambda_1$ is $\pi^2 = 9.86960$, and the error in $d^2\lambda_{1,2}$ is one part in ten thousand.)

Table 2-2 CALCULATION OF FIRST EIGENVALUE OF $V_{\text{I}}(\lambda, d)$ FOR UNIFORM $\overline{RC}$ NETWORK WITH $V_{\text{I}}'(\lambda, d) = 0$, $f(x) = g(x) = 1$

APPROXIMATING FUNCTION	SCHWARZ NUMBERS	$d^2\lambda_{1,n}$
$u_0 = (1 - x^2)$	$a_0 = 4/3$ $a_1 = 8/15$	2.50000
$u_1 = \frac{1}{12}(5 - 6x^2 + x^4)$	$a_2 = 68/315$ $a_3 = 248/2835$	2.47058 2.46774
$u_2 = \frac{1}{360}(61 - 75x^2 + 15x^4 - x^6)$	. . .	. . .

CALCULATION OF FIRST EIGENVALUE OF $V_{II}(\lambda, d)$ FOR UNIFORM $\overline{RC}$ NETWORK WITH $V_{II}(\lambda, 0) = V_{II}(\lambda, d) = 0, f(x) = g(x) = 1$

APPROXIMATING FUNCTION	SCHWARZ NUMBERS	$d^2\lambda_{1,n}$
$u_0 = x - x^2$	$a_0 = 1/3$ $a_1 = 1/30$	10.0000
$u_1 = \frac{1}{12}(x - 2x^3 + x^4)$	$a_2 = 17/5040$ $a_3 = 31/90720$	9.88023 9.87096
$u_2 = \frac{1}{360}[3x - 5x^3 + 3x^5 - x^6]$	. . .	. . .

The higher eigenvalues may be found by a variety of methods based on the Rayleigh principle.[23] Perhaps the simplest to apply is based on Temple's inequality, which can be rewritten in the form

$$\lambda_2 < \lambda_{2,n} < \frac{\lambda_{1,n} - \lambda_1}{\lambda_{1,n+1} - \lambda_1} \lambda_{1,n+1} \tag{2-98}$$

where λ_1 is the true value of the first eigenvalue, $\lambda_{1,n}$ $\lambda_{1,n+1}$ are approximations to λ_1; λ_2 is the true value of the second eigenvalue, and $\lambda_{2,n}$ is the nth approximation to λ_2.

The lower bound is

$$\lambda_2 > \lambda_{2,n} - \frac{\lambda_{2,n} - \lambda_{2,n+1}}{\dfrac{\lambda_3}{\lambda_{2,n+1}} - 1} \tag{2-99}$$

In general, the upper bound is

$$\lambda_N < \lambda_{N,n} < \frac{\lambda_{N-1,n} - \lambda_N}{\lambda_{N-1,n+1} - \lambda_N} \lambda_{N,n+1} \tag{2-100}$$

To illustrate, let us find the second eigenvalue of $V_I(\lambda, d)$ using Equation (2-98). First we must obtain a good estimate of λ_1 using the Rayleigh principle. Assume that we have found λ_1 correct to six figures; that is, $d^2\lambda_1 = 2.46740$. Then, from Equations (2-98), (2-93c), and (2-93d),

$$\begin{aligned} d^2\lambda_{2,1} &< \left(\frac{\lambda_{1,1} - \lambda_1}{\lambda_{1,2} - \lambda_1}\right) \lambda_{1,2} \\ &= \left(\frac{2.50000 - 2.46740}{2.47058 - 2.46740}\right) 2.47058 \\ &= 25.33 \end{aligned} \tag{2-101a}$$

[23] For example, the Rayleigh-Ritz method. See Kopal (Ref. 17).

$$d^2\lambda_{2,2} < \left(\frac{\lambda_{1,2} - \lambda_1}{\lambda_{1,3} - \lambda_1}\right)\lambda_{1,3}$$

$$= \left(\frac{2.47058 - 2.46740}{2.46774 - 2.46740}\right) 2.46774 \qquad \textbf{(2-101b)}$$

$$= 23.08$$

The procedure can be continued indefinitely until λ_2 is found to the desired accuracy. [The true value of $d^2\lambda_2$ is $9\pi^2/4 = 22.20660$, and Equation (2-101b) is 3.9 percent too high.] After λ_2 is established, λ_3 and higher eigenvalues may be determined by a similar process. However, the work involved to obtain the higher eigenvalues is formidable. In many cases, if approximate results are satisfactory, analysis and design based on the lowest few eigenvalues give good results. If the higher eigenvalues are needed an alternate procedure based on thc maximum-minimum principle[24] can be used. The latter procedure, which is also discussed by Collatz,[25] is referred to as the *enclosure theorem*. This theorem provides a simple means to bound all the eigenvalues by means of only one equation. It is particularly useful in the study of nonuniformly distributed networks and gives exact solutions for a number of tapered networks.

The *enclosure theorem* states that if there is a continuous function $U_0(x)$ and a comparison function $U_1(x)$ such that

$$\frac{d}{dx}\left[f(x)\,\frac{dU_1(x)}{dx}\right] = -\lambda g(x) U_0(x) \qquad \textbf{(2-102)}$$

and, moreover, if the function

$$\phi(x) = \frac{\dfrac{d}{dx}\left[f(x)\,\dfrac{dU_1(x)}{dx}\right]}{-g(x)U_1(x)} = \frac{U_0(x)}{U_1(x)} \qquad \textbf{(2-103)}$$

is bounded and does not change sign over the interval $0 < x < d$, then at least one eigenvalue, λ_n, lies between the maximum and minimum values of $\phi(x)$ in the interval $0 < x < d$. This theorem is stated here without proof. To apply the theorem, it is sufficient to select any comparison function $U_1(x)$ that satisfies the network boundary conditions, and then to find $U_0(x)$ as follows:

$$U_0(x) = -\frac{1}{g(x)}\frac{d}{dx}\left[f(x)\,\frac{dU_1(x)}{dx}\right] \qquad \textbf{(2-104)}$$

[24] R. Courant and D. Hilbert, *Methods of Mathematical Physics* (New York, Interscience, 1953), Vol. I, pp. 405–407.

[25] L. Collatz, *The Numerical Treatment of Differential Equations* (Berlin, Springer, 1960), pp. 202–213.

$U_0(x)$ need not satisfy any boundary conditions. However, better estimates are obtained when $U_1(x)$ is chosen so that $U_0(x)$ satisfies as many boundary conditions as possible.

Collatz has shown, for example, when $U_1(x) = f^k(x) \sin \alpha(x-d)$ the boundary condition $U_1(d) = 0$ is satisfied; also, the condition $U_1'(0) = 0$ is satisfied when

$$\alpha_n = \frac{kf'(0)}{f(0)} \tan \alpha_n d$$

The ratio $U_0(x)/U_1(x)$ is bounded when $k = -1/2$. Under these conditions,

$$\phi_{\text{I}}(x) = \frac{U_0(x)}{U_1(x)} = \frac{\alpha_n^2 - 1/4[f'(x)]^2 f^{-1}(x) + 1/2 f''(x)}{g(x)} \tag{2-105}$$

and the maxima and minima of $\phi_{\text{I}}(x)$ give bounds on the eigenvalues of V_{I}.

Also, when $U_1(x)$ is chosen as $f^k(x) \sin \beta x$, then $U_1(0) = U_1(d) = 0$, provided that $\beta_n = n\pi/d$. In this case, also, for $k = -1/2$, the ratio $U_0(x)/U_1(x)$ is bounded and the eigenvalues of V_{II} are enclosed by the maximum and minimum values of $\phi_{\text{II}}(x)$, where

$$\phi_{\text{II}}(x) = \frac{\beta_n^2 - 1/4[f'(x)]^2 f^{-1}(x) + 1/2 f''(x)}{g(x)} \tag{2-106}$$

Hence, the eigenvalues of V_{I} are enclosed by

$$\phi_{\text{I}}(x)\Big|_{\min} < \lambda < \phi_{\text{I}}(x)\Big|_{\max} \tag{2-107}$$

and the eigenvalues of V_{II} are enclosed by

$$\phi_{\text{II}}(x)\Big|_{\min} < \lambda < \phi_{\text{II}}(x)\Big|_{\max} \tag{2-108}$$

For example, the uniformly distributed RC network has $f(x) = g(x) = 1$, and the eigenvalues for $V_{\text{I}}(d)$ from (2-105) are enclosed by

$$\alpha_n^2 \leqslant \lambda_n \leqslant \alpha_n^2 \tag{2-109}$$

where $\alpha_n = (2n-1)\pi/2d$. Also, the eigenvalues of $V_{\text{II}}(d)$ are, from Equation (2-106), enclosed between the limits

$$\left(\frac{n\pi}{d}\right)^2 \leqslant \lambda_n \leqslant \left(\frac{n\pi}{d}\right)^2 \tag{2-110}$$

and the enclosure theorem gives exact results for the eigenvalues of $V_{\text{I}}(d)$ and $V_{\text{II}}(d)$ for the uniformly distributed RC network.

Consider, now, the linear tapered $\overline{RC}$ network where $f(x) = (1+Kx)$

and $g(x) = (1 - Kx)$. Then $f'(x) = +K, f''(x) = 0$, and the eigenvalues of $V_I(\lambda, d)$ are enclosed between

$$\alpha_n{}^2 - 1/4K^2 < \lambda_n < \alpha_n{}^2 - \frac{K^2}{4(1+Kd)^2} \tag{2-111}$$

where $\alpha_n = -1/2K \tan \alpha_n d$.

Similarly, the bounds on the eigenvalues of V_{II} from Equation (2-106) are given by the maxima and minima of

$$\left(\frac{n\pi}{d}\right)^2 - \frac{K^2}{4(1+K)^2} < \lambda_n < \left(\frac{n\pi}{d}\right)^2 - \frac{K^2}{4} \tag{2-112}$$

To illustrate the accuracy of the bounds on the eigenvalues obtained by the enclosure theorem, Table 2-3 shows the upper and lower bounds obtained for $K = 1$, with d normalized to unity for the linearly tapered network. It is noted from Table 2-3 that the percentage accuracy of the zero locations improves rapidly as the number of the zero increases. Note also that for larger value of K the bounds in (2-112) become progressively worse and the approximating functions are not so close to the true solution. For large K, more complex approximating functions are required in order to obtain tighter bounds.

Table 2-3 BOUNDS ON THE ZEROS OF V_I AND V_{II} FOR $K = 1$

		BOUNDS ON ZEROS OF V_I		BOUNDS ON ZEROS OF V_{II}		
n	α_n	$\phi_{I_{min}}$	$\phi_{I_{max}}$	β_n	$\phi_{II_{min}}$	$\phi_{II_{max}}$
1	1.8366	3.123	3.311	π	9.6191	9.8071
2	4.816	22.94	23.13	2π	39.298	39.416
3	7.917	62.43	62.62	3π	88.58	88.76
4	11.041	121.65	121.84	4π	157.66	157.85
5	14.173	200.61	200.81	5π	246.49	246.88
6	17.308	299.31	299.50	6π	355.06	355.25

PROBLEMS

2-1 A distortionless finite $RLCG$ line is excited by a unit step voltage. The source and the load resistance are R_S and R_L, respectively. Determine the voltage $v(t, d)$, if the line length is d. (Note that for a distortionless line $R/L = G/C = \alpha =$ a constant.)

2-2 Two uniform two-port distributed RC networks are cascaded as in Problem 1-6. In other words,

$$
\begin{aligned}
Z(s, x) &= r_1 = \frac{r_0}{W_1} && \text{for } x \text{ in the range } (0, d) \\
&= r_2 = \frac{r_0}{W_2} && \text{for } x \text{ in the range } (d, 2d) \\
Y(s, x) &= sc_1 = sc_0 W_1 && \text{for } x \text{ in the range } (0, d) \\
&= sc_2 = sc_0 W_2 && \text{for } x \text{ in the range } (d, 2d)
\end{aligned}
$$

Determine the voltage transfer function by Picard-Carson method if $W_1/W_2 = 0.1$. Only the first three terms of the series need be computed.

2-3 An exponentially tapered distributed RC network of length d has

$$r(x) = r_0 \epsilon^{2kx} \qquad c(x) = c_0 \epsilon^{-2kx}$$

a. Show that the open-circuit voltage transfer function is given by

$$T_V(s) = \frac{V_0}{V_{\text{in}}}(s) = \frac{\epsilon^{kd}}{\cosh \gamma d + \dfrac{kd}{\gamma d} \sinh \gamma d}$$

b. Show that the pole locations are given by

$$s_n T = \frac{1}{4}\left(\frac{2n-1}{\pi}\right)^2 \qquad n = 1, 2, \cdots$$

where $T = r_0 c_0 d^2$.

2-4 For the exponentially tapered RC network discussed in the text, page 55, find the solution for V_{II} using the Lagrangian three-point formula and the Richardson extrapolation procedures. Use $h = d/3$, $h = d/4$.

2-5 a. Determine the power series solution for $V_{\text{II}}(s, d)$ for the exponentially tapered $\overline{RLCG}$ network using the method of Frobenius.

$$Z(s, x) = (r_0 + sl_0)\epsilon^{2kx} \qquad Y(s, x) = (g_0 + sc_0)\epsilon^{-2kx}$$

Carry out the expansion to at least five terms—that is, b_5.

b. Rearrange the coefficients obtained in (a) to obtain a power-series expansion in s.

2-6 Show that if $I(s, x) = CI_c(s, x) + DI_d(s, x)$, then

$$V(s, x) = \frac{-1}{Y(s, x)}\left[C \frac{dI_c(s, x)}{dx} + D \frac{dI_d(s, x)}{dx}\right]$$

2-7 Given V_a and V_b as solutions (not a basic set) of the network voltage equation

a. Show that the driving-point admittance looking into a distributed network in the direction of increasing x is given by

$$Y_{\mathrm{IN}}(s, x) = \frac{-1}{Z(s, x)} \frac{\left| A \dfrac{dV_a}{dx} + B \dfrac{dV_b}{dx} \right|}{AV_a + BV_b}$$

b. If the network is terminated in a short circuit at $x = d$, show that the driving-point admittance at $x = 0$ is given by

$$Y_{11} = Y_{\mathrm{IN}}(s, 0) = \frac{I(s, 0)}{Y(s, 0)}$$

$$= \frac{-1}{Z(s, 0)} \frac{V_b(s, d) \dfrac{dV_a(s, 0)}{dx} - V_a(s, d) \dfrac{dV_b(s, 0)}{dx}}{V_a(s, 0)V_b(s, d) - V_b(s, 0)V_a(s, d)}$$

Hint: At $x = d$,

$$V(s, d) = AV_a(s, d) + BV_b(s, d) = 0$$

and hence

$$B = -A \frac{V_a(s, d)}{V_b(s, d)}$$

2-8 A linearly tapered distributed RC network of length d has

$$r(x) = \frac{r_0}{1 - ax} \qquad c(x) = c_0(1 - ax)$$

Determine the open-circuit voltage transfer function by the Picard-Carson method. Only the first three terms of the series need be computed.

2-9 For Problem 2-8 use the iterated structure approximation with three sections.

a. Determine $[M]_i$, for $i = 1, 2, 3, \ldots$.

b. Determine the open-circuit voltage transfer function.

2-10 Determine the pole locations of the open circuit voltage transfer function for a linearly tapered distributed RC network using

a. the Lagrangian method

b. the Collatz enclosure theorem. Let $a = 0.5$ and 1, and determine only the first three poles.

2-11 Consider a distributed RC network of length d with square electrical taper; that is,

$$r(x) = \frac{r_0}{(1+kx)^2} \qquad c(x) = c_0(1+kx)^2$$

Determine the magnitude of the first, second, and third poles of the open-circuit voltage transfer function using

a. the Lagrangian method.

b. the Rayleigh principle.

c. the Collatz enclosure theorem. Let $k = 0.5$, 1, and 2.

2-12 The voltage equation for the uniform lossless transmission line is given by

$$\frac{d^2V(s,x)}{dx^2} = s^2lcV(s,x)$$

where d is the network length. Determine the roots of $V_{\mathrm{I}}(s,d)$ and $V_{\mathrm{II}}(s,d)$ by the enclosure theorem. [Hint: Use $U_1 = \sin\alpha(x-d)$ for V_{I} and $U_1 = \sin\beta x$ for V_{II}.]

2-13 Consider an exponentially tapered $\overline{RCG}$ network of length d with $r(x) = r_0\epsilon^{2kx}$, $c(x) = c_0\epsilon^{-2kx}$, and $S = s + \Omega$ [where $\Omega = g(x)/c(x) =$ constant]. The differential equation for the voltage is given by

$$\frac{d}{dx}\left[\epsilon^{-2kx}\frac{dV(s,x)}{dx}\right] - Src\epsilon^{-2kx}V(s,x) = 0$$

Find the roots of $V_{\mathrm{I}}(s,d)$ and $V_{\mathrm{II}}(s,d)$ by the enclosure theorem, and compare them with those of the closed form solution. [Hint: Use $U_1 = \epsilon^{kx}\sin\alpha(x-d)$ for V_{I} and $U_1 = \epsilon^{kx}\sin\beta x$ for V_{II}.]

2-14 Show that, from Equation (2-26), the reciprocal relationship holds; that is, $AD - BC = 1$. [Hint: Take the derivative with respect to x and show that

$$\frac{d}{dx}(AD - BC) = 0$$

for all x.]

CHAPTER

3

Transient and Frequency Response of Distributed-Parameter Networks

3-1 Introduction

In this chapter the calculation of transient and frequency response of distributed-parameter networks of finite length is considered. Primary emphasis is placed on the uniform *RC* distributed network since the transient study of this type of network is straightforward and of practical interest. Simplified methods of calculating the key features of the frequency and transient response are also developed for the general distributed *RC* network. The techniques are applied to tapered distributed *RC* networks and it is shown that the methods are also applicable to a broad class of lumped-distributed systems.

In the following discussion it is assumed that the reader is familiar with elementary Laplace transform theory and its application in calculating the transient response of a lumped-parameter network.[1] The standard method for calculating the transient response of a distributed

[1] See, for example, M. S. Ghausi, *Principles and Design of Linear Active Circuits* (New York, McGraw-Hill, 1965), Chap. 16.

network via the residue approach is treated only briefly in Sections 3-2 and 3-3, since this material is treated in great detail in many books dealing with transmission lines.[2] We shall discuss in some detail other techniques. In particular, some simplified approximate methods of determining the transient response will be described.

3-2 Transient Response of a General Uniform Transmission Line

Consider the uniform transmission line ($\overline{RLCG}$) discussed in Section 1-1. The line is assumed to be initially relaxed. We shall determine $v(t, x)$ when a unit step voltage $v_0 = u(t)$ is applied at the input end $(x = 0)$ with the output end $(x = d)$ short-circuited. For this case the transform voltage along the line in terms of the transform voltage at the input is given by Problem 1-1.

$$V(s, x) = \frac{V_0(s, 0)}{\sinh \Gamma d} \sinh \Gamma(d - x) \tag{3-1}$$

where $\Gamma = \sqrt{(ls + r)(cs + g)}$. Since $v_0(t) = u(t)$, $V_0(s) = 1/s$ and Equation (3-1) becomes

$$V(s, x) = \frac{\sinh \Gamma(d - x)}{s \sinh \Gamma d} \tag{3-2}$$

It should be noted that in spite of the presence of the square root (Γ) in (3-2), there are no branch points. Equation (3-2) is meromorphic and its only singularities are poles. The poles of $V(s, x)$ are at $s = 0$ and the roots of $\sinh \Gamma d = 0$; that is,

$$\Gamma = \pm jk \frac{\pi}{d} \qquad k = 1, 2, 3, \ldots \tag{3-3}$$

Note that for $k = 0$ there is no pole, since the numerator and the denominator have roots that cancel each other. For convenience, we define

$$\Gamma = \sqrt{(ls + r)(cs + g)} = \sqrt{lc}\,\sqrt{(s + \alpha)^2 - \beta^2} \tag{3-4}$$

where
$$\alpha = \frac{1}{2}\left(\frac{r}{l} + \frac{g}{c}\right) \qquad \beta = \frac{1}{2}\left(\frac{r}{l} - \frac{g}{c}\right) \tag{3-5}$$

From Equations (3-3) and (3-4) we have

$$lc[(s + \alpha)^2 - \beta^2] = -\frac{k^2\pi^2}{d^2}$$

---

[2] See, for example, E. V. Bohn, *The Transform Analysis of Linear Systems* (Reading, Mass., Addison-Wesley, 1963).

or
$$s = -\alpha \pm \sqrt{\beta^2 - \frac{k^2\pi^2}{d^2lc}} \tag{3-6}$$

The poles of Equation (3-2) are given by (3-6) and are seen to be complex for large values of k. Some may be negative real for small values of k. For simplicity and without loss of generality we can assume that the poles are all complex in (3-6). Thus we can rewrite Equation (3-6) as

$$s = -\alpha \pm j\omega_k \tag{3-7}$$

where
$$\omega_k = \sqrt{\frac{k^2\pi^2}{d^2lc} - \beta^2} \qquad k = 1, 2, \ldots$$

To find the inverse Laplace transform of Eq. (3-2) we can use the residue theorem. It can be shown that the Jordan lemma is satisfied.[3] It should be noted that the conditions of the Jordan lemma should be checked, as Doetsch emphasizes, or else we are not sure that the sum of residues gives the correct answer. Hence, for $t > 0$,

$$v(t, x) = \sum \text{Res}\left[\frac{\sinh \Gamma(d-x)}{s \sinh \Gamma d}\,\epsilon^{st}\right] \tag{3-8a}$$

Therefore,

$$v(t, x) = \left[\frac{\sinh \Gamma(d-x)}{\sinh \Gamma d}\,\epsilon^{st}\right]_{s=0} + \sum_{k=1}^{\infty}\left[\frac{\sinh \Gamma(d-x)}{s\,\dfrac{d}{ds}(\sinh \Gamma d)}\,\epsilon^{st}\right]_{s=-\alpha\pm j\omega_k} \tag{3-8b}$$

At $s = 0$,

$$\Gamma = \sqrt{rg}$$

At $s = -\alpha + j\omega_k$,

$$\frac{d}{ds}(\sinh \Gamma d) = d\cosh \Gamma d\,\frac{d\Gamma}{ds} = (d \cosh \Gamma d)\left(lc\,\frac{s+\alpha}{\Gamma}\right)$$

$$= dlc(\cosh jk\pi)\,\frac{j\omega_k}{j\,\dfrac{k\pi}{d}} = \frac{(-1)^k\omega_k d^2lc}{k\pi} \tag{3-9}$$

(The reader is cautioned not to confuse the d of length with the d of differentiation.) Also expansion of $\sinh \Gamma(d-x)$ and the substitution of Equation (3-3) yields

$$\sinh \Gamma(d-x) = \sinh \Gamma d \cosh \Gamma x - \cosh \Gamma d \sinh \Gamma x$$

$$\sinh \Gamma(d-x) = 0 - (-1)^k j \sin\left(\frac{k\pi}{d}x\right) \tag{3-10}$$

[3] G. Doetsch, *Guide to the Applications of Laplace Transform* (Princeton, N. J., Van Nostrand, 1961), pp. 193–197.

From Equations (3-9) and (3-10) we obtain

$$\left[\frac{\sinh \Gamma(d-x)}{s\dfrac{d}{ds}(\sinh \Gamma d)}\right]_{s=-\alpha+j\omega_k} = -\frac{k\pi \sin k\pi x/d}{d^2 lc\omega_k(\omega_k + j\alpha)} \tag{3-11}$$

$$= -\frac{k\pi \sin k\pi x/d}{d^2 lc\omega_k\sqrt{\omega_k^2+\alpha^2}} \exp\left(-j\tan^{-1}\frac{\alpha}{\omega_k}\right)$$

Hence,

$$v(t,x) = \frac{\sinh\sqrt{rg}\,(d-x)}{\sinh\sqrt{rg}\,d}$$

$$-\sum_{k=1}^{\infty}\frac{k\pi \sin k\pi x/d}{d^2 lc\omega_k\sqrt{\omega_k^2+\alpha^2}}\exp\left(-\alpha t + j\omega_k t - j\tan^{-1}\frac{\alpha}{\omega_k}\right)$$

$$+ \text{CONJUGATE TERM}$$

$$= \frac{\sinh\sqrt{rg}\,(d-x)}{\sinh\sqrt{rg}\,d} - \frac{2\pi\epsilon^{-\alpha t}}{d^2 lc}\sum_{k=1}^{\infty}\frac{k\sin k\pi x/d}{\omega_k\sqrt{\alpha^2+\omega_k^2}}\cos\left(\omega_k t - \tan^{-1}\frac{\alpha}{\omega_k}\right) \tag{3-12}$$

In Equation (3-12) the first term represents the steady-state response and the second term is the transient part.

3-3 Lossless Line and RC Distributed Network

It is of interest to consider two special cases of the uniform *RLCG* line. The first case we consider is the lossless *ULC* line of length d. This is the special case in which $r = g = 0$. For this case, $\Gamma = \sqrt{lcs}$. The voltage $v(t, x)$ for a short-circuited end may be obtained directly from (3-12). The natural frequencies of the *ULC* line for a voltage excitation at the input are given by Equation (3-6) with $\alpha = \beta = 0$:

$$s = \pm j\omega_k = \pm j\frac{k\pi}{d\sqrt{lc}} \tag{3-13}$$

From Equation (3-12), by letting $\alpha = 0$, we obtain

$$v(t,x) = \frac{d-x}{d} - \frac{2\pi}{d^2 lc}\sum_{k=1}^{\infty}\frac{k\sin k\pi x/d}{\omega_k^2}\cos\omega_k t \tag{3-14}$$

We shall next consider a short-circuited $\overline{RC}$ network of length d—that is, an $\overline{RLCG}$ line in which l and g are zero. A unit step voltage is applied at $x = 0$ and $v(t, x)$ is to be determined; initial conditions are assumed to be zero. Although this result can be extracted from Equation

(3-12), since this type of network arises in integrated circuits we prefer to solve it directly.

For the short-circuited RC line, the transform of the voltage across the line as a function of position is given by Problem 1-1(b):

$$V(s,x) = \frac{V(s,0)}{\sinh \Gamma d} \sinh \Gamma(d-x) \tag{3-15}$$

where $\Gamma = \sqrt{rcs}$.

For a unit step voltage, $V(s,0) = 1/s$ and

$$V(s,x) = \frac{\sinh \Gamma(d-x)}{s \sinh \Gamma d} = \frac{\sinh \sqrt{rcs}\,(d-x)}{s \sinh(d\sqrt{rcs})} \tag{3-16}$$

Again there are no branch points, in spite of the radical sign in (3-16), so we have a meromorphic function. It can be shown that the Jordan lemma is satisfied[3] and thus the sum of residues gives the correct answer. The poles are at $s = 0$ and at the roots of $\sinh d\sqrt{rcs} = 0$. These roots are at

$$d\sqrt{rcs} = \pm jn\pi \qquad n = 1, 2, 3, \ldots$$
$$s = -\frac{n^2\pi^2}{d^2rc} \tag{3-17}$$

Therefore,

$$v(t,x) = \frac{d-x}{d} + \sum_{n=1}^{\infty} \left[\frac{(\sinh (d-x)\sqrt{rcs})\epsilon^{st}}{s \dfrac{d}{ds}(\sinh d\sqrt{rcs})} \right]_{s=-\frac{n^2\pi^2}{d^2rc}}$$

$$= \frac{d-x}{d} + \sum_{n=1}^{\infty} \left[\frac{\sinh (d-x)\sqrt{rcs}\epsilon^{st}}{\dfrac{d\sqrt{rcs}}{2} \cosh d\sqrt{rcs}} \right]_{s=-\frac{n^2\pi^2}{d^2rc}}$$

$$v(t,x) = \frac{d-x}{d} + \sum_{n=1}^{\infty} \frac{\pm j(-1)^{n+1} \sin xn\pi/d}{\pm (1/2) jn\pi(-1)^n} \exp\left(-\frac{n^2\pi^2}{d^2rc}t\right)$$

or

$$v(t,x) = \frac{d-x}{d} - \frac{2}{\pi} \sum_{n=1}^{\infty} \frac{\sin xn\pi/d}{n} \exp - \left(\frac{n^2\pi^2}{d^2rc}t\right) \tag{3-18}$$

3-4 Artificial *RC* Line—The Lumped-Parameter Approximation

Consider a short-circuited distributed RC network approximated by N identical sections, as shown in Figure 3-1. The RC line is initially at rest. A unit step voltage is applied at the input and we would like to determine $i_n(t)$, the current in the nth section.

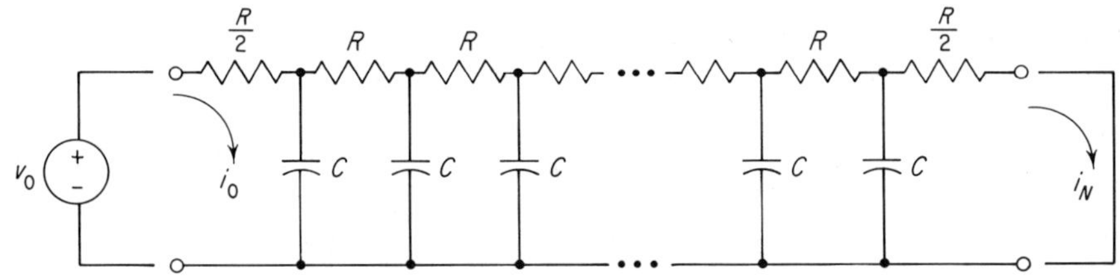

Figure 3-1 Iterative lumped approximation.

From Equation (1-38) the transform of current for the short-circuited *RC* line is

$$I_n(s) = V_0(s)\,\frac{\cosh\,(N-n)\tau}{Z_2\sinh\tau\,\sinh N\tau} \tag{3-19}$$

where

$$\tau = \cosh^{-1}\left(\frac{Z_1}{Z_2}+1\right) = \cosh^{-1}\left(\frac{RC}{2}\,s+1\right); \qquad Z_2 = \frac{1}{Cs}$$

If $v_0 = u(t)$, then $V_0(s) = 1/s$. Hence,

$$I_n(s) = \frac{1}{s}\,\frac{\cosh\,(N-n)\tau}{\dfrac{1}{Cs}\sinh\tau\,\sinh N\tau} = C\,\frac{\cosh\,(N-n)\tau}{\sinh\tau\,\sinh N\tau} \tag{3-20}$$

Note that Equation (3-20) is rational in s and proper, as is evident from Equations (1-46) and (1-47), and thus it can easily be shown that the singularities are poles and that the Jordan lemma holds. Hence, the inverse transform is obtained by evaluating the residues of $I_n(s)\epsilon^{st}$ at its poles. The poles of $I_n(s)$ are given by the roots of[4]

$$\sinh N\tau = 0, \text{ hence } N\tau_k = jk\pi \qquad k \text{ integer}$$

and

$$\sinh\tau = 0, \text{ hence } \tau_{k'} = jk'\pi \qquad k' \text{ integer} \tag{3-21}$$

---

[4] Alternatively, the poles of $I_n(s)$ are given by the roots of

$$\sinh\tau\,\sinh N\tau = 0$$

Using the identity of Equation (1-47), we can rewrite the above equation as

$$2^{N-1}\sinh^2\tau\prod_{n=1}^{N-1}\left(\cosh\tau - \cos\frac{n\pi}{N}\right) = 0$$

which is equivalent to

$$2^N RCs\left(1+\frac{RC}{2}s\right)\prod_{n=1}^{N-1}\left(1+\frac{RC}{2}s-\cos\frac{n\pi}{N}\right) = 0$$

From the above equation it is clear that there are exactly $(N+1)$ simple s-plane roots, as in Equation (3-22).

Therefore, $$1 + \frac{RC}{2} s_k = \cosh \tau_k = \cos \frac{k\pi}{N}$$

or $$s_k = -\frac{2}{RC}\left(1 - \cos \frac{k\pi}{N}\right) \qquad k = 0, 1, \ldots, N \tag{3-22}$$

The pole locations are shown in Figure 3-2. Note that at $\tau = 0$, we appear

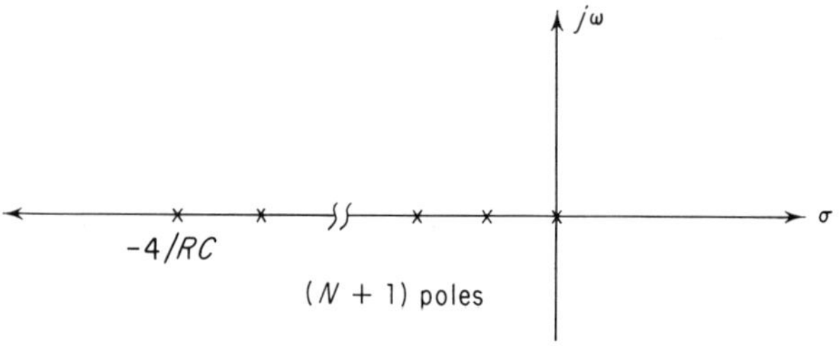

Figure 3-2 Poles of the ladder network.

to have a double pole in Equation (3-20). This is not actually the case, as will be shown shortly.

Since the ladder structure of Figure 3-1 has N capacitors with no capacitive tie sets or cut sets we expect N finite nonzero natural frequencies.[5] It should be noted that all the natural frequencies of the RC network lie on the negative real axis and are distinct. These facts are demonstrated in the following.

$$\begin{aligned} i_n(t) &= C \sum_{k=0}^{N} \left[\text{Res} \frac{\cosh (N-n)\tau}{\sinh \tau \sinh N\tau} \epsilon^{st} \right]_{s=s_k} \\ &= C \sum_{k=0}^{N} \left[\frac{\cosh (N-n)\tau_k}{\frac{d}{ds} [\sinh \tau \sinh N\tau]_{s_k}} \epsilon^{s_k t} \right] \end{aligned} \tag{3-23}$$

But $$\begin{aligned} \cosh (N-n)\tau_k &= \cosh N\tau_k \cosh n\tau_k - \sinh N\tau_k \sinh n\tau_k \\ &= \cos k\pi \cos \frac{kn\pi}{N} = (-1)^k \cos \frac{kn\pi}{N} \end{aligned} \tag{3-24}$$

from Equation (3-20). Recall that $\cosh \tau = 1 + RCs/2$; thus,

$$\begin{aligned} &\frac{d}{ds} [\sinh \tau \sinh N\tau] \\ &\qquad = [N \sinh \tau \cosh N\tau + \cosh \tau \sinh N\tau] \frac{d}{d \cosh \tau} \frac{d \cosh \tau}{ds} \end{aligned}$$

[5] See Ghausi (Ref. 1), pp. 21 and 32.

$$= [N \sinh \tau \cosh N\tau + \cosh \tau \sinh N\tau] \frac{1}{\sinh \tau} \frac{RC}{2}$$

$$= \frac{RC}{2} \left[N \cosh N\tau + \frac{\cosh \tau \sinh N\tau}{\sinh \tau} \right] \tag{3-25}$$

for $k = 1, 2, \ldots, N-1 \qquad \sinh N\tau_k = 0 \qquad \sinh \tau_k \neq 0$

Therefore, from Equation (3-25),

$$\frac{d}{ds} [\sinh \tau \sinh N\tau]_{s_k} = \frac{RC}{2} [N \cosh jk\pi] = (-1)^k \frac{N}{2} RC \tag{3-26}$$

for $\qquad k = 0 \qquad \sinh N\tau_k = 0 \qquad \sinh \tau_k = 0$

and

$$\lim_{\tau \to 0} \frac{\sinh N\tau}{\sinh \tau} = N \tag{3-27}$$

$$\frac{d}{ds} [\sinh \tau \sinh N\tau] \Bigg|_{s=0} = \frac{RC}{2} [N \cosh 0 + N \cosh 0] = NRC \tag{3-28}$$

for $\qquad k = N, \qquad \tau_k = j\pi$

and

$$\lim_{\tau \to j\pi} \frac{\sinh N\tau}{\sinh \tau} = \lim_{\delta \to 0} \frac{\sin N(\pi + \delta)}{\sin(\pi + \delta)} = (-1)^{N-1} N \tag{3-29}$$

Therefore,

$$\frac{d}{ds} [\sinh \tau \sinh N\tau] \Bigg|_{s=s_k} = \frac{RC}{2} [N \cosh jN\pi + (-1)^{N-1} N \cosh j\pi]$$

$$= (-1)^N NRC \tag{3-30}$$

Hence, $$i_n(t) = C \left[\frac{1}{NRC} + \sum_{k=1}^{N-1} \frac{\cos kn\pi/N}{NRC/2} \epsilon^{s_k t} + \frac{(-1)^n}{NRC} \epsilon^{s_N t} \right]$$

$$i_n(t) = \frac{1}{NR} + \frac{2}{NR} \sum_{k=1}^{N-1} (\cos kn\pi/N)\, \epsilon^{s_k t} + \frac{(-1)^n}{NR} \epsilon^{-4t/NR}$$

where

$$s_k = -\frac{2}{RC} (1 - \cos k\pi/N) \tag{3-31}$$

3-5 Transient Response of a Tapered Distributed *RGC* Network

Consider a tapered distributed RC network terminated in a resistive load, as shown in Figure 3-3. The dielectric loss may also be included in a simple fashion provided G/C = constant. The voltage transfer

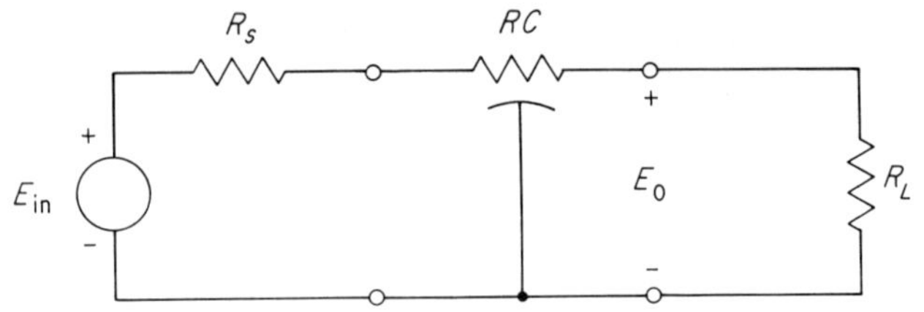

Figure 3-3

function $T_V(s)$ of the circuit is given by

$$T_V(s) \equiv \frac{E_0}{E_{in}}(s) = \frac{z_{21}R_L}{(z_{11}+R_s)\,(z_{22}+R_L) - z_{12}^{\,2}} \tag{3-32}$$

In Chapter 2 it was shown that for tapered distributed RGC networks, the open-circuit impedance parameters (or the short-circuit admittance parameters y_{ij}) can be expressed in the following forms

$$z_{11} = z_{11}(0)\,\frac{\prod_{i=1}^{\infty}\left(1+\dfrac{s}{\alpha_i}\right)}{\prod_{i=1}^{\infty}\left(1+\dfrac{s}{\sigma_i}\right)} = z_{11}(0)\,\frac{1+c_1s+c_2s^2+\cdots}{1+a_1s+a_2s^2+\cdots} \tag{3-33a}$$

$$z_{22} = z_{22}(0)\,\frac{\prod_{i=1}^{\infty}\left(1+\dfrac{s}{\beta_i}\right)}{\prod_{i=1}^{\infty}\left(1+\dfrac{s}{\sigma_i}\right)} = z_{22}(0)\,\frac{1+d_1s+d_2s^2+\cdots}{1+a_1s+a_2s^2+\cdots} \tag{3-33b}$$

$$z_{12} = z_{21} = z_{21}(0)\,\frac{1}{\prod_{i=1}^{\infty}\left(1+\dfrac{s}{\sigma_i}\right)} = z_{21}(0)\,\frac{1}{1+a_1s+a_2s^2+\cdots} \tag{3-33c}$$

where α_i, β_i, σ_i, a_i, c_i and d_i are real positive constants. Their specific values depend upon the taper function of the network and can be determined by the methods discussed in Sections 2-5 and 2-6.

From Equations (3-32) and (3-33) we obtain

$$T_V(s) \equiv \frac{E_0}{E_{in}}(s) = T_V(0)\,\frac{1+a_1s+a_2s^2+\cdots}{1+b_1s+b_2s^2+\cdots} \tag{3-34}$$

To find the key features of the transient response—that is, the rise and delay times for a step input—the conventional definition of 10 percent to 90 percent rise time and 50 percent delay time can be used, as shown in Figure 3-4. However, the exact calculations are quite involved and it is better to introduce some approximation techniques.

The transfer function in Equation (3-34) is a ratio of two entire functions. If the series in the numerator and denominator are terminated after i and j terms, respectively, we obtain a rational approximation:

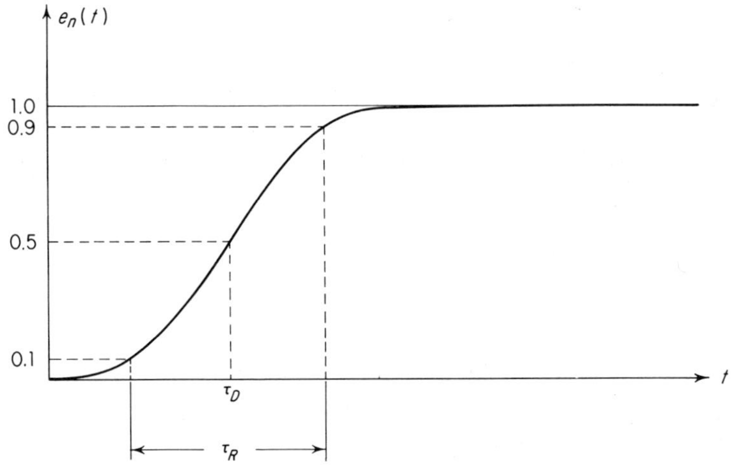

Figure 3-4 Definitions of 10 and 90 percent delay and rise time.

$$[T_V(s)]_{ij} = T_V(0)\,\frac{1 + a_1 s + a_2 s^2 + \cdots + a_i s^i}{1 + b_1 s + b_2 s^2 + \cdots + b_j s^j} \tag{3-35}$$

Usually $j > i$, since in most lumped physical networks the number of poles in a transfer function is larger than the number of zeros. Intuitively, it is obvious that a large number of terms would provide a good approximation. The transient response can be then determined in the usual manner. Unfortunately, for a given accuracy in the time domain, there is no general rule for determining the number of terms to be retained in the series. For a given $m = i + j$, many approximations are possible and these are known as the Padé approximants.[6]

A particularly convenient analytic method of computing rise time and delay time which is applicable for *monotonic (nonovershooting)* step response is given by Elmore's definitions,[7] as follows:

$$\tau_d = \int_0^\infty t e_n'(t)\, dt \tag{3-36}$$

$$\tau_r = \left[2\pi \int_0^\infty (t - \tau_d)^2 e_n'(t)\, dt\right]^{1/2} = \sqrt{2\pi}\left[\int_0^\infty t^2 e_n'(t)\, dt - \tau_d^{\,2}\right]^{1/2} \tag{3-37}$$

where
$$e_n'(t) = \frac{de_n}{dt}$$

is the impulse response of the network and

[6] For a detailed discussion of the Padé approximation see D. F. Tuttle, *Network Synthesis* (New York, Wiley, 1958), p. 761.

[7] W. C. Elmore, *J. Appl. Phys.*, **19** (1948), 55–63.

$$\int_0^\infty e_n'(t)\,dt = 1$$

that is, the area of the impulse response is normalized to unity. This normalization corresponds to $T_V(0) = 1$ in (3-34). The interpretations of (3-36) and (3-37) are shown in Figure 3-5(a) and (b). Some authors

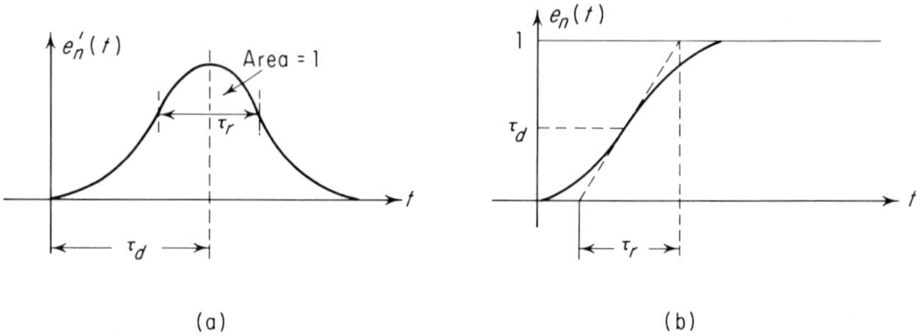

Figure 3-5 **(a)** Normalized impulse response. **(b)** Normalized step response.

use $h_n(t)$ for the normalized impulse response; that is, $h_n(t) = e_n'(t)$. The constant $\sqrt{2\pi}$ was arbitrarily chosen by Elmore so as to make the definition of rise time agree with another definition based on cascaded *RC* stages. For details, the reader is referred to Elmore's paper. Note that τ_d and τ_r are analogous to the mean and the standard deviation, respectively. It is interesting to note that, for the distributed *RC* networks when there are no transmission zeros in the finite plane, $e_n'(t)$ has the properties of the probability density function and thus

$$e_n(t) = \int_0^t e_n'(t)\,dt$$

behaves as a frequency distribution function. In other words, the step response $e_n(t)$ is a nondecreasing function of t and thus the condition of monotonicity is satisfied.

More generally the following can be shown to hold true.[8] If, for any lumped distributed *RC* network, the transfer function can be expressed as

$$H(s) = K\frac{s^m}{\phi(s)} \tag{3-38}$$

where K is a real constant and m a positive integer, then the impulse response $e_n'(t)$ or $h_n(t)$ has exactly m changes of sign. If the network is only lumped *RC*, $\phi(s)$ in (3-38) will be a polynomial of degree n with all the roots on the negative real axis. If, however, we have a distributed

[8] E. N. Protonotarious and O. Wing, *IEEE Trans. Circuit Theory*, **CT-14** (1967), p. 13–21.

RC network, $\phi(s)$ will be an infinite series or an infinite product with all the roots on the negative real axis.

A simple interpretation of the above property based on Equation (3-38) is shown in Figures 3-6 and 3-7. In Figure 3-6(a) the degree n

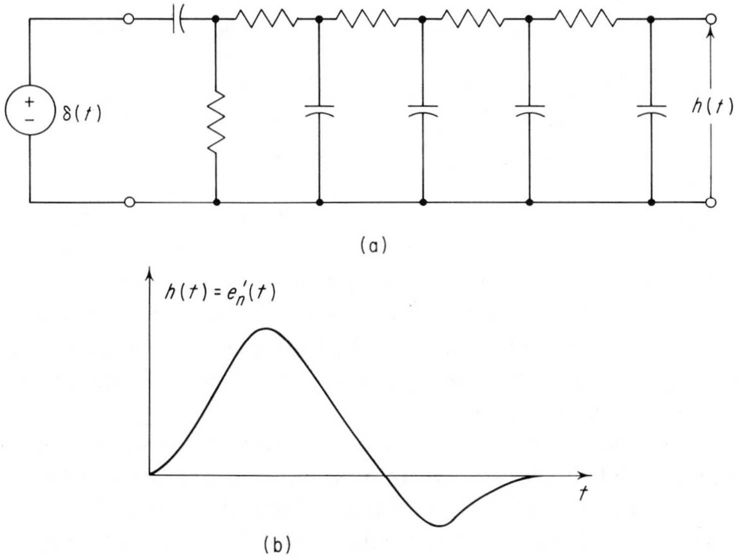

Figure 3-6 **(a)** Lumped *RC* network. **(b)** Impulse response of the network.

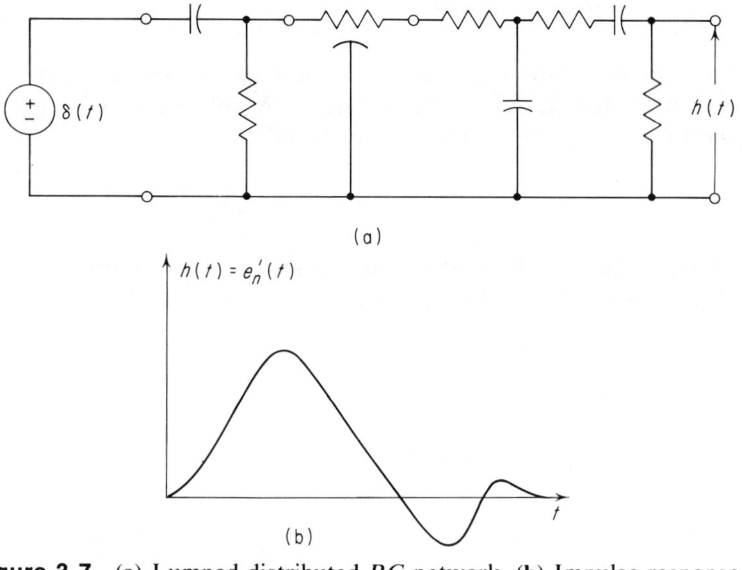

Figure 3-7 **(a)** Lumped distributed *RC* network. **(b)** Impulse response of the network.

of the polynomial $\phi(s)$ is $n = 5$ and $m = 1$; hence, the impulse response has only one change in sign and thus it can be quickly sketched as in Figure 3-6(b). For the network in Figure 3-7(a), the degree n in $\Phi(s)$ is infinity and $m = 2$; hence, the impulse response will have two changes in sign, as sketched in Figure 3-7(b). From the foregoing property it is readily seen that when $m = 0$ the normalized impulse response is positive for all t and behaves as a probability density function.

We use the subscripts d and r (Figure 3-5) in order to distinguish Elmore's definitions from the 50 percent delay time and 10 percent to 90 percent rise time definitions. For the latter we shall use the notation τ_D and τ_R (see Figure 3-4).

The application of (3-36) and (3-37) for the case in which the step response is a monotonic increasing function of time is illustrated further on in this section. The establishment of this monotonic increasing condition in general from Equation (3-34) is usually a difficult task. However, if (3-34) is expressed in such a form that the pole-zero locations are in evidence, it sometimes simplifies the task of establishing the monotonicity of the response.

In the following, we assume that the step response corresponding to Equation (3-34) is monotonic; that is, for e_{in} a unit step, the response $e_0(t)$ is a nondecreasing function of time. The transfer function, Equation (3-34), which could also be expressed as ratios of the current transforms, is written in the normalized form

$$H_n(s) = \frac{T_V(s)}{T_V(0)} = \frac{1 + a_1 s + a_2 s^2 + \cdots}{1 + b_1 s + b_2 s^2 + \cdots} \tag{3-39}$$

Now the impulse response is the inverse Laplace transform of $H(s)$. In other words, the derivative of the transient response to a step input is related to $H_n(s)$ by the Laplace transform

$$H_n(s) = \int_0^\infty e_n'(t)\epsilon^{-st}\,dt \tag{3-40}$$

where $e_n'(t)$ is the normalized impulse response, sometimes written as $h_n(t)$. Equation (3-40) can be expanded into a power series as

$$\begin{aligned} H_n(s) &= \int_0^\infty e_n'(t)\left[1 - st + \frac{s^2t^2}{2!} - \cdots\right] dt \\ &= \int_0^\infty e_n'(t)\,dt - s\int_0^\infty te_n'(t)\,dt + \frac{s^2}{2!}\int_0^\infty t^2e_n'(t)\,dt - \cdots \end{aligned} \tag{3-41}$$

Note that the poles of the transfer function are all in the left half plane and thus convergence is assured for small $|s|$. Substitution of Equations (3-36) and (3-37) into (3-41) yields

$$H_n(s) = 1 - s\tau_d + \frac{s^2}{2!}\left(\frac{\tau_r^{\,2}}{2\pi} + \tau_d^{\,2}\right) - \cdots \tag{3-42}$$

Equation (3-39) can also be expanded directly by long division as

$$H_n(s) = 1 - (b_1 - a_1)s + (b_1^{\,2} - a_1 b_1 + a_2 - b_2)s^2 + \cdots \tag{3-43}$$

Comparison of Equations (3-42) and (3-43) yields

$$\tau_d = b_1 - a_1 \tag{3-44}$$

$$\tau_r = \{2\pi[b_1^{\,2} - a_1^{\,2} + 2(a_2 - b_2)]\}^{1/2} \tag{3-45}$$

Remember that the application of Equations (3-44) and (3-45) is theoretically valid only when the a's and b's in (3-39) are such that the step response is monotonic and represents a low-pass network function. It is interesting to note that if the step response is monotonic in a low-pass network function the first two coefficients of the numerator and the denominator in (3-39) determine the delay and the rise times of the network, as defined by Elmore. In many practical situations where the overshoot for a step input is less than 5 percent, Equations (3-44) and (3-45) may still be used and the results are usually in close agreement with the conventional τ_D (50 percent) and τ_R (10 to 90 percent).

For some distributed networks, the closed-form expression may be available for the transfer function $H(s)$. If the monotonicity condition of the response for a step input is satisfied, then one can obtain τ_d and τ_r directly in terms of $H_n(s)$ in a closed form. The expressions are easily shown to be

$$\tau_d = -H_n'(0) \tag{3-46}$$

$$\tau_r = \sqrt{2\pi[H_n''(0) - \tau_d]} \tag{3-47}$$

where H_n is the normalized transfer function—that is, $H_n(0) = 1$—and $H_n'(0)$ and $H_n''(0)$ are the values of the first and second derivatives of $H_n(s)$ evaluated at $s = 0$, respectively.

3-6 Examples of the Application of Elmore's Definitions

As a first example let us consider a lumped parameter network designed to have a linear phase response. This class of networks has been studied thoroughly in the literature. The percent overshoot for a step input tends to zero as the order of the filter becomes very large. The frequency and transient response of this class of filters have also been tabulated.[9] In

[9] See, for example, M. S. Ghausi (Ref. 1), 88; also K. W. Henderson and W. H. Kautz, *IRE Trans. Circuit Theory*, **CT-5** (1958), 333–347.

particular let us consider a fifth-order filter (that is, a five-pole Thomson response). The normalized gain function for this filter (also referred to as maximally flat delay response) is given by

$$H_n(s) = \frac{1}{1 + s + 0.4444s^2 + 0.1112s^3 + 0.0159s^4 + 0.00106s^5} \tag{3-48}$$

Since the linear phase networks have negligible overshoot (less than 1 percent for any order filter), we can consider the response to be monotonic; thus, Elmore's definitions can be applied. From Equations (3-44), (3-45), and (3-48) we find

$$\tau_d = 1.0 \qquad \tau_r = 0.84$$

By the usual method of computing the 50 percent delay time τ_D and the 10 percent to 90 percent rise time τ_R, after lengthy computations from Eq. (3-48) (the reader may wish to verify this by carrying out the actual computations), we obtain

$$\tau_D = 0.99 \qquad \tau_R = 0.91$$

The results are close and, in addition, the time and effort saved by the use of Elmore's definitions are quite obvious.

For distributed RC networks, where the network functions have an infinite number of poles, the advantage of the use of Elmore's definitions becomes even greater as seen in the following.

Distributed *RC* network example. Consider a uniformly distributed RC network with $r(x) = r_0$, $c(x) = c_0$, and $g = l = 0$. The network length is equal to d. The network is shown in Figure 3-8. The voltage

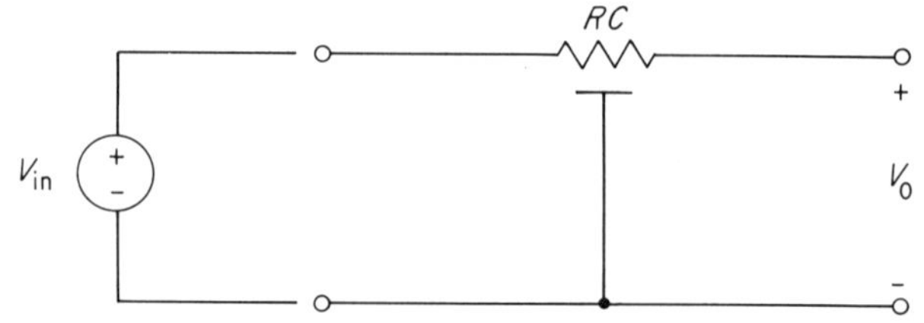

Figure 3-8 $\overline{URC}$ network.

transfer function for the network is given by

$$H(s) = \frac{V_0(s)}{V_{in}(s)} = -\frac{y_{21}}{y_{22}} \tag{3-49}$$

Substitution of the expressions for y_{ij} from Equation (1-21) into (3-49) yields

$$H(s) = \frac{1}{\cosh d\sqrt{r_0 c_0}\sqrt{s}} \tag{3-50}$$

For convenience, we normalize $d\sqrt{r_0 c_0}$ to unity. Expressing (3-50) in the form of (3-39), we have

$$H_n(s) = \frac{1}{1 + \frac{s}{2!} + \frac{s^2}{4!} + \frac{s^3}{6!} + \cdots} \tag{3-51}$$

Since the poles of Equation (3-50) are all on the negative real axis and are given by the zeros of y_{22} in (1-21a), and the transmission zeros are all at infinity, the transient response for a step input is monotonic. Applying Elmore's definition, from Equations (3-44), (3-45), and (3-51) we obtain

$$\tau_d = 0.5 \qquad \tau_r = 1.02$$

(Note that the time has been scaled by $1/d\sqrt{r_0 c_0}$).

Equation (3-50) is one of the simplest expressions arising in the analysis and synthesis of distributed *RC* networks. For this case it is easy to find the expression for the time response; for example, for a unit step input $V_{\text{in}}(s) = 1/s$, the output voltage (using the same frequency normalization) is

$$V_0(s) = \frac{1}{s}\frac{1}{\cosh\sqrt{s}} \tag{3-52}$$

Equation (3-52) may be expressed as

$$V_0(s) = \frac{1}{s}\frac{1}{\prod_{n=1}^{\infty}\left[1 + \frac{4s}{(2n-1)^2\pi^2}\right]} \tag{3-53}$$

The inverse Laplace transform of (3-53) is given by

$$v_0(t) = 1 + \frac{4}{\pi}\sum_{n=1}^{\infty}(-1)^n \frac{\exp\left[-\frac{(2n-1)^2\pi^2}{4}t\right]}{(2n-1)} \tag{3-54}$$

Equation (3-54) converges slowly for small t. To find the rise time τ_R and delay time τ_D requires the inclusion of many terms. Carrying out the computations, we find that

$$\tau_D = 0.38 \qquad \tau_R = 0.90$$

Again notice that the results are approximately in agreement with those obtained in Elmore's definiton.

Often when rise-time and delay-time calculations are to be made, it is very useful to obtain the time response in a form that converges very rapidly. Expansion in terms of the error function is convenient for this purpose. The error function (a tabulated function[10]) and the complementary error function are defined by

$$\operatorname{erfc} t = 1 - \operatorname{erf} t = 1 - \frac{2}{\sqrt{\pi}} \int_0^t \epsilon^{-x^2}\, dx \tag{3-55}$$

The inverse Laplace transform of Equation (3-52) in terms of the complementary error function, erfc t, is[11]

$$v_0(t) = 2 \sum_{n=1}^{\infty} (-1)^{n+1} \operatorname{erfc} \frac{(2n-1)}{2\sqrt{t}} \tag{3-56}$$

The infinite series in (3-56) converges very rapidly, and only the first few terms are necessary for reasonable accuracy. Again, however, evaluation of rise time and time delay involves tedious computations.

Note that the foregoing results are directly applicable to the other physical analog systems. For example, the short-circuit current gain of a common-base stage for a diffusion transistor is given by[12]

$$\frac{I_c}{I_e}(s) = \operatorname{sech} \theta = \operatorname{sech} \frac{W}{L} (1 + s\tau)^{1/2} \tag{3-57}$$

where W is the effective base width of the junction transistor, L and τ are minority carrier diffusion length and lifetime, respectively in the base region.

Tapered distributed *RGC* network example. Consider an arbitrarily tapered distributed RGC network (G represents the dielectric loss) or, in other words, a nonuniform $RLCG$ line with $l = 0$. The parameters $r(x)$ and $c(x)$ are piecewise continuous and bounded. The dielectric loss is assumed to be constrained by the relation $g(x)/c(x) = \Omega_0 =$ a constant.

The open-circuit voltage transfer function of the network shown in Figure 3-9 can be written as

$$T_V(s) = \frac{V_0(s)}{V_{\text{in}}(s)} = -\frac{y_{21}}{y_{22}} = \frac{1}{1 + B_1 s + B_2 s^2 + \cdots} \tag{3-58}$$

---

[10] E. Jahnke and F. Emde, Lösch *Table of Higher Functions* (New York, McGraw-Hill, 1960).

[11] See A. Erdelyi, *et al.*, *Tables of Integral Transforms* (New York, McGraw-Hill, 1954), Vol. I, p. 246.

$$\mathcal{L}^{-1}\left\{\frac{\exp\left[-N(a^2+bs)^{1/2}\right]}{s}\right\} = \frac{1}{2}\left[\epsilon^{-Na} \operatorname{erfc}\left(\frac{N}{2}\sqrt{\frac{b}{t}} - a\sqrt{\frac{b}{t}}\right) + \epsilon^{Na} \operatorname{erfc}\left(\frac{N}{2}\sqrt{\frac{b}{t}} + a\sqrt{\frac{t}{b}}\right)\right]$$

[12] See Ghausi, (Ref. 1), pp. 493.

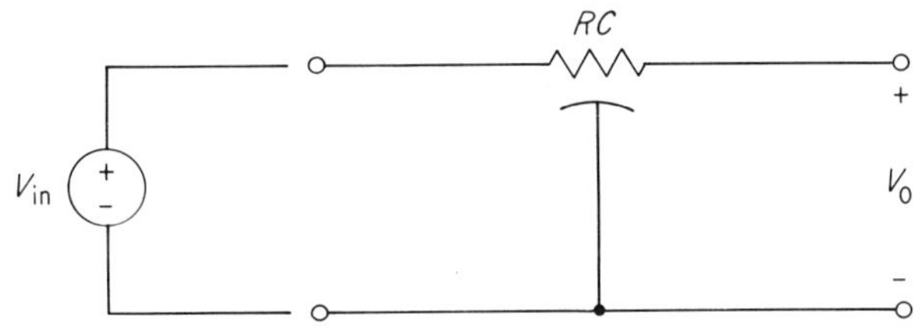

Figure 3-9 Tapered $\overline{RC}$ network.

where the constants B_i are determined either by the Picard-Carson method or by the basic-set product solution, as discussed in Sections 2-5 and 2-6, respectively. From Equation (3-58) and Table 2-1, it is readily seen that the denominator of $T_V(s)$ in (3-58) cannot have a pole in the finite s plane; in other words, the denominator is an entire function. Since the zeros of (3-58), which are the transmission zeros of the network, do not lie in the finite plane and the poles are all on the negative real axis, the step response for (3-58) is monotonic and Elmore's definitions apply. The delay and rise time are given by

$$\tau_d = B_1 \tag{3-59}$$

$$\tau_r = \sqrt{2\pi(B_1^2 - 2B_2)} \tag{3-60}$$

Uniformly distributed *RC* network with lumped *RC* termination. As a final example of the application of Elmore's method, consider a uniformly distributed RC network terminated by a series RC impedance, as shown in Figure 3-10.

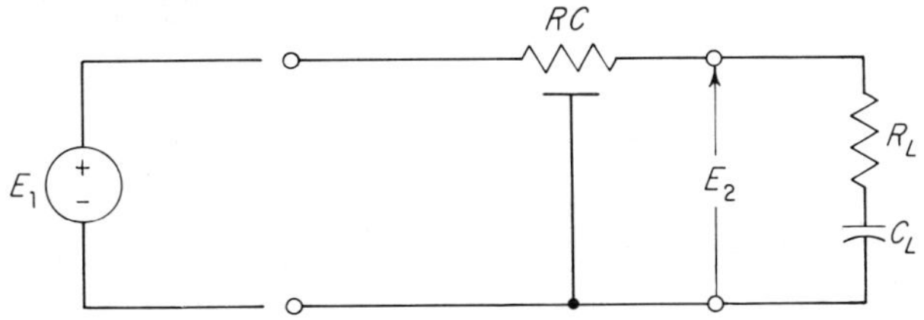

Figure 3-10 $\overline{URC}$ network terminated with a series RC impedance.

The voltage transfer function of this network is

$$H(s) = \frac{E_2}{E_1} = \frac{(T_L s + 1)\sqrt{Ts}}{(T_L s + 1)\sqrt{Ts}\cosh\sqrt{Ts} + RC_L s \sinh\sqrt{Ts}} \tag{3-61a}$$

where $T = r_0 c_0 d^2$ and $T_L = R_L C_L$. Equation (3-61a) may also be expressed as

$$H(s) = \frac{(1 + T_L s)}{1 + \left(T_L + \frac{T}{2} + r_0 d C_L\right)s + \left(\frac{T T_L}{2} + \frac{T^2}{24} + \frac{T r_0 d C_L}{6}\right)s^2 + \cdots} \tag{3-61b}$$

Note that in spite of the appearance of $\sqrt{Ts}$ in Equation (3-61a) there are no branch points in the transfer function, as is shown by (3-61b). The rise time, from Equations (3-61) and (3-45), is given by

$$\tau_r = (r_0 c_0 d^2)\left\{2\pi\left[\left(\frac{r_0 d C_L}{T}\right)^2 + \frac{1}{6} + 2\frac{r_0 d}{R_L}\left(\frac{T_L}{T}\right)^2 + \frac{2}{3}\left(\frac{C_L}{c_0 d}\right) - \frac{T_L}{T}\right]\right\}^{1/2} \tag{3-62}$$

It is instructive to compare the results in (3-62) with τ_R (the 10 percent to 90 percent rise time) as obtained by machine computation.[13]

For $\quad \dfrac{R_L}{r_0 d} = \dfrac{C_L}{c_0 d} = 0.1 \qquad \tau_r = 1.21T \qquad \tau_R = 1.20T$

$\quad \dfrac{R_L}{r_0 d} = \dfrac{C_L}{c_0 d} = 1.0 \qquad \tau_r = 4.22T \qquad \tau_R = 4.25T$

Note that the results are remarkably close. It should be noted, however, that the values of τ_d and τ_D in general will not be as close, due to the very nature of their defining equations.

3-7 Bandwidth Calculation for Distributed *RC* Networks

Consider the transfer function of a distributed *RC* network. For simplicity we shall consider first the case in which all the transmission zeros of the network function are at infinity (that is, there are no zeros in the finite plane). The transfer function may be expressed by

$$H(s) = \frac{H_0}{\prod_{i=1}^{\infty}\left(1 + \frac{s}{\sigma_i}\right)} \tag{3-63}$$

where H_0 is the value of $H(s)$ at zero frequency and $\sigma_1 < \sigma_2 < \sigma_3 < \cdots$. We shall determine the half-power frequency, ω_{3dB}. From Equation (3-63) we obtain the magnitude-squared function

$$|H(j\omega)|^2 = \frac{H_0^2}{\prod_{i=1}^{\infty}\left(1 + \frac{\omega^2}{\sigma_i^2}\right)} \tag{3-64}$$

At the 3-dB frequency,

[13] D. Starner, Lockheed Rept. LMSD-703095, Lockheed Missiles and Space Div., Sunnyvale, Calif., Sept. 1960.

$$\left|H(j\omega)\right|^2_{\omega=\omega_{3\,\mathrm{dB}}} = \frac{H_0^2}{2} \tag{3-65}$$

From Equations (3-64) and (3-65) we obtain

$$\frac{H_0^2}{2} = \frac{H_0^2}{\prod_{i=1}^{\infty}\left[1+\left(\frac{\omega_{3\,\mathrm{dB}}}{\sigma_i}\right)^2\right]} \tag{3-66}$$

Hence $\left[1+\left(\frac{\omega_{3\,\mathrm{dB}}}{\sigma_1}\right)^2\right]\left[1+\left(\frac{\omega_{3\,\mathrm{dB}}}{\sigma_2}\right)^2\right]\left[1+\left(\frac{\omega_{3\,\mathrm{dB}}}{\sigma_3}\right)^2\right]\cdots = 2$

or

$$1 + (\omega_{3\,\mathrm{dB}})^2\left[\frac{1}{\sigma_1^2}+\frac{1}{\sigma_2^2}+\frac{1}{\sigma_3^2}+\cdots\right] + (\omega_{3\,\mathrm{dB}})^4\left[\frac{1}{\sigma_1^2\sigma_2^2}+\frac{1}{\sigma_1^2\sigma_3^2}+\frac{1}{\sigma_2^2\sigma_3^2}+\cdots\right] + (\omega_{3\,\mathrm{dB}})^6\,[\cdots] + \cdots = 2 \tag{3-67}$$

Since $\omega_{3\,\mathrm{dB}} < \sigma_1 < \sigma_2 < \cdots$ and the individual series are absolutely convergent we neglect the terms above $\omega_{3\,\mathrm{dB}}^2$ and we have, to a first approximation,

$$1 + (\omega_{3\,\mathrm{dB}})^2\left[\frac{1}{\sigma_1^2}+\frac{1}{\sigma_2^2}+\frac{1}{\sigma_3^2}+\cdots\right] \approx 2 \tag{3-68}$$

or

$$\frac{1}{\omega_{3\,\mathrm{dB}}} \simeq \sqrt{\frac{1}{\sigma_1^2}+\frac{1}{\sigma_2^2}+\cdots} = \sqrt{\sum_i^N\left(\frac{1}{\sigma_i}\right)^2} \tag{3-69}$$

In Equation (3-69) the series is truncated after N terms; the error can be made small by a proper choice of N. In practice, for distributed RC networks with a transfer function, as in Equation (3-63), the value $N = 4$ is satisfactory for many cases; that is, only the first four poles need be considered in (3-69).

In some cases the distributed RC network is represented by an iterated finite lumped network. Of course the method of approximating a distributed network by an iterated finite lumped network is also valid for tapered distributed RC networks. For such networks, however, the element values of each section obviously are not the same as in the case of uniform networks (see Problem 2-10). The question of how many sections to use depends upon the frequency range of interest, the time constant of the line and the desired accuracy.

If the step response of a distributed network is a monotonically increasing function of time, a quick approximate method of determining the 3-dB frequency is to use the empirical formula

$$\tau_r f_{3\,\mathrm{dB}} \simeq 0.35 \tag{3-70}$$

where τ_r is the rise time determined by Equation (3-45). In Equation (3-70) the 10 percent to 90 percent rise time definition (that is, τ_R) can also be used if it is available. However, as we have already shown in Equation (3-60), it is a simple matter to find τ_r if the transfer function is given, provided that the step response is monotonic. If the monotonicity condition is satisfied for the transfer function of the form

$$H(s) = \frac{1 + a_1 s + a_2 s^2 + \cdots}{1 + b_1 s + b_2 s^2 + \cdots} \tag{3-71}$$

then from Equation (3-70), (3-71), and (3-45) we have

$$\omega_{3\,\mathrm{dB}} \simeq \frac{0.35\sqrt{2\pi}}{[b_1^2 - a_1^2 + 2(a_2 - b_2)]^{1/2}} \tag{3-72}$$

It should be noted that the monotonicity condition of the step response is generally not easy to establish; therefore, Equations (3-72) and (3-45) should be used with caution. In practice, Equations (3-72) and (3-45) can also be used without significant error if the step response has an overshoot of less than 5 percent.

As an example, consider the open-circuit voltage transfer function of a uniform *RC* line as given by Equation (3-51). For this case, the step response is monotonic, and we determine $\tau_r = 1.02$. From Equation (3-70) we obtain $f_{3\,\mathrm{dB}} \approx 0.35$. The exact value of the 3-dB frequency for this case is $f_{3\,\mathrm{dB}} = 0.387$. Note that the rise time is normalized with respect to $d\sqrt{r_0 c_0}$; thus, $f_{3\,\mathrm{dB}} \approx 0.35/d\sqrt{r_0 c_0}$.

3-8 The Equivalent Dominant-Pole and Excess-Phase Approximations

The concept of dominant poles and zeros plays an important role in simplifying the analysis and design of linear networks. In many physical situations the behavior of a system is of interest in the region where the dominant poles and zeros are located and the actual system can be approximated satisfactorily by a low-order transfer function consisting only of the dominant poles and zeros.[14] For a lumped-parameter system in which the locations of the dominant poles and zeros are known, the approximate calculation of the frequency and transient response is simplified considerably.

The idea of dominant poles and zeros can also be extended to a distributed-parameter network. For example, the intrinsic short-circuit

[14] D. O. Pederson and G. H. Wilson, *IEEE Trans. Circuit Theory*, **CT-11** (March 1964), 104–108.

current gain of the diffusion transistor in the common-base connection, termed alpha, is given by[15]

$$\alpha(s) = \frac{1}{\cosh \frac{W}{L}(1 + s\tau)^{1/2}} \tag{3-73}$$

where W is the base width, L is the diffusion length, τ is the minority carrier lifetime in the base region, and s is the complex frequency variable. Note that Equation (3-73) is similar to the open-circuit voltage transfer function of the $\overline{URC}$ network, and is a representative distributed network function. The network function has a countably infinite number of poles. The low-frequency behavior of the short-circuit gain is usually of greatest interest and the expression for alpha is customarily approximated by the simplified expression.

$$\alpha(j\omega) \simeq \frac{\alpha_0}{[1 + j(\omega/\omega_\alpha)]} \epsilon^{-j(\omega m/\omega_\alpha)} \tag{3-74}$$

where α_0 is the zero frequency value of alpha, ω_α is the 3-dB frequency, in radians per second, m is the excess phase factor, and ω is the frequency variable in radians per second. The magnitude and phase of alpha, and of the approximating function, are shown for comparison in Figure 3-11.

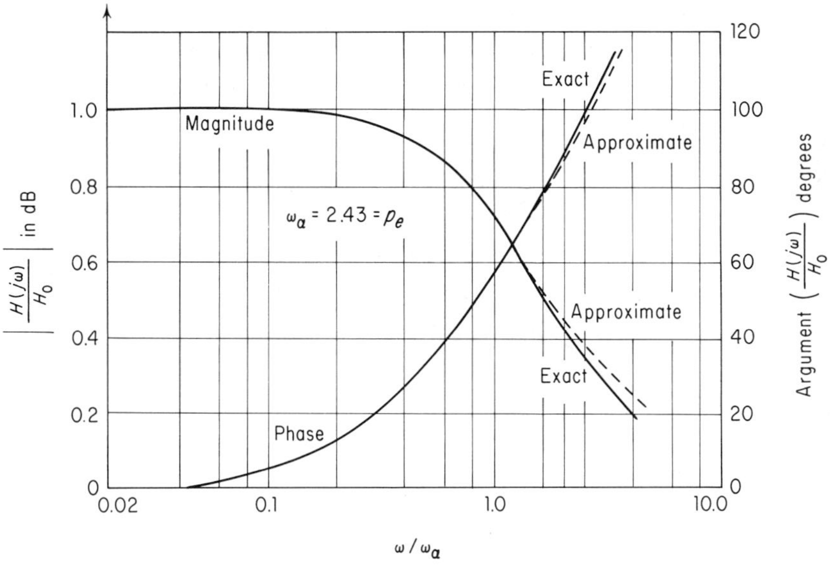

Figure 3-11 Magnitude and phase of $H(j\omega)/H_0$ (exact versus approximate).

[15] See R. L. Pritchard, *Proc. IRE,* **40** (1952), 1746–1781. Also Ghausi (Ref. 1), 189–190.

Note that the simplified approximating function, Equation (3-74), has substantially the same magnitude and phase response as the true function over the frequency range from zero frequency to a frequency about twice ω_α.

The simplified expression for alpha is obtained by determining ω_α and m. The 3-dB radian frequency ω_α is the radian frequency at which the magnitude of alpha is 3 dB below its zero frequency value, while m is the phase, in radians, in excess of $\pi/4$ radians at ω_α.

The transient response to step function inputs is also readily determined from the approximating function when $j\omega$ is replaced by s in Equation (3-74). Thus, for a unit step input the short-circuit output current of the intrinsic common-base diffusion transistor is found from the inverse Laplace transformation of

$$I(s) \simeq \frac{1}{s} \frac{\alpha_0}{\left(1 + \dfrac{s}{\omega_\alpha}\right)} \epsilon^{-sm/\omega_\alpha} \tag{3-75}$$

which yields

$$i(t) \simeq \alpha_0 \left[1 - \exp - \left(t - \frac{m}{\omega_\alpha}\right)\right] u\left(t - \frac{m}{\omega_\alpha}\right) \tag{3-76}$$

where $u(t - m/\omega_\alpha)$ is the Heaviside unit step; that is, $u(t - m/\omega_\alpha) = 1$ for $t > m/\omega_\alpha$ and is zero for $t < m/\omega_\alpha$.

The exact unit step response, and the approximate response calculated from Equation (3-76) are shown for comparison in Figure 3-12. Note

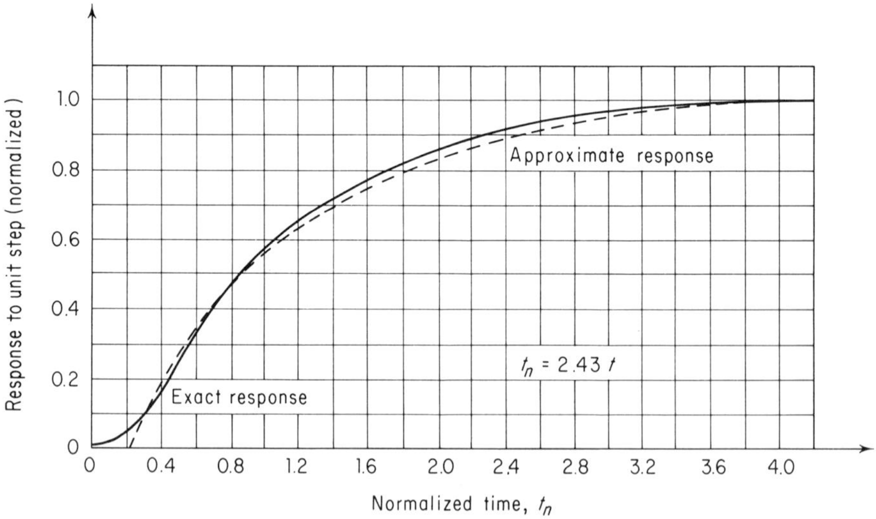

Figure 3-12 Comparison of exact and approximate step-function response of $\overline{URC}$ network.

the close correspondence of the response functions, particularly with respect to time delay and rise time.

As shown in this example, much useful information about the behavior of distributed network functions in the frequency and time domains can be obtained from a relatively simple approximating function. For instance, the open-circuit voltage transfer function of the $\overline{URC}$ network is

$$H(s) = \frac{1}{\cosh d\sqrt{s\tau}} \tag{3-77}$$

where d is the network length and $\tau = r_0 c_0$. This expression is very similar to Equation (3-73), and thus we may infer that the open-circuit voltage transfer function of the $\overline{URC}$ network can be approximated by

$$H(s) \approx \frac{H(0)}{\left(1 + \dfrac{s}{p_e}\right)} \epsilon^{-sm/p_e} \equiv H_1(s) \tag{3-78}$$

where $H(0)$ is the zero-frequency value, p_e is the 3-dB radian frequency (equivalent dominant pole), and m is the excess phase factor. Thus, the comparisons shown in Figure 3-11 and 3-12 also apply to the open-circuit voltage transfer function of the $\overline{URC}$ network, as well as to the alpha of the common-base diffusion transistor.

Now, we will develop a generalization of the equivalent dominant pole and excess phase concept to the point where it can be applied to tapered $\overline{RC}$ networks, and to networks made up of lumped and distributed elements intermixed.

From the results of Chapter 2, we know that the transfer function of a distributed linear network can be expressed either by a ratio of two Taylor's series expansions as

$$H(s) = H_0 \frac{1 + A_1 s + A_2 s^2 + \cdots}{1 + B_1 s + B_2 s^2 + \cdots} = H_0 \frac{\sum_{i=0}^{\infty} A_i s^i}{\sum_{i=0}^{\infty} B_i s^i} \tag{3-79}$$

where $$A_0 = B_0 = 1$$

or by a ratio of two infinite-product expansions as

$$H(s) = H_0 \frac{\left(1 + \dfrac{s}{z_1}\right)\left(1 + \dfrac{s}{z_2}\right) \cdots}{\left(1 + \dfrac{s}{p_1}\right)\left(1 + \dfrac{s}{p_2}\right) \cdots} = H_0 \frac{\prod_{i=1}^{\infty} \left(1 + \dfrac{s}{z_i}\right)}{\prod_{i=1}^{\infty} \left(1 + \dfrac{s}{p_i}\right)} \tag{3-80}$$

Because we may obtain the two-port parameters in either the form of (3-79) or of (3-80), we shall treat each form in turn.

First consider an all-pole transfer function

$$H(s) = \frac{H_0}{Q(s)} = \frac{H_0}{1 + B_1 s + B_2 s^2 + \cdots} = \frac{H_0}{\sum_{i=0}^{\infty} B_i s^i} \tag{3-81}$$

The equivalent infinite-product form of (3-81) is

$$H(s) = \frac{H_0}{Q(s)} = \frac{H_0}{\left(1 + \frac{s}{p_1}\right)\left(1 + \frac{s}{p_2}\right) \cdots} = \frac{H_0}{\prod_{i=1}^{\infty} \left(1 + \frac{s}{p_i}\right)} \tag{3-82}$$

In passing, we note that the constants B_i and p_i are related as follows:

$$\begin{aligned} B_0 &= 1 \\ B_1 &= \sum_{i=1}^{\infty} \frac{1}{p_i} \\ B_2 &= \sum_{i_1=1}^{\infty} \sum_{i_2=i_1+1}^{\infty} \frac{1}{p_{i_1}} \frac{1}{p_{i_2}} \\ B_n &= \sum_{i_1=1}^{\infty} \sum_{i_2=i_1+1}^{\infty} \cdots \sum_{i_n=i_{n-1}+1}^{\infty} \frac{1}{p_{i_1}} \frac{1}{p_{i_2}} \cdots \frac{1}{p_{i_n}} \end{aligned} \tag{3-83}$$

and hence a sufficient condition that the B_i are all positive is that the p_i are all positive.

We then determine the equivalent dominant pole p_e and the excess phase factor m from Equation (3-81) or (3-82). Let us begin with Equation (3-81). To find p_e, we must determine the 3-dB radian frequency of $|H(j\omega)|$ from (3-81), or what is equivalent, the radian frequency at which $|H(j\omega)|^2 = H_0^2/2$. To find the excess phase factor m, we must evaluate the phase of $H(j\omega)$ at $\omega = p_e$ from (3-81).

The magnitude squared function, $|H(j\omega)|^2$ is determined by taking the product

$$|H(j\omega)|^2 = H(j\omega)H(-j\omega) \tag{3-84}$$

In series form, the magnitude-squared function is

$$\left|\frac{H(\omega)}{H_0}\right|^2 = \frac{1}{1 + C_2\omega^2 + C_4\omega^4 + \cdots} = \frac{1}{\sum_{i=0}^{\infty} C_{2i}\omega^{2i}} \tag{3-85}$$

where

$$\begin{aligned} C_0 &= 1 \\ C_2 &= B_1^2 - 2B_2 \qquad C_4 = B_2^2 - 2B_1B_2 + B_4^2 \\ C_{2n} &= \sum_{j=-1}^{j=+1} (-1)^{n+j} (B_{n+j})(B_{n-j}) \end{aligned}$$

Equation (3-85) gives no information about the algebraic sign of C_i.

However, if we take the magnitude-squared function from the infinite product form of (3-82), we find

$$\left|\frac{H(\omega)}{H_0}\right|^2 = \frac{1}{\prod_{i=1}^{\infty}\left(1+\frac{j\omega}{p_i}\right)} \frac{1}{\prod_{i=1}^{\infty}\left(1-\frac{j\omega}{p_i}\right)} \tag{3-86a}$$

or

$$\left|\frac{H(\omega)}{H_0}\right|^2 = \frac{1}{\prod_{i=1}^{\infty}\left(1+\frac{\omega^2}{p_i^2}\right)} \tag{3-86b}$$

and on carrying out the product

$$\left|\frac{H(\omega)}{H_0}\right|^2 = \frac{1}{1+C_2\omega^2+C_4\omega^4+\cdots} = \frac{1}{\sum_{i=0}^{\infty} C_{2i}\omega^{2i}} \tag{3-87}$$

Comparison of Equations (3-86) and (3-87) leads to

$$C_0 = 1$$

$$C_2 = \sum_{i=1}^{\infty}\frac{1}{p_i^2} \qquad C_4 = \sum_{i_1=1}^{\infty}\sum_{i_2=i_1+1}^{\infty}\left(\frac{1}{p_{i_1}^2}\right)\left(\frac{1}{p_{i_2}^2}\right)$$

$$C_{2n} = \sum_{i=1}^{\infty}\sum_{i_2=i_1+1}^{\infty}\cdots\sum_{i_n=i_{n-1}+1}^{\infty}\left(\frac{1}{p_{i_1}^2}\right)\left(\frac{1}{p_{i_2}^2}\right)\cdots\left(\frac{1}{p_{i_n}^2}\right)$$

and hence we demonstrate that the algebraic signs of C_i are positive when all p_i are real. The relationships between the series and product forms are summarized in Table 3-1.

Table 3-1 SUMMARY OF RELATIONS BETWEEN SERIES AND PRODUCT FORMS

FUNCTION	SERIES FORM OF $Q(s)$	PRODUCT FORM OF $Q(s)$	RELATION BETWEEN SERIES AND PRODUCT FORMS
$\frac{H_0}{H(s)}$	$\sum_{i=0}^{\infty} B_i s^i$	$\prod_{i=1}^{\infty}\left(1+\frac{s}{p_i}\right)$	$B_0 = 1$ $B_n = \sum_{i_1=1}^{\infty}\sum_{i_2=i_1+1}^{\infty}\cdots\sum_{i_n=i_{n-1}+1}^{\infty}\left(\frac{1}{p_{i_1}}\right)\left(\frac{1}{p_{i_2}}\right)\cdots\left(\frac{1}{p_{i_n}}\right)$
$\left\|\frac{H_0}{H(s)}\right\|^2$	$\sum_{i=0}^{\infty}(-1)^i C_{2i}s^{2i}$	$\prod_{i=1}^{\infty}\left[1+\left(\frac{s}{p_i}\right)^2\right]$	$C_0 = 1$ $C_{2n} = \sum_{i_1=1}^{\infty}\sum_{i_2=i_1+1}^{\infty}\cdots\sum_{i_n=i_{n-1}+1}^{\infty}\left(\frac{1}{p_{i_1}}\right)^2\left(\frac{1}{p_{i_2}}\right)^2\cdots\left(\frac{1}{p_{i_n}}\right)^2$
$\left\|\frac{H_0}{H(\omega)}\right\|^2$	$\sum_{i=0}^{\infty} C_{2i}\omega^{2i}$	$\prod_{i=1}^{\infty}\left[1+\left(\frac{\omega}{p_i}\right)^2\right]$	$C_0 = 1$ $C_{2n} = \sum_{i_1=1}^{\infty}\sum_{i_2=i_1+1}^{\infty}\cdots\sum_{i_n=i_{n-1}+1}^{\infty}\left(\frac{1}{p_{i_1}}\right)^2\left(\frac{1}{p_{i_2}}\right)^2\cdots\left(\frac{1}{p_{i_n}}\right)^2$
$\phi(j\omega)$	$\tan^{-1}\left[\frac{B_1\omega-B_3\omega^3+\cdots}{B_0-B_2\omega^2+\cdots}\right]$	$\sum_{i=1}^{\infty}\tan^{-1}\left(\frac{\omega}{p_i}\right)$	$m = \frac{\pi}{4} - \phi(j\omega)\Big\|_{\omega=p_e}$

To find the equivalent dominant pole p_e from Equation (3-85) we must find the solution of the equation

$$2 = 1 + C_2 p_e^2 + C_4 p_e^4 + \cdots = \sum_{i=0}^{\infty} C_{2i} p_e^{2i} \tag{3-88}$$

This is readily done by the method of successive approximations or iteration, illustrated in Figure 3-13 (see also Appendix E). From Equation (3-88),

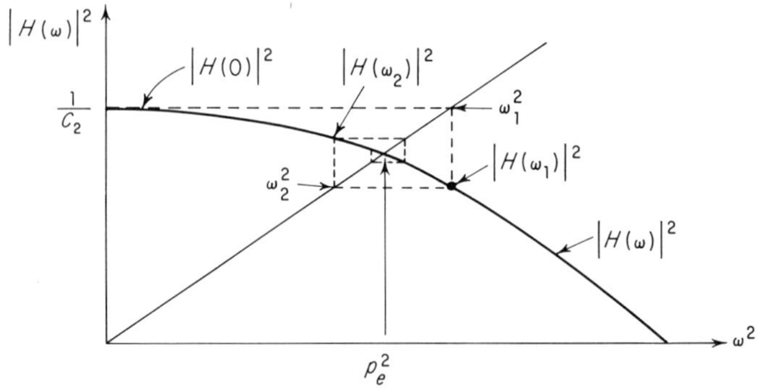

Figure 3-13 Iteration procedure for finding p_e.

$$p_e^2 = \frac{1 - C_4 p_e^4 - \cdots}{C_2} \tag{3-89}$$

In most cases, $C_2 >> C_4 \ldots >> C_n$, and after two iterations we obtain the approximate solution

$$p_e^2 \approx \frac{C_2^2 - C_4}{C_2^3} \tag{3-90}$$

For most cases, further iteration has a negligible effect on the result. Hence, we use the expression

$$p_e \approx \sqrt{\frac{C_2^2 - C_4}{C_2^3}} \tag{3-91}$$

The same type of iteration procedure may be used to relate p_1, the dominant pole of $H(s)$, to C_2 and C_4. By setting the product $Q(s)Q(-s)$ equal to zero and using the iteration scheme, we have

$$p_1 \approx \sqrt{\frac{C_2^2 + C_4}{C_3^2}} \tag{3-92}$$

We define

$$\delta = \frac{C_4}{C_2^2} \tag{3-93}$$

From Equations (3-91) and (3-92) we find the relation between the equivalent dominant pole p_e and the dominant pole p_1 to be

$$\left(\frac{p_1}{p_e}\right)^2 \approx \frac{1+\delta}{1-\delta} \tag{3-94}$$

For $\delta < 0.1$, Equation (3-94) can be further approximated by

$$p_e \approx \frac{p_1}{1+\delta} \tag{3-95}$$

We repeat that in Equation (3-95), p_e is the *equivalent dominant pole* and is identical to the 3-dB radian frequency of $|H(j\omega)|$. Thus, the approximation to the magnitude function is given by

$$\left|\frac{H(j\omega)}{H_0}\right| \simeq \left|\frac{H_1(j\omega)}{H_0}\right| = \left|\frac{1}{1 + j\omega/p_e}\right| \tag{3-96}$$

where $|H_1(j\omega)/H_0|$ is the magnitude of the approximating function.

Next, we compute the excess phase factor m by setting the phase error of the approximating function equal to zero at $\omega = p_e$. From Equation (3-82), the phase of $H(j\omega)$ is

$$\arg H(j\omega) = -\sum_{i=1}^{\infty} \tan^{-1} \frac{\omega}{p_i} \tag{3-97}$$

The phase of the approximating function of Equation (3-78) is

$$\arg H_1(j\omega) = -\tan^{-1} \frac{\omega}{p_e} - \frac{m\omega}{p_e} \tag{3-98}$$

Using the identity

$$\tan^{-1} A - \tan^{-1} B = \tan^{-1}\left(\frac{A-B}{1+AB}\right) \tag{3-99}$$

we find the phase difference $e_p(j\omega)$ as

$$e_p(j\omega) = \arg H_1(j\omega) - \arg H(j\omega)$$

$$= \tan^{-1}\left(\frac{\dfrac{\omega}{p_1} - \dfrac{\omega}{p_e}}{1 + \omega^2/p_1 p_e}\right) + \sum_{i=2}^{\infty} \tan^{-1} \frac{\omega}{p_i} - m\frac{\omega}{p_e} \tag{3-100}$$

Since $\tan x \approx x$ for small values of x, Equation (3-100) may be written as

$$e_p \simeq \tan^{-1} \omega \left[\frac{p_e - p_1}{\omega^2 + p_e p_1}\right] + \sum_{i=2}^{\infty} \frac{\omega}{p_i} - m\frac{\omega}{p_e} \tag{3-101}$$

Since m is chosen to make the phase error zero at $\omega = p_e$, we have, from Equations (3-101) and (3-95),

$$m \approx \tan^{-1}\left(\frac{-\delta}{2+\delta}\right) + p_e \sum_{i=2}^{\infty} \frac{1}{p_i}$$

$$\approx -\frac{\delta}{2+\delta} + p_e \sum_{i=2}^{\infty} \frac{1}{p_i} \qquad \textbf{(3-102)}$$

The complete expression for the approximating function is

$$\frac{H(j\omega)}{H_0} \simeq \frac{H_1(j\omega)}{H_0} = \frac{1}{1 + j\omega/p_e}\,\epsilon^{-j\omega m/p_e} \qquad \textbf{(3-103)}$$

with p_e given by Equation (3-95) and m given by Equation (3-102). The results are summarized in Table 3-2.

Table 3-2 CONSTANTS OF THE EQUIVALENT DOMINANT-POLE AND EXCESS-PHASE APPROXIMATION

$Q(s)$ in infinite-series form $\sum_{n=0}^{\infty} B_n s^n$ $B_0 = 1$	$p_e \approx \left[\frac{C_2^2 - C_4}{C_2^3}\right]^{1/2}$ $C_2 = B_1^2 - 2B_2$ $C_4 = B_2^2 - 2B_1B_3 + B_4^2$	$m \approx \frac{-\delta}{2+\delta} + p_e\left(B_1 - \frac{1}{p_1}\right)$ $p_1 \approx (1+\delta)p_e$ $\delta \approx \frac{C_4}{C_2^2}$
$Q(s)$ in infinite-product form $\prod_{n=1}^{\infty}\left(1 + \frac{s}{p_n}\right)$	$p_e \approx \frac{p_1}{1+\delta}$ $\delta \approx p_1^2 \sum_{i=2}^{\infty} \frac{1}{p_i^2}$	$m \approx \frac{-\delta}{2+\delta} + p_e\left(B_1 - \frac{1}{p_1}\right)$ $B_1 = \sum_{i=1}^{\infty} \frac{1}{p_i}$

Consider now the errors in magnitude and phase in the approximating function. The magnitude error in the denominator of the approximating function $e_n(\omega^2)$ is found directly as

$$e_n(\omega^2) = (1 + C_2\omega^2 + C_4\omega^4 + \cdots) - \left(1 + \frac{\omega^2}{p_e^2}\right) \qquad \textbf{(3-104)}$$

Ignoring the terms beyond $C_4\omega^4$, and using the relations

$$p_e^2 = \frac{1-\delta}{C_2} \qquad C_4 = \delta C_2^2$$

we find

$$e_n(\omega^2) \simeq \frac{C_2\omega^2}{1-\delta}\left[(1-\delta)C_2\omega^2 - 1\right]$$

$$= \delta \frac{\omega^2}{p_e^{\,2}}\left[\frac{(1-\delta)^2\omega^2}{p_e^{\,2}} - 1\right] \tag{3-105}$$

Note that $e_n(\omega^2)$ is zero at $\omega^2 = 0$, and at $\omega^2 = p_e^{\,2}/(1-\delta)$.

By setting the derivative of Equation (3-105) equal to zero, we find that $e_n(\omega^2)$ has a local maximum at

$$\omega_m^{\,2} \simeq \frac{p_e^{\,2}}{2(1-\delta)^2} \simeq \frac{p_1^{\,2}}{2} \tag{3-106}$$

At ω_m, the maximum magnitude error is

$$e_n(\omega_m^{\,2}) = \frac{-\delta}{4(1-\delta)^2} \tag{3-107}$$

Now, let us find the relative magnitude error. The true value of the function can be written, using (3-104), as

$$H^2(\omega^2) = \frac{H_0^{\,2}}{1 + \left(\frac{\omega}{p_e}\right)^2 + e_n^{\,2}} \tag{3-108}$$

Defining the relative magnitude error by

$$e_R = \frac{H_1^{\,2} - H^2}{H^2} \tag{3-109}$$

we find, using (3-108), that

$$e_R = \frac{e_n}{1 + \frac{\omega^2}{p_e^{\,2}}} = \frac{\delta\left(\frac{\omega}{p_e}\right)^2\left[(1-\delta)^2\left(\frac{\omega}{p_e}\right)^2 - 1\right]}{1 + \left(\frac{\omega}{p_e}\right)^2} \tag{3-110}$$

At ω_m, the relative magnitude error is

$$e_R = \frac{-\delta}{6 - 8\delta + 4\delta^2} \tag{3-111}$$

For the majority of applications, $\delta << 1$, and the magnitude-squared error can be expressed in decibels[16] by the simple relation

$$\begin{aligned} e_{\text{dB}} &= 10 \log_{10}\left[\frac{H_1^{\,2}(\omega^2)}{H^2(\omega^2)}\right] \\ &\simeq -4.34 e_R \\ &\simeq \frac{4.34\delta}{6 - 8\delta}\ \text{dB} \end{aligned} \tag{3-112}$$

---

[16] For small x, $\log_\epsilon (1 + x) \simeq x$, and $\log_{10} (1 + x) = 0.434 \log_\epsilon (1 + x)$.

The phase error $e_p(\omega)$ is defined as

$$e_p(\omega) = \arg H_1(\omega) - \arg H(\omega)$$
$$\approx -\tan^{-1} \frac{\delta\omega p_e}{\omega^2 + (1+\delta)p_e^2} + \frac{\delta\omega}{(2+\delta)p_e} \quad \text{(3-113)}$$

Since for small δ the angles are very small, the angle can be replaced by its tangent and, after simplification, we find that

$$e_p(\omega) \approx \frac{\delta\omega\,[\omega^2 - p_e^2]}{(2+\delta)p_e\,[\omega^2 + (1+\delta)p_e^2]} \quad \text{(3-114)}$$

The phase error has a local maximum (Problem 3-18) at $\omega_p = p_1/2$. The maximum phase error is

$$e_{p_m} \approx \frac{-(3-4.1\delta)\delta}{20} \approx \frac{-3\delta}{20} \text{ radians} \quad \text{(3-115)}$$

The magnitude and phase-error relationships are summarized in Table 3-3.

The region over which the simple single-pole approximating function can be used is determined by the allowable magnitude and phase errors. In general, the simple single-pole approximation (with excess phase factor) has limited usefulness for frequencies much greater than $\omega = p_1$. However, this limitation can be removed by using more complex approximating functions. Thus, given

$$\frac{H(j\omega)}{H_0} = \frac{1}{\prod_{i=1}^{\infty}\left(1 + \frac{j\omega}{p_i}\right)} \quad \text{(3-116)}$$

the first pole can be factored out and an equivalent dominant-pole and excess-phase-factor approximation determined for the remainder. Thus, we can approximate the function $H(j\omega)$ over a greater range of frequencies by the expression

Table 3-3 FREQUENCY-DOMAIN ERRORS OF THE APPROXIMATION

MAGNITUDE ERRORS AT $\omega_M' = p_1/\sqrt{2}$	PHASE ERROR AT $\omega_p = p_1/2$
$e_M = \frac{-\delta}{4(1-\delta)^2}$	$e_p = \frac{-(3-4.1\delta)\delta}{20}$ (radians)
$e_R = \frac{-\delta}{6-8\delta}$	$e_p = -8.6\delta + 11.7\delta$ (degrees)
$e_{dB} = \frac{4.34\delta}{6-8\delta}$ dB	

$$\frac{H(j\omega)}{H_0} \simeq \frac{1}{\left(1+j\dfrac{\omega}{p_1}\right)} \frac{\epsilon^{-jm/p_e}}{\left(1+j\dfrac{\omega}{p_e}\right)} \tag{3-117}$$

where p_1 is the dominant pole of $H(j\omega)$, and p_e and m are the equivalent dominant pole and excess phase factor of

$$\frac{(1+j\omega/p_1)H(j\omega)}{H_0} = \frac{1}{\prod_{i=2}^{\infty}\left(1+j\dfrac{\omega}{p_i}\right)} \tag{3-118}$$

In general, Equation (3-117) has acceptably low magnitude and phase errors over the frequency range $0 \leqslant \omega \leqslant p_2$, where p_2 is the second pole of $H(j\omega)$. The procedure can be extended further if desired. However, the simplicity and the attractiveness of this method is reduced if more complicated expressions are used.

As a final comment, if the network function consists of a numerator and denominator—both of which are infinite series or products—we can treat numerator and denominator separately and obtain equivalent dominant roots and excess phase terms for each.

3-9 Examples of the Application of Equivalent Dominant-Pole and Excess-Phase Approximations

In order to demonstrate the ease of application and usefulness of the equivalent dominant-pole and excess-phase approximation, we shall demonstrate a few detailed examples.

Consider the open-circuit voltage transfer function of the uniformly distributed RC network as given in Equation (3-50). Using the normalization factor $d\sqrt{r_0 c_0}$, we have

$$H(s) = \frac{1}{\cosh\sqrt{s}} = \frac{1}{Q(s)} \tag{3-119}$$

For this case $Q(s)$ can be expressed easily in the infinite-series or infinite-product forms

$$Q(s) = 1 + \frac{s}{2!} + \frac{s^2}{4!} + \cdots = \sum_{n=0}^{\infty} \frac{s^n}{n!} \tag{3-120a}$$

or

$$Q(s) = \prod_{n=1}^{\infty}\left(1 + \frac{4s}{(2n-1)^2\pi^2}\right) \tag{3-120b}$$

From the infinite series:

$$B_0 = 1 \qquad B_1 = 0.5 \qquad B_2 = 0.0417$$
$$B_3 = 1.389 \times 10^{-3} \qquad B_4 = 2.48 \times 10^{-5}$$

From Equation (3-85) we obtain the coefficients of the magnitude-squared function:

$$C_0 = 1 \qquad C_2 = 0.1666 \qquad C_4 = 3.968 \times 10^{-4}$$

From Equation (3-91), the equivalent dominant pole is

$$p_e = \sqrt{\frac{C_2^2 - C_4}{C_2^3}} = 2.43 \tag{3-121}$$

From Equation (3-92), the dominant pole p_1 is

$$p_1 = \sqrt{\frac{C_2^2 + C_4}{C_2^3}} = 2.47$$

Notice that if the product expansion is given, p_1 is the lowest critical frequency. From Equation (3-120b), $|p_1| = \pi^2/4 = 2.47$. Also, from Equation (3-93),

$$\delta = \frac{C_4}{C_2^2} = 0.0143$$

From Equation (3-106), the frequency of maximum magnitude error is

$$\omega_m \approx \frac{p_e}{\sqrt{2}\,(1-\delta)} = 1.75$$

The maximum magnitude error is

$$e_{M_m} = \frac{-\delta}{4(1-\delta)^2} = 0.00362$$

The error in decibels is

$$e_{\text{dB}} \approx \frac{4.34\delta}{6 - 8\delta} = 0.01 \text{ dB}$$

From Equation (3-102) the excess phase factor is determined. First the infinite summation may be written as follows:

$$\sum_{n=2}^{\infty} \frac{1}{p_n} = B_1 - \frac{1}{p_1} = 0.5 - \frac{1}{2.47} = 0.095$$

since

$$B_1 = \sum_{n=1}^{\infty} \frac{1}{p_n}$$

Hence,

$$m = -\frac{\delta}{2+\delta} + p_e \sum_{n=2}^{\infty} \frac{1}{p_n} = \frac{-0.0143}{2.0143} + 2.43(0.095) = 0.224 \tag{3-122}$$

The phase error is maximum at $\omega_p = p_1/2 = 1.23$. From Equation (3-115), the maximum phase error is

$$e_p \approx -0.15\delta = -0.00215 \text{ rad} = -0.123°$$

The foregoing error calculations were carried out here in order to clarify the formulas developed in the previous section.

The equivalent dominant pole and excess phase approximation for Equation (3-119) is

$$H(s) \approx \frac{1}{\left(1+\frac{s}{2.43}\right)\exp\left(+\frac{0.224s}{2.43}\right)} = \frac{1}{\left(1+\frac{s}{2.43}\right)} \epsilon^{-0.092s} \tag{3-123}$$

The frequency response and transient response for a unit step of the exact expression, Equation (3-119), and the approximate expression, Equation (3-123), are shown in Figures 3-11 and 3-12, respectively.

Example of an exponentially tapered *RC* network. An exponentially tapered RC network of length d has the following resistance and capacitance variations:

$$r(x) = r_0\epsilon^{2kx} \qquad c(x) = c_0\epsilon^{-2kx}$$

where r_0 and c_0 are resistance and capacitance per unit length and k is the taper factor (which is real and may be positive or negative). For this network, the open-circuit voltage transfer function $T(s)$ is given by

$$T(s) = \frac{-y_{12}}{y_{22}} = \frac{\epsilon^{kd}}{\cosh \gamma d + \frac{kd}{\gamma d}\sinh \gamma d} \tag{3-124}$$

where $\gamma = \sqrt{k^2 + r_0c_0s}$.

We now develop an approximation in the form of an equivalent dominant pole and excess phase for Equation (3-124); that is,

$$T(s) \approx \frac{T_0\epsilon^{-ms/p_e}}{\left(1+\frac{s}{p_e}\right)} \tag{3-125}$$

where T_0 is the value of $T(s)$ for $s = 0$.

We also determine the frequency response and the transient response for a step input and compare them with those of the exact case. The poles of Equation (3-124) occur at the zeros of the denominator. Hence setting the denominator of (3-124) equal to zero we obtain

$$\cosh \gamma d + \frac{kd}{\gamma d}(\sinh \gamma d) = 0 \tag{3-126}$$

The solutions of (3-126) may be divided for convenience into two classes, those for positive and those for negative taper.

We shall determine the roots of Equation (3-126) and consider the positive-taper ($k > 0$) case in the following. The negative-taper case, which is similar, is left as an exercise for the reader. For $kd \geqslant 0$, the roots of (3-126) are all complex and lie on the imaginary axis of γd plane. This can be verified by direct evaluation of (3-126). For positive taper, then, let $\gamma_n d = j\theta_n$, where the subscript n indicates the number of the root. Substitution of $j\theta_n$ for γd in (3-126) yields

$$\cos \theta_n + \frac{kd \sin \theta_n}{\theta_n} = 0 \tag{3-127}$$

where

$$j\theta_n = \sqrt{k^2d^2 + T_0 s} \qquad T_0 = r_0 c_0 d^2 \tag{3-128}$$

In the s plane, the poles of the transfer function lie on the negative real axis. These are designated by σ_n. From Equation (3-128),

$$\sigma_n = -\frac{1}{T_0}(k^2d^2 + \theta_n{}^2) \tag{3-129}$$

A sketch of $kd \sin \theta_n/\theta_n$ and $\cos \theta_n$ for Equation (3-127) reveals that the solutions for θ_n lie in the neighborhood of $(2n-1)\pi/2$ for $n = 1, 2, 3, \ldots$. To develop the series solution for θ_n, let $\theta_n = \alpha_n + (2n-1)\pi/2$, and substitute this into Equation (3-127), which may be rewritten as[17]

$$\theta_n = -kd \tan \theta_n \tag{3-130}$$

substitution of $\theta_n = (1/2)\pi(2n-1) + \alpha_n$ into (3-130) yields

$$(1/2)\pi(2n-1) + \alpha_n = -kd \tan[(1/2)\pi(2n-1) + \alpha_n] = -kd \cot \alpha_n$$

or

$$\alpha_n = -\cot^{-1}\left[\frac{(1/2)\pi(2n-1) + \alpha_n}{kd}\right] \tag{3-131}$$

Rewriting Equation (3-131), we have

$$\tan \alpha_n = \frac{-kd}{(1/2)\pi(2n-1) + \alpha_n} \tag{3-132}$$

which can be solved easily by iteration. Noting from Equation (3-132) that when $\alpha_n << 1$, the tangent can be replaced by the angle, giving

$$\alpha_n \approx \frac{-kd}{(1/2)\pi(2n-1) + \alpha_n} \tag{3-133}$$

With one iteration (see Appendix E), we have

[17] The principal solutions of Equation (3-130) for various kd values are tabulated in *Handbook of Mathematical Functions* (Washington, D. C., GPO, 1964), U.S. Dept. of Commerce, Appl. Math. Ser. 55.

$$\alpha_n \approx \frac{-kd}{(1/2)\pi(2n-1) - \dfrac{kd}{(1/2)\pi(2n-1)+\alpha_n}}$$

$$\approx \frac{-(1/2)\pi(2n-1)kd}{(1/4)\pi^2(2n-1)^2 - kd} \tag{3-134}$$

The error between the exact value of α_n and the approximate value given by Equation (3-134) is less than 3 percent for $kd \leqslant 8$. In practice, kd is usually smaller than 8. From Equation (3-134), θ_n can be written as

$$\theta_n \approx \frac{\pi(2n-1)}{2}\left[1+\frac{4kd}{(2n-1)^2\pi^2+4kd}\right]_{n=1,2,\ldots} \tag{3-135}$$

Since θ_n equals α_n plus a known exact function of π, the error in θ_n is less than the error in α_n. For $kd \leqslant 8$, the error in θ_n is less than 1.2 percent. Figure 3-14 shows the position of the first three poles of the open-circuit voltage transfer function of the exponentially tapered RC network, computed from Equations (3-135) and (3-129). For zero taper factor (that is, $kd = 0$) the pole locations are those of the uniform distributed RC network. As the taper factor kd assumes larger values, the tapering of the $\overline{ERC}$ causes the poles of Equation (3-124) to move away from the positions occupied by the poles of the $\overline{URC}$ network. In particular, the poles nearest the origin are shifted by an amount proportionately greater than the more remote poles, as can readily be seen from Figure 3-14.

In particular, let us consider the value of $kd = 2$. For this case the pole locations can be found from (3-129) and (3-135) to be

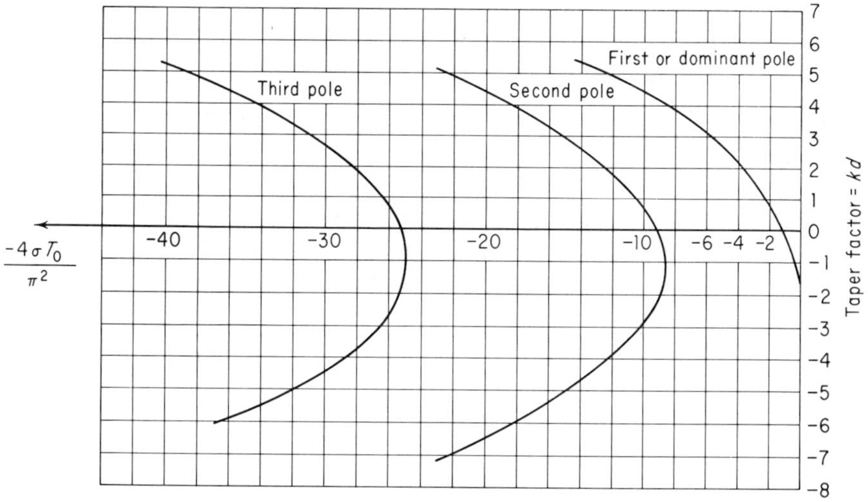

Figure 3-14 Positions of first, second, and third poles of the $\overline{ERC}$ network as a function of taper.

$$T(s) \approx \frac{T_0}{\left(1+\frac{s}{9.16}\right)\left(1+\frac{s}{30.1}\right)\left(1+\frac{s}{69.8}\right)\cdots} \qquad \textbf{(3-136)}$$

To obtain the equivalent dominant-pole and excess-phase approximation we apply the formulas of the previous section to Equation (3-136) and obtain $p_e = 8.27$ and $m = 0.50$. Hence,

$$T(s) \approx \frac{T_0}{\left(1+\frac{s}{8.27}\right)\exp\left(\frac{0.5s}{8.27}\right)} = \frac{T_0}{\left(1+\frac{s}{8.27}\right)}\epsilon^{-0.0603s} \qquad \textbf{(3-137)}$$

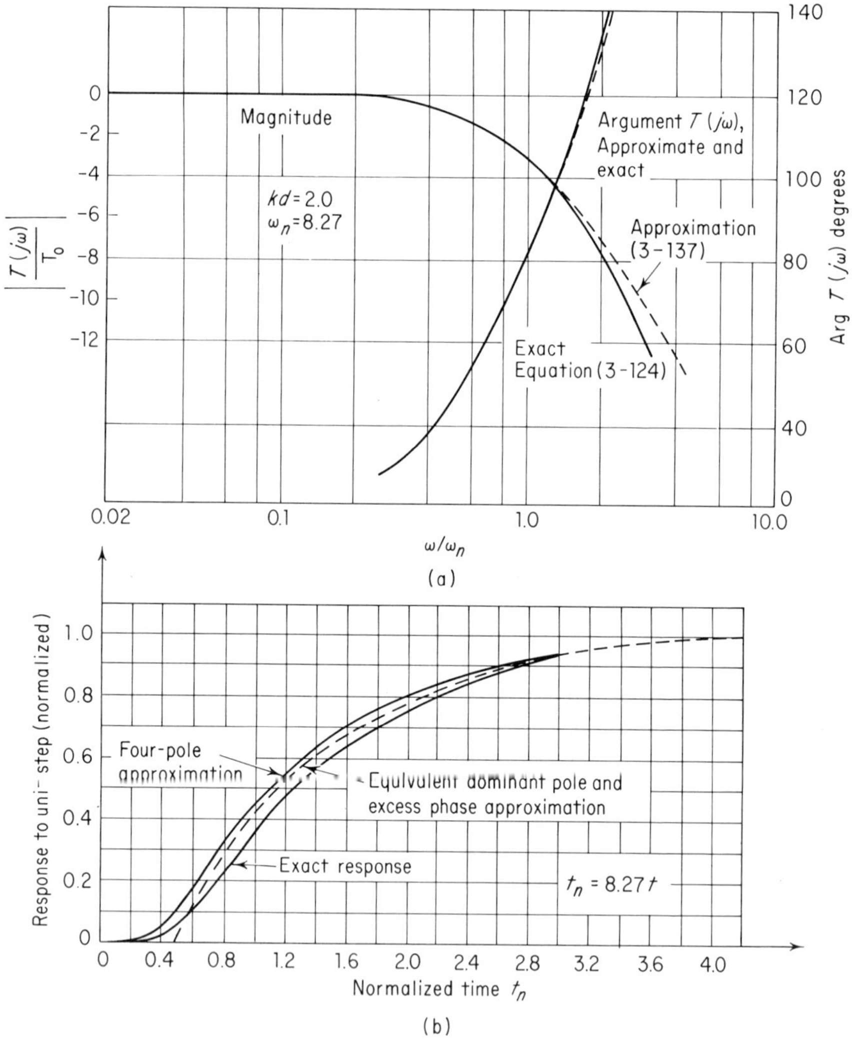

Figure 3-15 **(a)** Frequency response of $\overline{ERC}$. **(b)** Comparison of exact and approximate step-function response of $\overline{ERC}$ network.

The frequency and transient response (for a step input) of the approximate expression (3-137) and the exact expression (3-124) are shown in Figures 3-15(a) and (b). In Figure 3-15(b) the step response of Equation (3-136), as found by including only the lowest four poles, is also shown. Again notice that the results are very close to each other. The rise time and the 3-dB bandwidth for the exponentially tapered $\overline{RC}$ network as computed by the equivalent dominant-pole and excess-phase approximation are

$$\tau_R = \frac{2.2}{p_e} = 0.266 \qquad \omega_{3\,\text{dB}} = p_e = 8.27$$

Note that the normalization factor is $r_0 c_0 d^2$. On the basis of Elmore's definitions—that is, by expanding Equation (3-124) into a series and then applying (3-45) and (3-70)—the bandwidth and the rise time versus the taper factor are shown in Figures 3-16(a) and 3-16(b), respectively. The two methods give results that are in close agreement.

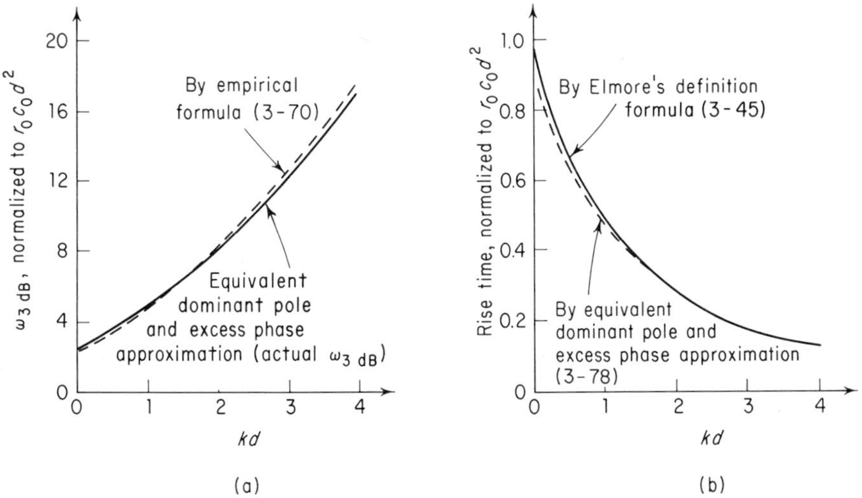

Figure 3-16 Comparison of empirical formula and Elmore's definition for $\omega_{3\text{dB}}$ and rise time of $\overline{ERC}$.

Common-emitter short-circuit current gain of diffusion transistor. In a previous example, we considered the common-base short-circuit current gain (alpha) of the diffusion transistor. It was similar in form to the open-circuit voltage transfer function of the $\overline{URC}$ network. Here, we consider the common-emitter short-circuit current gain (beta) of the diffusion transistor. Beta, like alpha, is a distributed network function. It is defined as

$$\beta = \frac{\alpha}{1-\alpha} = \frac{1}{\cosh \frac{W}{L}\sqrt{1+s\tau} - 1} \tag{3-138}$$

where W is the base width, L is the diffusion length, and τ is the minority carrier lifetime. We now derive an equivalent dominant-pole and excess phase factor for β. Perhaps the simplest approach to take is to determine the product form of beta. From Equation (3-138), it is seen that the poles of beta occur where

$$\cosh \frac{W}{L}\sqrt{1+s\tau} = 1$$

that is, where

$$\frac{W}{L}\sqrt{1+s\tau} = \pm j(2n\pi) \tag{3-139}$$

From Equation (3-139), the s-plane pole locations are

$$\sigma_n = \frac{1}{\tau}\left[1 + \left(\frac{L}{W}\right)^2 4n^2\pi^2\right] \tag{3-140}$$

Examination of Equation (3-138), by differentiating the denominator, shows that the dominant pole, $s_0 = -1/\tau$, is simple, whereas all the others are second order. Hence, the product expansion of β is written as

$$\beta = \frac{\beta_0}{(1+s\tau)\prod_{n=1}^{\infty}\left(1+\frac{s}{\sigma_n}\right)^2} \tag{3-141}$$

For typical diffusion transistors, $(W/L)^2 \leqslant 0.1$ and, from Equation (3-140), $\sigma_1 \geqslant 394\sigma_0$. Because of this wide separation between the dominant and nondominant poles, the equivalent dominant-pole and excess-phase approximation is valid in a wide frequency range. From Equation (3-141), the magnitude-squared function is

$$\frac{|\beta(\omega^2)|}{\beta_0{}^2} = \frac{1}{1 + C_2\omega^2 + C_4\omega^4 + \cdots} \tag{3-142}$$

where

$$C_2 \approx \tau^2\left[1 + \frac{W^4}{8L^4\pi^4}\sum_{n=1}^{\infty}\frac{1}{n^4}\right] \approx \tau^2$$

and

$$C_4 = \sum_{n=1}^{\infty}\sum_{k=n+1}^{\infty}\left(\frac{1}{\sigma_n}\right)^2\left(\frac{1}{\sigma_k}\right)^2 \approx 0$$

Hence, the effective dominant pole p_e is given by

$$p_e = \sqrt{\frac{1}{C_2}} = \frac{1}{\tau} \tag{3-143}$$

The phase of β is

$$\phi(\omega) = -\tan^{-1}(\omega\tau) - 2\sum_{n=1}^{\infty}\tan^{-1}\left(\frac{\omega}{\sigma_n}\right) \approx -\tan^{-1}\omega\tau - \frac{\omega\tau}{12}\left(\frac{W}{L}\right)^2 \quad \text{(3-144)}$$

and the excess phase is obtained simply from the second term in Equation (3-144); that is,

$$m\left(\frac{\omega}{p_e}\right) = m\omega\tau = \frac{\omega\tau}{12}\left(\frac{W}{L}\right)^2 \quad \text{(3-145)}$$

so that

$$m = \frac{1}{12}\left(\frac{W}{L}\right)^2 \quad \text{(3-146)}$$

Hence, the equivalent dominant-pole and excess-phase approximation to β is

$$\beta = \frac{\beta_0}{1+j\omega\tau}\exp\left[-j\frac{\omega\tau}{12}\left(\frac{W}{L}\right)^2\right] \quad \text{(3-147)}$$

The diffusion transistor just treated is a special case of the graded-base or drift transistor in which an impurity gradient in the base region produces an accelerating field. The graded-base transistor has been studied by Kroemer[18] and β is given by

$$\beta = \frac{\epsilon^{\eta}}{\cosh Z + \dfrac{\eta}{Z}\sinh Z - \epsilon^{\eta}}$$

where

$$Z = \sqrt{\eta^2 + \theta^2} \qquad \theta = \frac{W}{L}\sqrt{1+s\tau}$$

and

$$\eta = \text{base impurity gradient factor} = \frac{q\mathcal{E}_0 W}{2kT} \quad \text{(3-148)}$$

where q is the electronic charge, $\mathcal{E}_0$ is the electric field in the base region, k is Boltzmann's constant, and T is the absolute temperature.

The equivalent dominant-pole and excess-phase approximation discussed earlier is also applicable to the drift transistor. However, the details are quite involved and will not be given here.[19] A Bode plot of drift transistor β for various values of η is shown in Figure 3-17. Note that the case $\eta = 0$ corresponds to the β of the diffusion transistor, with equivalent dominant-pole and excess-phase approximation given by Equation (3-147).

---

[18] H. Kroemer, in *Transistor Manual* (Camden, N.J., RCA, 1956), Vol. 1, pp. 202–220. See also Ghausi (Ref. 1), pp. 220–230.

[19] J. Kelly, Tech. Rept. 400–98, New York University, New York, N.Y., July 1964.

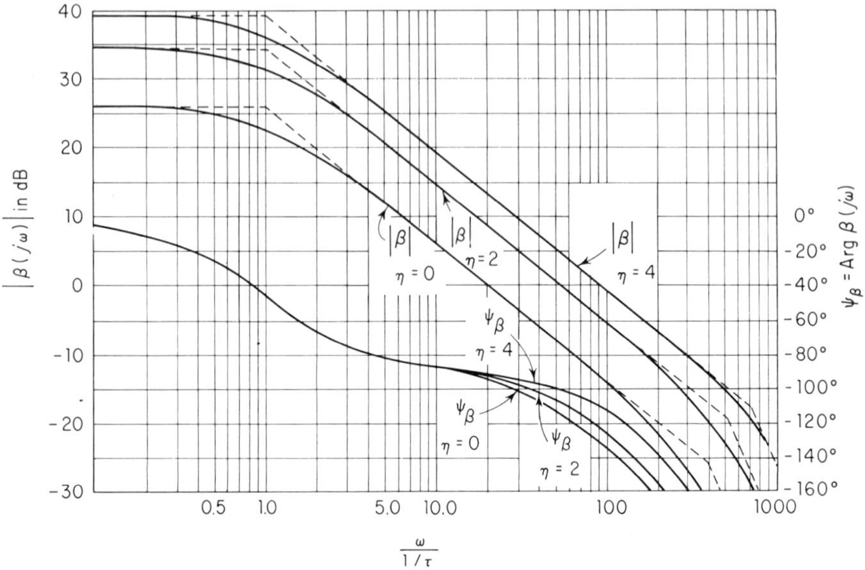

Figure 3-17 Magnitude and phase of $\beta(j\omega)$ versus frequency for $\eta = 0, 2, 4$; $(W/L)^2 = 0.1$.

3-10 Numerical Inversion of the Laplace Transform

In conclusion, we shall mention the numerical inversion of the Laplace transform for distributed-parameter networks. With the availability of fast computers and efficient algorithms these numerical techniques are now quite useful. There are a number of known methods of numerical inversion of Laplace transform. Interested readers are referred to the literature.[20]

PROBLEMS

3-1 For the general uniform transmission line $\overline{RLCG}$ of length d, the output is short-circuited. The line is initially relaxed. Derive the expression for $i(t, x)$ if the input is $v_0(t) = u(t)$.

[20] A. Papoulis, *Quart. Applied Math.*, **14** (1955), 405.
H. E. Salzer, *J. Math. Phys.*, **37** (1958), 89–109.
W. Weeks, *J. Assoc. Comput. Mach.*, **13** (1966), 419–426.
C. F. Chen, *IEEE Internat'l Conv. Record,* **14** (1966), 7, 281–285.
J. W. Cooley and J. W. Tukey, *Math. Comput.*, **19** (1965), 297–301.
O. Wing, *J. Comput.*, **2** (1967), 153–166.
C. Lancoz, *Applied Analysis* (Englewood Cliffs, N. J., Prentice-Hall, 1956).

3-2 An open-circuited lossless transmission line, initially at rest, is excited at the input by a unit step voltage. Show that, for $t > 0$,

$$v(t, x) = 1 - \frac{4}{\pi} \sum_{k=1}^{\infty} \frac{1}{2k-1} \sin\left[\frac{(2k-1)\pi}{2d} x\right] \cos\left[\frac{(2k-1)\pi}{2d\sqrt{lc}} t\right]$$

3-3 If the line in Problem 3-1 is approximated by N identical T sections, show that

$$i_n(t) = \frac{1}{N}\sqrt{\frac{c}{l}} \sum_{k=1}^{N} \frac{\cos\left[\frac{(2k-1)n}{N}\frac{\pi}{2}\right]}{\sin\left[\frac{2k-1}{N}\frac{\pi}{4}\right]} \sin \omega_k t$$

where
$$\omega_k = \frac{2}{\sqrt{lc}} \sin \frac{(2k-1)\pi}{4N}$$

and
$$\frac{Z_1}{2} = \frac{sld}{2} \qquad Z_2 = \frac{1}{scd}$$

3-4 For a short-circuited RC line of length d, which is initially at rest, what is the current $i(t, x)$ when a unit step voltage is applied at $x = 0$? Show that, for $t > 0$,

$$i(t, d) = \frac{1}{rd}\left[1 + 2\sum_{n=1}^{\infty} (-1)^n \exp\left(\frac{-n^2\pi^2 t}{rcd^2}\right)\right]$$

3-5 A uniformly distributed RC network is made of a resistive sheet of 2 kΩ/cm^2 and a capacitive sheet of 200 pF/cm^2. The length and the width of the network are 5 cm and 2 cm, respectively. The network is excited at the input by a unit step voltage. The line is initially relaxed and the output is short-circuited. Find the short-circuited current:

a. by using the distributed-parameter approach.
b. by using the artificial-line method with four sections.

3-6 For the network of Figure 3-1, if the output is open-circuited, find $v_N(t)$.

3-7 **a.** For a uniform RC line of length d, with $r(x) = r_0$ and $c(x) = c_0$, show that

$$\tau_d = \frac{r_0 c_0 d^2}{2}$$

$$\tau_r = \sqrt{\frac{\pi}{3}}\, r_0 c_0 d^2$$

b. What are the expressions for τ_d and τ_r if the line is leaky with $g(x) = g_0$?
c. For part (b) if $r_0 = 2\ \text{k}\Omega/\text{cm}$, $c_0 = 200\ \text{pF/cm}$, $\Omega_0 = 4 \times 10^{-7}$ rad/s, width $= 1$ cm, and $d = 2$ cm, find the numerical values of τ_d and τ_r.

3-8 **a.** For an exponentially tapered distributed RC network of length d with $r(x) = r_0\epsilon^{2kx}$, $c(x) = c_0\epsilon^{-2kx}$, and $g = 0$, obtain the expression for the open-circuit voltage transfer function and show that

$$\tau_d = (r_0c_0d^2)\ \frac{kd - \epsilon^{-kd}\sinh kd}{2(kd)^2}$$

$$\tau_r = \sqrt{\frac{\pi}{2}}\ (r_0c_0d^2)\ \frac{[2kd\epsilon^{-2kd} + \epsilon^{-2kd}\sinh^2 kd - 3\epsilon^{-kd}\sinh kd + kd]^{1/2}}{(kd)^2}$$

b. If the dielectric loss is included—that is, if $g(x)/c(x) = \Omega_0$—what are the corresponding expressions for τ_d and τ_r?

3-9 An exponentially tapered RC line [that is, $r(x) = r_0\epsilon^{2kx}$, $c(x) = c_0\epsilon^{-2kx}$] has the following parameter values: $r_0 = 2 \times 10^3 \Omega/\text{cm}$, $c_0 = 200\ \text{pF/cm}$, $d = 2$ cm, and $k = 1\ \text{cm}^{-1}$. Determine $f_{3\,\text{dB}}$ of the short-circuit current transfer function by using Equation (3-69).

3-10 For n monotonic cascaded stages show that, by Elmore's definition,

$$(\tau_d)_o = \sum_i^n (\tau_d)_i$$

$$(\tau_r)_o = \left[\sum_i^n (\tau_r)_i^2\right]^{1/2}$$

where the subscripts o and i stand for overall and individual stages, respectively.

3-11 Derive Equation (3-56).

3-12 For an exponentially tapered RC network, if the taper factor is given by $kd = -1$, determine the poles of the transfer function for Equation (3-124). Determine the 3-dB frequency and the rise time (for a step input) of the network by whatever method you please.

3-13 An exponentially tapered RC network with taper kd is loaded by a lumped resistive load R_L.

a. Show that the transfer function for this case is given by

$$T_v(s) = \frac{\epsilon^{kd}}{(\cosh \gamma d) + \left(kd + \frac{r_0 d\epsilon^{2kd}}{R_L}\right)\left(\frac{\sinh \gamma d}{\gamma d}\right)}$$

b. Determine the 3-dB frequency and the rise time (for a step input) of the network for $R_L = 28r_0 d$ and $kd = 2$. Hint: Make the following substitution:

$$k'd = kd + \frac{r_0 d}{R_L}\epsilon^{2kd}$$

3-14 For a uniform $\overline{RGC}$ network find $f_{3\text{ dB}}, \tau_r$, and τ_d if $g/c = \Omega_0$.

3-15 Determine τ_r and τ_d for Problem 1-6.

3-16 Determine τ_r and τ_d for Problem 1-7. What is the approximate $\omega_{3\text{ dB}}$?

3-17 Determine τ_r and τ_d for Problem 2-9.

3-18 Derive Equations (3-114) and (3-115), and show that e_p has a local maximum at $\omega = p_1/2$.

CHAPTER

4

Closed-Form Solutions and Equivalent Tapered Distributed Networks

4-1 Introduction

In the preceding chapters we discussed means for obtaining infinite-series and infinite-product solutions for distributed-network functions. However, it is sometimes desirable to obtain two-port parameters in closed form because the expressions are compact and because similarities between different types of tapered networks are more easily recognized.

The purpose of this chapter is to describe methods of obtaining closed-form solutions for tapered distributed networks. Several different techniques are covered. One technique involves a change of dependent variable in the network differential equation to identify types of tapers that lead to similar immittance functions. Another technique involves a change of independent variable in the voltage differential equation of the network to identify equivalent distributed networks—that is, networks with identical immittance functions but different types of electrical tapers. Some of the equivalent lines may be desirable from the standpoint of construction. A third technique involves choosing a suitable voltage function as the solution of a distributed-network voltage differential equation, and then determining the types of tapered networks that produce the chosen voltage function. In the final portion of the chapter, a class of distributed *RC* networks with rational transfer functions is described.

There are some applications for tapered distributed networks. For example, tapered lossless networks are used for impedance matching at microwave frequencies. Tapered *RC* networks are used to obtain increased phase shift at lower attenuation levels for phase-shift oscillators. A knowledge of the behavior of tapered distributed networks is helpful for an efficient design of such networks.

Finally, we note that in some applications, the distributed-network structure is purposely fabricated as a tapered structure; such devices as the graded-base or drift transistor fall into this category. For these cases, the immittance parameters can be expressed in closed-form expressions and can be found using the methods that follow.

4-2 Immittance Parameters of Some Tapered Distributed Networks

In this section, we treat some cases of tapered distributed networks whose immittance parameters can be expressed conveniently in closed form. For simplicity, we treat only those networks in which the per-unit-length series impedance $Z(s, x)$ and the per-unit-length shunt admittance $Y(s, x)$ can be separated into functions of s and x and in which the product $Z(s, x)Y(s, x)$ is constant independent of x. That is, we restrict the following discussion to networks where

$$Z(s, x) = \frac{Z(s)}{p(x)} \quad \text{and} \quad Y(s, x) = Y(s)\,p(x)$$

and $p(x)$ describes the variations in Z and Y. Under these restrictions, we shall show how a number of different types of electrically tapered networks can be gathered into a single class of networks with similar immittance parameters.

Next, we shall show that when different types of *RC* tapered networks have the same per-unit-length series impedance and shunt admittance at both input and output ports and when the impedance and admittance variations are of the same general form over the network length, the open-circuit voltage transfer functions of the networks are quite similar. This result is important from a computational viewpoint because many tapered *RC* networks have very complicated expressions for their immittance parameters—and it is useful to know that these complicated functions under some conditions have numerical values almost equal to those of the simpler functions of sines and cosines. However, for pure *LC* or $\overline{RLGC}$ networks, the magnitude and phase of the network functions are very sensitive to the pair of poles and/or zeros closest to the $j\omega$ axis. For these cases, substantial differences can be obtained in the real and imaginary parts of the network functions by tapering the networks.[1]

Now, let us consider a tapered distributed network. Using the notation as in Chapter 2, the general expressions for voltage and current at any point x in the network, assuming zero initial conditions, are given by

$$\frac{dV(s,x)}{dx} = -Z(s,x)I(s,x) \quad \textbf{(4-1a)}$$

$$\frac{dI(s,x)}{dx} = -Y(s,x)V(s,x) \quad \textbf{(4-1b)}$$

where $Z = [r(x) + sl(x)] = Z_0/p(x)$ and $Y = [g(x) + sc(x)] = Y_0p(x)$; also $Z_0 = [r_0 + sl_0]$, $Y_0 = [g_0 + sc_0]$; $r(x)$ and $l(x)$ are the series resistance and inductance per unit length and $g(x)$ and $c(x)$ are the shunt conductance and capacitance per unit length. The function $p(x)$ is the electrical taper of the network. For example, for an exponential taper, we have $p(x) = p_0\epsilon^{\pm 2kx}$.

For the case at hand, the network voltage and current equations are

$$\frac{dV}{dx} = -[Z_0/p(x)]I \quad \textbf{(4-2a)}$$

$$\frac{dI}{dx} = -[Y_0p(x)]V \quad \textbf{(4-2b)}$$

In general, $p(x)$ is always a finite, positive, nonzero function; also, except at discontinuities, $p(x)$ always has a derivative. Therefore, in the region where the network is continuous, Equation (4-2) can be differentiated with respect to x and rearranged to give the Sturm equation for the tapered network, as follows:

$$\frac{d}{dx}\left[p(x)\frac{dV}{dx}\right] - \lambda^2 p(x)V = 0 \quad \textbf{(4-3)}$$

where $\lambda^2 = Z_0Y_0$. As noted in Chapter 2, basic-set solutions, V_I and V_{II}, of Equation (4-3) give the distributed network two-port parameters. For Equation (4-3), the short-circuit admittance parameters in terms of Z and p are

$$y_{11} = \frac{1}{Z(0)}\frac{V_I(s,d)}{V_{II}(s,d)} = \frac{1}{Z_0}\frac{V_I(s,d)}{V_{II}(s,d)} \quad \textbf{(4-4a)}$$

$$y_{12} = y_{21} = \frac{-1}{Z(0)}\frac{1}{V_{II}(s,d)} = \frac{-1}{Z_0}\frac{1}{V_{II}(s,d)} \quad \textbf{(4-4b)}$$

[1] H. Olsen, *Acoustical Engineering* (Princeton, N.J., Van Nostrand, 1958), Chap. 5.

$$y_{22} = \frac{1}{Z(d)} \frac{V_{\text{II}}'(s, d)}{V_{\text{II}}(s, d)} = \frac{p(d)}{Z_0} \frac{V_{\text{II}}'(s, d)}{V_{\text{II}}(s, d)} \tag{4-4c}$$

In general, when $p(x)$ is an arbitrary, continuous, nonzero function of x such as a polynomial with no roots in the interval $0 \leqslant x \leqslant d$, it is not possible to obtain solutions of Equation (4-3) that are simple, tabulated functions. For this reason, we shall now show how a change of dependent variable in (4-3) can sometimes simplify the procedure of obtaining the immittance parameters of tapered distributed networks. The change of dependent variable also helps identify a class of taper functions that produce networks with similar immittance parameters.

Solution by change of variable. To define a class of networks with similar immittance functions but different tapers, we can investigate a standard form for writing the voltage equation (4-3). Although $p(x)$ represents the network taper, a change in dependent variable via an integrating factor transforms (4-3) into a *normal form*, which is identical for many types of taper. This change of variable is often used to simplify second-order linear differential equations.[2] Let us define the network voltage V as the product of two functions, U and W, so that

$$V = UW \tag{4-5}$$

Note that, under the change of variable,

$$\frac{dV}{dx} = UW' + U'W$$

$$\frac{d^2V}{dx^2} = UW'' + 2U'W' + U''W \tag{4-6}$$

and the original voltage relation, Equation (4-3), becomes

$$UW'' + \left(2U' + U\frac{p'}{p}\right) W' + \left(U'' + U'\frac{p'}{p} - \lambda^2 U\right) W = 0 \tag{4-7}$$

Now, if the coefficient of W' is zero, that is,

$$\left(2U' + U\frac{p'}{p}\right) = 0 \tag{4-8}$$

which occurs when

$$U = \frac{1}{\sqrt{p(x)}} \tag{4-9}$$

[2] See, for example, E. L. Ince, *Ordinary Differential Equations* (New York, Dover, 1956), p. 394.

then on substitution $V = UW = W/\sqrt{p(x)}$ in Equation (4-3), and clearing common factors, we obtain

$$\frac{d^2W}{dx^2} + \mathscr{I}(x) = 0 \tag{4-10}$$

Equation (4-10) is called the normal form of the differential equation and $\mathscr{I}(x)$ is called the *invariant*. Equations with the same normal form are said to be *equivalent*.

The invariant, $\mathscr{I}(x)$, is related to the network taper $p(x)$ by the differential equation[3]

$$\mathscr{I}(x) = -\left[\lambda^2 + \frac{p''}{2p} - \frac{1}{4}\left(\frac{p'}{p}\right)^2\right] \tag{4-11a}$$

and by the alternate expression[4]

$$\mathscr{I}(x) = -(\lambda^2 + q'/2 + q^2/4) \tag{4-11b}$$

where $q = d[\ln p(x)]/dx$. Provided that $\mathscr{I}(x)$ does not become infinite over the network length, $0 \leqslant x \leqslant d$, then two analytic and linearly independent solutions, W_A and W_B, are obtained for W. Thus, since $V = UW$, and $U = (p)^{-1/2}$, we have

$$V = p^{-1/2}[AW_A + BW_B] \tag{4-12a}$$

and, from Equation (4-2a),

$$\mathscr{I} = \frac{p^{1/2}}{Z(s)}\left[\frac{(AW_A + BW_B)p'}{2p} - (AW_A' + BW_B')\right] \tag{4-12b}$$

Following a line of reasoning similar to that employed in Chapter 2, we find the short-circuit admittance parameters of the tapered network from Equation (4-12). These are listed in Table 4-1. Further, when W_A and W_B are basic-set solutions, W_{I} and W_{II}, the expressions are greatly simplified. These, also, are listed in Table 4-1.

---

[3] It should be noted that when the variable λ is very large, as compared to the other terms in Equation (4-11a), the invariant approaches $-\lambda^2$ asymptotically. This means that the solutions for tapered networks asymptotically approach those of the uniform case. We have already observed in Chapter 2 the fact that the pole-zero locations of tapered networks, for large s, are close to those of the uniform case.

[4] Note that instead of introducing q, there is another change of variable that simplifies $\mathscr{I}(x)$. In other words let $\Omega = 1/U = \sqrt{p(x)}$. Then $\mathscr{I}(x) = -(\lambda^2 + \Omega''/\Omega)$. For $\mathscr{I}(x) = $ a constant, a linear differential equation in Ω with constant coefficients results. This avoids the Riccati differential equation (see Problem 4-12).

Table 4-1 SHORT-CIRCUIT ADMITTANCE PARAMETERS FOR TAPERED NETWORKS ($V = UW$)

PARAMETER	GENERAL SOLUTION W_A, W_B	BASIC-SET SOLUTION W_{I}, W_{II}
y_{11}	$\dfrac{1}{Z(s,0)}\left[\dfrac{p'(0)}{2p(0)} + \dfrac{W_A(d)W_B'(0) - W_A'(0)W_B(d)}{W_A(0)W_B(d) - W_A(d)W_B(0)}\right]$	$\dfrac{1}{Z(s,0)}\left[\dfrac{p'(0)}{2p(0)} + \dfrac{W_{\mathrm{I}}(d)}{W_{\mathrm{II}}(d)}\right]$
y_{12} y_{21}	$\dfrac{-1}{Z(s,d)}\sqrt{\dfrac{p(0)}{p(d)}}\left[\dfrac{1}{W_A(0)W_B(d) - W_A(d)W_B(0)}\right]$	$\dfrac{-1}{Z(s,d)}\sqrt{\dfrac{p(0)}{p(d)}}\left[\dfrac{1}{W_{\mathrm{II}}(d)}\right]$
y_{22}	$\dfrac{1}{Z(s,d)}\left[\dfrac{W_A'(d)W_B(0) - W_A(0)W_B'(d)}{W_A(d)W_B(0) - W_A(0)W_B(d)} - \dfrac{p'(d)}{2p(d)}\right]$	$\dfrac{1}{Z(s,d)}\left[\dfrac{W_{\mathrm{II}}'(d)}{W_{\mathrm{II}}(d)} + \dfrac{p'(d)}{2p(d)}\right]$

Networks with similar immittances. We have seen that under the change of variable, $V = UW$ tapered networks have short-circuit admittance parameters as given in Table 4-1. Further, on referring back to Equation (4-10), we see that all tapered networks that have the same invariant, $\mathscr{I}(x)$, must also have the same solutions in W. Hence, all tapered networks with the same invariant have essentially the same form for their admittance parameters, which are given in Table 4-1. The principal difference in admittance functions, when the invariant is the same, is in the additive constants

$$\frac{p'(0)}{2p(0)} \quad \text{and} \quad \frac{p'(d)}{2p(d)}$$

These constants usually have a small effect on pole-zero positions, as will be seen later in this section. This result is important for it enables us to compare networks with different tapers in a straightforward fashion. Let us now study the short-circuit admittance parameters of the class of networks for which $\mathscr{I}(x) = -[\lambda^2 + k^2]$, where k^2 is a constant. From Equation (4-11b),

$$2q' + q^2 = 4k^2 \tag{4-13}$$

where $q = d[\ln p(x)]/dx$. Note that the taper need not be constant.

For these networks, we have

$$\frac{d^2W}{dx^2} - (\lambda^2 + k^2)W = 0 \tag{4-14}$$

with basic-set solutions

$$W_{\mathrm{I}}(s,x) = \cosh x\sqrt{\lambda^2 + k^2} \tag{4-15a}$$

$$W_{\mathrm{II}}(s,x) = \frac{\sinh x\sqrt{\lambda^2 + k^2}}{\sqrt{\lambda^2 + k^2}} \tag{4-15b}$$

Upon substitution in Table 4-1, the two-port $[y_{ij}]$ parameters are found to be

$$y_{11} = \frac{1}{Z(s,0)}\left[\frac{\theta \coth \theta}{d} + \frac{1}{2}\frac{p'(0)}{p(0)}\right] \tag{4-16a}$$

$$y_{12} = y_{21} = -\frac{1}{Z(s,d)} \cdot \frac{1}{d}\sqrt{\frac{p(0)}{p(d)}}\left(\frac{\theta}{\sinh \theta}\right) \tag{4-16b}$$

$$y_{22} = \frac{1}{Z(s,d)}\left[\frac{\theta \coth \theta}{d} - \frac{1}{2}\frac{p'(d)}{p(d)}\right] \tag{4-16c}$$

where $\theta = d\sqrt{\lambda^2 + k^2}$.

Now, let us identify the various tapers for which $\mathcal{I}(x) = -[\lambda^2 + k^2]$. Since

$$\mathcal{I}(x) = -(\lambda^2 + q'/2 + q^2/4)$$

the tapers in question are found from the solutions of the Riccati differential equation, Equation (4-13), rewritten for convenience as follows:

$$2q' = 4k^2 - q^2 \tag{4-17}$$

The type of solution obtained for Equation (4-17) is determined by k^2. Thus, for $k^2 = 0$,

$$q' = -\frac{q^2}{2} \tag{4-18a}$$

which upon integration gives

$$q = -\frac{q^3}{6} + C_0 \tag{4-18b}$$

where C_0 is the constant of integration. One consistent solution of Equation (4-18b) has $q = 0$, from which $p(x) = p_0$, a constant. Another solution, from Equation (4-17), has $q' = 0$, and $q = (\pm 2k)$, from which $p(x) = p_o \epsilon^{\pm 2kx}$. The first solution defines the uniform distributed network ($\overline{U}$) and the second defines the exponential distributed network ($\overline{E}$).

In all, there are six types of tapers defined by Equation (4-17); these are listed in Table 4-2. Each tapered network is described by the admittance parameters given in Table 4-1. As listed, these tapers include the hyperbolic-cosine-squared ($\overline{HC}$), exponential ($\overline{E}$), uniform ($\overline{U}$), hyperbolic-sine-squared ($\overline{HS}$), square or Bessel taper ($\overline{S}$), and trigonometric-cosine-squared ($\overline{TC}$) distributed networks.

Up to this point, we have kept the development quite general, the only restriction being YZ = constant independent of x. Hence, the two-port $[y_{ij}]$ parameters given by Equation (4-14) apply to the lossless line, the distributed RC network, and to the general four-parameter distributed network ($\overline{RLCG}$). For each type of network, all that is required to find

Table 4-2 TAPERS DEFINED BY $2q' = 4k^2 - q^2$, WHERE $q = d[\ln p(x)]/dx$

TYPE OF TAPER	k	$q(x)$	VARIATION OF WIDTH $p(x)$
Hyperbolic-cosine-squared $(\overline{HC})$	$k^2 > 0$ $q^2 < 4k^2$	$2k \tanh [k(x + c_1)]$	$p_o \cosh^2 [k(x + c_1)]$
Exponential $(\overline{E})$	$k^2 > 0$ $q^2 = 4k^2$	$2k$	$p_0 \epsilon^{2kx}$
Uniform $(\overline{U})$	$k^2 = 0$ $q = 0$	0	p_0
Hyperbolic-sine-squared $(\overline{HS})$	$k^2 > 0$ $q^2 > 4k^2$	$2k \coth [k(x + c_1)]$	$p_0 \sinh^2 [k(x + c_1)]$ $(x + c_1) \neq 0$
Square (Bessel) $(\overline{S})$	$k^2 = 0$ $q^2 \neq 0$	$\dfrac{2}{c_1 + x}$	$p_0\left(1 + \dfrac{x}{c_1}\right)^2$ $(x + c_1) \neq 0$
Trigonometric-cosine-squared $(\overline{TC})$	$k^2 < 0$	$-2\|k\| \tan [\|k\|(x + c_1)]$	$p_0 \cos^2 [\|k\|(x + c_1)]$ $\|k\|(x + c_1) \neq \pm \frac{1}{2}\pi(2n + 1)$ $n = 0, 1, 2, \ldots$

the $[y_{ij}]$ parameters is the proper substitution of λ^2. Thus, for the lossless network,

$$\lambda^2 = Z_0 Y_0 = s^2 l_0 c_0$$

For the distributed *RC* network,

$$\lambda^2 = Z_0 Y_0 = s r_0 c_0$$

For the four-parameter network,

$$\lambda^2 = Z_0 Y_0 = (s l_0 + r_0)(s c_0 + g_0)$$

Hence, for the lossless network,

$$y_{11} = \frac{1}{\sqrt{s^2 l_0 c_0}} \left[\frac{\sqrt{s^2 l_0 c_0 + k^2} \cosh d\sqrt{s^2 l_0 c_0 + k^2}}{\sinh d\sqrt{s^2 l_0 c_0 + k^2}} + \frac{1}{2} \frac{p'(0)}{p(0)} \right] \tag{4-19a}$$

For the distributed *RC* network,

$$y_{11} = \frac{1}{\sqrt{sr_0c_0}} \left[\frac{\sqrt{sr_0c_0 + k^2} \cosh d\sqrt{sr_0c_0 + k^2}}{\sinh d\sqrt{sr_0c_0 + k^2}} + \frac{1}{2} \frac{p'(0)}{p(0)} \right] \tag{4-19b}$$

For the $\overline{RLGC}$ network,

$$y_{11} = \frac{1}{\sqrt{(r_0 + sl_0)(g_0 + sc_0)}} \times \left[\frac{\sqrt{(r_0 + sl_0)(g_0 + sc_0) + k^2} \cosh d\sqrt{(r_0 + sl_0)(g_0 + sc_0) + k^2}}{\sinh d\sqrt{(r_0 + sl_0)(g_0 + sc_0) + k^2}} + \frac{1}{2} \frac{p'(0)}{p(0)} \right] \tag{4-19c}$$

An important special case of the four-parameter network is the so-called distortionless network. This network has the property that

$$\frac{r_0}{l_0} = \frac{g_0}{c_0} = \Omega$$

Hence, λ^2 can be written as $\lambda^2 = l_0c_0(s + \Omega)^2$. This is equivalent to a lossless network with all s-plane poles and zeros shifted to the left by an amount Ω. The pole-zero locations are identical to those of a lossy delay line with $p'(x) = 0$. For the distortionless line

$$y_{11} = \frac{1}{\sqrt{(s + \Omega)^2 l_0c_0}} \times \left[\frac{\sqrt{(s + \Omega)^2 l_0c_0 + k^2} \cosh d\sqrt{(s + \Omega)^2 l_0c_0 + k^2}}{\sinh d\sqrt{(s + \Omega)^2 l_0c_0 + k^2}} + \frac{1}{2} \frac{p'(0)}{p(0)} \right] \tag{4-19d}$$

As shown in Equations (4-19), the use of an integration factor to put the voltage equation in normal form is a powerful tool for identifying various similar types of electrically tapered distributed networks.

It is useful to point out that the poles and zeros of $[y_{ij}]$ for the simple class of tapers for which the invariant is constant can be found from Equation (4-16). Aside from the contribution of $Z(s, d)$, the poles of the admittances are the solutions of

$$\frac{\sinh \theta}{\theta} = 0 \tag{4-20a}$$

and there are an infinite number of solutions at θ equal to a multiple of $j\pi$.[5] Thus, the poles of $[y_{ij}]$ occur where

$$\theta_n = \pm jn\pi \qquad n = 1, 2, 3, \ldots \tag{4-20b}$$

Since $\theta = d\sqrt{\lambda^2 + k^2}$, the poles lie at

$$\lambda^2 = -\left(\frac{n^2\pi^2}{d^2} + k^2\right)$$

For the $\overline{LC}$ network, where $\lambda^2 = s^2 l_0 c_0$, the poles are located at

$$s = \pm j\sqrt{\frac{n^2\pi^2}{l_0 c_0 d^2} + \frac{k^2}{l_0 c_0}} \tag{4-21a}$$

For the $\overline{RC}$ network, $\lambda^2 = s r_0 c_0$, and the poles are located at

$$s = -\frac{1}{r_0 c_0}\left[\frac{n^2\pi^2}{d^2} + k^2\right] \tag{4-21b}$$

For the $\overline{RLCG}$ distortionless network, $\lambda^2 = l_0 c_0 (s + \Omega)^2$, and the poles are located at

$$s = -\Omega \pm j\sqrt{\frac{n^2\pi^2}{l_0 c_0 d^2} + \frac{k^2}{l_0 c_0}} \tag{4-21c}$$

The zeros of y_{11} and y_{22} are found from the solutions of

$$\frac{\theta \coth \theta}{d} = -\frac{1}{2}\frac{p'(0)}{p(0)} \tag{4-22a}$$

and

$$\frac{\theta \coth \theta}{d} = \frac{1}{2}\frac{p'(d)}{p(d)} \tag{4-22b}$$

respectively. Again, there are an infinite number of solutions.[6] These solutions were discussed in Chapter 3. [See Equation (3-126).]

Before leaving the discussion of tapered networks with closed-form solutions, let us investigate the Bessel tapers—that is, the networks with a taper function $p(x) = kx^a$. This class also has solutions in the closed form. In this discussion, we must remember that $p(x) \neq 0$.[7] For this taper function, the voltage equation becomes

$$\frac{d^2V}{dx^2} + \frac{a}{x}\frac{dV}{dx} - \lambda^2 V = 0 \tag{4-23}$$

---

[5] Note that

$$y_{12} = y_{21} = -\frac{1}{dZ(s,d)}\sqrt{\frac{p(0)}{p(d)}}\frac{\theta}{\sinh\theta}$$

and that

$$\lim_{\theta\to 0}\frac{\theta}{\sinh\theta} = 1$$

Hence y_{12} is an all pole function, if $Z(s, d)$ contributes no zeros, with poles at the s-plane roots of $\sinh\theta/\theta = 0$. These poles are the only poles of y_{11} and y_{22}.

[6] In general, Equation (4-22) may have one real root under certain conditions, and always has an infinite number of imaginary roots, at $\theta_n = j\phi_n$. A limited number of solutions of $\tan\phi_n = \pm K\phi_n$ and $\cot\phi_n = \pm K\phi_n$ are listed in *Handbook of Mathematical Functions*, (Washington, D. C., GPO, 1964), U.S. Dept. of Commerce, Appl. Math., Sec. 55, pp. 224–225.

[7] Note that one could write $p(x) = (1 + kx)^a$. However, this translation in x complicates the expressions considerably and is not used here. It is simpler to make the substitution $x^a = (1 + ku)^a$ in the final result.

and is a standard form of Bessel's equation. There are two types of solutions to Eq. (4-23), the applicable type depending on whether $(a-1)/2$ is an integer or not. For $(a-1)/2$ an integer, that is, for $a = 1, 3, 5, \ldots$, the two linearly independent solutions of Equation (4-23) are[8]

$$V = x^{-(a-1)/2}[A J_{(a-1)/2}(j\lambda x) + BY_{(a-1)/2}(j\lambda x)] \qquad a = 1, 3, 5, \ldots \tag{4-24}$$

where $J_{(a-1)/2}(j\lambda x)$ is a Bessel function of the first kind and $Y_{(a-1)/2}$ is a Bessel function of the second kind.

For nonintegral values of $(a-1)/2$, the voltage equation has the solution

$$V = x^{-(a-1)/2}[A J_{(a-1)/2}(j\lambda x) + B J_{-(a-1)/2}(j\lambda x)] \qquad a = 0, 2, 4, 6, \ldots \tag{4-25}$$

where $J_{(a-1)/2}(j\lambda x)$ are half-order Bessel functions of the first kind. The solutions of Equation (4-25) are expressible as combinations of sine and cosine functions.[9] Thus, for $a = 0$, we have the uniformly distributed network, and

$$J_{-1/2}(j\lambda x) = \left(\frac{2}{j\pi\lambda x}\right)^{1/2} \cos j\lambda x \tag{4-26a}$$

$$J_{-1/2}(j\lambda x) = \left(\frac{2}{j\pi\lambda x}\right)^{1/2} \sin j\lambda x \tag{4-26b}$$

Substitution of Equations (4-26) into (4-25) and redefining the arbitrary constants gives

$$V = A \cosh \lambda x + \frac{B \sinh \lambda x}{\lambda} \tag{4-27}$$

as obtained previously for the uniformly distributed network. Similar manipulation for $a = 2, 4, 6, \ldots$ will put the voltage solution in the form of a combinations of sines and cosines. (See Table 4-3 for the half-order Bessel functions.)

The cases where $a = 1, 3, 5, \ldots$, with voltage solutions as in Equation (4-24), are more difficult to handle numerically. The difficulty lies in evaluating the integral-order Bessel functions of complex argument. For instance, for the RC network, $\lambda = \sqrt{s\tau}$; on the $j\omega$ axis, for the linear taper we have to evaluate expressions of the form

$$\begin{aligned} J_0(j\lambda x) &= J_0(j\sqrt{j\omega}\, x) \\ &= \text{ber } x + j \text{ bei } x \end{aligned} \tag{4-28}$$

---

[8] See F. Bowman, *Introduction to Bessel Functions* (New York, Dover, 1958), pp. 117–118; also N. W. McLachlan, *Bessel Functions for Engineers* (New York, Oxford, 1934).

[9] See H. B. Dwight, *Tables of Integrals and Other Mathematical Data* (New York, Macmillan, 1961).

Table 4-3 HALF-ORDER BESSEL FUNCTIONS

$J_{1/2}(u) = \left(\frac{2}{\pi u}\right)^{1/2} \sin u$	$J_{-1/2}(u) = \left(\frac{2}{\pi u}\right)^{1/2} \cos u$
$J_{3/2}(u) = \left(\frac{2}{\pi u}\right)^{1/2} \left(\frac{\sin u}{u} - \cos u\right)$	$J_{-3/2}(u) = \left(\frac{2}{\pi u}\right)^{1/2} \left(-\sin u - \frac{\cos u}{u}\right)$
$J_{5/2}(u) = \left(\frac{2}{\pi u}\right)^{1/2} \left[\left(\frac{3}{u^2} - 1\right) \sin u - \frac{3}{u} \cos u\right]$	$J_{-5/2}(u) = \left(\frac{2}{\pi u}\right)^{1/2} \left[\frac{3}{u} \sin u + \left(\frac{3}{u^2} - 1\right) \cos u\right]$

where ber x and bei x are Thomson functions.[10] Thus, each quantity in Equation (4-24) becomes a pair of complex conjugate quantities when evaluated on the j axis, and the immittance parameters are correspondingly more difficult to evaluate.[11]

Comparison of tapered networks. Because of the difficulty in interpreting the network behavior from the voltage solution for the linearly tapered network, we seek an alternative means for comparing tapered network performance. In order to make a meaningful comparison, we shall define a network parameter called taper ratio, denoted by M. The taper ratio is defined as the ratio of network incremental impedance at port 1 to network incremental impedance at port 2; that is,

$$M = \frac{Z(s, 0)}{Z(s, d)} = \frac{p(d)}{p(0)} \tag{4-29}$$

where $p(x)$ is the network taper function.

Several types of network taper functions with the same taper ratio are shown in Figure 4-1. These are the square taper and exponential taper, as well as the linear taper. The linear taper does not belong to the same class of networks as the square and exponential tapers, as we have seen. It does not have simple closed-form immittance functions; the linear taper is defined by $p(x) = p_0(1 + kx)$. As shown in Figure 4-1, the various taper functions are roughly the same and we have good reason to expect the corresponding networks to have substantially the same electrical performance characteristics. To illustrate this point with a specific example, let us investigate the open-circuit voltage transfer functions T_V of three types of tapered distributed networks whose taper functions are shown in Figure 4-1.

[10] McLachlan (Ref. 8); also W. Flügge, *Four-Place Tables of Transcendental Functions* (New York, McGraw-Hill, 1954).

[11] W. M. Kaufman and S. J. Garret, *IRE Trans. Circuit Theory*, **CT-9** (1962), 329–336.

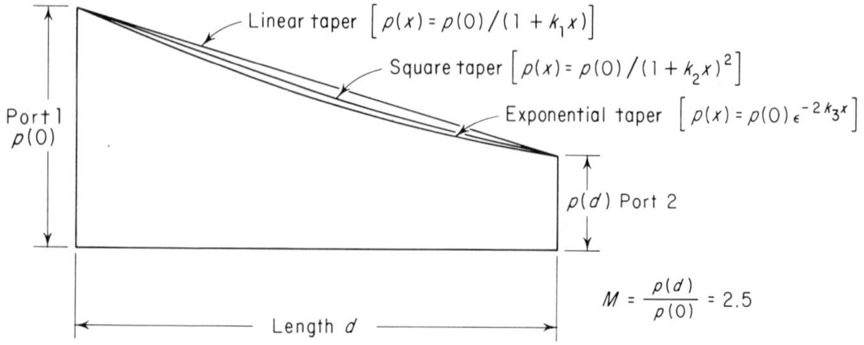

Figure 4-1 Taper functions for exponential, square, and linear tapers of the same taper ratio M.

For our basis of comparison, let us determine the open-circuit voltage transfer functions T_V of the networks using the Picard-Carson method. From Table 2-1,

$$T_V = \frac{V_2}{V_1} = \frac{y_{21}}{y_{22}} = \frac{1}{V_{\mathrm{I}}} \tag{4-30}$$

where V_{I} is found from Equations (2-23) and (2-24). Using these equations, we shall obtain a series expansion for T_V of the form

$$T_V = \frac{V_2}{V_1} = \frac{1}{1 + a_1 s + a_2 s^2 + a_3 s^3 + \cdots} \tag{4-31}$$

From Equation (2-24),

$$\begin{aligned} \psi_1 &= \int_0^x Y_0\,dx \qquad \zeta_2 = a_1 = \int_0^x Z_0 \psi_1\,dx \\ \psi_3 &= \int_0^x Y_0 \zeta_2\,dx \quad \zeta_4 = a_2 = \int_0^x Z_0 \psi_3\,dx \end{aligned} \tag{4-32}$$

The results for the exponential, square, and linear taper factors are summarized in Table 4-4, in which general expressions for a_1, a_2, and a_3 are given in terms of the taper ratio M. For purposes of comparison, we evaluate the coefficients at a taper ratio of 2.5. The numerical values are listed in Table 4-5.

As shown in Table 4-5, the coefficients in the power-series expansion of T_V are substantially the same for the three types of taper; hence the dominant poles and the low-frequency network performance of each is substantially the same. To be specific, consider an RC network, where

Table 4-4 OPEN-CIRCUIT VOLTAGE TRANSFER FUNCTION OF EXPONENTIAL, SQUARE, AND LINEAR TAPERS

$$T_V = \frac{1}{1 + a_1 s + a_2 s^2 + a_3 s^3 + \cdots}$$

EXPONENTIAL TAPER: $Z = z_0 \epsilon^{-2k_1 x}$ $\quad Y = y_0 \epsilon^{+2k_1 x}$ $\quad M = \epsilon^{+2k_1 d}$

$$a_1 = \frac{z_0 y_0 d^2}{(\ln M)^2}\left[\ln M + \frac{1}{M} - 1\right]$$

$$a_2 = \frac{(z_0 y_0 d^2)^2}{(\ln M)^4}\left[3\left(\frac{M-1}{M}\right) + \frac{(\ln M)^2}{2} - \left(\frac{1+2M}{M}\right)\ln M\right]$$

$$a_3 = \frac{(z_0 y_0 d^2)^3}{(\ln M)^6}\left[\frac{(\ln M)^3}{3} + \frac{2(3M+2)}{M}\ln M - \left(\frac{3M-1}{2M}\right)(\ln M)^2 - 10\left(\frac{M-1}{M}\right)\right]$$

SQUARE TAPER: $Z = \dfrac{z_0}{(1 + k_2 x)^2}$ $\quad Y = y_0(1 + k_2 x)^2$ $\quad M = (1 + k_2 d)^2$

$$a_1 = \frac{z_0 y_0 d^2}{3!(\sqrt{M} - 1)^2}\left[M + \frac{2}{\sqrt{M}} - 3\right]$$

$$a_2 = \frac{(z_0 y_0 d^2)^2}{5!(\sqrt{M} - 1)^4}\left[M^2 - 10M + 20\sqrt{M} + \frac{4}{\sqrt{M}} - 15\right]$$

$$a_3 = \frac{(z_0 y_0 d^2)^3}{7!(\sqrt{M} - 1)^6}\left[M^3 - 21M^2 + 70M^{3/2} - 105M + 84\sqrt{M} - 35 + \frac{6}{\sqrt{M}}\right]$$

LINEAR TAPER: $Z = \dfrac{z_0}{(1 + k_3 x)}$ $\quad Y = y_0(1 + k_3 x)$ $\quad M = (1 + k_3 d)$

$$a_1 = \frac{z_0 y_0 d^2}{4(M-1)^2}\,[M^2 - 1 - 2\ln M]$$

$$a_2 = \frac{(z_0 y_0 d^2)^2}{64(M-1)^4}\,[M^4 + 4M^2 - 5 + 4(2M^2 + 1)\ln M]$$

$$a_3 = \frac{(z_0 y_0 d^2)^3}{64(M-1)^6}\,[M^6 + 18M^4 - 9M^2 - (6 + 36M^2 + 18M^4)\ln M - 10]$$

Table 4-5

$M = 2.5$	a_1	a_2	a_3
Exponential	0.377	0.0291	0.00094
Square	0.377	0.0293	0.00095
Linear	0.379	0.0296	0.00095

$Z_0Y_0 = sr_0c_0 = s\tau$. Then, for a taper ratio of 2.5, the exponential network has

$$T_V = \frac{1}{1 + 0.377s\tau + 0.0291(s\tau)^2 + 0.00094(s\tau)^3 + \ldots} \tag{4-33}$$

To complete the comparison for RC networks, the equivalent dominant pole $\omega_{3\,\mathrm{dB}}$ and rise time τ_r (see Chapter 3) for the three types of tapered RC networks are shown in Figure 4-2 for taper ratios ranging from 0.1 to 10. Figure 4-3 shows the variation in excess phase factor m

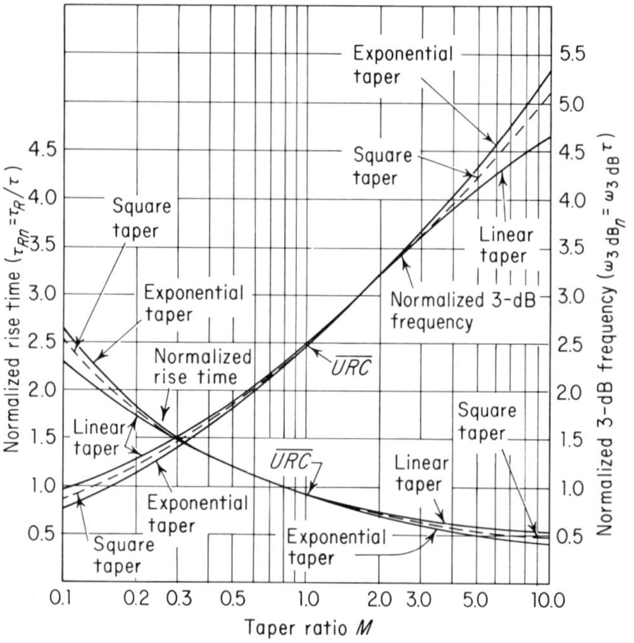

Figure 4-2 Rise time and 3-dB frequency for $T_V(j\omega)$ versus taper ratio (linear, square, and exponential tapers).

and time delay τ_d as functions of taper ratio. (Rise time is normalized to $\tau = r_0c_0d^2$; $\omega_{3\,\mathrm{dB}}$ is normalized to $1/\tau$.)

The curves show that for moderate taper ratios, the network performance is essentially the same for the three types of networks treated. Hence, we conclude that when tapering is used it is expedient to choose the network with the simplest expressions for its immittance functions to simplify and reduce the labor of calculation.

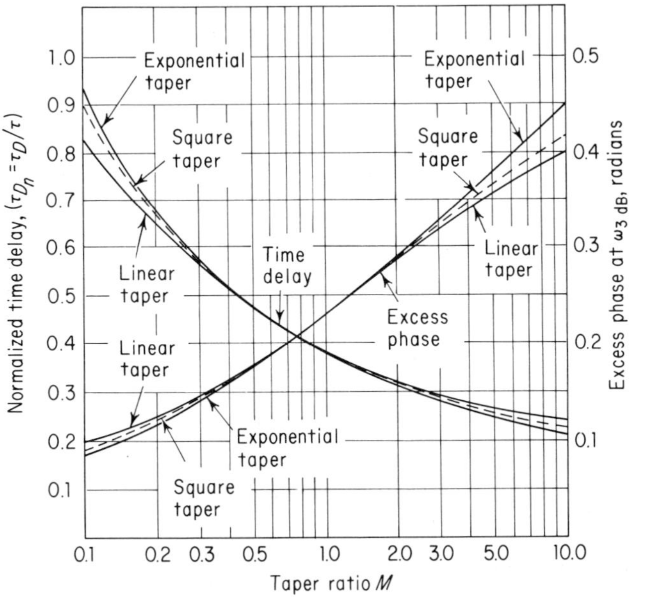

Figure 4-3 Time delay and excess phase versus taper ratio (linear, square, and exponential tapers).

4-3 Equivalent Tapered Networks

In this section, we shall describe a method for determining the immittance parameters of equivalent tapered networks when

$$Z(s, x) = Z_0(s) f_a(x) \quad \text{and} \quad Y(s, x) = Y_0(s) f_b(x)$$

Two distributed networks are equivalent when they are electrically indistinguishable at their terminals. In other words, the two-port network parameters of two equivalent distributed networks are identical at some fixed values of network lengths. The method involves a change of the independent variable.[12] Further, if the solution to the voltage or current equation for a network with given taper functions is known, the method provides solutions for a wide variety of other taper functions in a direct fashion.

Consider the tapered network with $Z = Z_0(s) f_1$ and $Y = Y_0(s) f_2$. If we suppose that the voltage solution is known; that is, given the telegrapher's equations

[12] H. Berger, *IEEE Trans. Circuit Theory,* **CT-13** (1966), 92–93.

$$\frac{dV}{du} = -Z_0(s) f_1(u) I \tag{4-34a}$$

$$\frac{dI}{du} = -Y_0(s) f_2(u) V \tag{4-34b}$$

where $f_1(u)$ and $f_2(u)$ are differentiable positive functions over the interval $0 \leqslant u \leqslant d_1$, the known solution is

$$V(\lambda, u) = AV_{\text{I}}(\lambda, u) + BV_{\text{II}}(\lambda, u) \tag{4-34c}$$

where λ is defined by $\lambda^2 = Z_0(s)\, Y_0(s)$.

The solution to a different network with

$$\frac{dV}{dx} = -Z_0(s) f_a(x) I \tag{4-35a}$$

$$\frac{dI}{dx} = -Y_0(s) f_b(x) V \tag{4-35b}$$

can be found when either $f_a(x)$ or $f_b(x)$ is specified.

Since
$$\frac{dV}{dx} = \frac{dV}{du}\frac{du}{dx} \qquad \frac{dI}{dx} = \frac{dI}{du}\frac{du}{dx} \tag{4-36}$$

then under change of independent variable, Equations (4-35a) and (4-35b) become

$$\frac{dV}{du}\frac{du}{dx} = -Z_0(s) f_a(x) I \tag{4-37a}$$

$$\frac{dI}{du}\frac{du}{dx} = -Y_0(s) f_b(x) V \tag{4-37b}$$

where $f_a(x)$ and $f_b(x)$ are related to $f_1(u)$ and $f_2(u)$ by

$$f_a(x) = f_1(u)\frac{du}{dx} \tag{4-38a}$$

$$f_b(x) = f_2(u)\frac{du}{dx} \tag{4-38b}$$

Upon cancellation of the common factor du/dx, Equations (4-37a) and (4-37b) are transformed into Equations (4-34a) and (4-34b), the solution of which is given by (4-34c).

To use this method, we define u in terms of the new variable x as

$$u = h(x) \tag{4-39}$$

With the reference point at port 1 we have the condition that $u = 0$ when $x = 0$. Next, if we are given $f_a(x)$, we equate the integrals as shown in the following

$$\int_0^u f_1(u)\,du = \int_0^x f_a(x)\,dx \tag{4-40a}$$

and obtain the result

$$F_1(u) = F_a(x) \tag{4-40b}$$

where $F_1(u)$ and $F_a(x)$ are the integrated expressions from Equation (4-40a), which we solve to determine $u = h(x)$. If $f_b(x)$ is given, we integrate and determine $u = h(x)$ from

$$F_2(u) = F_b(x) \tag{4-40c}$$

From Equation (4-38) we find that $f_a(x)$ and $f_b(x)$ are related by the expression

$$f_a(x) = f_b(x)\,\frac{f_1(u)}{f_2(u)} \tag{4-41}$$

Recall that, for a physical network, $f_1(u)$ and $f_2(u)$ are nonzero and positive. The voltage solution to Equation (4-34) is

$$V(\lambda, u) = AV_{\text{I}}(\lambda, u) + BV_{\text{II}}(\lambda, u) \tag{4-42}$$

For network taper functions as defined by (4-41), the voltage solution is

$$V[\lambda, h(x)] = AV_{\text{I}}[\lambda, h(x)] + BV_{\text{II}}[\lambda, h(x)] \tag{4-43}$$

At the terminals of the network

$$x = 0 \qquad u = 0$$

and

$$x = d \qquad u = h(d)$$

and the voltage solution at port 2 is $V[\lambda, h(d)]$. Hence, using basic-set notation for the $[y_{ij}]$ short-circuit admittance parameters (see also Table 2-1),

$$y_{11} = \frac{1}{Z_0}\,\frac{V_{\text{I}}[\lambda, h(d)]}{V_{\text{II}}[\lambda, h(d)]}$$

$$y_{12} = y_{21} = \frac{-1}{Z_0}\,\frac{1}{V_{\text{II}}[\lambda, h(d)]}$$

$$y_{22} = \frac{1}{Z_0}\,\frac{V'_{\text{II}}[\lambda, h(d)]}{V_{\text{II}}[\lambda, h(d)]} \tag{4-44}$$

Let us illustrate the method by two examples.

Example 1

Given the uniform distributed network with $Z(s, u) = Z_0(s)$, $Y(s, u) = Y_0(s)$, that is, $f_1(u) = f_2(u) = 1$, what is the equivalent network with $Z(s, x) = Z_0(s)\epsilon^{\alpha x}$?

First, let us determine $u = h(x)$. From the given information, $f_a(x) = \epsilon^{\alpha x}$. Therefore, using Equation (4-40),

$$\int_0^u du = \int_0^x \epsilon^{\alpha x}\, dx \tag{4-45a}$$

we find

$$u = \frac{1}{\alpha}(\epsilon^{\alpha x} - 1) \tag{4-45b}$$

Also, from Equation (4-41),

$$f_b(x) = \epsilon^{\alpha x} \tag{4-46}$$

Thus, a tapered network with $Z(s, x) = Z_0(s)\epsilon^{\alpha x}$ and $Y(s, x) = Y_0(s)\epsilon^{\alpha x}$ is equivalent to a uniformly distributed network. The $[y_{ij}]$ parameters are

$$y_{11} = y_{22} = \frac{1}{Z_0(s)} \frac{\lambda \cosh\left(\dfrac{\epsilon^{\alpha d} - 1}{\alpha}\right)\lambda}{\sinh\left(\dfrac{\epsilon^{\alpha d} - 1}{\alpha}\right)\lambda} \tag{4-47a}$$

$$y_{12} = y_{21} = \frac{-1}{Z_0(s)} \frac{\lambda}{\sinh\left(\dfrac{\epsilon^{\alpha d} - 1}{\alpha}\right)\lambda} \tag{4-47b}$$

In other words for $(\epsilon^{\alpha d} - 1)/\alpha$ equal to d_1, for example, Equation (4-47) has the same pole-zero configuration as Equation (1-18), which represents the admittance parameters of uniformly distributed network of length d_1.

To generalize further, it is obvious from Equations (4-40) and (4-41) that all tapered networks with $f_a(x) = f_b(x)$ are equivalent to uniform networks, with

$$h(d) = \int_0^d f_a(x)\, dx$$

Hence all tapered networks with $Z(s, x) = Z_0(s) f_a(x)$, $Y(s, x) = Y_0(s) f_a(x)$ have the two-port short-circuit admittance parameters

$$y_{11} = y_{22} = \frac{1}{Z_0(s)} \lambda \frac{\cosh \lambda\, h(d)}{\sinh \lambda\, h(d)} \tag{4-48a}$$

$$y_{12} = y_{21} = \frac{-1}{Z_0(s)} \frac{\lambda}{\sinh \lambda\, h(d)} \tag{4-48b}$$

For our second example, we shall consider tapered networks equivalent to the exponentially tapered network.

Example 2

The exponentially tapered network has $f_1(u) = \epsilon^{2ku}$ and $f_2(u) = \epsilon^{-2ku}$ Let us find an equivalent network with $f_a(x) = 1$. From Equation (4-40a).

$$\int_0^u \epsilon^{2ku}\, du = \int_0^x dx \tag{4-49a}$$

which leads to the relation

$$u = \frac{1}{2k} \ln (2kx + 1) \tag{4-49b}$$

$$h(d) = \frac{1}{2k} \ln (2kd + 1) \tag{4-49c}$$

Also, from Equation (4-41), we find

$$f_b(x) = \epsilon^{-4ku} = \frac{1}{(2kx + 1)^2} \tag{4-50}$$

Thus, networks with

$$Z(s, x) = Z_0(s) \qquad Y(s, x) = \frac{Y_0(s)}{(2kx + 1)^2}$$

are equivalent to the exponentially tapered network.

We conclude by noting that the change of independent variable as described in this section provides a simple and straightforward method for determining the network properties of distributed two-ports when one taper function is specified.

The method used in this section in combination with reduction to the normal form, as discussed in Section 4-2, can also be used to obtain additional closed-form solutions. The interested reader is referred to the literature.[13]

4-4 Determination of Network Taper Functions

In the work we have described so far, we have shown some methods for analyzing tapered distributed networks by finding the voltage solution of the differential equation when $Z(s, x)$, $Y(s, x)$ are given. At this point, we shall show another approach in which, having specified the form of the voltage solution, we find the network parameters $Z(s, x)$, $Y(s, x)$ that produce the specified voltage. There are restrictions on the method and the reader is also cautioned not to regard this method as a synthesis procedure.

The determination of the network functions $Z(s, x)$ and $Y(s, x)$ is straightforward when the voltage solutions are specified.[14] The method also applies when the current solutions are specified, since the equations are of identical form. Thus in order not to duplicate the results we shall consider voltage solutions exclusively. For the distributed network with $Z(s, x) = Z_0(s) f_1(x)$, $Y(s, x) = Y_0(s) f_2(x)$ the voltage solutions satisfy a differential equation of the form

[13] K. J. Gough and R. N. Gould, *IEEE Trans. Circuit Theory*, **CT-13** (1966), 453–454.

[14] L. Gruner, *IEEE Trans. Circuit Theory*, **CT-12** (1965), 241–247.

$$\frac{d^2V}{dx^2} - P(x)\,\frac{dV}{dx} - \lambda^2 Q(x) V = 0 \tag{4-51}$$

where $P(x) = f_1'(x)/f_1(x)$, $\lambda^2 = Z_0(s)Y_0(s)$, and $Q(x) = f_1(x)f_2(x)$. Now Equation (4-51) has two linearly independent voltage solutions, V_A and V_B. If we substitute V_A and V_B in turn into Equation (4-51), we can determine $P(x)$ and $\lambda^2 Q(x)$ in terms of V_A, V_B, and their derivatives (see Problem 4-9). Thus, we relate $P(x)$ and $\lambda^2 Q(x)$ to V_A and V_B and find

$$P(x) = \frac{V_A V_B'' - V_A'' V_B}{V_A V_B' - V_A' V_B} \tag{4-52a}$$

and

$$\lambda^2 Q(x) = -\frac{[V_A' V_B'' - V_A'' V_B']}{[V_A V_B' - V_A' V_B]} \tag{4-52b}$$

where the prime represents differentiation with respect to x. Note that the term in the denominator of Equation (4-52) is the Wronskian of the differential equation and is never zero and that the first and second derivatives of V_A and V_B must exist, since they satisfy Equation (4-51). Further, since $P(x)$ is related to $Z(s,x)$ and $\lambda^2 Q(x)$ is related to the product $Z(s,x)\;Y(s,x)$, we readily find that

$$Z(s,x) = Z_0(s)(V_A V_B' - V_A' V_B) \tag{4-53a}$$

$$Y(s,x) = \frac{-1}{Z_0(s)}\,\frac{[V_A' V_B'' - V_A'' V_B']}{[V_A' V_B'' - V_A' V_B]} \tag{4-53b}$$

Hence, Equation (4-53) shows that if any two linearly independent voltage solutions for a distributed parameter network are known, the impedance and admittance functions Z and Y are easily determined.

For example, given the solutions

$$V_A = \cosh \lambda x \qquad V_B = \frac{\sinh \lambda x}{\lambda} \tag{4-54}$$

we immediately find from Equation (4-53) that

$$Z(s,x) = Z_0(s)\;[\cosh^2 \lambda x - \sinh^2 \lambda x] = Z_0(s) \tag{4-55a}$$

$$Y(s) = \frac{-1}{Z_0(s)}\;\frac{[\lambda^2 \sinh^2 \lambda x - \lambda^2 \cosh^2 \lambda x]}{[\cosh^2 \lambda x - \sinh^2 \lambda x]} = Y_0(s) \tag{4-55b}$$

which is the result expected for the uniform distributed network.

To use the method, it is necessary to know V_A and V_B since $P(x)$ is also unknown. Given V_A and V_B, a catalog of networks can be found having the specified voltage solutions. Equation (4-52) which is a study of the appropriate terms of Eq. (4-51), shows that both V_A and V_B cannot each be a product of a function of x and another of only λ, since no choice of these functions can yield an equation with the coefficients as in Equation (4-51). Hence, one of the suitable forms for V_A and V_B is

$$V_A = U(x)W(x)^{\sqrt{\lambda^2+\beta}} \tag{4-56a}$$

$$V_B = U(x)W(x)^{-\sqrt{\lambda^2+\beta}} \tag{4-56b}$$

where $\beta = \pm\alpha^2$ and α is an arbitrary real constant and $\lambda^2 = Z_0(s)Y_0(s)$ as before. Equation (4-56) can be verified by direct substitution into Equations (4-51) and (4-52). This process also shows that the function $W(x)$, which is an arbitrary real function, is related to $U(x)$ by

$$U(x) = [C_1W(x)^{\sqrt{\beta}} + C_2W(x)^{-\sqrt{\beta}}]^{-1} \tag{4-57}$$

where C_1 and C_2 are arbitrary constants. We could alternatively select an arbitrary $U(x)$ and then determine $W(x)$. From Equations (4-56) and (4-57) we see that one pair of appropriate choices for V_A and V_B is

$$V_A = \frac{W(x)^{\sqrt{\lambda^2+\beta}}}{C_1W(x)^{\sqrt{\beta}} + C_2W(x)^{-\sqrt{\beta}}} \tag{4-58a}$$

$$V_B = \frac{W(x)^{-\sqrt{\lambda^2+\beta}}}{C_1W(x)^{\sqrt{\beta}} + C_2W(x)^{-\sqrt{\beta}}} \tag{4-58b}$$

Table 4-6 IMPEDANCE AND ADMITTANCE FUNCTIONS FROM THE VOLTAGE SOLUTION

V_A OR V_B	$Z(x)$	$Y(x)$
$\dfrac{W^{\pm\sqrt{\lambda^2+\beta}}}{C_1W^{\sqrt{\beta}} + C_2W^{-\sqrt{\beta}}}$ $\beta = \pm\alpha^2$	$Z_0(s)\dfrac{W'}{W}\left[C_1W^{\sqrt{\beta}} + C_2W^{-\sqrt{\beta}}\right]^{-2}$	$Y_0(s)\dfrac{W'}{W}\left[C_1W^{\sqrt{\beta}} + C_2W^{-\sqrt{\beta}}\right]^{2}$
$\dfrac{[C_1W + (-1)^n\sqrt{C_1^2W^2 + C_2}]^{\pm\sqrt{\lambda^2+\beta}/\sqrt{\beta}}}{W}$ $n = 0$ or 1	$Z_0(s)\dfrac{W'}{W^2\sqrt{C_1^2W^2 + C_2}}$	$Y_0(s)\dfrac{W'W^2}{\sqrt{C_1^2W^2 + C_2}}$
$W^{(1+a)/2}Z_{(1+a)/m}\left(\dfrac{2\sqrt{-\lambda^2}}{m}W^{m/2}\right)$*	$Z_0(s)W^aW'$	$Y_0(s)W^{-a+m^{-2}}W'$
$\left[\dfrac{1}{\cos x}\dfrac{d}{dx}\right]^n \epsilon^{\pm ix\sqrt{n^2-\lambda^2}}$	$Z_0(s)\cos^{-2n}x$	$Y_0(s)\cos^{2n}x$
$\cos^{2n+1}x\left[\dfrac{1}{\cos x}\dfrac{d}{dx}\right]^{n+1} \epsilon^{\pm ix\sqrt{n^2-\lambda^2}}$	$Z_0(s)\cos^{2n}x$	$Y_0(s)\cos^{-2n}x$

* $Z_{(1+a)/m}$ represents the pair of linearly independent solutions of the Bessel differential equation, where one of the pair could be identified as V_A and the other as V_B.

By choosing different values for β and C_1 and C_2, we may catalog a number of different tapered networks, as shown in Table 4-6.

Other voltage solutions that provide the proper terms in Equation (4-51) are also listed in Table 4-6, along with the corresponding impedance and admittance functions. Note that the function $W(x)$ is an arbitrary real function of x, subject to V_A, V_B, $Z(x)$, and $Y(x)$ being finite for $0 \leq x \leq d$, whereas β, a, and m are arbitrary constants. Table 4-6 is representative of applications of the method. It is not complete, since there are literally an infinite number of pairs of solutions to the voltage equation for which the method can be used—some in closed form, as in Table 4-6,[14] and others existing in the form of infinite series.[15]

4-5 Distributed *RC* Networks with Rational Immittances

The distributed networks treated so far all have had transcendental immittance parameters. A specially tapered two-port distributed *RC* structure[16] ideally has rational transfer functions and one rational driving-point function. Attempts also have been made to realize the structure in practical $\overline{RC}$ networks. The structure proposed by Heizer is described in the following.

As shown in Figure 4-4, a multilayer sandwich composed of a resistive film covered by dielectric and conducting planes is the basic structure for potential realization of rational immittance parameters.

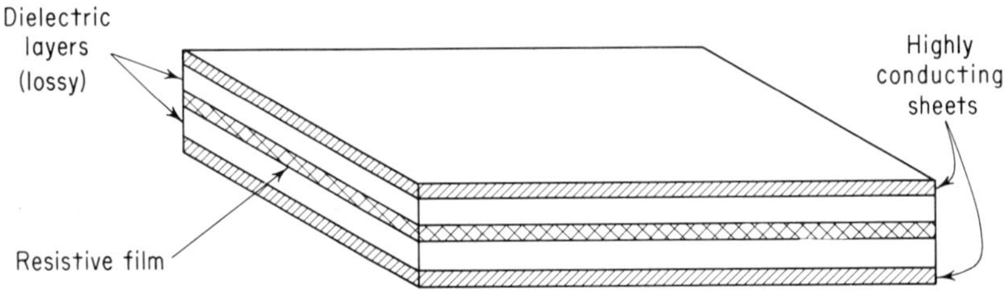

Figure 4-4 $\overline{RC}$ layered structure.

When treated as a two-port, the connection of Figure 4-5 can yield a rational y_{12}, y_{21}, and y_{22}; the connection of Figure 4-6 can yield a rational z_{12}, z_{21}, and z_{11}. These rational functions are obtained when certain constraints are imposed on the per-unit-length shunt admittances between the resistive film and the upper and lower conducting planes.

---

[15] For applications in acoustics see V. Salmon, *J. Acoust. Soc. Am.*, **17** (1946), 212.

[16] K. W. Heizer, *IEEE Trans. Circuit Theory*, **CT-9** (1962), 356–362.

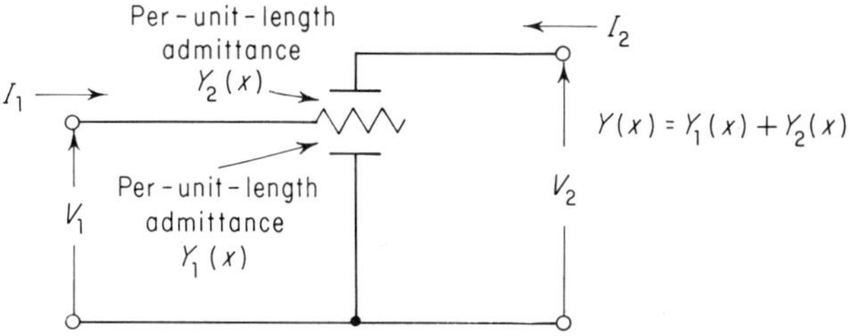

Figure 4-5 Two-port connection for rational y_{12}, y_{21}, y_{22} (y_{11} transcendental).

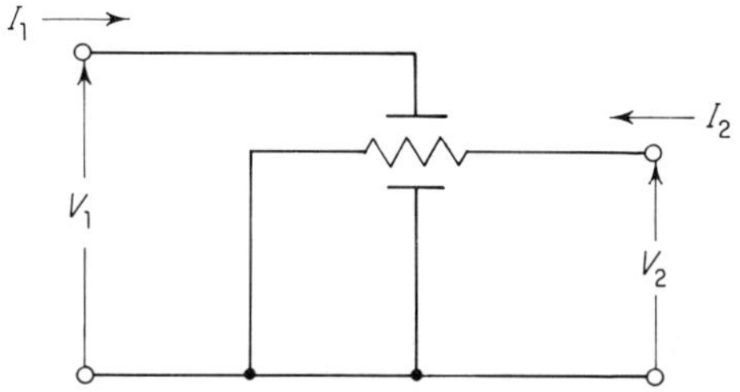

Figure 4-6 Two-port connection for rational z_{11}, z_{12}, z_{21} (z_{22} transcendental).

If we call $Y_1(x)$ the per-unit-length admittance between the resistive film and the ground-plane conductor and $Y_2(x)$ the per-unit-length admittance between the resistive film and the conducting plane connected to port 2 in Figure 4-5, and if we further require that $Y_1(x) + Y_2(x) = Y$, where Y is independent of x, then the network of Figure 4-5 upon short circuit at port 2 is equivalent to a $\overline{URC}$ with port 2 open-circuited.

The solution of the $\overline{URC}$ network equation [Problem 1-1(c)] shows that with V_2 of Figure 4-5 zero (that is, for I_2 of $\overline{URC}$ equal to zero), the potential $V(s, x)$ at any point along the resistive film is given by

$$V(s,x) = V_1(s,0)\,\frac{\cosh \lambda(d-x)}{\cosh \lambda d} \tag{4-59}$$

where $V_1(s, 0)$ is the potential at port 1, $\lambda = \sqrt{r(g+sc)}$ and d is the network length. Let the shunt admittance of port 2 be

$$Y_2(x) = g_2(x) + sc_2(x) \tag{4-60}$$

where $g_2(x)$ and $c_2(x)$ are described by the Fourier series with finite number of terms

$$g_2(x) = \sum_{n=0}^{N} b_n \sin\,(2n+1)\,\frac{\pi x}{2d} \tag{4-61a}$$

and $$c_2(x) = \sum_{n=0}^{N} a_n \sin (2n+1) \frac{\pi x}{2d} \tag{4-61b}$$

Note that $g_2(x)$ and $c_2(x)$ are non-negative and it is also understood that the sum

$$Y_1(x) + Y_2(x) = Y = \text{a constant} \tag{4-62}$$

The current flowing into port 2 is given by the integral

$$I_2 = \int_0^d V[g_2 + sc_2]\, dx \tag{4-63}$$

Substitution of Equation (4-59) and (4-61) into Equation (4-63) and performing the integration yields

$$I_2 = -V_1 \sum_{n=0}^{N} \frac{(2n+1)\pi(b_n + sa_n)}{2d\lambda^2 + \dfrac{(2n+1)^2\,\pi^2}{2d}} \tag{4-64}$$

where $$\lambda^2 = Z_0(s)Y_0(s) = r(g+sc) \tag{4-65}$$

Hence, the short-circuit transfer admittance y_{21}, from Equation (4-64), is found directly as

$$y_{21} = \frac{-\pi}{2drc} \sum_{n=0}^{N} \frac{(2n+1)(b_n + sa_n)}{s + \dfrac{g}{c} + \dfrac{(2n+1)^2\pi^2}{4d^2rc}} \tag{4-66}$$

We note that this function is rational for finite N.

Further, we note that the poles of y_{21} in Equation (4-66) coincide with the poles of y_{21} of a conventional $\overline{URC}$ network having the dielectric loss, g/c = constant. Hence, the transfer admittance of Equation (4-66) closely resembles that of a $\overline{URC}$ network in the dominant frequency region.

To find y_{11}, we evaluate I_1 with $V_2 = 0$. From the familiar telegrapher's equations,

$$I = \frac{-1}{Z(s,x)} \frac{dV}{dx} \tag{4-67a}$$

Therefore, from Equations (4-59) and (4-67), with $Z(s,x) = r$, we have

$$I_1 = V_1 \frac{\lambda d \sinh \lambda d}{rd \cosh \lambda d} \tag{4-67b}$$

Hence, $$y_{11} = \left.\frac{I_1}{V_1}\right|_{V_2=0} = \frac{\lambda d \tanh \lambda d}{rd} \tag{4-68}$$

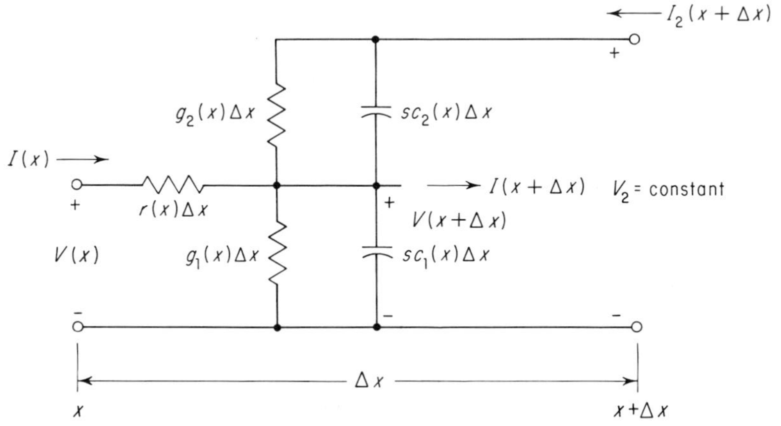

Figure 4-7 Incremental network for calculation of y_{22}.

The remaining task is to find y_{22}. First we set $V_1 = 0$ and find $V(x)$. The incremental network is as shown in Figure 4-7. The network voltage equation results in a nonhomogeneous differential equation and can be solved by a number of standard techniques, including the method of undetermined coefficients.[17] The network equation is obtained as follows. From Figure 4-7,

$$\frac{\Delta I}{\Delta x} = [g_2 + sc_2(x)]V_2 - [g + sc]V(x) \tag{4-69a}$$

$$\frac{\Delta V}{\Delta x} = -rI(x) \tag{4-69b}$$

where $g = g_1(x) + g_2(x)$ and $c = c_1(x) + c_2(x)$. In the limit as $\Delta x \rightarrow 0$, from Equation (4-69b),

$$I(x) \rightarrow \frac{-1}{r}\frac{dV}{dx}$$

and

$$\frac{dI(x)}{dx} = \frac{-1}{r}\frac{d^2V}{dx^2} \tag{4-70}$$

Upon substitution of Equation (4-70) into (4-69a), we get

$$\frac{d^2V}{dx^2} - srcV = -r[g_2 + sc_2]V_2 \tag{4-71}$$

Recall that g_2 and c_2 are given by Equation (4-61). The complementary and particular solutions of Equation (4-71) are given by

[17] W. Kaplan, *Ordinary Differential Equations* (Reading, Mass., Addison-Wesley, 1958).

$$V_c = A \cosh \lambda x + B \frac{\sinh \lambda x}{\lambda} \tag{4-71a}$$

$$V_p = \sum_{n=0}^{N} \frac{(b_n + sa_n) r V_2}{\dfrac{(2n+1)^2 \pi^2}{4d} + r(g + sc)} \sin (2n+1) \frac{\pi x}{2d} \tag{4-71b}$$

Hence the solution of Equation (4-71) is

$$V(s, x) = V_c(s, x) + V_p(s, x) \tag{4-72}$$

Now to find y_{22} the constraints are $V(s, 0) = 0$, and $I(s, d) = 0$. From these two constraints, we find that the constants A and B in Equation (4-71a) are equal to zero. Thus $V(s, x) = V_p(s, x)$. Substitution of λ^2 from Equation (4-65) in $V_p(s, x)$ yields

$$V(s, x) = r V_2 \sum_{n=0}^{N} \frac{(b_n + sa_n) \sin (2n+1) \dfrac{\pi x}{2d}}{\lambda^2 + \dfrac{(2n+1)^2 \pi^2}{4d^2}} \tag{4-73}$$

Now

$$I_2(s, d) = -\int_0^d [V_2 - V(s, x)][g_2(x) + sc_2(x)]\, dx \tag{4-74}$$

and from Equations (4-73) and (4-74) we find that

$$y_{22} = \frac{2d}{\pi} \sum_{n=0}^{N} \left[\frac{b_n + sc_n}{2n+1} - \frac{\pi}{4c} \frac{(b_n + sc_n)^2}{s + \dfrac{g}{c} + \dfrac{(2n+1)^2 \pi^2}{4d^2 rc}} \right] \tag{4-75}$$

We note that the poles of Equation (4-75) are the same as in (4-66), as expected. The short-circuit admittance parameters are summarized in Table 4-7. One approximate physical realization for this case, as given by Heizer, is shown in Figure 4-8.

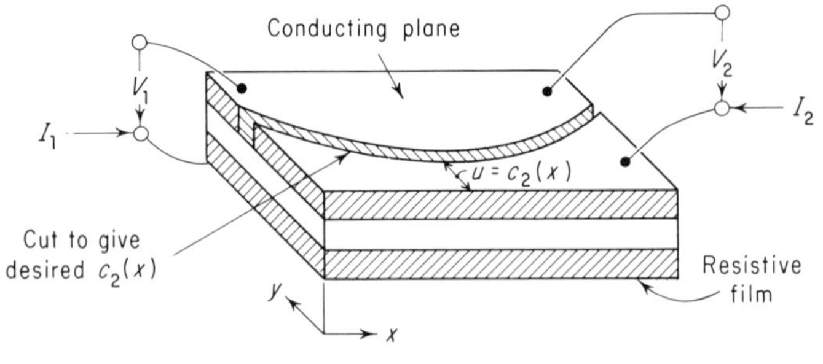

Figure 4-8 An approximate realization of rational y_{12}, y_{21}, y_{22}.

We note that the total area of the conducting plane is constant over the body of the network structure and hence, where the two conducting segments are connected electrically, we have a uniform network with constant r, c, and g. When a thin cut is made in the conducting plane, as shown, the capacitance to the conducting planes is divided into two parts, c_1 and c_2, with $c_1 + c_2 = c$. Under the assumptions that the current flow is one-dimensional and that capacitance is proportional to the width of the conducting plane, the function

$$c_2 = \sum_{n=0}^{N} a_n \sin\,(2n+1)\,\frac{\pi x}{2d}$$

can be realized approximately by an appropriate shape of the cut.

It should be noted that several approximations and assumptions are made[16] in obtaining the capacitance variations as in Equation (4-61b) by the structure of Figure 4-8. There are also restrictions on the coefficients of Equation (4-61); hence, a careful examination of the approximations and assumptions is needed whenever use is made of this structure.

Table 4-7 SHORT-CIRCUIT ADMITTANCE PARAMETERS

$$y_{11} = \frac{\lambda d}{rd}\tanh \lambda d$$

$$y_{12} = y_{21} = \frac{-\pi}{2rcd}\sum_{n=0}^{N}\frac{(b_n + sc_n)(2n+1)}{s + \dfrac{g}{c} + \dfrac{(2n+1)^2\pi^2}{4d^2rc}}$$

$$y_{22} = \frac{2d}{\pi}\sum_{n=0}^{N}\left[\frac{b_n + sc_n}{2n+1} - \frac{\pi}{4c}\,\frac{(b_n+sc_n)^2}{s + \dfrac{g}{c} + \dfrac{(2n+1)^2\pi^2}{4d^2rc}}\right]$$

PROBLEMS

4-1 Show that the Sturm equation for the current differential equation is

$$\frac{d}{dx}\left[\frac{1}{p(x)}\frac{dI}{dx}\right] - \left[\frac{Z_0Y_0}{p(x)}\right] I = 0$$

when
$$Z(s,x) = \frac{Z_0}{p(x)} \qquad Y(s,x) = Y_0 p(x)$$

4-2 Consider the exponentially tapered distributed RC network $(\overline{ERC})$ where $r(x) = r_0\epsilon^{2kx}$, $c(x) = c_0\epsilon^{-2kx}$, and k is a constant.

a. Show that the short-circuit admittance parameters of the exponentially tapered RC network are given by the following matrix:

$$[y_{ij}] = \frac{1}{r_0 d}\begin{bmatrix} \dfrac{\gamma_0 d}{\tanh \gamma_0 d} - kd & -\dfrac{\gamma_0 d \epsilon^{kd}}{\sinh \gamma_0 d} \\ -\dfrac{d\epsilon^{kd}}{\sinh \gamma_0 d} & \epsilon^{2kd}\left(\dfrac{\gamma_0 d}{\tanh \gamma_0 d} + kd\right) \end{bmatrix}$$

$$\gamma_0 = \sqrt{k^2 + s r_0 c_0} \qquad d = \text{network length}$$

b. Show that the open-circuit impedance parameters of the exponentially tapered RC network are given by

$$[z_{ij}] = \frac{1}{s c_0 d}\begin{bmatrix} kd + \dfrac{\gamma_0 d}{\tanh \gamma_0 d} & \dfrac{\gamma_0 d \epsilon^{kd}}{\sinh \gamma_0 d} \\ \dfrac{\gamma_0 d \epsilon^{kd}}{\sinh \gamma_0 d} & \epsilon^{2kd}\left(\dfrac{\gamma_0 d}{\tanh \gamma_0 d} - kd\right) \end{bmatrix}$$

4-3 Using the definitions of the short-circuit admittance parameters and the solution of the voltage equation

$$V(s, x) = \frac{1}{\sqrt{p(x)}}\,[A W_{\mathrm{I}}(s, x) + B W_{\mathrm{II}}(s, x)]$$

derive the $[y_{ij}]$ parameters using the appropriate boundary conditions. Compare the results with Table 4-1.

4-4 Given $2q' = 4k^2 - q^2$, where $q = d[\ln p(x)]/dx$. Find $p(x)$ for

a. $k^2 > 0$.

b. $k^2 \geqslant 0$.

c. $k^2 = 0$.

d. $k^2 < 0$.

Compare the results with Table 4-2.

4-5 Show that the open-circuit voltage transfer function T_V for the Bessel ($\overline{S}$) network is unity for $s = 0$. Use the results of Table 4-1.

4-6 For the distributed RC network shown in Figure 4-6, find y_{22} using the method of undetermined coefficients.

4-7 Given the voltage and current solutions to a two-port distributed network of length d:

$$V(s, x) = K_A V_A(s, x) + K_B V_B(s, x)$$

$$I(s, x) = \frac{-1}{Z(s, 0)}\,[K_A V_A'(s, x) + K_B V_B'(s, x)]$$

The *ABCD* parameters are defined by

$$\begin{bmatrix} V(0) \\ I(0) \end{bmatrix} = \begin{bmatrix} A & B \\ C & D \end{bmatrix} \begin{bmatrix} V(d) \\ I(d) \end{bmatrix}$$

Show that the *ABCD* parameters can be formed as

$$\begin{bmatrix} A & B \\ C & D \end{bmatrix} = \begin{bmatrix} \dfrac{\Delta\begin{pmatrix} 0 \\ d' \end{pmatrix}}{\Delta\begin{pmatrix} d \\ d' \end{pmatrix}} & Z_0(s)\,\dfrac{\Delta\begin{pmatrix} 0 \\ d \end{pmatrix}}{\Delta\begin{pmatrix} 0 \\ 0' \end{pmatrix}} \\ \dfrac{1}{Z_0(s)}\,\dfrac{\Delta\begin{pmatrix} d' \\ 0' \end{pmatrix}}{\Delta\begin{pmatrix} d \\ d' \end{pmatrix}} & \dfrac{\Delta\begin{pmatrix} d \\ 0' \end{pmatrix}}{\Delta\begin{pmatrix} 0 \\ 0' \end{pmatrix}} \end{bmatrix}$$

where

$$\Delta\begin{pmatrix} 0 \\ d' \end{pmatrix} = \begin{bmatrix} V_A(s,0) & V_B(s,0) \\ V_A'(s,d) & V_B'(s,d) \end{bmatrix}$$

and $\Delta\begin{pmatrix} d' \\ d \end{pmatrix}$, $\Delta\begin{pmatrix} 0' \\ 0 \end{pmatrix}$ are defined in a similar manner.

4-8 Repeat Problem 4-7 with the basic-set voltage and current solutions

$$V(s,x) = K_1V_{\mathrm{I}}(s,x) + K_2V_{\mathrm{II}}(s,x)$$

$$I(s,x) = \frac{-1}{Z_0(s)}\left[K_1V_{\mathrm{I}}'(s,x) + K_2V_{\mathrm{II}}'(s,x)\right]$$

and compare the results with Table 2-1. [In basic-set notation, $V_{\mathrm{I}}(s,0) = V_{\mathrm{II}}'(s,0) = 1$, $V_{\mathrm{I}}'(s,0) = V_{\mathrm{II}}(s,0) = 0$.]

4-9 Given that V_A and V_B are solutions of the distributed network Equation (4-51),

a. Derive Equations (4-52a) and (4-52b).

b. Show that for the distributed network,

$$P(x) = \frac{Z'(s,x)}{Z(s,x)} = \frac{f_1'(x)}{f_1(x)}$$

$$\lambda^2 Q(x) = Z_0(s)Y_0(s)f_1(x)f_2(x)$$

c. Using the results of (a) and (b) derive Equations (4-53a) and (4-53b).

4-10 Verify the first row of Table 4-6.

4-11 **a.** Show that under the change of independent variable the following differential equation

$$\frac{d^2V}{dx^2} = \frac{1}{Z}\frac{dZ}{dx}\frac{dV}{dx} - ZYV = 0$$

becomes
$$\frac{d^2V}{du^2} - \frac{d}{du}\left(\ln\sqrt{\frac{Z(u)}{Y(u)}}\right)\frac{dV}{du} - \lambda^2 V = 0$$

where $\lambda^2 = Z_0(s)Y_0(s)$.
Hint: use

$$u = \int_0^x \sqrt{Z(x)Y(x)}\, dx$$

Note that for the same ratio of $Z(u)/Y(u)$, the network behavior is equivalent.
b. Show that if two networks are compared and if

$$\int_0^x \sqrt{Z_1Y_1}\, dx = \int_0^x \sqrt{Z_2Y_2}\, dx$$

the networks are equivalent.

4-12 Given

$$\mathcal{I}(x) = -\left(\lambda^2 + \frac{\Omega''}{\Omega}\right)$$

where $\Omega = \sqrt{p(x)}$. For $\mathcal{I}(x) = K^2$ find $p(x)$ for K^2 positive, negative, and equal to zero, respectively. Compare your results with those of Table 4-2.

CHAPTER

5

The Root-Locus Technique and Stability of Active Lumped Distributed Networks

5-1 Introduction

This chapter deals with the analysis and stability of combinations of active lumped distributed networks with particular emphasis on the determination of the natural frequencies of the system. In a broader sense we wish to determine the pole-zero locations of the lumped-distributed network and then obtain certain information pertaining to the performance of the system. In order to do so, we make use of the root-locus technique. Since we deal with systems which include distributed-parameter networks, the conventional root locus must be generalized so as to be applicable for a countably infinite number of singularities. The generalized root-locus technique, in addition to providing insight into the behavior of the system, provides a valuable tool for studying the stability of distributed-parameter networks. Other stability criteria are also examined.

5-2 Natural Frequencies

Consider a linear active lumped distributed network in the frequency domain. We assume that the system has no isolated parts. The distributed networks in the system may be $\overline{RC}$, $\overline{LC}$, or others, with equal or different but finite lengths. The distributed networks are treated as two-ports, and thus only the input-output terminals are accessible. We shall consider the methods of finding the natural frequencies of the system.

The frequencies at which a signal can be present in a system without applied excitation are defined as the natural frequencies. In other words, the natural frequencies are the poles of the network function with initial conditions set equal to zero. The network function is defined by the following excitation-response relationship:

$$\begin{pmatrix} \text{RESPONSE} \\ \text{FUNCTION} \\ \Phi_r(s) \end{pmatrix} = \begin{pmatrix} \text{NETWORK} \\ \text{FUNCTION} \\ N(s) \end{pmatrix} \begin{pmatrix} \text{EXCITATION} \\ \text{FUNCTION} \\ \Phi_e(s) \end{pmatrix} \tag{5-1}$$

Here, $\Phi_r(s)$ and $\Phi_e(s)$ are the transforms of current and/or voltage quantities and the subscripts r and e designate response and excitation, respectively. The poles of $N(s)$ are the natural frequencies of the system. For certain response quantities, it is possible for pole-zero cancellation to occur. In this case, the natural frequencies do not appear explicitly in certain response functions of the network. Since the system may consist of lumped distributed elements, the natural frequencies of the system will be infinite in number. The natural frequencies may be determined by the following methods:

1. Loop-impedance method. The loop impedance around *any* loop in the absence of excitation must be zero at the natural frequencies. Consider for example the system shown schematically in Figure 5-1. We break open the loop at x and set the loop impedance equal to zero

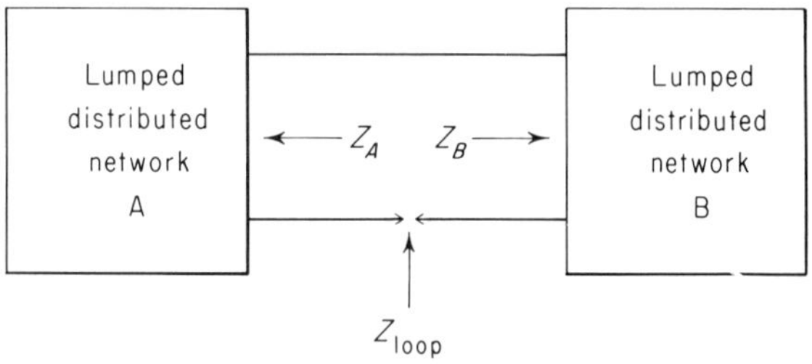

Figure 5-1 Determination of natural frequencies.

$$Z_{\text{loop}} = Z_A + Z_B = 0 \tag{5-2}$$

The zeros of Z_{loop} are the natural frequencies of the system. Equation (5-2) is also called the characteristic equation of the system.

2. Nodal-admittance method. The nodal admittance across *any* node pair in the absence of excitation is zero at the natural frequencies; for example, consider Figure 5-1.

$$Y_{\text{node}} = \frac{1}{Z_A} + \frac{1}{Z_B} = 0 \tag{5-3}$$

The zeros of Y_{node} are the natural frequencies of the system. Note that Equations (5-2) and (5-3) give the same results as we would expect since

$$\frac{1}{Z_A} + \frac{1}{Z_B} = \frac{Z_A + Z_B}{Z_A Z_B} = 0 \tag{5-4}$$

or $Z_A + Z_B = 0$, since Z_A and $Z_B \neq 0$.

3. The circuit determinant method. To find the natural frequencies of the network, set the circuit determinant from nodal (or mesh) analysis equal to zero. The roots of the determinant are the natural frequencies.

Consider the voltage transfer function associated with the arrangement shown in Figure 5-2. The network N is a two-port supplied by a

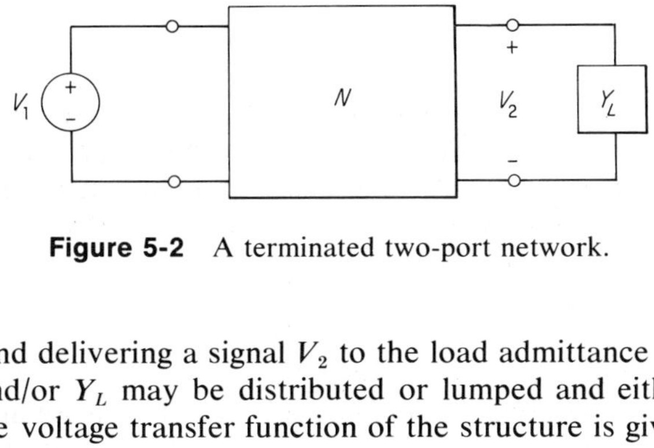

Figure 5-2 A terminated two-port network.

source V_1 and delivering a signal V_2 to the load admittance Y_L. The networks N and/or Y_L may be distributed or lumped and either active or passive. The voltage transfer function of the structure is given by

$$T_V = \frac{V_2}{V_1} = -\frac{y_{21}(s)}{y_{22}(s) + Y_L(s)} \tag{5-5}$$

where y_{ij} are the short-circuit admittance parameters of the two-port network N. If both N and Y_L are lumped structures, $y_{21}(s)$, $y_{22}(s)$, and $Y_L(s)$ are rational functions. One finds, therefore, that the poles and zeros are obtained by the solution of two algebraic equations which result from setting denominator and numerator polynomials equal to zero. Furthermore, if one wishes to study, for example, the effect of changing the scale factor associated with the admittance $Y_L(s)$, one deals with the characteristic equation of the form

$$R(s) = F_1(s) + KF_2(s) = 0 \tag{5-6}$$

where K is a parameter, a real number independent of s. Root-locus techniques[1] have provided a powerful means for studying the behavior of equations of the form of Equation (5-6) when $F_1(s)$ and $F_2(s)$ are polynomials, which is the case for lumped networks.

Suppose that network N is a tapered distributed RC network. In Chapter 2 it was shown that the short-circuit admittance parameters of such structures can be expressed in an infinite product expansion of the following form

$$y_{11}(s) = y_{11}(0)\frac{\prod_{i=1}^{\infty}\left(1+\frac{s}{\alpha_i}\right)}{\prod_{i=1}^{\infty}\left(1+\frac{s}{\sigma_i}\right)}$$

$$y_{21}(s) = y_{12}(s) = y_{12}(0)\frac{1}{\prod_{i=1}^{\infty}\left(1+\frac{s}{\sigma_i}\right)} \tag{5-7}$$

$$y_{22}(s) = y_{22}(0)\frac{\prod_{i=1}^{\infty}\left(1+\frac{s}{\lambda_i}\right)}{\prod_{i=1}^{\infty}\left(1+\frac{s}{\sigma_i}\right)}$$

where α_i, σ_i, and λ_i are all real and positive and have the dimensions of $(\text{time})^{-1}$. Their values depend upon the taper of the network, but the critical frequencies of the driving-point admittance functions alternate with each other as one would expect for RC networks. A lumped-load admittance Y_L is expressible as

$$Y_L(s) = K_D\frac{N_L(s)}{D_L(s)} \tag{5-8}$$

where $N_L(s)$ and $D_L(s)$ are polynomials in s, and K_D is a constant. If one assumes that a distributed network is connected to a lumped-load admittance, as shown in Figure 5-3, the voltage function formed using Equation (5-5) becomes

$$T_V = \frac{1}{\prod_{i=1}^{\infty}\left(1+\frac{s}{\lambda_i}\right) + K\frac{N_L(s)}{D_L(s)}\prod_{i=1}^{\infty}\left(1+\frac{s}{\sigma_i}\right)} \tag{5-9}$$

where K_D has been absorbed in the constant K. To determine the natural

---

[1] J. G. Truxal, *Control System Synthesis* (New York, McGraw-Hill, 1955), Chap. 4.

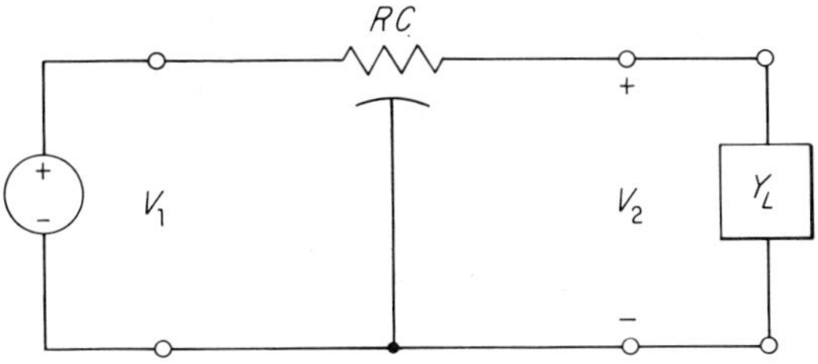

Figure 5-3

frequencies one is faced with the problem of finding the poles of $T_V(s)$ – that is, the values of s_i that satisfy the equation

$$R(s) = D_L(s) \prod_{i=1}^{\infty}\left(1 + \frac{s}{\lambda_i}\right) + KN_L(s) \prod_{i=1}^{\infty}\left(1 + \frac{s}{\sigma_i}\right) = 0 \qquad \textbf{(5-10)}$$

It is of interest to note that if Y_L were a distributed network rather than a lumped network, $N_L(s)$ and $D_L(s)$ would be expressible in the infinite product form associated with $y_{11}(s)$ and $y_{22}(s)$. In some instances, the load admittance and the short-circuit admittance functions associated with the two-port N would be available as transcendental functions. The formulas in Appendix C can be used to express the transcendental functions in product form.

From the foregoing it is evident that in dealing with distributed systems or with lumped distributed systems, one obtains characteristic equations of the form of Equation (5-6) in which $F_1(s)$ and $F_2(s)$ may be algebraic or transcendental functions. In view of the usefulness of root-locus techniques when these two functions are polynomials, one is naturally led to inquire whether a generalization of the technique to include functions with an infinite number of critical frequencies is possible. It is now of value to examine what modifications of the construction techniques normally used with lumped systems are necessary in order to treat the functions encountered in distributed systems in a meaningful fashion.

5-3 Root-Locus Construction for Distributed-Parameter Networks[2]

A convenient way of determining the values of s that satisfy Equation (5-6) is to express it in the form

$$K \frac{F_2(s)}{F_1(s)} = -1 \qquad \textbf{(5-11)}$$

[2] J. J. Kelly, M. S. Ghausi, and J. H. Mulligan, Jr., *IEEE Internat'l Conv. Record,* pt. 7, (1966), 308–318.

Typically, one is interested in the variation of the roots of this equation as K is varied from 0 to ∞ or $-\infty$ to $+\infty$, remaining real throughout the process. The paths in the s plane followed by the roots of Equations (5-6) and (5-11) are known as the root loci associated with $R(s)$.

In a lumped system, $F_1(s)$ and $F_2(s)$ are both polynomials. Hence, Equation (5-11), for a lumped system, may be expressed as

$$K_1 \frac{\prod_{i}^{k} (s + z_i)}{\prod_{j}^{m} (s + p_j)} = \epsilon^{\pm jn\pi} \tag{5-12}$$

where n is odd for K positive and even for K negative, respectively. The root loci constitute all s-plane points for which Equation (5-12) is satisfied.

Rules for the construction of the loci for lumped systems are well known (Problem 5-1). Some of these rules may be applied directly to the functions associated with distributed and lumped distributed systems. For example, if the Weierstrass factor theorem[3] is employed, it becomes evident that the following rules may be used without change to analyze systems in which $F_1(s)$ and $F_2(s)$ satisfy the conjugacy conditions, that is, $F_1{}^*(s) = F_1(s^*)$ and $F_2{}^*(s) = F_2(s^*)$ and have either a finite or countably infinite number of zeros.

Start and termination. The loci start ($K = 0$) at the zeros of $F_1(s)$ and terminate ($K = \infty$) on the zeros of $F_2(s)$ as K varies from zero to infinity.

Number of loci. The number of separate loci is equal to the number of zeros of $F_1(s)$ or of $F_2(s)$, whichever is the larger. If either $F_1(s)$ or $F_2(s)$ is a transcendental function, there are an infinite number of loci.

Symmetry. The loci are symmetrical about the real axis.

Loci on real axis. The loci include those sections of the real axis that lie to the left of an odd number of zeros of $F_1(s)$ and $F_2(s)$ for K positive and to the left of an even number of the zeros of the two functions for K negative.

When a portion of the real axis between two successive zeros of $F_1(s)$ or two successive zeros of $F_2(s)$ is part of the root locus, there will be a particular value of K for which $R(s)$ will have a second-order

[3] The Weierstrass factor theorem states that a function with no singularities in the finite complex plane can be expressed as a product of linear factors in s, multiplied by an arbitrary entire function. Most distributed networks of finite length meet this requirement. (See Appendix B.)

root on the real axis. This root is known as the breakaway point. When $F_1(s)$ and $F_2(s)$ are polynomials, the breakaway point is usually found by formulating an algebraic equation based on the angular relations necessary to satisfy Equation (5-11). The following approach, though used infrequently, is particularly convenient to apply when $F_1(s)$ and $F_2(s)$ are not polynomials.

Breakaway point. The points at which the loci break away from the real axis are found as solutions of the equation

$$F_1(s)F_2'(s) = F_1'(s)F_2(s) \tag{5-13}$$

This equation is derived in the following manner. At a breakaway point $(s = s_b)$, two or more of the loci have a common root, and thus $R(s)$ has at least a second-order zero at s_b. From a consideration of the Taylor-series expansion about s, this implies that $R(s_b)$ and $R'(s_b)$ are zero. As a consequence, the condition that s_b be a breakaway point is

$$R'(s_b) = 0 = F_1'(s_b) + KF_2'(s_b) \tag{5-14}$$

From Equation (5-11), K may be expressed in terms of $F_1(s)$ and $F_2(s)$ which permits the last equation to be written in the form

$$F_1(s_b)F_2'(s_b) = F_1'(s_b)F_2(s_b) \tag{5-15}$$

Note that the breakaway points can occur anywhere in the complex plane, not just on the real axis. The complex roots of Equation (5-15) are an indication of this fact.

Angles of arrival and departure. If s_i is a simple zero of $F_1(s)$, the angle of departure of the locus from s_i is given by

$$\phi_d = \pi + \arg \frac{F_2(s_i)}{F_1'(s_i)} \tag{5-16}$$

If s_j is a simple zero of $F_2(s)$, the angle of arrival of the locus at s_j is given by

$$\phi_a = \pi + \arg \frac{F_1(s_j)}{F_2'(s_j)} \tag{5-17}$$

The foregoing results are obtained readily by considering a Taylor-series expansion in the vicinity of the zeros of $R(s)$ at the points s_i and s_j, respectively. To locate points on the locus in the vicinity of s_i, we consider the function $R(s)$ defined in Equation (5-6), assigning to K values near zero. (The points s_i correspond to $K = 0$.) Let K_1 be a particular small value of K. To locate a point on the locus in the neighborhood of s_i, which is to be designated s_{i1}, the function $R(s) = F_1(s)$

$+ K_1F_2(s)$ is expanded in a Taylor series about s_i. This has the form

$$R(s) = R(s_i) + R'(s_i)(s - s_i) + \tfrac{1}{2} R''(s_i)(s - s_i)^2 + \cdots \tag{5-18}$$

Furthermore, in view of the zero of $F_1(s)$ at s_i, it is noted that

$$R(s_i) = F_1(s_i) + K_1F_2(s_i) = K_1F_2(s_i) \tag{5-19}$$

whereas the first derivative can be expressed as

$$R'(s_i) = F_1'(s_i) + K_1F_2'(s_i) \tag{5-20}$$

Thus, for points in the immediate vicinity of s_i corresponding to values of K_1 infinitesimally close to zero, the function $R(s)$ can be approximated by the first two terms of the series expansion; that is,

$$R(s) \approx K_1F_2(s_i) + [F_1'(s_i) + K_1F_2'(s_i)](s - s_i) \tag{5-21}$$

The condition that s_{i1} be a point on the locus corresponding to $K = K_1$ is

$$R(s_{i1}) = 0 \tag{5-22}$$

Imposing this condition on the preceding equation enables us to locate s_{i1}. It is found that

$$s_{i1} - s_i = -\frac{K_1F_2(s_i)}{F_1'(s_i) + K_1F_2'(s_i)} \tag{5-23}$$

which reduces to the simpler form

$$s_{i1} - s_i \approx -\frac{K_1F_2(s_i)}{F_1'(s_i)} \tag{5-24}$$

as K_1 becomes sufficiently small. The angle of departure of the locus from s_i is identified readily from the Equation (5-24) as that given as Equation (5-16), since $\phi_d = \arg\,(s_{i1} - s_i)$.

A corresponding development is used to obtain Equation (5-17). In the vicinity of the points s_j, by definition a zero of $R(s)$, is a solution of Equation (5-6) with K assigned a large value, $K = K_2$. In view of the fact that $R(s)$ is analytic at s_j, it may be expanded in a Taylor series about that point, and one may obtain the counterpart of Equation (5-21) as

$$\frac{1}{K_2} R(s) \approx \frac{1}{K_2} F_1(s_j) + \left[F_2'(s_j) + \frac{1}{K_2} F_1'(s_j) \right] (s - s_j) \tag{5-25}$$

To locate a point s_{j2} on the locus corresponding to $K = K_2$, we impose the condition

$$R(s_{j2}) = 0 \tag{5-26}$$

which yields

$$s_{j2} - s_j = -\frac{\dfrac{1}{K_2} F_1(s_j)}{F_2'(s_j) + \dfrac{1}{K_2} F_1'(s_j)} \tag{5-27}$$

The locus approaches s_j as K_2 becomes infinite, and thus in the immediate vicinity of s_j, the last equation reduces to

$$s_{j2} - s_j \approx -\frac{\dfrac{1}{K_2} F_1(s_j)}{F_2'(s_j)} \tag{5-28}$$

The expression for the angle of arrival follows directly from consideration of Equation (2-8), since $\phi_a = \arg\,(s_{j2} - s_j)$, and K_2 is a non-negative real number.

To treat cases in which $F_1(s)$ or $F_2(s)$ have multiple zeros, the techniques used in Equations (5-21) and (5-25) must be extended to include the first nonzero derivatives of $F_1(s)$ or $F_2(s)$, respectively. This yields higher-order derivatives for $(s - s_i)$ or $(s - s_j)$, which lead to equations similar to (5-24) and (5-28).

Intersections with imaginary axis. In dealing with lumped systems for which $F_1(s)$ and $F_2(s)$ are always polynomials, it is convenient to locate the points of intersection of the loci and the imaginary axis by the use of Routh's criterion.[4] The points of intersection and the values of K for which they occur are of considerable practical and theoretical interest inasmuch as the $j\omega$-axis crossings represent the transition between stability and instability for a system whose transfer function contains $R(s)$ in its denominator. Whenever $F_1(s)$ or $F_2(s)$ is not a polynomial, however, Routh's criterion fails to provide an effective means of determining the necessary information. In fact, it is advantageous to proceed directly from Equation (5-11) and note that for $K > 0$ the intersections of the loci with the imaginary axis occur at those values ω_c for which

$$\arg\left[\frac{F_2(j\omega_c)}{F_2(j\omega_c)}\right] = \pm(2n+1)\pi \qquad n = 0, 1, 2, \ldots \tag{5-29a}$$

and for $K < 0$ the corresponding values of ω_c are found from

$$\arg\left[\frac{F_2(j\omega_c)}{F_1(j\omega_c)}\right] = \pm 2n\pi \qquad n = 0, 1, 2, \ldots \tag{5-29b}$$

[4] M. F. Gardner and J. L. Barnes, *Transients in Linear Systems* (New York, Wiley, 1942), Vol. 1, pp. 197–201.

Equation (5-29) permits us to establish an equation that may be used to compute the various values of ω_c where the loci intersect the imaginary axis. In some instances the equation derived from the last result is sufficiently simple that the values of ω_c are obtained with little trouble. In some other cases the use of the Nyquist diagram or the Bode plot may be preferable, as discussed in Section 5-5. For certain forms of $F_1(s)$ and $F_2(s)$, however, there are advantages in expanding the ratio of $F_2(j\omega_c)$ to $F_1(j\omega_c)$ in a Taylor series and completing the solution for the values of ω_c by an iterative numerical calculation. In some cases the equation for the $j\omega$-axis intercept may be directly found by setting Im $[R(s)] =$ Re $[R(s)] = 0$, where Im and Re designate the imaginary and real parts, respectively. To find the $j\omega$-axis intercept, set $s = j\omega_c$ and obtain the desired equation. This procedure is illustrated in one of the examples given in Section 5-4.

Asymptotic behavior. Of considerable interest in assessing the behavior of a system is the variation of the roots of $R(s)$ for large values of K. When we consider lumped systems such that $F_1(s)$ and $F_2(s)$ are polynomials of different degree, the loci approach straight lines, which intersect at a point on the real axis; see Problem 5-1(d). When we are dealing with lumped distributed systems or pure distributed systems, however, the limiting form taken by the loci differ, in general, from this pattern.

To study the behavior of the loci as K becomes infinite, it is convenient to examine the actual form of the equation for the loci or an approximation thereto which is valid for large values of K.

It is convenient to write Equation (5-6) in a form that emphasizes the dependence on σ and ω and to define in terms of these quantities the real and imaginary parts of the functions $F_1(s)$ and $F_2(s)$; that is,

$$F_1(\sigma, \omega) = F_{1R}(\sigma, \omega) + jF_{1I}(\sigma, \omega) \tag{5-30}$$

$$F_2(\sigma, \omega) = F_{2R}(\sigma, \omega) + jF_{2I}(\sigma, \omega) \tag{5-31}$$

where the subscripts R and I denote the real and the imaginary parts, respectively. The condition that $R(s) = 0$ is then expressible as

$$F_{1R}(\sigma, \omega) + jF_{1I}(\sigma, \omega) + KF_{2R}(\sigma, \omega) + jKF_{2I}(\sigma, \omega) = 0 \tag{5-32}$$

which may also be written as the two equations

$$F_{1R}(\sigma, \omega) + KF_{2R}(\sigma, \omega) = 0 \tag{5-33}$$

$$F_{1I}(\sigma, \omega) + KF_{2I}(\sigma, \omega) = 0 \tag{5-34}$$

Elimination of K between these two equations defines the root loci. Thus, we obtain for the loci the expressions

$$\frac{F_{1R}(\sigma, \omega)}{F_{2R}(\sigma, \omega)} = \frac{F_{1I}(\sigma, \omega)}{F_{2I}(\sigma, \omega)} \quad \text{(5-35)}$$

When Equation (5-35) is used, care should be exercised about the sign of K that has been eliminated. As written, the equation defines the loci for both positive and negative values of K. For this reason, Equations (5-33) and (5-34) are often preferable. The use of these equations is demonstrated in an example in Section 5-4.

In some applications we encounter functional forms for $F_1(s)$ and $F_2(s)$ that are sufficiently simple that by using Equation (5-35) we can obtain an explicit expression for the loci. This expression is of value in determining imaginary-axis crossings as well as asymptotic behavior. When more complicated functional forms are involved, however, Equation (5-35) can be used to obtain the asymptotic form of the loci by substituting expressions in the equation that are valid for large values of σ or ω or both. To determine the behavior in a specific instance, we employ an asymptotic form of (5-35) in conjunction with (5-33) or (5-34) to establish the region of the s plane in which the locus exists as K becomes infinite. The asymptotic boundaries of the loci can be intersecting straight lines, parallel straight lines, or curves of general form, depending upon the nature of $F_1(s)$ and $F_2(s)$.

5-4 Representative Examples

In this section we examine various examples which illustrate the use of the results established in the previous section. As our first example let us consider a simple delay line.[5]

A simple feedback system with constant time delay. Consider the schematic representation of a simple feedback system with a single pole and a constant time delay of 0.1 second, as shown in Figure 5-4. Physi-

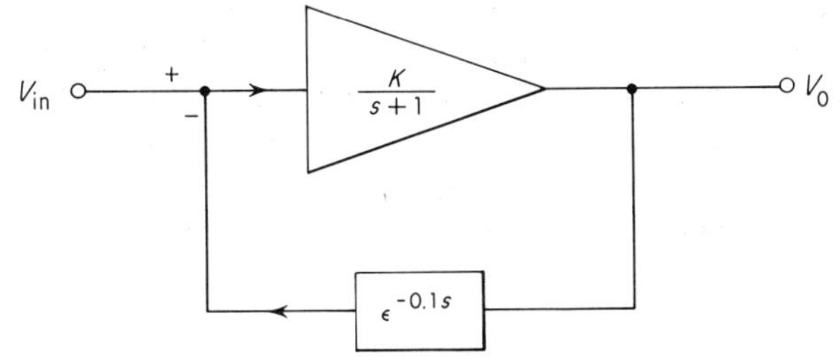

Figure 5-4 Feedback with transportation lag.

[5] Y. Chu, *Trans. AIEE*, **71** (1952) pt. II, 291–298.

cally, in an active device, the time delay may be caused by the excess phase of a transistor and associated with the amplifier block. As shown in Chapter 3, the excess-phase term approximates the distributed nature of the device. The delay may also be attributable to a passive network, such as a delay line, which is the case considered in Figure 5-4.

The closed-loop transfer function of the system is given by

$$\frac{V_0}{V_{\text{in}}}(s) = \frac{K}{(s+1) + K\epsilon^{-0.1s}} \tag{5-36}$$

The natural frequencies of the system are given by the roots of the characteristic equation, namely

$$(s+1) + K\epsilon^{-0.1s} = 0 \tag{5-37}$$

Identification of the functions $F_1(s)$ and $F_2(s)$ yields

$$F_1(s) = s + 1 \tag{5-38}$$

$$F_2(s) = \epsilon^{-0.1s} \tag{5-39}$$

Application of Equation (5-13) gives the equation for the determination of the breakaway point as

$$-(s+1)(0.1)\epsilon^{-0.1s} = \epsilon^{-0.1s} \tag{5-40}$$

From Equation (5-40), it is found that the breakaway point is at $s = -11$.

In order to find the intersections of the loci with the imaginary axis, using Equation (5-29), we can write

$$\arg\left[\frac{\epsilon^{-j0.1\omega_c}}{1 + j\omega_c}\right] = \pm(2n+1)\pi \tag{5-41}$$

From Equation (5-41), another equation whose solutions are the axis crossings is found to be

$$-0.1\omega_c - \tan^{-1}\omega_c = \pm(2n+1)\pi \tag{5-42}$$

The first two roots of this equation are 16.3 and 78.4. Since Equation (5-42) is valid for both positive and negative K, one must be careful to choose the correct strips for the appropriate sign of K, as shown in Figure 5-5. In this case, for example, 47.1 is not an axis crossing point for K positive; it is a crossing point for K negative.

To study the asymptotic behavior of the loci, Equation (5-35) is used. In applying it, one notes first that

$$F_1(\sigma, \omega) = 1 + \sigma + j\omega \tag{5-43}$$

$$\begin{aligned} F_2(\sigma, \omega) &= \epsilon^{-0.1(\sigma + j\omega)} \\ &= \epsilon^{-0.1\sigma}(\cos 0.1\omega - j\sin 0.1\omega) \end{aligned} \tag{5-44}$$

Thus, the loci are defined by the relation

$$\frac{1+\sigma}{\epsilon^{-0.1\sigma}\cos 0.1\omega} = -\frac{\omega}{\epsilon^{-0.1\sigma}\sin 0.1\omega} \tag{5-45}$$

which can be written in the simpler form

$$\sigma = -(1 + \omega \cot 0.1\omega) \tag{5-46}$$

By consideration of Equation (5-46), it is found that the loci are confined to regions of the s plane bounded by lines parallel to the real axis. The loci approach these straight lines for large positive and negative values of σ. Solution of Equation (5-46) for ω for large values of σ yields the first three intersections of the asymptotes with the imaginary axis at $\omega = 31.4$, 62.7, and 94.1, respectively.

The root loci for the system are shown in Figure 5-5; the various

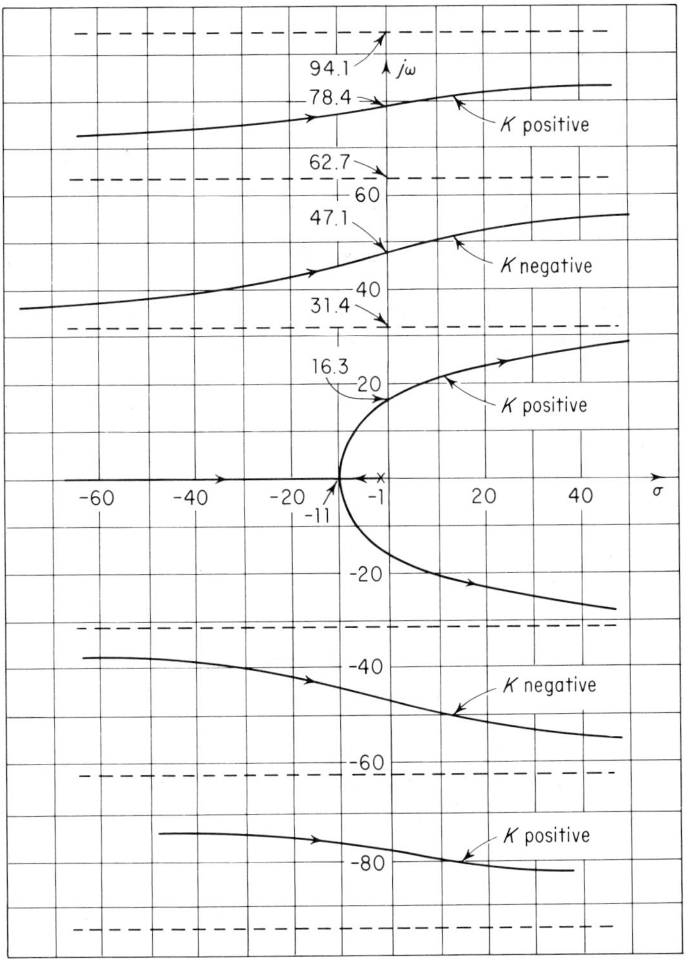

Figure 5-5 Root locus.

characteristics that have just been calculated are also indicated. For this particular system, once the breakaway point and the asymptotic behavior are determined, sketching the essential features of the loci is a simple matter. Note that the principal branch (the branch with lowest $j\omega$-axis crossover) crosses the $j\omega$ axis at $\omega = 16.3$. The value of K at this frequency is readily determined to be equal to 16.32. In other words, the system becomes unstable for any gain $K > 16.32$. The stability criterion is examined in some detail in Section 5.5.

Distributed *RC* two-port and lumped load. Consider now the case in which a network N is a uniform $\overline{RC}$ network and Y_L is a lumped RC load, as depicted in Figure 5-6. For the $\overline{URC}$ network, assumed to be of

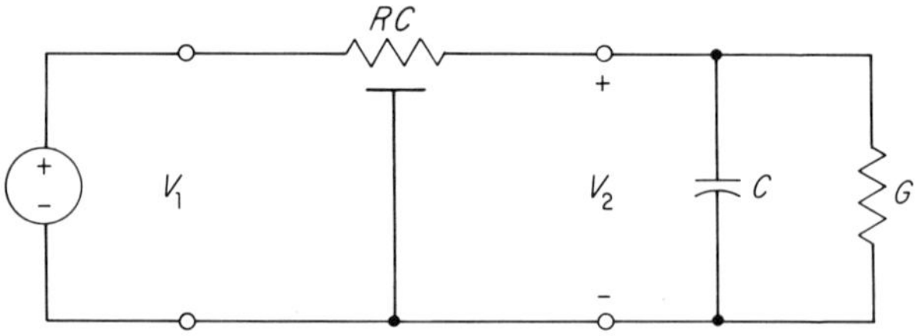

Figure 5-6

length d and having per-unit resistance and capacitance r_0 and c_0, the short-circuit admittance parameters [see Equation (1-21)] are

$$y_{11}(s) = y_{22}(s) = g\theta \coth \theta = g \frac{\prod_{n=0}^{\infty}\left[1 + \dfrac{4sT}{(2n+1)^2\pi^2}\right]}{\prod_{m=1}^{\infty}\left(1 + \dfrac{sT}{m^2\pi^2}\right)} \tag{5-47}$$

$$y_{12}(s) = y_{21}(s) = -g\theta \operatorname{csch} \theta = -g \frac{1}{\prod_{m=1}^{\infty}\left(1 + \dfrac{sT}{m^2\pi^2}\right)}$$

where $\theta = \sqrt{sT}$, $T = r_0 c_0 d^2$, and $g = 1/r_0 d$. The load admittance Y_L is

$$Y_L = G(1 + sT_L) \tag{5-48}$$

where G and C are the conductance and capacitance of the load, respectively, and $T_L = C/G$. By substitution of Equations (5-47) and (5-48) into Equation (5-5), we obtain, for the voltage transfer function of the system,

$$T_V = \frac{1}{\cosh \sqrt{sT} + K(1 + sT_L)\dfrac{\sinh \sqrt{sT}}{\sqrt{sT}}} = \frac{1}{R(s)} \tag{5-49}$$

where $K = Gr_0 d = G/g$. The functions $F_1(s)$ and $F_2(s)$, which have been used in the preceding development, are identified as

$$F_1(s) = \cosh \sqrt{sT} = \prod_{n=0}^{\infty} \left[1 + \frac{4sT}{(2n+1)^2 \pi^2} \right] \tag{5-50}$$

$$F_2(s) = (1 + sT_L) \prod_{m=1}^{\infty} \left(1 + \frac{sT}{m^2 \pi^2} \right) \tag{5-51}$$

By examination of the preceding two equations, it follows that the zeros of $F_1(s)$ are located at

$$s_n = -\frac{(2n+1)^2 \pi^2}{4T} \qquad n = 0, 1, 2, 3, \ldots \tag{5-52}$$

Those of $F_2(s)$ occur at

$$s_L = -\frac{1}{T_L} = -\frac{G}{C} \quad \text{and} \quad s_m = -\frac{m^2 \pi^2}{T} \qquad m = 1, 2, 3, \ldots \tag{5-53}$$

Note that the successive s_i and s_j alternate with one another; the value of s_L, determined entirely by the loci admittance Y_L, bears no relation to s_n and s_m, which depend on the structure of the distributed network.

Loci associated with $R(s)$ for various assumptions concerning the load admittance are shown in Figure 5-7. In view of the fact that s_L, s_m, and s_n are all real and that the s_m and s_n alternate, the loci are confined to the real axis and their locations are readily identified. Figure 5-7(a) shows the behavior for the condition $G = 0$ and $C = 0$, which corresponds to an open-circuited line. This is the condition wherein $R(s)$ degenerates to the single term $\cosh \sqrt{sT}$ whose zeros are given by Equation (5-52). In Figure 5-7(b) and (c), the loci are shown for the special situations in which $C = 0$, $G \neq 0$ and $G = 0$, $C \neq 0$, respectively. Note that in the latter case, the expression $K(1 + sT_L)$ reduces to $sr_0 dC$, and thus, the loci illustrate the variation of the roots of $R(s)$ as C varies from zero to infinity. In Figures 5-7(d) through 5-7(f), the quantity $1/T_L$ in the zero of $F_2(s)$ contributed by the load admittance is assumed to be less than, equal to, or greater than $\pi^2/4T$, the first zero contributed to $F(s)$ by the distributed structure. Pole-zero cancellation is indicated in Figure 5-7(e).

Certain interesting conclusions regarding the performance of the lumped distributed system can be obtained by consideration of Figure 5-7. From Figure 5-7(b), it can be seen that shunting the output terminal of the distributed network with a resistance broadens the bandwidth of the frequency response characteristic of the network; the two extremes of the first pole location of $T_V(s)$ are immediately apparent. In Figure 5-7(c), the effect of a pure capacitive load is indicated, and it is noted that the bandwidth is steadily decreased as C is increased from zero.

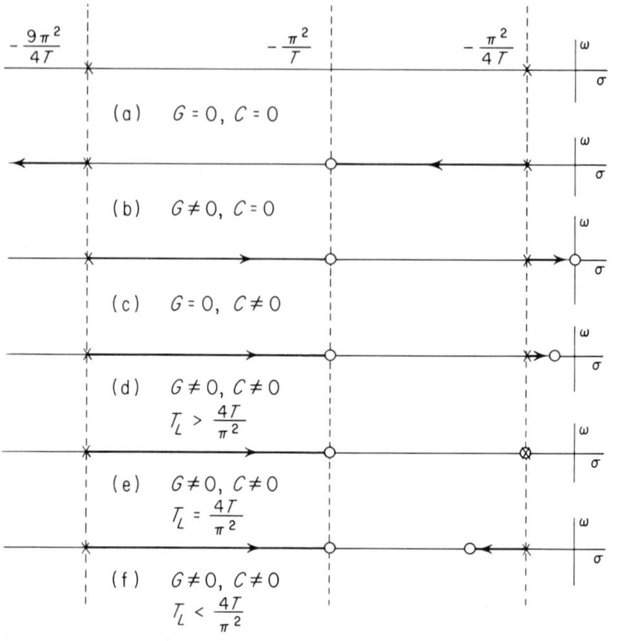

Figure 5-7 Root locus.

From Figure 5-7(d), (e), and (f) the effect of the nature of $Y_L(s)$ on the voltage transfer function is indicated; it can be seen that the bandwidth may be increased or decreased depending on the value of T_L relative to the time constant of the distributed structure.

Distributed *RC* two-port and distributed *RC* load. Another system of interest is that in which network N is a uniform $\overline{RC}$ network. The configuration is shown in Figure 5-8. For simplicity in numerical calcu-

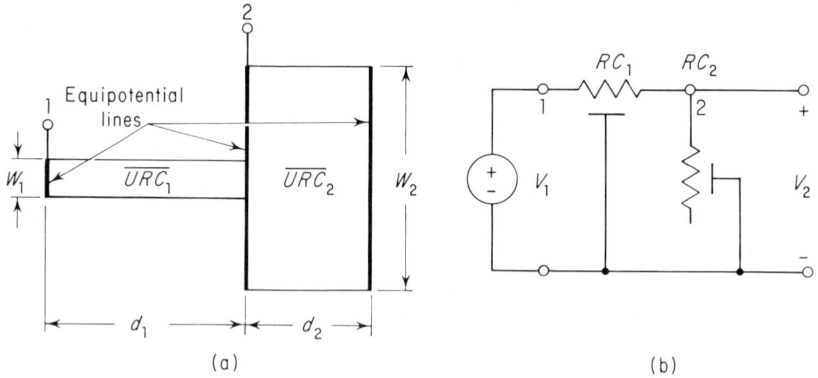

Figure 5-8

lations, it will be assumed that the distributed networks are made up of the same material; they differ only in their lengths and widths. The problem to be investigated will be the variation produced in the voltage transfer function T_V as the ratio of the width W_1 to W_2 is varied.

The critical frequencies of the two networks are obtained from Equation (5-47) by the introduction of appropriate subscripts 1 and 2 for identification of the individual structures. Consequently, the load admittance has the form

$$Y_L(s) = g_2\theta_2 \tanh \theta_2 \tag{5-54}$$

and by the use of Equation (5-5), the required transfer function is found to be

$$T_V = \frac{g_1\theta_1 \operatorname{csch} \theta_1}{g_1\theta_1 \coth \theta_1 + g_2\theta_2 \tanh \theta_2} \tag{5-55}$$

This equation may be simplified to the following form without any assumptions concerning θ_1 and θ_2:

$$T_V = \frac{\cosh \theta_2}{\cosh \theta_1 \cosh \theta_2 + \dfrac{g_2\theta_2}{g_1\theta_1} \sinh \theta_1 \sinh \theta_2} \tag{5-56}$$

For networks of the same material and sheet thickness, one may write

$$\frac{g_2\theta_2}{g_1\theta_1} = \frac{W_2}{W_1}$$

Let this ratio be designated by K_1. Hence, Equation (5-56) may be written as

$$T_V = \frac{\cosh \theta_2}{\cosh \theta_1 \cosh \theta_2 + K_1 \sinh \theta_1 \sinh \theta_2} \tag{5-57}$$

Consider now the characteristic equation of the network, which is the denominator of Equation (5-57):

$$R(s) = \cosh \theta_1 \cosh \theta_2 + K_1 \sinh \theta_1 \sinh \theta_2 \tag{5-58}$$

This equation may be expressed as

$$R(s) = F_1(s) + K_1F_2(s) \tag{5-59}$$

where
$$F_1(s) = \cosh \theta_1 \cosh \theta_2 \tag{5-60a}$$

and
$$F_2(s) = \sinh \theta_1 \sinh \theta_2 \tag{5-60b}$$

The transcendental functions in Equations (5-60a) and (5-60b) may be expressed in the product expansion form

$$F_1(s) = \prod_{n=0}^{\infty} \left[1 + \frac{4sT_1}{(2n+1)^2\pi^2}\right]\left[1 + \frac{4sT_2}{(2n+1)^2\pi^2}\right] \tag{5-61a}$$

$$F_2(s) = \sqrt{T_1 T_2}\, s^2 \prod_{m=1}^{\infty} \left[1 + \frac{T_1 s}{m^2 \pi^2}\right]\left[1 + \frac{T_2 s}{m^2 \pi^2}\right] \tag{5-61b}$$

Noting that $K_1 = W_2/W_1$, $T_1 = r_1 c_1 d_1^2$, $T_2 = r_2 c_2 d_2^2$ and that for similar material $r_1 c_1 = r_2 c_2$, we may rewrite Equation (5-58) as

$$R(s) = \prod_{n=0}^{\infty} \left[1 + \frac{4T_1 s}{(2n+1)^2 \pi^2}\right]\left[1 + \frac{4T_2 s}{(2n+1)^2 \pi^2}\right] + \frac{W_2}{W_1}\frac{d_1}{d_2} T_2 s \prod_{m=1}^{\infty}\left(1 + \frac{T_1 s}{m^2 \pi^2}\right)\left(1 + \frac{T_2 s}{m^2 \pi^2}\right) \tag{5-62}$$

For convenience, we introduce a normalization factor

$$\Omega_0 = \frac{\pi^2}{4T_2} \tag{5-63}$$

Employing this factor, Equation (5-62) becomes

$$R(s) = \prod_{n=0}^{\infty}\left[1 + \frac{(T_1/T_2)}{(2n+1)^2}\left(\frac{s}{\Omega_0}\right)\right]\left[1 + \frac{1}{(2n+1)^2}\left(\frac{s}{\Omega_0}\right)\right] + \frac{W_2}{W_1}\frac{d_1}{d_2}\frac{\pi^2}{4}\left(\frac{s}{\Omega_0}\right)\prod_{m=1}^{\infty}\left[1 + \frac{(T_1/T_2)}{4m^2}\frac{s}{\Omega_0}\right)\left]\left[1 + \frac{1}{4m^2}\left(\frac{s}{\Omega_0}\right)\right] \tag{5-64}$$

Equation (5-64) is a product expansion for Equation (5-58); however, the constants multiplying $F_2(s)$ are different. We denote the new constant by $K = W_2 d_1/W_1 d_2$. The respective zeros of $F_1(s)$ and $F_2(s)$ are:

$$F_1(s):\begin{cases} s_{na} = -\dfrac{(2n+1)^2 T_2 \Omega_0}{T_1} = -(2n+1)^2\dfrac{\pi^2}{4T_1} \\ \qquad\qquad\qquad\qquad\qquad\qquad n = 0, 1, 2, \ldots \\ s_{nb} = -(2n+1)^2\Omega_0 = -(2n+1)^2\dfrac{\pi^2}{4T_2} \end{cases} \tag{5-65}$$

$$F_2(s):\begin{cases} s_{ma} = -\dfrac{4m^2 T_2 \Omega_0}{T_1} = -\dfrac{m^2\pi^2}{T_1} \\ \qquad\qquad\qquad\qquad\qquad\qquad m = 1, 2, 3, \ldots \\ s_{mb} = -4m^2\Omega_0 = -\dfrac{m^2\pi^2}{T_2} \end{cases} \tag{5-66}$$

and $\qquad s_0 = 0$

Because of the nature of m and n, the values of s_{nb} and s_{mb} can never be equal. Note, however, that there are ratios of T_1 to T_2 that cause s_{nb} (zeros of cosh θ_2) and s_{ma} (zeros of sinh θ_1/θ_2) to be equal. If we define $T_1/T_2 = 4k^2$, the roots of $F_1(s)$ and $F_2(s)$ take the form

$$s_{na} = -\frac{(2n+1)^2}{4k^2}\Omega_0 \qquad s_{ma} = -\left(\frac{m}{k}\right)^2\Omega_0 \tag{5-67}$$

$$s_{nb} = -(2n+1)^2\Omega_0 \qquad s_{mb} = -4m^2\Omega_0 \qquad s_0 = 0$$

If the ratio m/k is an odd integer, there are values of m for which s_{nb} equals s_{ma} and then $F_1(s)$ and $F_2(s)$ have a common factor, which is a zero of $\cosh\theta_2$. Thus, for this value of $k = \frac{1}{2}\sqrt{T_1/T_2}$, $T_V(s)$ as given in Equation (5-56) is an all-pole function. In addition, whenever m/k is an even integer, the corresponding s_{ma} coincides with one of the zeros s_{mb}, yielding a second-order zero of $F_2(s)$.

The root-locus diagram for the general case, Equation (5-64), is shown in Figure 5-9 as

$$K = \frac{T_1 d_1^2}{T_2 d_2^2} = \frac{W_2 d_1}{W_1 d_2}$$

varies. Note that this variation can be achieved by changing either the widths, lengths, or both.

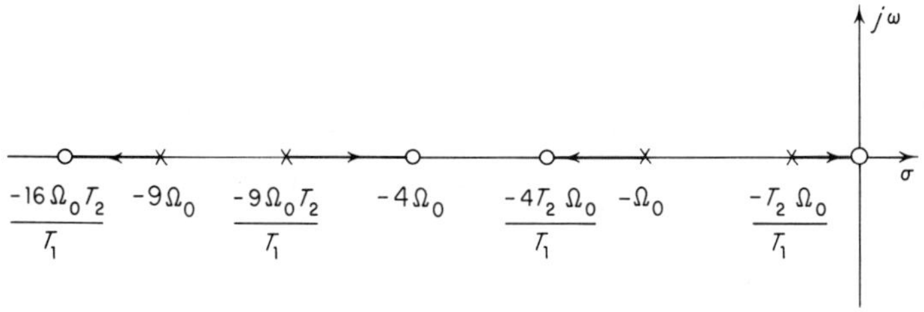

Figure 5-9 Root locus for Equation (5-64).

It is of interest to consider the special case of $k = 1$, that is, $T_1/T_2 = 4$. For this condition, Equation (5-56) becomes

$$T_V(s) = \frac{1}{\prod_{n=0}^{\infty}\left[1 + \frac{16T_2 s}{(2n+1)^2\pi^2}\right] + 2\left(\frac{W_2}{W_1}\right) T_2 s \prod_{m=1}^{\infty}\left(1 + \frac{T_2 s}{m^2\pi^2}\right)^2} \tag{5-68}$$

The root locus for this case, obtained by varying W_2/W_1, is given in Figure 5-10. From the figure, one notes that the bandwidth of the composite system is decreased as the ratio W_2/W_1 increases. Furthermore, in view of the separation between the first and second loci (as counted

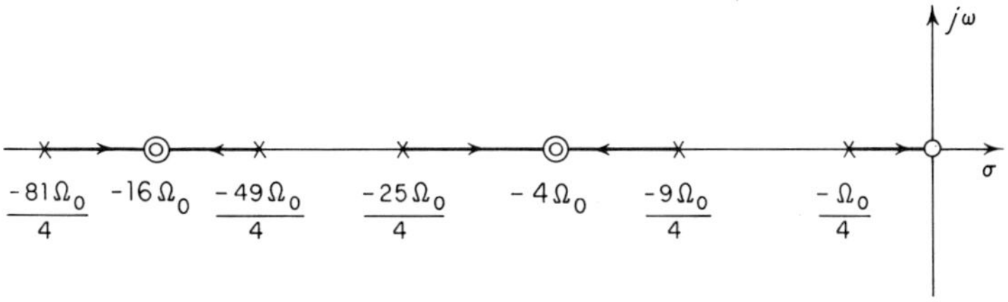

Figure 5-10 Root locus for Equation (5-68).

from the origin), it is evident that a very good approximation to the behavior of the system can be obtained up to the 6-dB frequency by use of a transfer function consisting of a single pole.

Lumped distributed two-port. Consider the lumped distributed networks shown in Figure 5-11. These two networks play similar roles as the bridged-T and the twin-T lumped *RC* networks. In other words,

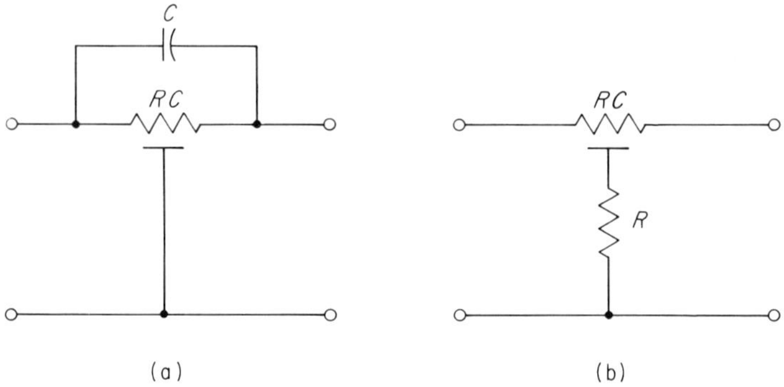

Figure 5-11 $\overline{RC}$ notch networks.

both networks can have complex transmission zeros. The transmission zeros of the network can be designed to lie on the $j\omega$ axis. Consequently, if this network is placed in the feedback path of a simple single-loop feedback amplifier as shown in Figure 5-12, bandpass transmission[6] takes place (see also Section 7-5).

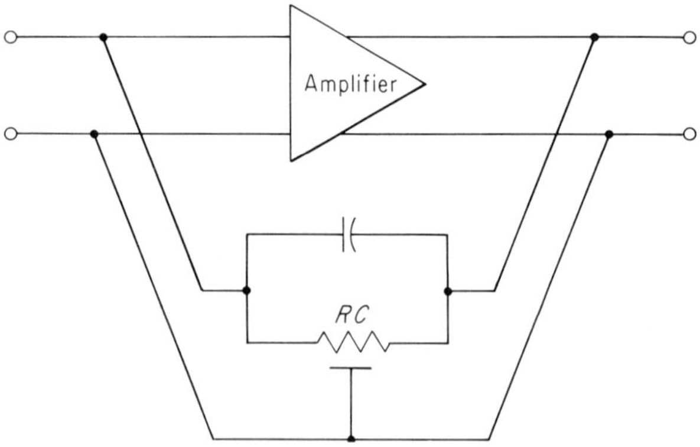

Figure 5-12 $\overline{RC}$ active bandpass circuit.

[6] W. M. Kaufman, *Proc. IRE*, **48** (1960), 1540–1545.

The voltage transfer functions of these two structures, Figure 5-11(a) and (b), have the same form; that is,

$$T_V = -\frac{y_{21}}{y_{22}} = \frac{1 + K\theta \sinh \theta}{\cosh \theta + K\theta \sinh \theta} \tag{5-69}$$

where $\theta = \sqrt{sT}$, $T = r_0 c_0 d^2$, and $K = C/c_0 d$ for the structure in Figure 5-11(a) and $K = R/r_0 d$ for that of Figure 5-11(b).

The denominator of T_V has the same form as the functions studied in the previous example (Figure 5-6) with the element G of the lumped load admittance set equal to zero; see Equation (5-49). The loci of the natural frequencies are shown in Figure 5-7(c).

For the circuits in Figure 5-11 we shall also consider the location of the transmission zeros. They are of particular interest since they are not restricted to the negative real axis and can be designed to be on $j\omega$ axis and thus yield a notch filter. The equation defining the loci is

$$R(s) = 1 + K\theta \sinh \theta = 1 + K\sqrt{sT} \sinh \sqrt{sT} \tag{5-70}$$

The functions $F_1(s)$ and $F_2(s)$ are found to be

$$F_1(s) = 1 \tag{5-71}$$

$$F_2(s) = \sqrt{sT} \sinh \sqrt{sT} = sT \prod_{m=1}^{\infty} \left(1 + \frac{sT}{m^2\pi^2}\right) \tag{5-72}$$

From these expressions, it is noted that only zeros of $F_2(s)$ are present, all of which are of first order. They are located on the negative real axis at

$$s_m = -\frac{m^2\pi^2}{T} \qquad m = 0, 1, 2, \ldots \tag{5-73}$$

The first few zeros are shown in Figure 5-13. Because of the absence of zeros in $F_1(s)$, the loci will not be confined to the negative real axis. It is of interest to locate the breakaway points, which are located between successive pairs of zeros. Imposition of the condition given in Equation (5-13) provides the equation whose solutions are the breakaway points; that is,

$$F_2'(s) = 0 \tag{5-74}$$

Differentiating Equation (5-72), we find the necessary equation to be

$$\tanh \sqrt{sT} = -\sqrt{sT} \tag{5-75}$$

Examination of this equation reveals that its roots are located on the negative real axis, and if the substitution $(sT) = -x^2$ is made, the desired points can be found by solving the equation pair

$$\tan x = -x \tag{5-76a}$$

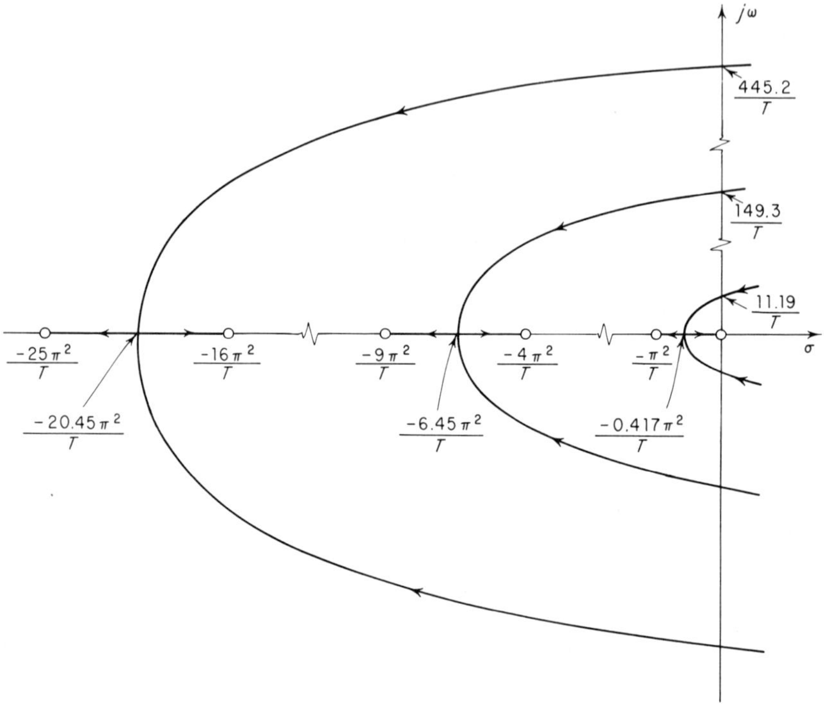

Figure 5-13 Root locus for notch filter (not to scale).

and from Equation (5-70), with $F_2(s) = -x \sin x$, we have

$$\frac{1}{K} = x \sin x \tag{5-76b}$$

For positive K, $\sin x$ must be positive and also satisfy Equation (5-76a). For negative K, $\sin x$ must be negative and also satisfy Equation (5-76a).

Figure 5-14(a) immediately shows that the solutions for positive K, lie in the range,

$$\frac{(4n+1)\pi}{2} < x < (2n+1)\pi \qquad n = 0, 1, 2, \ldots \tag{5-77a}$$

For negative K, the solutions lie in the range

$$\frac{(4n+3)\pi}{2} < x < 2n\pi \qquad n = 1, 2, 3, \ldots \tag{5-77b}$$

Thus, for K positive, from Equation (5-77a) the solution for x may be written as

$$x = (4n+1)\frac{\pi}{2} + \delta_n \tag{5-78}$$

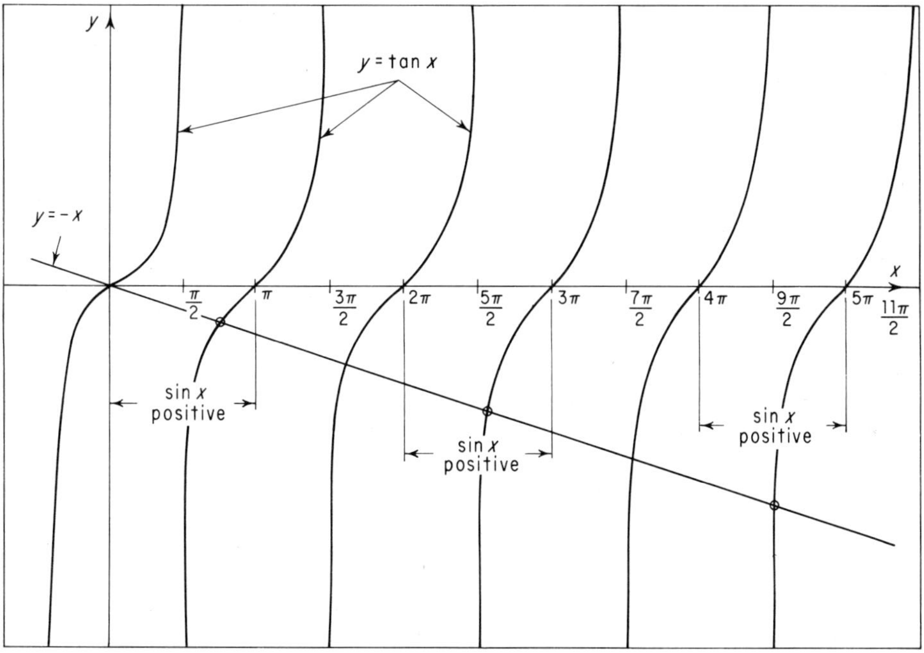

Figure 5-14 (a) Solutions of tan $x = -x$ for positive sin x.

where $\delta_n < 0.34$ radian for $n = 0$ and approaches zero for large values of n. Since

$$\tan\left[(4n+1)\frac{\pi}{2} + \delta_n\right] = \frac{\tan\,(4n+1)(\pi/2) + \tan\,\delta_n}{1 - \tan\,(4n+1)(\pi/2)\,\tan\,\delta_n} \tag{5-79}$$

$$= -\frac{1}{\tan\,\delta_n}$$

from Equations (5-79), (5-78), and (5-76a),

$$\tan\,\delta_n = \frac{1}{(4n+1)(\pi/2) + \delta_n} \tag{5-80}$$

To solve this equation, the approximation $\tan\,\delta_n \approx \delta_n$ will be used. For $n = 0$, the error in approximation is 0.4 percent in Equation (5-80) and becomes much smaller as n increases. The use of this approximation in Equation (5-80) yields

$$\delta_n = \frac{1}{(4n+1)\dfrac{\pi}{2} + \dfrac{1}{(4n+1)(\pi/2) + \delta_n}} \tag{5-81}$$

Equation (5-81) is in the continued fraction form. Stopping the iteration (see Appendix E) at the second step, we have

$$\delta_n = \frac{(4n+1)(\pi/2)}{(4n+1)^2(\pi^2/4)+1} \tag{5-82}$$

and

$$x_n \approx (4n+1)\frac{\pi}{2}\left[1+\frac{4}{(4n+1)^2\pi^2+4}\right] \tag{5-83}$$

Since $s=-x^2/T$, Equation (5-83) may be written as

$$s_{bn} \approx -\frac{1}{T}(4n+1)^2\frac{\pi^2}{4}\left[1+\frac{4}{(4n+1)^2\pi^2+4}\right]^2 \tag{5-84}$$

The first three of these and the corresponding values of K as found from Equation (5-84) are

BREAKAWAY POINTS

n	s_{bn}	K at s_{bn}
1	$-0.417\ \pi^2/T$	0.552
2	$-6.45\ \pi^2/T$	0.126
3	$-20.45\ \pi^2/T$	0.0704

Because of the forms of Equations (5-76a) and (5-70) there are an infinite number of loci associated with $R(s)$. To determine where the loci cross the imaginary axis, assuming for the moment that such intersections occur, the last method of solution suggested in Section 5-3 shall be used. In Equation (5-70), we set

$$\text{Im}\,[R(s)] = K[v \sinh u \cos v + u \cosh u \sin v] = 0 \tag{5-85}$$

$$\text{Re}\,[R(s)] = 1 + K[u \sinh u \cos v - v \cosh u \sin v] = 0 \tag{5-86}$$

where $\theta = u + jv$ and $s = \theta^2/T = 1/T\,[u^2 - v^2 + j2uv]$. Note that on the $j\omega$ axis $s = j\omega_c$; thus, $u = v$ and Equation (5-85) reduces to

$$\tanh u = -\tan u \tag{5-87}$$

A sketch of Equation (5-87), see Figure 5-14(b), reveals that the values of u satisfying Equation (5-87) for positive K [that is, $F_2(s)$ negative] are bounded by

$$\frac{(4n+1)\pi}{2} < u < (2n+1)\pi \qquad n = 0, 1, 2, \ldots \tag{5-88}$$

For $u \geqslant 3$, $\tanh u \approx 1$ to better than 0.5 percent, and for $u \geqslant 2$, $\tanh u \approx 1$ to better than 3.6 percent. Thus using the approximation $\tanh u \approx 1$ in Equation (5-87) for $u \geqslant 3$, we obtain $\tan u = -1$. This has the solution

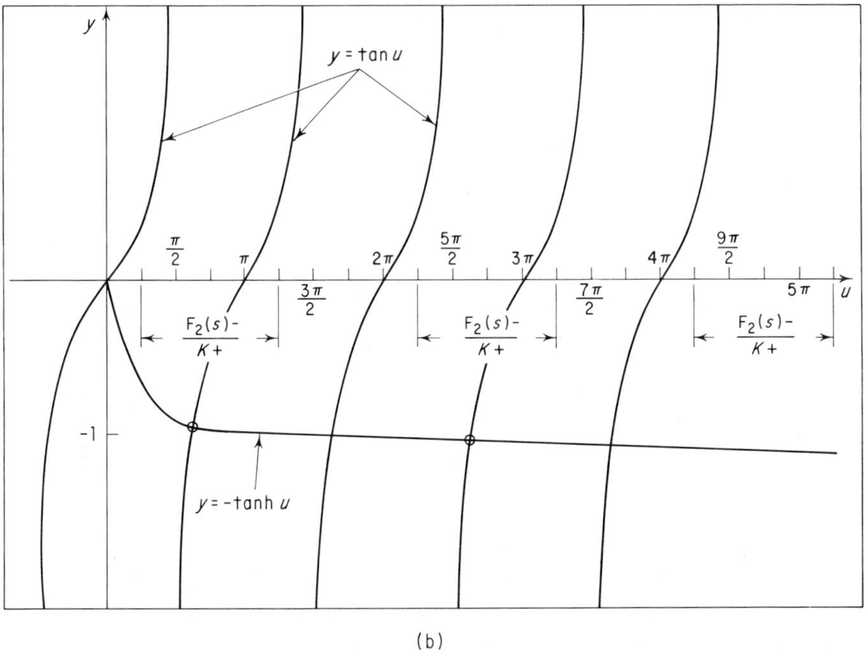

Figure 5-14 (b) Solutions of tan $u = -\tanh u$ for K positive.

$$u \approx \left[(4n+1)\frac{\pi}{2} + \frac{\pi}{4} \right] = (8n+3)\frac{\pi}{4} \tag{5-89}$$

Consequently,

$$\omega_c = \frac{2uv}{T} = \frac{1}{T}(8n+3)^2\frac{\pi^2}{8} \qquad n = 0, 1, 2, \ldots \tag{5-90}$$

It should be noted that for $n = 0$, $u = 2.36$ and the error incurred by approximating $\tanh u \approx 1$ is only about 2 percent. The first three of the $j\omega$-axis intercepts and the values of K associated with each are

$j\omega$-AXIS INTERCEPT	K AT THE INTERCEPT
$\omega_{c1} = \pm 11.19/T$	5.62×10^{-2}
$\omega_{c2} = \pm 149.3/T$	2.90×10^{-5}
$\omega_{c3} = \pm 445.2/T$	6.29×10^{-8}

It is of interest to note two other methods which may be applied in the solution of Equation (5-29a) to determine the intersection with the imaginary axis nearest to the origin. Their use frequently offers a considerable simplification in numerical calculations. To illustrate the first technique, the function of θ in Equation (5-70) is expanded into a Taylor series yielding

$$R(s) = 1 + K\left(\theta^2 + \frac{\theta^4}{3!} + \frac{\theta^6}{5!} + \frac{\theta^8}{7!} + \cdots\right) \tag{5-91}$$

which can in turn be written in terms of ω_c as

$$R(s) = 1 + K\left[j\omega_c T - \frac{(\omega_c T)^2}{3!} - j\frac{(\omega_c T)^3}{5!} + \frac{(\omega_c T)^4}{7!} + \cdots\right] \tag{5-92}$$

Separating the infinite series into a real and imaginary part and applying the condition of Equation (5-29a), we obtain

$$\arg\left[\frac{F_2(j\omega_c)}{F_1(j\omega_c)}\right] = \tan^{-1}\left[\frac{\omega_c T - \dfrac{(\omega_c T)^3}{5!} + \dfrac{(\omega_c T)^5}{9!} - \cdots}{-\dfrac{(\omega_c T)^2}{3!} + \dfrac{(\omega_c T)^4}{7!} - \dfrac{(\omega_c T)^6}{11!} - \cdots}\right]$$

$$= \pm(2k+1)\pi \tag{5-93}$$

At solutions of Equation (5-93), the tangent of the angle equals zero provided $\omega_c > 0$. Hence, in order to obtain an approximate value of the location of the intersection nearest the origin, we seek the smallest value of ω_c for which

$$\omega_c T - \frac{(\omega_c T)^3}{5!} + \frac{(\omega_c T)^5}{9!} - \cdots = 0 \qquad \omega_c > 0$$

Using the iteration technique, this smallest value of ω_c is closely approximated by the solution of the equation

$$1 - \frac{(\omega_c T)^2}{5!} = 0 \tag{5-94}$$

which yields $\omega_c \approx 10.95/T$. A second iteration using this value as a basis with the equation

$$\omega_c T - \frac{(\omega_c T)^3}{5!} + \frac{(\omega_c T)^5}{9!} = 0 \tag{5-95}$$

yields the corrected value of $\omega_c \approx 11.19/T$. Further iteration does not affect the result to the indicated accuracy.

A second approach to the determination of the first crossing of the imaginary axis employs the concept of the equivalent dominant-pole and excess-phase approximation as discussed in Section 3-8. In the present application, $F_2(s)$ is approximated by the expression

$$F_2(s) = \sqrt{sT}\sinh\sqrt{sT} = sT\left(1 + \frac{sT}{9.13}\right)\epsilon^{0.558sT} \tag{5-96}$$

The large separation between successive zeros, as indicated by Equation (5-73), makes this form of approximation a particularly accurate one. Use of Equations (5-96) and (5-29a) yields the following equation for ω_c:

$$\tan^{-1}\frac{\omega_c T}{9.13} + 0.558\,\omega_c T - \frac{\pi}{2} = 0 \qquad \textbf{(5-97)}$$

The lowest ω_c in the solution of Equation (5-97) is $\omega_c = 11.19/T$, which is the same result as obtained in the two previous calculations.

The root locus is shown in Figure 5-13. The various key points that have been calculated are indicated in the figure.

It is of interest to consider next the asymptotic behavior of the loci. For this purpose one may use Equations (5-33) and (5-34). From Equation (5-85), which has already made use of (5-34),

$$u = -v\,\frac{\tanh u}{\tan v} \qquad \textbf{(5-98)}$$

Substituting Equation (5-98) into (5-86), noting that (5-86) is the expanded form of (5-33), we find that

$$1 - K\left(\frac{v}{\sin v}\right)\left[\frac{\sinh^2 u \cos^2 v + \cosh^2 u \sin^2 v}{\cosh u}\right] = 0 \qquad \textbf{(5-99)}$$

Note that to satisfy Equation (5-99) for K positive, $(v/\sin v)$ must be positive, because the expression in the product is always positive. For the asymptotic behavior, one considers u very large, thus Equation (5-98) reduces to

$$\tan v \simeq -\frac{v}{u} \approx 0 \qquad u \geqslant 5 \qquad \textbf{(5-100)}$$

Hence

$$v_n \simeq (2n+1)\pi \qquad \text{for } K \text{ positive} \qquad \textbf{(5-101)}$$

$$v_n \approx 2n\pi \qquad \text{for } K \text{ negative} \qquad \textbf{(5-102)}$$

Since

$$s = \sigma + j\omega = \frac{u^2 - v^2 + j2uv}{T} \qquad \textbf{(5-103)}$$

The equations for asymptotic family of curves for positive K are therefore obtained from Equations (5-103) and (5-101) as follows:

$$\sigma + j\omega \approx \frac{u^2 - (2n+1)^2\pi^2 + j2(2n+1)\pi u}{T} \qquad \textbf{(5-104)}$$

Eliminating u in Equation (5-104), we obtain

$$\sigma = \frac{1}{T}\left\{\left[\frac{\omega T}{2(2n+1)\pi}\right]^2 - (2n+1)^2\pi^2\right\} \tag{5-105}$$

Equation (5-105) is recognized to define parabolas which pass through

$$\sigma = -\frac{(2n+1)^2\pi^2}{T}$$

Note that in this case the asymptotic curves are parabolas. This is in contrast to the lumped system in which case the asymptotic curves are always straight lines intersecting at one point.

5-5 Stability of Lumped Distributed Active Networks

Stability of systems with rational transfer functions can be determined by a number of methods. If all the natural frequencies of the system are known, the stability can be established by inspection. In other words, the pole that is farthest to the right must have a nonpositive real part.

When the transfer function is not rational, the stability criterion, in the bounded-input bounded-output sense, is not a trivial problem; for example, consider the function defined by[7]

$$y(t) = t^2 \sin t^2 \qquad t \geqslant 0 \tag{5-106}$$

The transform of Equation (5-106) is analytic for all finite s. In other words, its Laplace transform is an entire function, hence, when this function is part of the system function, determining stability by examining the real part of the farthest pole to the right is meaningless, since the transform of Equation (5-106) has no poles in the finite plane. However, it is readily seen that the function $t^2 \sin t^2$ takes arbitrarily large values for $t \to \infty$ and describes an unstable situation. Thus, if we look at the pole farthest to the right, the instability produced by the entire function remains entirely unobserved.

If the transfer function is not rational, but expressible in an infinite-product form, exhibiting the countably infinite number of singularities, and *if* it has no additional term which is an entire function, then one can settle stability by merely inspecting the real part of the pole farthest to the right.

The problem of establishing stability in a linear lumped distributed system is usually done in the frequency domain. In this case the number of natural frequencies is countably infinite. For the system to be stable, all the natural frequencies must be in the left half plane (that is, Re

[7] G. Doetsch, *Guide to the Applications of Laplace Transforms* (Princeton, N. J., Van Nostrand, 1961), p. 218.

$s_i < 0$ for $i = 1, 2, \ldots$), provided there is no additional entire function in the characteristic equation.

The analytic approach, in general, is not simple and techniques similar to those discussed in Section 5-4 may be used. Alternatively one may approximate the transcendental functions by algebraic expressions and then use a standard method such as the Routh-Hurwitz test to determine stability of the system. However, the required accuracy of approximation is not known beforehand and any satisfactory approximation is usually complicated and requires high-degree polynomial approximants. Thus, in general, graphical procedures seem to be attractive for the stability analysis of lumped distributed active systems. Among these, the root-locus technique, the Nyquist diagram, and the Bode plot are particularly attractive. These methods do not require any approximations and are discussed briefly in the following. We assume that the reader is familiar with these methods for lumped systems.[8]

Distributed two-port network with an active *RC* load. We first consider the application of root-locus techniques for the stability analysis of active lumped distributed systems. Consider the arrangement shown in Figure 5-15. Let the active *RC* network driving-point admittance be given by

$$Y_{\text{in}} = K \frac{(s_n - 2)^2 + 4}{(s_n + 4)^2 + 4} \tag{5-107}$$

where $s_n = s4T/\pi^2$ and K is a real positive variable.

We would like to find the locus of the natural frequencies and examine the stability of the system. The natural frequencies of the system are given, using Equation (5-3), by the roots of the following equation:

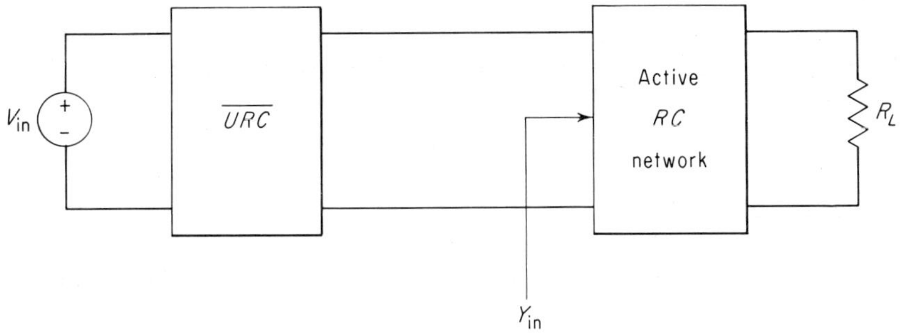

Figure 5-15 Active $\overline{RC}$ network.

[8] See, for example, Truxal (Ref. 1).

$$(y_{22})_{\overline{RC}} + Y_{\text{in}} = 0 \tag{5-108}$$

For the uniformly distributed RC network of length d, y_{22} is given by Equation (1-21a); that is,

$$y_{22} = \frac{1}{r_0 d} \sqrt{sT} \coth \sqrt{sT} = \frac{1}{r_0 d} \frac{\cosh \sqrt{sT}}{\dfrac{\sinh \sqrt{sT}}{\sqrt{sT}}} \tag{5-109}$$

where $T = r_0 c_0 d^2$. Substitution of Equations (5-109) and (5-107) into Equation (5-108) yields

$$[(s_n + 4)^2 + 4] \cosh \pi\sqrt{s_n}/2 + K_0[(s_n - 2)^2 + 4] \frac{\sinh \pi\sqrt{s_n}/2}{\pi\sqrt{s_n}/2} = 0 \tag{5-110}$$

where $K_0 = K/r_o d$. Equation (5-110) may be written in the form of

$$F_1(s_n) + K_0 F_2(s_n) = 0$$

where

$$F_1(s_n) = [(s_n + 4)^2 + 4] \cosh \pi\sqrt{s_n}/2 = [(s_n + 4)^2 + 4] \prod_{m=1}^{\infty} \left(1 + \frac{s_n}{(2m-1)^2}\right) \tag{5-111a}$$

$$F_2(s_n) = [(s_n - 2)^2 + 4] \frac{\sinh \pi\sqrt{s_n}/2}{\pi\sqrt{s_n}/2} = [(s_n - 2)^2 + 4] \prod_{m=1}^{\infty} \left(1 + \frac{s_n}{4m^2}\right) \tag{5-111b}$$

In order to draw the root locus, we now determine a few key parameters. The angle of departure is given by Equation (5-16); that is,

$$\phi_d = \pi + \arg \frac{F_2(s_i)}{F_1'(s_i)}$$

Consider the pole $s_{ni} = -4 + j2$. Here,

$$\arg F_2(s_{ni}) = \arg [(s_n - 2)^2 + 4] \left. \frac{\sinh \pi\sqrt{s_n}/2}{\pi\sqrt{s_n}/2} \right|_{s_n = -4+j2} \approx 76^\circ \tag{5-112a}$$

Further, since $\cosh \pi\sqrt{s_n}/2$ has no complex roots, we have

$$F_1'(s_{ni}) = (\cosh \pi\sqrt{s_n}) \left. \frac{d}{ds} [(s_n + 4)^2 + 4] \right|_{s_n = -4+j2}$$

$$= 2(s_n + 4) \cosh \pi\sqrt{s_n}/2\big|_{s_n=-4+j2} \tag{5-112b}$$

and

$$\arg F_1'(s_{ni}) \approx -87° \tag{5-112c}$$

Hence,

$$\phi_d = 180 + 76 + 87° \approx -17° + 2\pi \tag{5-113}$$

The arrival angle at $s_{ni} = 2 + j2$ is, from Equation (5-17),

$$\phi_a = \pi + \arg \frac{F_1(s_i)}{F_2'(s_i)}$$

At $s_{ni} = 2 + j2$,

$$\arg F_1(s_{ni}) = \arg\,[(s_n + 4)^2 + 4] \cosh \pi\sqrt{s_n}/2\big|_{s_n=2+j2} = 91° \tag{5-114a}$$

Also,

$$\arg F_2'(s_{ni}) = \arg \left\{ \frac{\sinh \pi\sqrt{s_n}/2}{\pi\sqrt{s_n}/2} \frac{d}{ds} [(s_n - 2)^2 + 4] \right\} \Bigg|_{s_n=2+j2}$$

$$\arg F_2'(s_{ni}) = \arg \left[\left(\frac{\sinh \pi\sqrt{s_n}/2}{\pi\sqrt{s_n}/2} \right) 2(s_n - 2) \right] \Bigg|_{s_n=2+j2} \approx 125° \tag{5-114b}$$

Hence,

$$\phi_a = 180 + 91 - 125° = 146° \tag{5-115}$$

The intersection with the imaginary axis is, from Equation (5-29a),

$$\arg \frac{F_2(j\omega_c)}{F_1(j\omega_c)} = \pm(2k + 1)\pi \qquad k = 0, 1, 2, \ldots$$

For this case, it is obvious that there is only one $j\omega$-axis intersection. From the arrival and departure angles (see Figure 5-16) the intersection appears to be in the range $1 < \omega_c < 3$. The easiest way to determine this is by trial and error or by an iteration technique, as discussed in Appendix E. The solution is found to be

$$\omega_c = 2.49 \tag{5-116}$$

At the crossing frequency the value of $\overline{K}_0$ is given by

$$\overline{K}_0 = -\frac{F_1(j2.49)}{F_2(j2.49)} \approx 5.64 \tag{5-117}$$

Hence the system will be unstable for

$$K \geqslant 5.64 r_0 d \tag{5-118}$$

The root locus is shown in Figure 5-16.

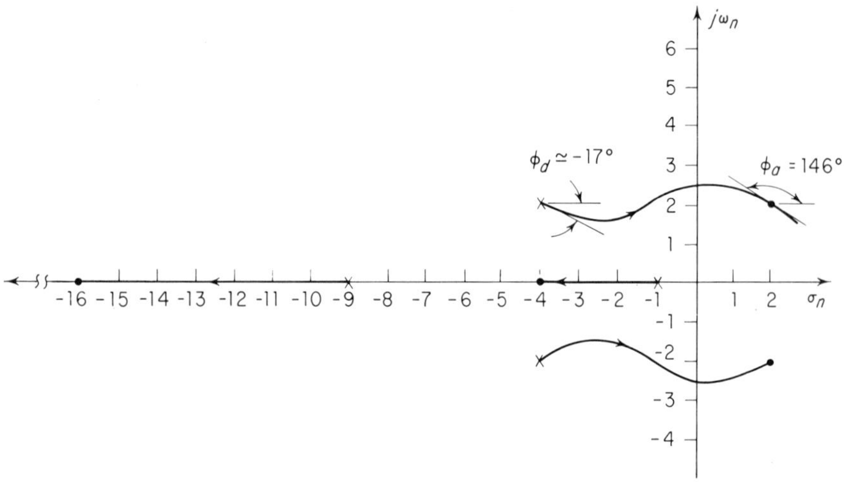

Figure 5-16 Root locus for active $\overline{RC}$ network.

Feedback system with time delay. Consider the feedback system with transportation lag as shown by the block diagram in Figure 5-17. We shall examine the stability of the system by the Nyquist diagram[9] and the Bode plot.

The characteristic equation of the system is given by

$$1 + \frac{20\epsilon^{-s\tau}}{(s + 1)(s + 2)} = 0 \tag{5-119}$$

Of course, τ is positive for a physically realizable system. In either the Nyquist diagram or the Bode plot, the multiplication of the open-loop transfer function by $\epsilon^{-j\omega\tau}$ represents a phase shift varying linearly with

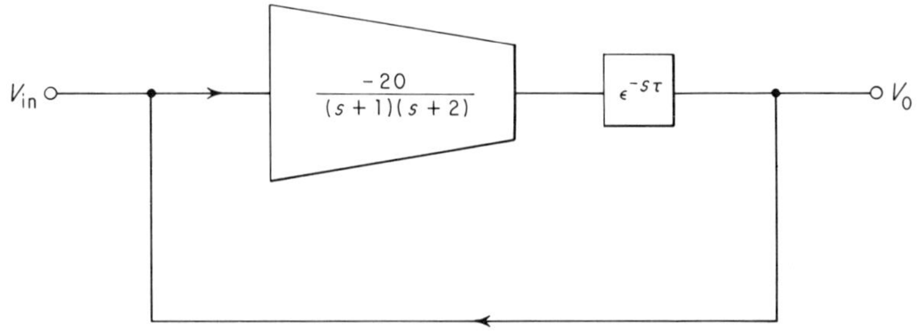

Figure 5-17 Feedback system with time delay.

[9] C. A. Desoer, *IEEE Trans. Circuit Theory*, **CT-12** (1965), 230–234.

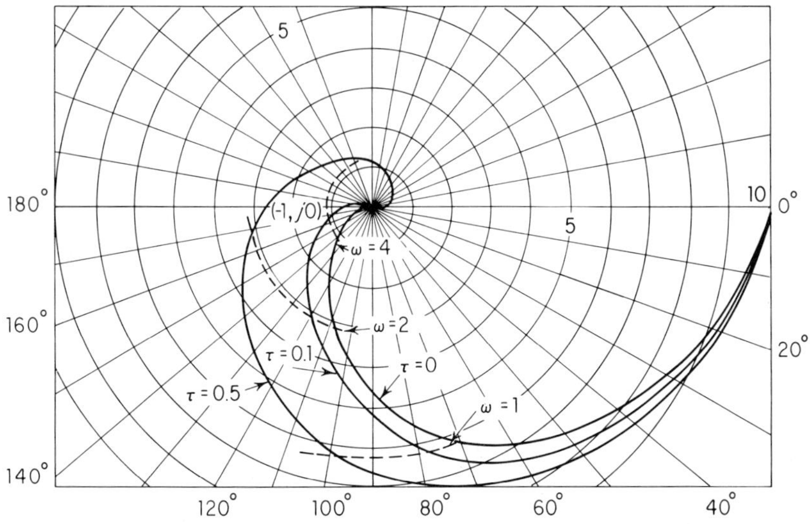

Figure 5-18 Nyquist diagram for $\dfrac{20\epsilon^{-s\tau}}{(s+1)(s+2)}$.

frequency. In the Nyquist diagram, each point in the diagram is rotated by an angle of $-\omega\tau$ radians as indicated in Figure 5-18. Note that the system is stable for $\tau = 0.1$ and unstable for $\tau = 0.5$. In the Bode plot, the magnitude is unchanged by the introduction of the lag factor, whereas the phase lag is increased by an amount proportional to frequency. Figure 5-19 shows the Bode plot of the open-loop transfer function for the system shown in Fig. 5-17. For $\tau = 0.5$ the system is unstable, since at the frequency where the phase is $-180°$ the gain is larger than unity (0 dB). For the system of Figure 5-17, one can readily find the maximum value of τ for which the system is stable (Problem 5-11).

In sampled data systems, the Z transform,[10] which is a transformation $z = \epsilon^{sT}$, has been found to be very useful. The stability test of a sampled-data system is simplified if one considers the z plane directly. The transformation $z = \epsilon^{sT}$ maps the right half of the s plane into the exterior of the unit circle in the z plane. Thus, in terms of the z variable, the system is stable if there are no roots of the characteristic equation outside the unit circle. This approach can also be useful in the stability analysis of distributed networks.

When only ideal active devices and uniformly distributed RC networks are present in a system, sometimes it may be convenient to

[10] Truxal (Ref. 1), Chap. 9, 1955.

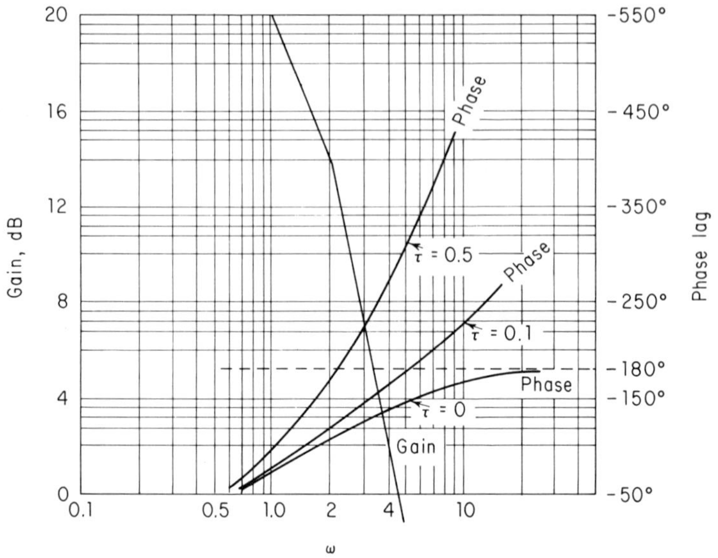

Figure 5-19 Bode plot for $\dfrac{20\epsilon^{-s\tau}}{(s+1)(s+2)}$.

introduce the transformation $W = \epsilon^{\sqrt{Ts}}$. For such a system the transfer function can be expressed as

$$H(s) = \frac{N(\epsilon^{\sqrt{Ts}})}{D(\epsilon^{\sqrt{Ts}})} \qquad \textbf{(5-120)}$$

where N and D are polynomials in $\epsilon^{\sqrt{Ts}}$ only. Thus, by introducing the transformation $W = \epsilon^{\sqrt{Ts}}$, Equation (5-120) reduces to a rational function of W. Stability can then be examined directly in the W plane. This study has been made with the following result.[11]

A necessary and sufficient condition for bounded-input bounded-output stability of a system for which the transfer function is rational in $W = \epsilon^{\sqrt{Ts}}$, and the degree of the numerator is not greater than the degree of the numerator, is that all poles of the transfer function occur within that region of the W plane bounded by $\epsilon^{|\phi|+j\phi}$ where $-\pi \leqslant \phi = \arg W \leqslant \pi$. The region is shown in Figure 5-20.

As an example consider the system shown in Figure 5-21. The gain constant is real $-\infty < K < \infty$.

The characteristic equation of the system is

$$1 + K\epsilon^{-\sqrt{Ts}} = 0 \qquad \textbf{(5-121)}$$

[11] J. Bourquin and T. N. Trick, *Proc. 10th Midwest Symp. Circuit Theory*, Purdue, 1967.

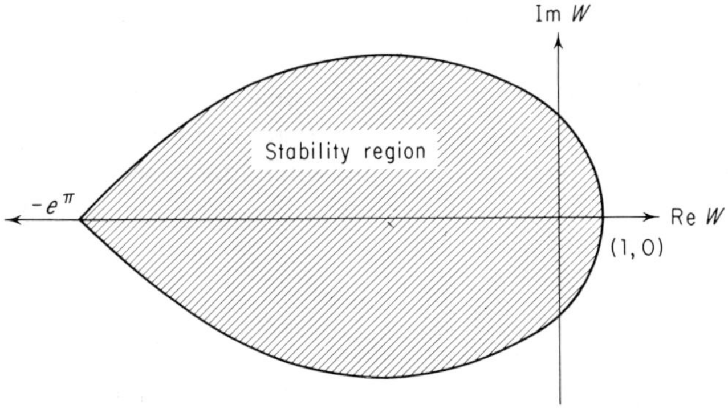

Figure 5-20 Stability region in the W plane.

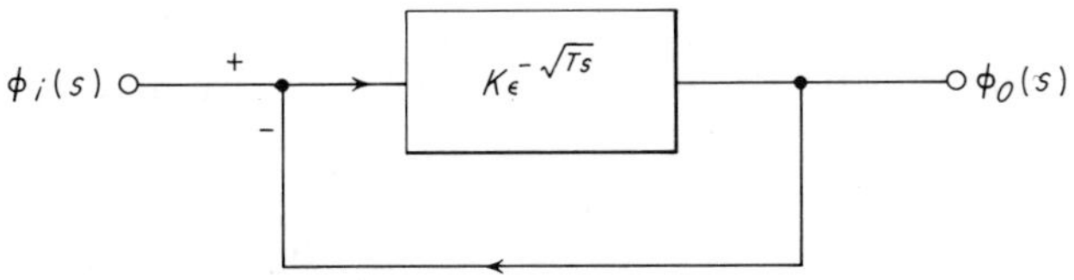

Figure 5-21

Introducing the transformation $W = \epsilon^{\sqrt{Ts}}$ we have, from Equation (5-121),

$$1 + \frac{K}{W} = 0 \tag{5-122}$$

The root locus for Equation (5-122) in the W plane is shown in Figure 5-22. From Figures 5-20 and 5-22, it is seen that (for $K < 0$) when the locus passes the point $(1, 0)$, the system is unstable; that is, for $|K| > 1$ the system is unstable. For $K > 0$, which represents negative feedback, the system becomes unstable when the locus crosses the point $(\epsilon^{-\pi}, 0)$; that is, for $K > \epsilon^{\pi}$ the system is unstable.

Other transformations useful in distributed network synthesis have also been introduced and are discussed in the next chapter. Note the

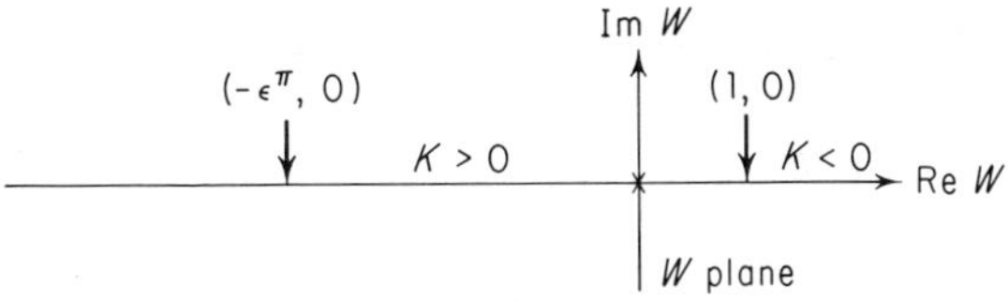

Figure 5-22 Root locus in the W plane.

stability region for the transformation $P = \cosh \sqrt{sT}$, is shown in Figure 6-38.

Finally, it should be noted that an analytic method is available to test the stability of a purely distributed parameter system.[12] The stability criterion applies to systems whose network functions are ratios of finite sums of exponentials. In other words, the criterion tests whether all the zeros of a function of the form

$$F(s) = \sum_{n=0}^{N} C_n \epsilon^{s\mu_n} \tag{5-123}$$

(where C_n and μ_n are real, $\mu_0 = 0$, $\mu_{n+1} > \mu_n$) lie within the interior of the left half s plane. Interested readers are referred to the literature.[12]

PROBLEMS

5-1 The characteristic equation of a lumped system may be written as

$$1 + KG(s) = 1 + K \frac{\prod_{i}^{k} (s + z_i)}{\prod_{j}^{m} (s + p_j)} = 0 \qquad K \geqslant 0$$

Establish the following rules:

a. The loci start from the poles and terminate at the zeros of $G(s)$.

b. The root loci are symmetrical about the real axis.

c. The number of separate loci equals the number of poles or zeros of $G(s)$, whichever number is larger.

d. The asymptotes of the loci approach straight lines whose angles are given by $\theta_i = \pm n\pi/(m-k)$, where n is an odd integer. The asymptotes intersect on the real axis at σ_0 which is determined from

$$\sigma_0 = \frac{\sum^{m} \text{poles} - \sum^{k} \text{zeros}}{m - k}$$

e. The parts of the real axis that comprise sections of the loci are to the left of an odd number of critical frequencies (poles and zeros) of $G(s)$.

f. The angle of departure from a pole p_x is given by

$$\phi_d = \sum_{j=1}^{k} \arg\,(p_x - z_j) - \sum_{\substack{i=1 \\ i \neq x}}^{m} \arg\,(p_x - p_i) \mp 180°$$

---

[12] B. K. Kinariwala and A. Gersho, *Bell System Tech. J.*, **45** (1966), 1153–1155.

g. The angle of arrival at a zero z_x is given by

$$\phi_a = \sum_{i=1}^{m} \arg\,(z_x - p_i) - \sum_{\substack{j=1 \\ j\neq x}}^{k} \arg\,(z_x - z_j) \mp 180^\circ$$

h. The breakaway points are determined by solving

$$\frac{dK}{ds} = \frac{d}{ds}\,[G(s)] = 0$$

i. The intersection of the loci with the imaginary axis is determined by the Routh-Hurwitz test.

Which of these rules do not apply to a distributed-parameter system?

5-2 Determine the key features of the root loci for

$$KG(s) = \frac{K}{(s+1)(s+2)(s+3)}$$

using the conventional lumped network rules and using the general rules developed for distributed networks. In particular, find

a. The breakaway points.
b. The imaginary-axis intercepts.
c. The angle of the asymptotes.
d. The intersection of the asymptotes with the negative real axis.

5-3 For a feedback system with transportation lag, the characteristic equation is given by

$$1 + K\frac{\epsilon^{-0.1s}}{(s+1)(s+2)} = 0$$

Draw the root locus showing the lowest two $j\omega$-axis crossover points. What is the lowest value of K for which the system becomes unstable?

5-4 For the configuration shown, sketch the root-locus of the natural frequencies as the length of $\overline{ULC}$ is varied. The $\overline{URC}$ network has a length d. Indicate the key features in the plot. (Use appropriate normalization.)

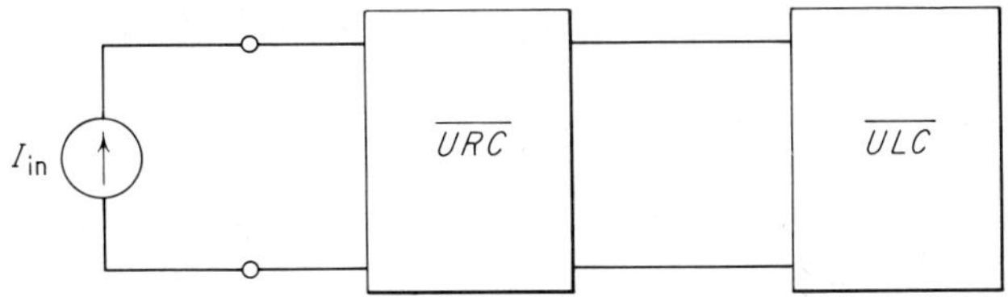

5-5 For the active network shown the amplifier is an ideal voltage controlled voltage source. Let $R = 1\ \Omega$, $C = 10$ fd, where $R = r_c d$ and $C = c_c d$, respectively.

a. For what value of A_0 can an approximate two-pole maximally flat magnitude response be obtained?

b. Can this circuit become unstable by varying the gain constant A_0? If so, what is the smallest value of A_0 for instability?

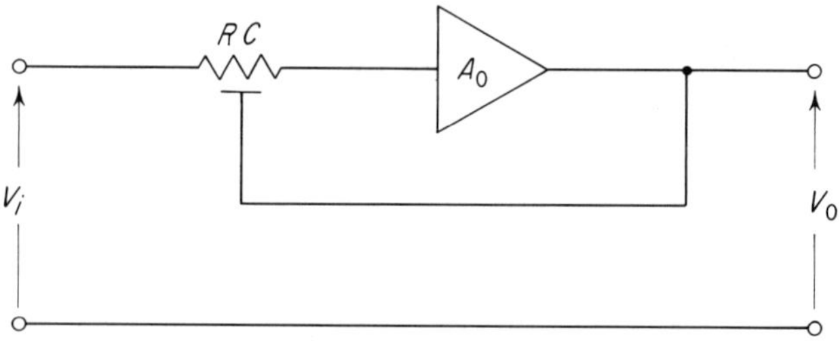

5-6 A $\overline{URC}$ network is bridged by a lumped capacitance C as shown. Given that the parameters are $\theta = \sqrt{s r_0 c_0 d^2}$, $R = r_0 d$, and $C = K c_0 d$, find the network voltage transfer function T_V in terms of r_0, c_0, and θ. Sketch the loci of the zeros of T_V as the parameter K is varied. In particular, determine

a. the positions of the first two breakaway points,

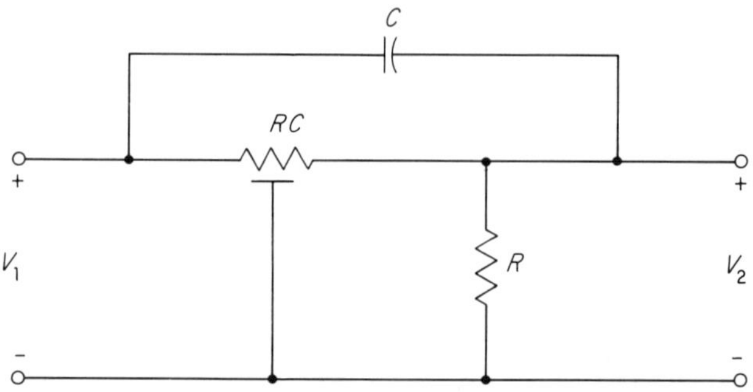

b. the first two pairs of imaginary axis crossovers,

c. the asymptotes of the loci.

Compare these loci with the loci of the network for which $R = \infty$.

5-7 For the active network shown:

a. Determine the values of total resistance ($R = r_0 d$) and total capacitance ($C = c_0 d$) of the URC such that the transmission zero is at $\pm j1$. (Hint: See table on p. 169.)

b. If $C_1 = 0.2$ fd, and the values of part (a) hold, can the system become unstable if the amplifier is an ideal voltage controlled voltage source? If so, what is the smallest value of A_0 for instability?

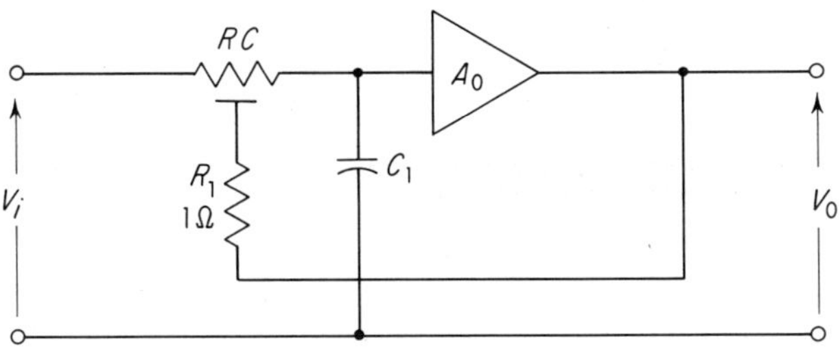

where $K_1 = W_2/W_1$, $K_2 = G_L/g_2$, $g_2 = r_{0_2}d_2$, $\theta_1 = d_1\sqrt{sr_0c_0}$. Determine the approximate rise time and the 3 dB bandwidth of the network for $K_1 = K_2 = 4$ by whatever method you choose.

5-8 Draw the Nyquist diagram and the Bode plot for the system shown in Figure 5-21. Determine the value of K, using the Nyquist plot, that will cause the system to become unstable. Check your results with the Bode plot.

5-9 The characteristic equation of a linear system is given by

$$1 + K\sqrt{sT}\sinh\sqrt{sT}$$

Determine, by Nyquist diagram or Bode plot, the lowest value of K for which the system becomes unstable.

5-10 Establish the stability region given in Figure 5-20.

5-11 For the system shown in Figure 5-17, determine the maximum value of τ for which the system is stable.

CHAPTER

6

Synthesis of Distributed Networks

6-1 Introduction

In this chapter we present elementary synthesis procedures for driving-point and transfer functions using distributed networks. Attention is focused on uniformly distributed networks with emphasis on *RC* distributed networks. This choice is made for simplicity and because distributed *RC* networks are encountered in integrated circuits. Since the complexities involved in multiport synthesis require a background in network synthesis, we limit ourselves to a few basic, simple, and useful techniques.

No background in network synthesis is required to understand this chapter. However, some familiarity with elementary two-element-type synthesis procedures will be of help[1] and we have included here a brief

[1] See, for example, M. Van Valkenberg, *Introduction to Modern Network Synthesis* (New York, Wiley, 1960) or E. S. Kuh and D. O. Pederson, *Principles of Circuit Synthesis* (New York, McGraw-Hill, 1958).

discussion of this topic. We have covered lumped and distributed two-element network synthesis. Transfer function synthesis, utilizing active element and one-port lumped *RC* networks and active distributed *RC* one-port networks, is also discussed. Illustrative synthesis examples are given to reinforce the understanding of the materials covered in each section.

6-2 Realizability of Lumped Passive Driving-Point Functions

In the synthesis of linear passive networks, the concept of positive real (abbreviated as p-r) functions, originated by Otto Brune,[2] plays a fundamental role. Positive real functions are the foundation of passive network synthesis and are defined as functions satisfying the two requirements.

$$\text{Re } W(s) \geqslant 0 \qquad \text{for Re } s \geqslant 0 \tag{6-1}$$

and

$$W(s) \text{ real when } s \text{ is real}$$

where $W(s)$ is a driving-point immittance (impedance and/or admittance) function. A convenient method of testing a function for its p-r character is the so-called *abc* of p-r testing. The *abc* conditions are as follows:

(a) The function is regular in the right-half complex-frequency plane.
(b) Any poles on the $j\omega$ axis must be simple with real and positive residue.
(c) The real part of the function is non-negative on the entire $j\omega$ axis.

Any function that meets *all* of the *abc* conditions is realizable by a network composed of *RLC* elements. For convenience we list some of the important properties of p-r functions in Table 6-1.

We shall not cover here the synthesis of *RLC* driving-point functions. Various methods exist for general *RLC* driving-point synthesis; the interested reader may refer to the ample references on this subject.[3] However, we shall consider the synthesis of two-element one-port networks, such as *RC* and *LC* networks, briefly in the next section, since these methods can also be extended in distributed *RC* network synthesis via appropriate transformations. Moreover *RC* one-ports and practical amplifiers can also be used in the synthesis of transfer functions for integrated circuits.

---

[2] O. Brune, *J. Math. Phys.*, **10** (1931), 191–236.

[3] Van Valkenberg (Ref. 1); also N. Balabanian, *Network Synthesis* (Prentice-Hall, Englewood Cliffs, N. J., 1958).

Table 6-1 PROPERTIES OF POSITIVE REAL FUNCTIONS

1. For lumped networks, the driving-point immittance function is rational.

2. The coefficients of the numerator and denominator polynomials in $W(s) = P(s)/Q(s)$ are real and positive. As a consequence of this,
   a. Complex poles and zeros of $W(s)$ occur in conjugate pairs.
   b. $W(s)$ is real when s is real.
   c. The scale factor $W(0) = a_0/b_0$ is real and positive.

3. The poles and zeros of $W(s)$ have nonpositive real parts.

4. The degrees of the numerator and denominator polynomials in $W(s)$ differ at most by unity.

5. Poles of $W(s)$ on the $j\omega$ axis must be simple with real positive residue.

6. The exponent of the lowest power of s in the numerator and denominator polynomial of $W(s)$ can differ at most by unity.

7. At real frequencies ($s = j\omega$) the real part of $W(s)$ is an even function of ω and the imaginary part is an odd function of ω.

6-3 Synthesis of Two-Element One-Port Lumped Networks

When the driving-point immittance function is restricted to be of the two-element kind, considerable simplification results in the synthesis. We shall first consider the case of LC one-ports and then consider RC and RL one-port networks. We omit the proofs, since they can be found in almost all of the textbooks referenced in this chapter.

***LC* one-port network synthesis.** The necessary and sufficient conditions for $W(s)$ to be the driving point immittance of an LC network are the following:

All poles of $W(s)$
(a) lie on the $j\omega$ axis
(b) are simple
(c) have real positive residues **(6-2)**

The properties of LC one-port networks are listed in Table 6-2. An LC driving-point immittance function can be expressed as

$$W_{LC}(s) = K \frac{(s^2 + \omega_1{}^2)(s^2 + \omega_3{}^2) \cdots (s^2 + \omega_{2n+1}{}^2)}{s(s^2 + \omega_2{}^2)(s^2 + \omega_4{}^2) \cdots (s^2 + \omega_{2n}{}^2)} \tag{6-3}$$

Table 6-2 PROPERTIES OF LC ONE-PORT NETWORKS

1. The immittance $W(s)$ is an odd rational function.

2. The real part of $W(j\omega)$ equals zero.

3. The slope of the reactance function $dX/d\omega$ is always non-negative [where $W(j\omega) = jX(\omega)$]. In fact,

$$\frac{dX}{d\omega} \geqslant \left|\frac{X}{\omega}\right|$$

4. Poles and zeros of $W(s)$ are on the $j\omega$ axis. They alternate and the poles have positive real residues.

5. $W(s)$ is realizable in two Foster forms and two Cauer forms, with the minimum number of elements equal to the highest power of s.

6. $W(s)$ must have a pole or a zero at the origin and at infinity.

By expanding Equation (6-3) in partial fractions we obtain the following expressions for $Z(s)$ and $Y(s)$:

$$Z_{LC}(s) = K_\infty s + \frac{K_0}{s} + \sum_i^N \frac{2K_i s}{(s^2 + \omega_i^2)} \tag{6-4}$$

$$Y_{LC}(s) = H_\infty s + \frac{H_0}{s} + \sum_j^N \frac{2H_j s}{(s^2 + \omega_j^2)} \tag{6-5}$$

where all the K's and H's are non-negative constants. The synthesis of Equations (6-4) and (6-5) are obvious from Figure 6-1(a) and (b). A network element or a pair of elements can be associated with each term in Equation (6-4) or (6-5). This leads directly to the two Foster canonical forms shown in Figure 6-2.

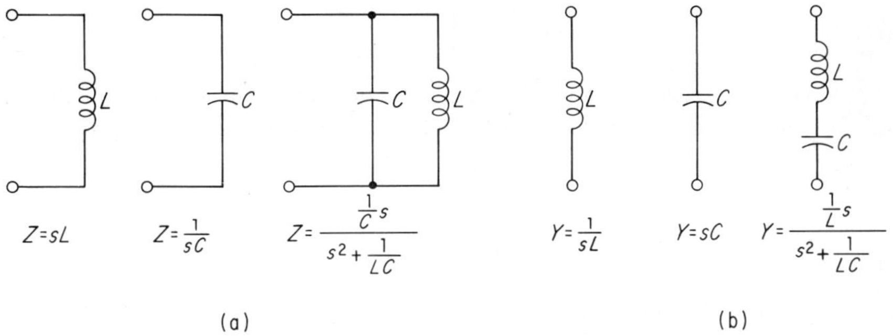

Figure 6-1

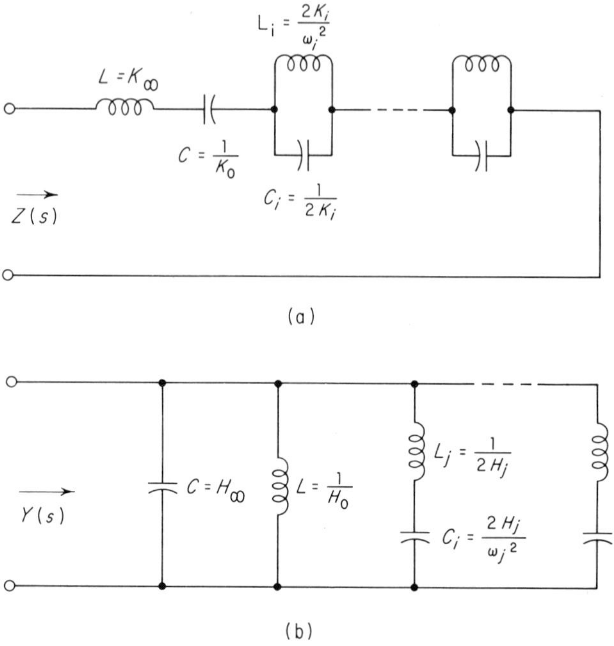

Figure 6-2 **(a)** Foster's first canonical form. **(b)** Foster's second canonical form.

Example 1

Let

$$Z(s) = \frac{s(s^2+4)(s^2+16)}{(s^2+1)(s^2+9)}$$

To obtain the first Foster canonical form we expand $Z(s)$ into a partial fraction expansion

$$Z(s) = s + \frac{45}{8}\frac{s}{s^2+1} + \frac{35}{8}\frac{s}{s^2+9}$$

The realization is shown in Figure 6-3(a). To obtain the second Foster canonical form we expand $Y(s)$ into a partial fraction expansion

$$Y(s) = \frac{1}{Z(s)} = \frac{9}{64}\frac{1}{s} + \frac{5}{16}\frac{s}{s^2+4} + \frac{35}{64}\frac{s}{s^2+16}$$

The realization is shown in Figure 6-3(b).

The Cauer canonical forms are obtained through continued division. This method of realization leads to low-pass and high-pass ladders shown in Figure 6-4(a) and (b), respectively. Notice that the input impedance of the network shown in Figure 6-4(a) can be expressed as

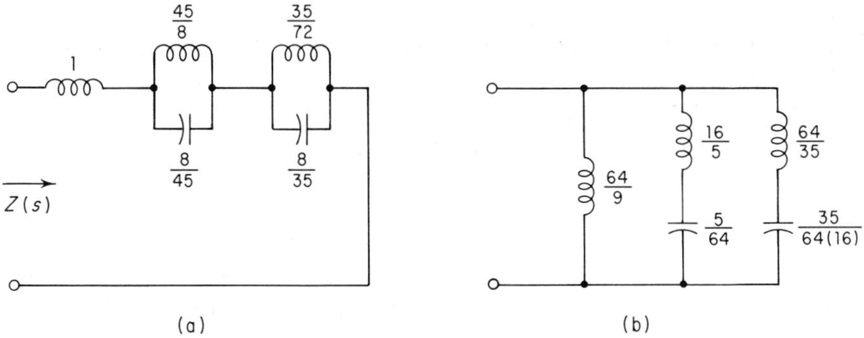

Figure 6-3 **(a)** First and **(b)** second Foster form.

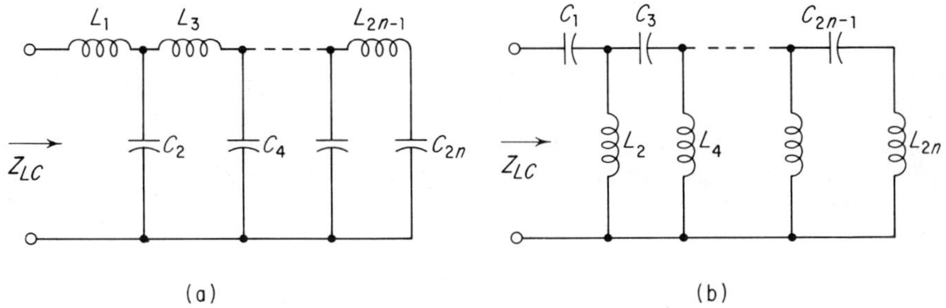

Figure 6-4 **(a)** First and **(b)** second Cauer form.

$$Z_{LC}(s) = L_1 s + \cfrac{1}{C_2 s + \cfrac{1}{L_3 s + \cfrac{1}{\ddots \, C_n s}}} \tag{6-6}$$

and that of Figure 6-4(b) can be expressed as

$$Z_{LC}(s) = \frac{1}{C_1 s} + \cfrac{1}{\cfrac{1}{L_2 s} + \cfrac{1}{\cfrac{1}{C_3 s} + \cfrac{1}{\ddots \, \cfrac{1}{L_n s}}}} \tag{6-7}$$

Since Equations (6-6) and (6-7) are finite continued fractions, the realization method is sometimes called a continued-fraction expansion.

To obtain the realization of Z_{LC} in the first Cauer form, arrange the numerator and denominator polynomials in descending order. Perform the continued division and assign the quotient of the divisions as branch immittances of the ladder network; see Figure 6-4(a). If the degree of the numerator of Z_{LC} is less than the degree of the denominator, there is no series inductance; therefore, start with Y_{LC}.

To obtain the realization of Z_{LC} in the second Cauer form, arrange the numerator and denominator polynomials in ascending order. Perform the continued division and assign the quotient of the divisions as branch immittances of the ladder network; see Figure 6-4(b). If the degree of the numerator of Z_{LC} is larger than the degree of the denominator, there is no series capacitance; therefore, start with Y_{LC}.

Example 2

Let

$$Z(s) = \frac{s(s^2+4)(s^2+16)}{(s^2+1)(s^2+9)} = \frac{s^5+20s^3+64s}{s^4+10s^2+9} \tag{6-8}$$

To obtain the first Cauer form we apply continued division on Z_{LC}, since the degree of the numerator of Z_{LC} is higher than the degree of the denominator.

$$\begin{array}{lll}
s^4+10s^2+9 \,\big)\, s^5+20s^3+64s & 1s & \leftarrow L \\
\quad s^5+10s^3+9s & & \\
10s^3+55s \,\big)\, s^4+10s^2+9 & 0.1s & \leftarrow C \\
\quad s^4+5.5s^2 & & \\
4.5s^2+9 \,\big)\, 10s^3+55s & 2.222s & \leftarrow L \\
\quad 10s^3+20s & & \\
35s \,\big)\, 4.5s^2+9 & 0.128s & \leftarrow C \\
\quad 4.5s^2 & & \\
9 \,\big)\, 35s & 3.89s & \leftarrow L \\
\quad 35s & & \\
\quad 0 & &
\end{array}$$

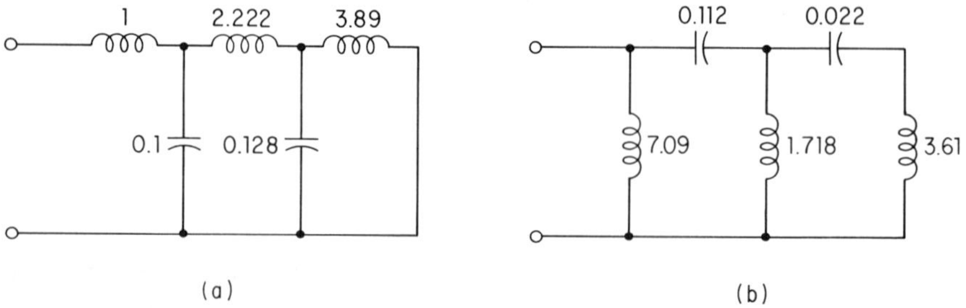

Figure 6-5 **(a)** First and **(b)** second Cauer form.

The realization is shown in Figure 6-5(a).

To obtain the second Cauer form, we arrange the numerator and denominator polynomials of Z_{LC} in ascending order. However, since the degree of the numerator of Z_{LC} is larger than the degree of the denominator, there is no series capacitance and we omit the first step and thus start with Y_{LC}.

$$
\begin{array}{l}
64s+20s^3+s^5\,\overline{)\,9+10s^2+s^4} \qquad 0.141\frac{1}{s} \leftarrow \frac{1}{L}\\
\qquad\quad \underline{9+2.80s^2+0.14s^4}\\
\qquad\quad 7.20s^2+0.86s^4\,\overline{)\,64s+20s^3+s^5} \qquad 8.90\frac{1}{s} \leftarrow \frac{1}{C}\\
\qquad\qquad\qquad\qquad \underline{64s+7.67s^3}\\
\qquad\qquad\qquad\qquad 12.33s^3+s^5\,\overline{)\,7.20s^2+0.86s^4} \qquad 0.582\frac{1}{s} \leftarrow \frac{1}{L}\\
\qquad\qquad\qquad\qquad\qquad\qquad \underline{7.20s^2+0.583s^4}\\
\qquad\qquad\qquad\qquad\qquad\qquad 0.277s^4\,\overline{)\,12.33s^3+s^5} \qquad 44.5\frac{1}{s} \leftarrow \frac{1}{C}\\
\qquad\qquad\qquad\qquad\qquad\qquad\qquad\quad \underline{12.33s^3}\\
\qquad\qquad\qquad\qquad\qquad\qquad\qquad\quad s^5\,\overline{)\,0.277s^4} \qquad 0.277\frac{1}{s} \leftarrow \frac{1}{L}\\
\qquad\qquad\qquad\qquad\qquad\qquad\qquad\qquad \underline{0.277s^4}\\
\qquad\qquad\qquad\qquad\qquad\qquad\qquad\qquad 0
\end{array}
$$

The realization is shown in Figure 6-5(b).

We can obtain other canonical forms of realization by using a combination of both the Foster and Cauer forms. These are known as mixed forms; for example, in Figure 6-4(a), instead of L's and C's we can have series LC and shunt LC elements, and so forth. Nonseries parallel realization different from the Foster and Cauer forms is also possible,[4] as shown in Figure 6-6.

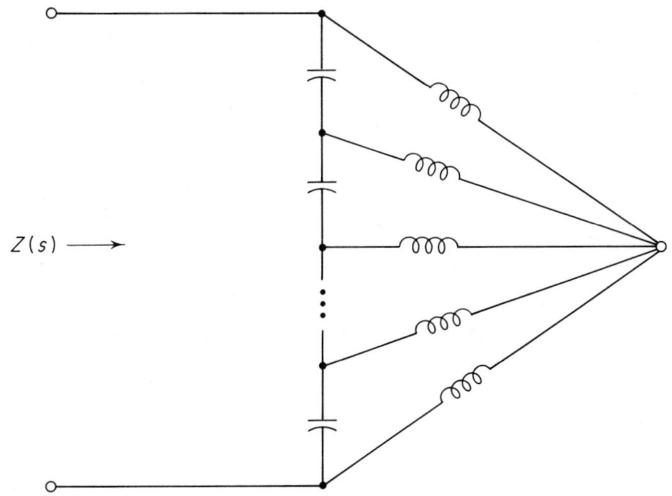

Figure 6-6 A nonseries-parallel realization.

[4] H. B. Lee, *IEEE Trans. Circuit Theory,* **CT-10** (1963), 81–85; also H. B. Lee, *IEEE Trans. Circuit Theory,* **CT-11** (1964), 313–315.

This realization contains one more than the minimum number of circuit elements and thus it is not canonic. The superfluous circuit element may be used to obtain a better desensitivity in the network function.

Note that if $Z_{LC}(s)$ is not given in a factored form it is often more convenient to use a realization in the Cauer forms rather than in the Foster forms.

RC and RL one-port network synthesis. Since many of the properties of RC and RL networks are very similar, we shall mainly consider RC synthesis and the reader can easily apply the methods to RL synthesis.

The results of LC synthesis can readily be applied to RC or RL synthesis by the use of Cauer transformation $s = p^2$, as given by Equations (1-61), (1-62), and (1-63). For RC networks the transformation is illustrated in Figure 6-7.

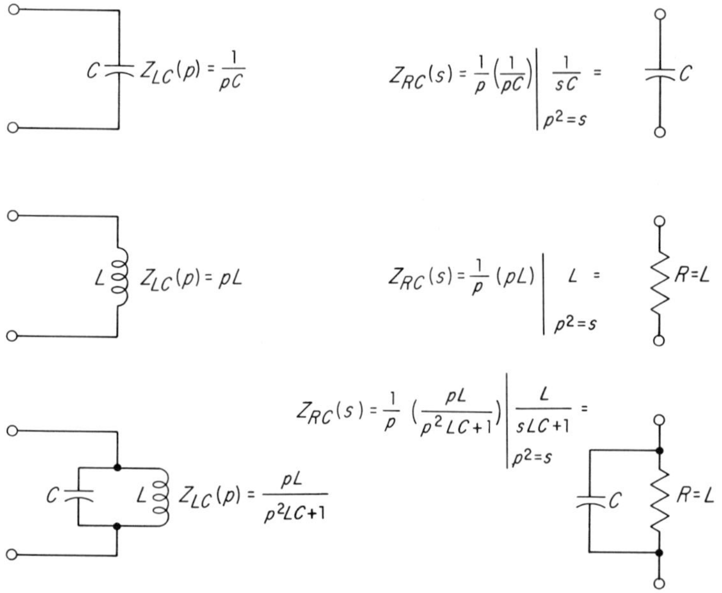

Figure 6-7 Transformation of LC networks into RC networks, for

$$Z_{RC}(s) = \frac{1}{p} Z_{LC}(p)\Big|_{p^2 = s}$$

In order to gain some insight into RC synthesis we consider briefly the topic of RC synthesis by itself in the following discussion.

The necessary and sufficient conditions for $W(s)$ to be the driving-point immittance of an RC or RL network are given in Table 6-3.

Table 6-3 NECESSARY AND SUFFICIENT CONDITIONS FOR $W(s)$

$W = Z_{RC}, Y_{RL}$	$W = Y_{RC}, Z_{RL}$
(a) All poles of $W(s)$ are simple and restricted to the σ axis.	(a) Same.
(b) Residues of $W(s)$ at all poles are real and positive.	(b) Residues of $W(s)/s$ at all poles are real and positive.
(c) No poles of $W(s)$ at infinity.	(c) No poles of $W(s)$ at the origin.

The properties of RC and RL one-port networks are listed in Table 6-4. The driving-point impedance and admittance functions of an RC one-port network can be always expressed in a partial fraction expansion

Table 6-4 PROPERTIES OF RC AND RL ONE-PORT NETWORKS

$Z_{RC} \longleftrightarrow Y_{RL}$	$Y_{RC} \longleftrightarrow Z_{RL}$
(a) All poles and zeros lie on negative σ axis and are simple.	(a) Same.
(b) Poles and zeros interlace.	(b) Same.
(c) The lowest critical frequency is a pole which may be at $s = 0$.	(c) The lowest critical frequency is a zero which may be at $s = 0$.
(d) The highest critical frequency is a zero which may be at $s = \infty$.	(d) The highest critical frequency is a pole which may be at $s = \infty$.
(e) The slopes $\left.\frac{dZ}{d\sigma}\right\|_{RC}$, and $\left.\frac{dY}{d\sigma}\right\|_{RL}$ are always negative.	(e) The slope $\left.\frac{dY}{d\sigma}\right\|_{RC}$ and $\left.\frac{dZ}{d\sigma}\right\|_{RL}$ are always positive.
(f) $Z_{RC}(0) > Z_{RC}(\infty), Z_{RL}(\infty) > Z_{RL}(0)$.	(f) $Y_{RC}(\infty) > Y_{RC}(0), Z_{RL}(\infty) > Z_{RL}(0)$.
(g) The minima of Re $Z_{RC}(j\omega)$ and of Re $Y_{RL}(j\omega)$ occur at $\omega = \infty$.	(g) The minima of Re $Y_{RC}(j\omega)$ and Re $Z_{RL}(j\omega)$ occur at $\omega = 0$.
(h) The maxima of Re $Z_{RC}(j\omega)$ and of Re $Y_{RL}(j\omega)$ occur at $\omega = 0$.	(h) The maxima of Re $Y_{RC}(j\omega)$ and Re $Z_{RL}(j\omega)$ occur at $\omega = \infty$.
(i) Im Z_{RC} and Im Y_{RL} are never positive.	(i) Im Y_{RC} and Im Z_{RL} are never negative.
(j) The minimum number of elements in a realization is equal to the number of finite nonzero critical frequencies plus one.	(j) Same.

as

$$Z_{RC}(s) = K_\infty + \frac{K_0}{s} + \sum_i^N \frac{K_i}{s+\sigma_i} \tag{6-9}$$

$$Y_{RC}(s) = H_0 + H_\infty s + \sum_j^N \frac{H_j s}{s+\sigma_j} \tag{6-10}$$

where all the K's, H's, and σ's are real, positive constants. The synthesis of Equations (6-9) and (6-10) are obvious from a glance at Figure 6-8(a)

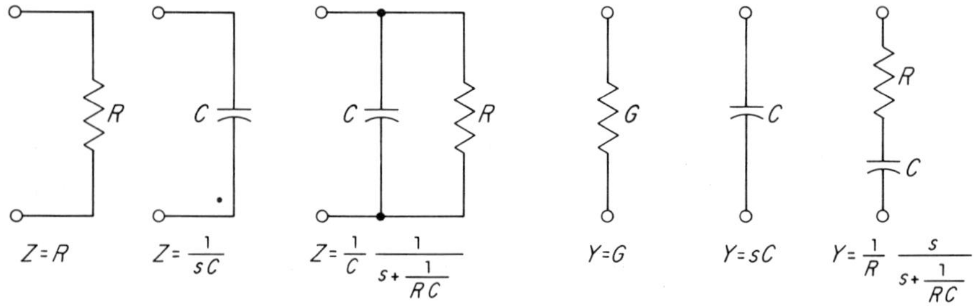

Figure 6-8

and (b), respectively, in which it is shown how a network element or a pair of elements can be associated with each term in Equations (6-9) and (6-10). Hence, a partial fraction expansion of $Z_{RC}(s)$ and $Y_{RC}(s)/s$ yields the two Foster forms, since all the residues are real and positive. The two Foster forms are shown in Figure 6-9.

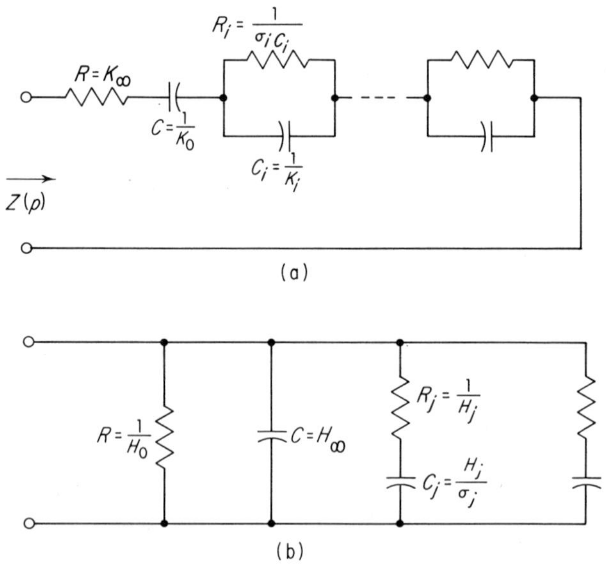

Figure 6-9 **(a)** Foster's first form. **(b)** Foster's second form.

Example 3

Let
$$Z(s) = \frac{(s+2)(s+4)}{(s+1)(s+3)}$$

To obtain the first Foster canonical RC network, we expand $Z(s)$ into partial fraction expansion:

$$Z(s) = \frac{(s+2)(s+4)}{(s+1)(s+3)} = 1 + \frac{\frac{3}{2}}{s+1} + \frac{\frac{1}{2}}{s+3}$$

The realization is shown in Figure 6-10(a).

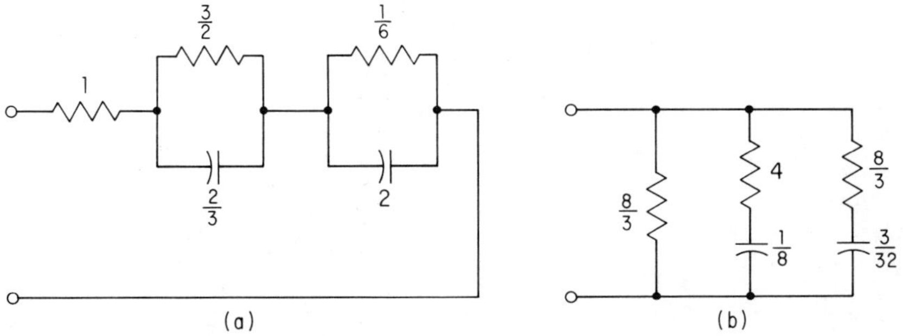

Figure 6-10 **(a)** First and **(b)** second Foster form.

To obtain the second Foster form, we expand $Y_{RC}(s)/s$ in a partial fraction expansion. Note that a partial fraction expansion of $Y_{RC}(s)$ does not lead to a physical realization because of the resulting negative residues. For $Y_{RC}(s)/s$ the residues are positive and, from Equation (6-10), realization is achieved; thus,

$$\frac{1}{s}Y(s) = \frac{1}{s}\,\frac{(s+1)(s+3)}{(s+2)(s+4)} = \frac{\frac{3}{8}}{s} + \frac{\frac{1}{4}}{s+2} + \frac{\frac{3}{8}}{s+4}$$

Hence,
$$Y(s) = \frac{3}{8} + \frac{1}{4}\,\frac{s}{s+2} + \frac{3}{8}\,\frac{s}{s+4}$$

The realization is shown in Figure 6-10(b).

The two Cauer forms of realization are shown in Figure 6-11. The

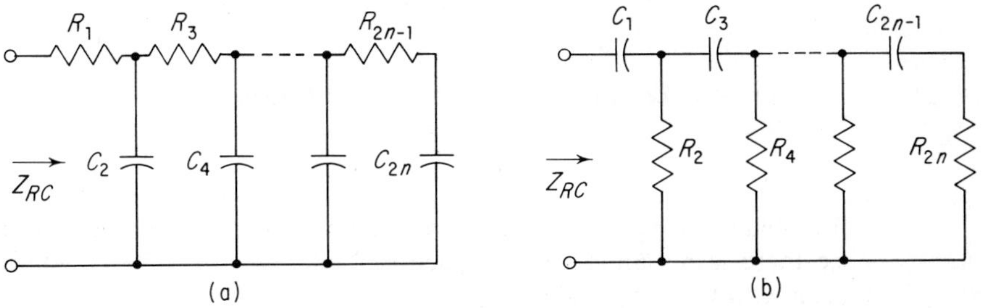

Figure 6-11 **(a)** First and **(b)** second Cauer form.

method of obtaining the Cauer forms is identical to the one discussed for LC networks, and is not repeated here. An example illustrates the procedure.

Example 4

Consider the driving-point impedance function of the previous example:

$$Z(s) = \frac{s^2 + 6s + 8}{s^2 + 4s + 3}$$

To obtain the first Cauer form perform the continued division

$$\begin{array}{l}
s^2+4s+3\,\big)\,s^2+6s+8\,\big(\,1 \leftarrow R \\
\qquad\qquad\quad\; \underline{s^2+4s+3} \\
\qquad\qquad\qquad 2s+5\,\big)\,s^2+4s+3\,\big(\,\tfrac{1}{2}s \leftarrow C \\
\qquad\qquad\qquad\qquad\quad \underline{s^2+\tfrac{5}{2}s} \\
\qquad\qquad\qquad\qquad\quad \tfrac{3}{2}s+3\,\big)\,2s+5\,\big(\,\tfrac{4}{3} \leftarrow R \\
\qquad\qquad\qquad\qquad\qquad\qquad\quad \underline{2s+4} \\
\qquad\qquad\qquad\qquad\qquad\qquad\qquad 1\,\big)\,\tfrac{3}{2}s+3\,\big(\,\tfrac{3}{2}s \leftarrow C \\
\qquad\qquad\qquad\qquad\qquad\qquad\qquad\quad \underline{\tfrac{3}{2}s} \\
\qquad\qquad\qquad\qquad\qquad\qquad\qquad\qquad 3\,\big)\,1\,\big(\,\tfrac{1}{3} \leftarrow R \\
\qquad\qquad\qquad\qquad\qquad\qquad\qquad\qquad\qquad \underline{1} \\
\qquad\qquad\qquad\qquad\qquad\qquad\qquad\qquad\qquad 0
\end{array}$$

The realization is shown in Figure 6-12(a).

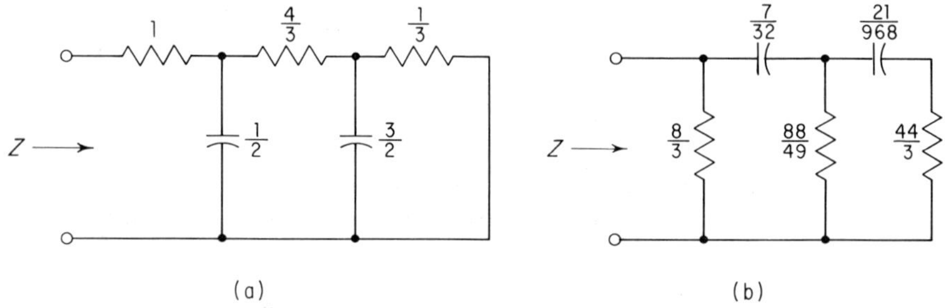

Figure 6-12 (a) First and (b) second Cauer form.

To obtain the second Cauer form we note that $Z(0)$ is not infinite, hence there is no initial series capacitor. Thus, we begin the continued division with the second step, $Y(s)$.

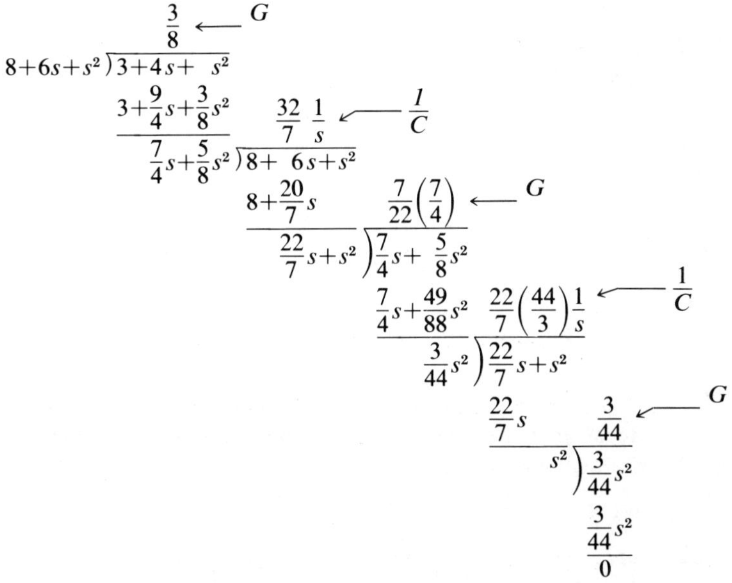

The realization is shown in Figure 6-12(b). Again, as in the case of *LC* networks, other canonical forms for *RC* networks are also possible.

The reader now readily recognizes that the synthesis steps for *RL* networks are identical to those of *RC* synthesis. An example illustrates the procedure.

Example 5

$$Z(s) = \frac{s(s+2)(s+4)}{(s+1)(s+3)}$$

To obtain the first Foster form we expand $Z_{RL}(s)/s$. Note that a partial fraction expansion of $Z_{RL}(s)$ does not lead to a physical realization because of the resulting negative residues. For $Z_{RL}(s)/s$ the residues are always positive; thus,

Let
$$\frac{Z(s)}{s} = \frac{s(s+2)(s+4)}{s(s+1)(s+3)} = 1 + \frac{3}{2}\frac{1}{s+1} + \frac{1}{2}\frac{1}{s+3}$$

and
$$Z(s) = s + \frac{3}{2}\frac{s}{s+1} + \frac{1}{2}\frac{s}{s+3}$$

The realization is shown in Figure 6-13(a).

To obtain the second Foster form we expand $Y_{RL}(s)$

$$Y(s) = \frac{(s+1)(s+3)}{s(s+2)(s+4)} = \frac{\frac{3}{8}}{s} + \frac{\frac{1}{4}}{s+2} + \frac{\frac{3}{8}}{s+4}$$

The realization is shown in Figure 6-13(b).

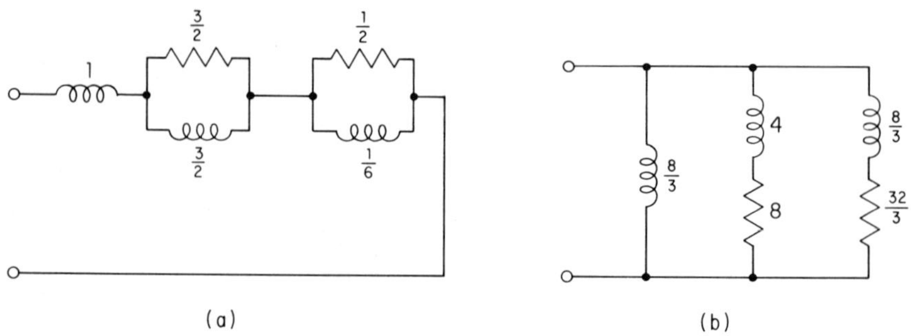

Figure 6-13 **(a)** First and **(b)** second Foster form.

The two Cauer forms for RL networks are shown in Figure 6-14. Recall that the first form is a low-pass structure, while the second form is a high-pass structure.

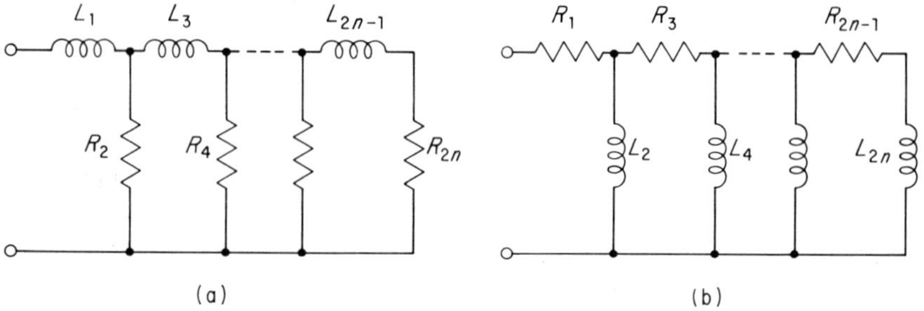

Figure 6-14 **(a)** First and **(b)** second Cauer form.

To obtain the first Cauer form we begin with continued division

$$
\begin{array}{l}
s^2+4s+3\,\overline{)\,s^3+6s^2+8s\,}\quad 1s \leftarrow L \\
\qquad\quad \underline{s^3+4s^2+3s} \\
\qquad\quad 2s^2+5s\,\overline{)\,s^2+4s+3\,}\quad \tfrac{1}{2} \leftarrow G \\
\qquad\qquad\quad \underline{s^2+\tfrac{5}{2}s} \\
\qquad\qquad\quad \tfrac{3}{2}s+3\,\overline{)\,2s^2+5s\,}\quad \tfrac{4}{3}s \leftarrow L \\
\qquad\qquad\qquad\quad \underline{2s^2+4s} \\
\qquad\qquad\qquad\quad s\,\overline{)\,\tfrac{3}{2}s+3\,}\quad \tfrac{3}{2} \leftarrow G \\
\qquad\qquad\qquad\qquad \underline{\tfrac{3}{2}s} \\
\qquad\qquad\qquad\qquad 3\,\overline{)\,s\,}\quad \tfrac{1}{3}s \leftarrow L \\
\qquad\qquad\qquad\qquad\quad \underline{s} \\
\qquad\qquad\qquad\qquad\quad 0
\end{array}
$$

The realization is shown in Figure 6-15(a).

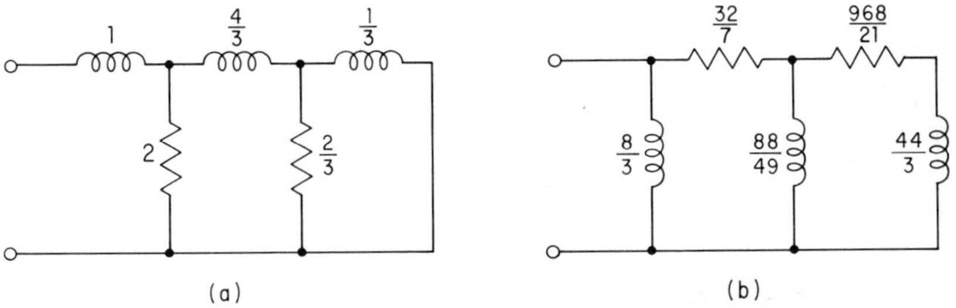

Figure 6-15 **(a)** First and **(b)** second Cauer form.

To obtain the second Cauer form, we note that $Z(0)$ is equal to zero, hence the first series resistance is missing. We therefore start the continued division with $Y(s)$.

$$8s+6s^2+s^3 \,\overline{\big)\, 3+4s+s^2} \qquad \frac{3}{8}\left(\frac{1}{s}\right) \longleftarrow \frac{1}{L}$$

$$\frac{3+\frac{9}{4}s+\frac{3}{8}s^2}{\frac{7}{4}s+\frac{5}{8}s^2} \,\overline{\big)\, 8s+6s^2+s^3} \qquad 8\left(\frac{4}{7}\right) \longleftarrow R$$

$$\frac{8s+\frac{20}{7}s^2}{\frac{22}{7}s^2+s^3} \,\overline{\big)\, \frac{7}{4}s+\frac{5}{8}s^2} \qquad \left(\frac{7}{4}\right)\left(\frac{7}{22}\right)\frac{1}{s} \longleftarrow \frac{1}{L}$$

$$\frac{\frac{7}{4}s+\frac{49}{88}s^2}{\frac{3}{44}s^2} \,\overline{\big)\, \frac{22}{7}s^2+s^3} \qquad \left(\frac{44}{3}\right)\frac{22}{7} \longleftarrow R$$

$$\frac{\frac{22}{7}s^2}{s^3} \,\overline{\big)\, \frac{3}{44}s^2} \qquad \frac{3}{44}\frac{1}{s} \longleftarrow \frac{1}{L}$$

$$\frac{\frac{3}{44}s^2}{0}$$

The realization is shown in Figure 6-15(b).

Finally, in passing it should be noted that the method of two-element network synthesis can also be readily applied to special situations of *RLC* driving-point functions. The special situation may have either the series or the parallel form, as shown in Figure 6-16. Problems of this nature are given as exercises at the end of this chapter and should pose no difficulty.

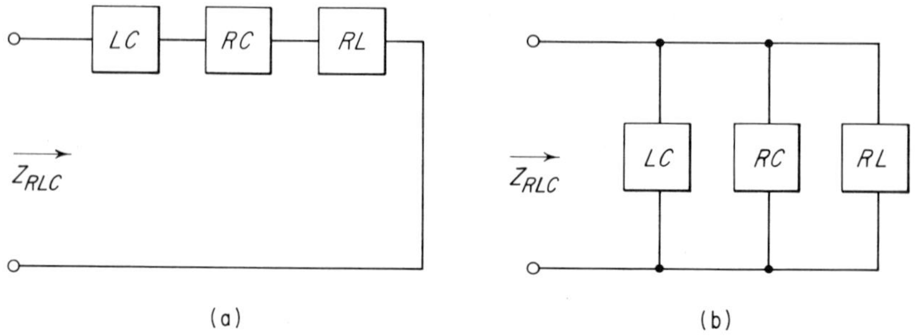

Figure 6-16 (a) Series and (b) shunt RLC network.

6-4 Driving-Point Synthesis of Resistive Uniform-Transmission-Line Networks

In the case of lumped networks, the network functions are defined by rational functions of the complex frequency variable. Further, it is well known that the positive real condition Equation (6-1), is the necessary and sufficient condition for driving-point-immittance realization. When distributed elements are present, the network functions involve transcendental functions of the complex variable, as we have seen in the previous chapters. For a certain class of distributed networks the methods and techniques of lumped network synthesis can be applied under an appropriate transformation of the frequency variable. For example, consider the uniform lossless transmission lines of equal electrical length, $d\sqrt{lc}$. Note that electrical length is not the same as the physical length d of the line. The electrical length derives its name from the common usage and reference to the fractions of the wavelength. From Equation (1-20) and Table 1-1 for the uniform lossless line, the open-circuit and short-circuit driving-point impedances are given by

$$Z_{oc}\Big|_{LC} = z_{11} = \sqrt{\frac{l}{c}}\coth sd\sqrt{lc} = Z_0 \coth \frac{s}{\Omega_0} \tag{6-11}$$

$$Z_{sc}\Big|_{LC} = \frac{1}{y_{11}} = \sqrt{\frac{l}{c}}\tanh sd\sqrt{lc} = Z_0 \tanh \frac{s}{\Omega_0} \tag{6-12}$$

where $Z_0 \equiv \sqrt{l/c}$ and $\Omega_0^{-1} \equiv d\sqrt{lc}$ are the characteristic impedance and the electrical length of the line, respectively.

If we employ Richards' transformation,[5] that is, if we introduce a new frequency variable

[5] P. I. Richards, *Proc. IRE,* **30** (1948), 217–220.

$$\lambda = \tanh \frac{s}{\Omega_0} = \frac{\epsilon^{2s/\Omega_0} - 1}{\epsilon^{2s/\Omega_0} + 1} \tag{6-13}$$

Then Equations (6-11) and (6-12) upon substitution of (6-13) reduce to

$$Z_{oc} = \frac{Z_0}{\lambda} \tag{6-14}$$

$$Z_{sc} = Z_0\lambda \tag{6-15}$$

Note that Equations (6-14) and (6-15) are of the same form as the impedances of a capacitor and an inductor, respectively, in the new frequency variable λ. Moreover, the restriction that the line's electrical length be *commensurate* insures that only terms of the form $(\epsilon^{2s/\Omega_0})^n$ will appear, where n is an integer. Hence, $Z(s)$ is a rational function of ϵ^{2s/Ω_0}. But

$$\epsilon^{2s/\Omega_0} = \frac{1+\lambda}{1-\lambda}$$

hence, $Z(\lambda)$ is a rational function of λ. Thus, Brune's necessary and sufficient conditions apply to networks of resistors and uniform transmission lines of commensurate length. Thus, $Z(\lambda)$ must be a p-r function in the λ plane. It follows then that networks composed of commensurate lines and of resistors may be treated as lumped-parameter networks in the λ-plane. Thus many techniques and results of lumped-parameter network synthesis can be carried over in the design of this class of distributed networks. It should be noted, however, that when the actual frequency ω is considered, $\lambda = j\tan(\omega/\Omega_0)$ is a periodic function. Therefore, the characteristic of the network is also a periodic function of ω.

If the structure is restricted to have only uniformly distributed lossless lines and no resistors, then it is obvious, at least formally, that the lumped synthesis of two-element *LC*, discussed in Section 6-2, can be used. From the practical viewpoint, it is usually desirable to have a cascaded structure rather than a series or parallel configuration. Often a resistive termination may also be specified. Interested readers are referred to a paper by Ozaki and Ishii.[6] A recent paper by Kinariwala[7] extends the methods to include lossless transmission lines of arbitrary electrical length.

We shall next consider in some detail the synthesis of uniformly distributed *RC* networks. This topic is useful in the design of integrated circuits.

---

[6] H. Ozaki and J. Ishii, *IRE Trans. Circuit Theory,* **CT-2** (1955), 325–336.

[7] B. K. Kinariwala, *Bell System Tech. J.,* **45** (1966), 631–651.

6-5 Synthesis of Uniformly Distributed *RC* Driving-Point Functions

Consider the uniformly distributed *RC* network shown in Figure 6-17. The two-port open-circuit impedance parameters and the short-circuit admittance parameters of this network, from Equations (1-17) and (1-18), with $\Gamma = d\sqrt{sr_0c_0}$ and $Z_0 = \sqrt{r_0/c_0s}$, are

$$[Z] = \begin{bmatrix} \dfrac{r_0}{\sqrt{sr_0c_0}} \coth d\sqrt{sr_0c_0} & \dfrac{r_0}{\sqrt{sr_0c_0}} \operatorname{csch} d\sqrt{sr_0c_0} \\ \dfrac{r_0}{\sqrt{sr_0c_0}} \operatorname{csch} d\sqrt{sr_0c_0} & \dfrac{r_0}{\sqrt{sr_0c_0}} \coth d\sqrt{sr_0c_0} \end{bmatrix} \tag{6-16}$$

$$[Y] = \begin{bmatrix} \dfrac{\sqrt{sr_0c_0}}{r_0} \coth d\sqrt{sr_0c_0} & -\dfrac{\sqrt{sr_0c_0}}{r_0} \operatorname{csch} d\sqrt{sr_0c_0} \\ -\dfrac{\sqrt{sr_0c_0}}{r_0} \operatorname{csch} d\sqrt{sr_0c_0} & \dfrac{\sqrt{sr_0c_0}}{r_0} \coth d\sqrt{sr_0c_0} \end{bmatrix} \tag{6-17}$$

From Equations (6-16) and (6-17), the open-circuit and short-circuit driving-point impedances of the network are

$$Z_{oc}\Big|_{\overline{RC}} = z_{11} = \frac{r_0}{\sqrt{sr_0c_0}} \coth d\sqrt{sr_0c_0} \tag{6-18}$$

$$Z_{sc}\Big|_{\overline{RC}} = \frac{1}{y_{11}} = \frac{r_0}{\sqrt{sr_0c_0}} \tanh d\sqrt{sr_0c_0} \tag{6-19}$$

The network representation for Equations (6-18) and (6-19) are shown in Figure 6-18.

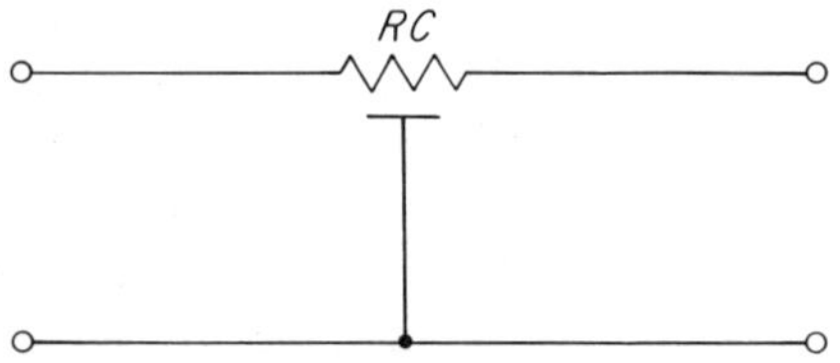

Figure 6-17 Uniformly distributed network.

Two other one-port configurations that can be obtained from Figure 6-17 are shown in Figure 6-19 with their corresponding one-port impedances. We shall consider here only the one-port configurations in Figure 6-18. (Those in Figure 6-19 are used exclusively in Sections 6-7 through 6-10.) However, note the equivalency of the expressions for Figure 6-18 with that of Figure 6-19, the only difference being in the time constants.

A transformation that is very useful for the synthesis of distributed

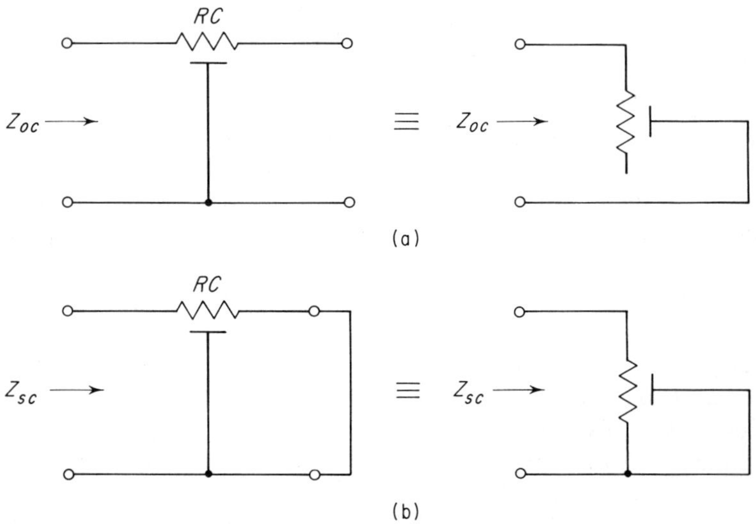

Figure 6-18 Network representations for (**a**) open-circuited and (**b**) short-circuited $\overline{URC}$.

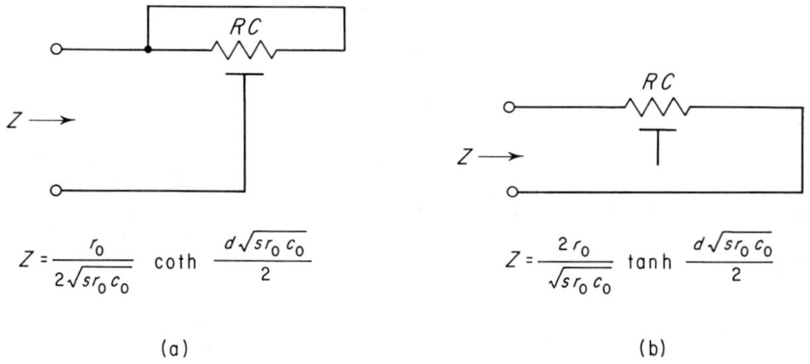

Figure 6-19

RC networks is a variation of Richard's transformation, as follows:

$$\Lambda = \tanh a\sqrt{s} \tag{6-20}$$

where $a = \sqrt{r_0 c_0 d^2} = \sqrt{RC} =$ a constant.[8]

From Equations (6-18), (6-19), and (6-20) we obtain the following:

$$\sqrt{s}\, Z_{oc}\Big|_{\overline{RC}} = \sqrt{\frac{r_0}{c_0}}\,\frac{1}{\Lambda} \tag{6-21}$$

[8] A. Tachibana, *J. Inst. Electron. Commun. Eng. (Japan),* **46** (1963), 55–59, May 1963; also R. W. Wyndrum, Jr., Tech. Rep. 400–76, New York University, May 1963.

$$\sqrt{s}\, Z_{sc}\Big|_{\overline{RC}} = \sqrt{\frac{r_0}{c_0}}\, \Lambda \tag{6-22}$$

Equations (6-21) and (6-22) are readily recognized to be the driving-point impedance of a lumped capacitance and inductance, respectively, in the Λ plane. Hence the lumped synthesis procedure of two-element LC, as discussed in Section 6-3, can be directly applied to any structure consisting only of one-port $Z_{oc}|_{\overline{RC}}$ and $Z_{sc}|_{\overline{RC}}$ networks. This is quite different from the lossless line case, where the inclusion of resistances does not destroy the lumped nature of the network in the λ plane. The presence of a lumped resistance in the distributed RC structure destroys this property because the resistance must be multiplied by $\sqrt{s}$ and thus one must resort to approximations in such cases.

For purely distributed RC networks of equal electrical length, the elementary networks in the Λ plane are shown in Figure 6-20. These are

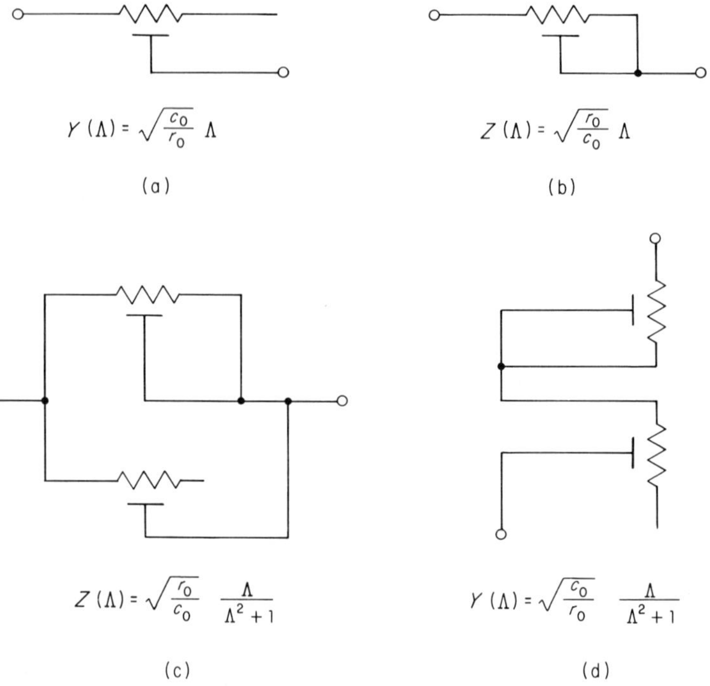

Figure 6-20

exactly the same functional form in the Λ plane as are L and C lumped networks in the s plane. Thus it is readily seen that the necessary and sufficient conditions for the realizability of $Z(s)$ as a driving-point immittance of a finite number of elemental $Z_{oc}|_{\overline{RC}}$ and $Z_{sc}|_{\overline{RC}}$ networks are that $Z(s)$ may be expressed as

$$Z(s) = \frac{k_\infty}{\sqrt{s}} \tanh a\sqrt{s} + \frac{k_0}{\sqrt{s} \tanh a\sqrt{s}} + \sum_{i=1}^{N} \frac{2k_i \tanh a\sqrt{s}}{\sqrt{s}\,(\tanh^2 a\sqrt{s} + b_i^2)} \tag{6-23}$$

where k_∞, k_0, and k_i are all $\geqslant 0$. Note that Equation (6-23) allows uniformly distributed networks of different r and c but that the product $\sqrt{r_i c_i}$ and the length d must be the same for each elemental network; in other words, identical electrical lengths, but not necessarily the same physical lengths, are required. However, for $\overline{RC}$ networks of identical materials, $r_i c_i$ = constant, which calls for equal length d. Note further that $\sqrt{s}Z(s)$ is a rational function of $\epsilon^{a\sqrt{s}}$. In the Λ plane, Equation (6-23) may be written as

$$Z(\Lambda) = \sqrt{s}\; Z(s) = k_\infty \Lambda + \frac{k_0}{\Lambda} + \sum_{i=1}^{N} \frac{2k_i \Lambda}{\Lambda^2 + b_i^2} \tag{6-24}$$

Comparison of Equation (6-24) with Equation (6-4) shows that the synthesis in the Λ plane is identical to the synthesis of $Z_{LC}(s)$ in the s plane. Hence the synthesis procedure follows the steps shown in Figure 6-21.

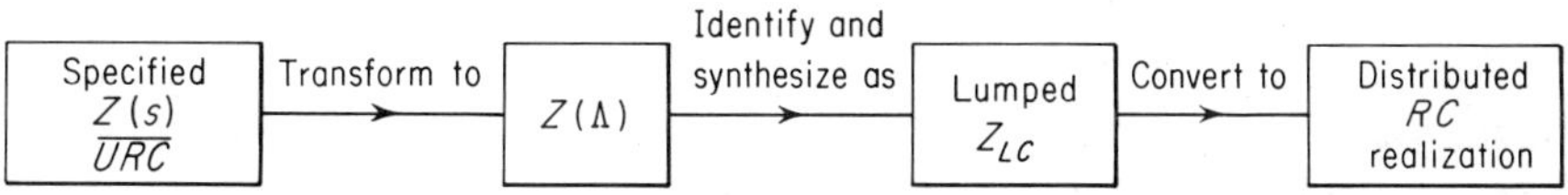

Figure 6-21 Steps in the synthesis of $\overline{URC}$.

It should be noted again that the transformation from the s plane to the Λ plane is not a one-to-one transformation. The multiple equivalency of the s plane to the Λ plane has transformed an infinite number of pole-zero locations in the s plane into a single pole-zero location in the Λ plane. Also note that the transformation is positive real; that is, a p-r function in the s plane is mapped into a p-r function in the Λ plane.

From Figure 6-21 and the material of Section 6-3, it is clear that the synthesis procedure of two-element lumped LC driving-point functions can be utilized for the uniformly distributed RC network of equal electrical length. The synthesis procedure yields the Foster forms, Cauer forms, and mixed forms.

Example 6

Let
$$Z(s) = \frac{1}{\sqrt{s}}\left[\frac{(\tanh \sqrt{s})(\tanh^2 \sqrt{s} + 4)}{(\tanh^2 \sqrt{s} + 1)(\tanh^2 \sqrt{s} + 9)}\right] \tag{6-25}$$

Transforming the s into Λ plane, and noting that $a = 1$, we obtain

$$Z(\Lambda) = \sqrt{s}\, Z(s) = \frac{\Lambda(\Lambda^2 + 4)}{(\Lambda^2 + 1)(\Lambda^2 + 9)} \tag{6-26}$$

Partial fraction expansions of Equation (6-26) yield

$$Z(\Lambda) = \frac{\frac{3}{8}\Lambda}{\Lambda^2 + 1} + \frac{\frac{5}{8}\Lambda}{\Lambda^2 + 9}$$

$$Y(\Lambda) = \frac{9}{4\Lambda} + \frac{\frac{15}{4}\Lambda}{\Lambda^2 + 4} + \Lambda$$

The LC realizations in the Foster forms are shown in Figure 6-22.

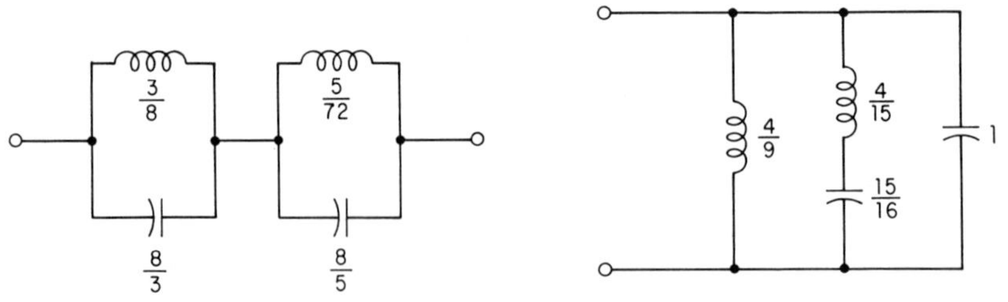

Figure 6-22 Lumped LC realization.

The corresponding distributed RC network realizations are shown in Figure 6-23. The realizations in the Cauer forms are straightforward and are left as an exercise for the reader.

This type of synthesis, although mathematically acceptable, has the main drawback of leading to a clumsy interconnection which is not desirable from the viewpoint of microelectronic fabrication. A configuration that is preferable for integrated-circuit fabrication is the cascade

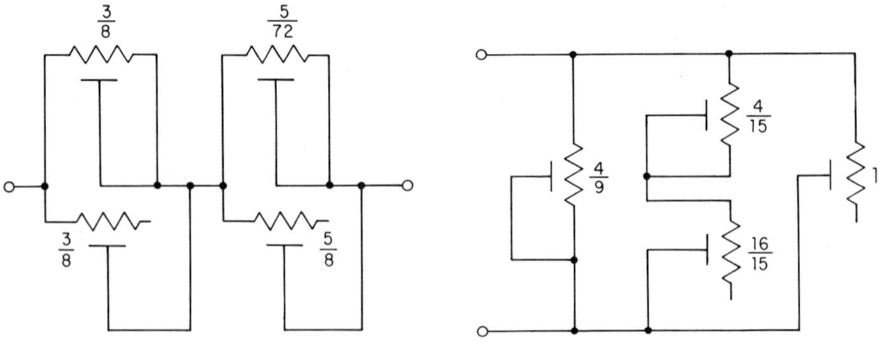

Note: The numbers indicate the values of the resistances in ohms.

Figure 6-23 $\overline{URC}$ realization.

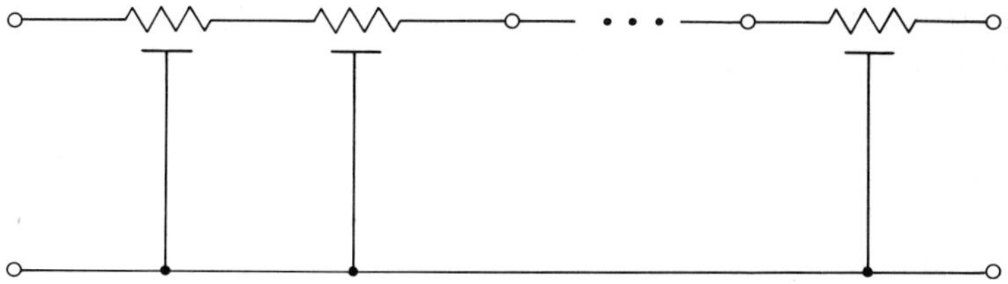

Figure 6-24 Cascade of $\overline{URC}$ networks.

configuration. A cascade configuration utilizing $Z_{oc}|_{\overline{RC}}$ networks is shown in Figure 6-24. This structure may also be viewed as a cascaded interconnection of unloaded two-ports. In any event, this configuration minimizes the number of fabrication steps and eliminates most of the interconnections that would otherwise be required. The physical embodiment of the cascade configuration is shown in Figure 6-25. We shall next consider the cascade synthesis of uniformly distributed *RC* lines.

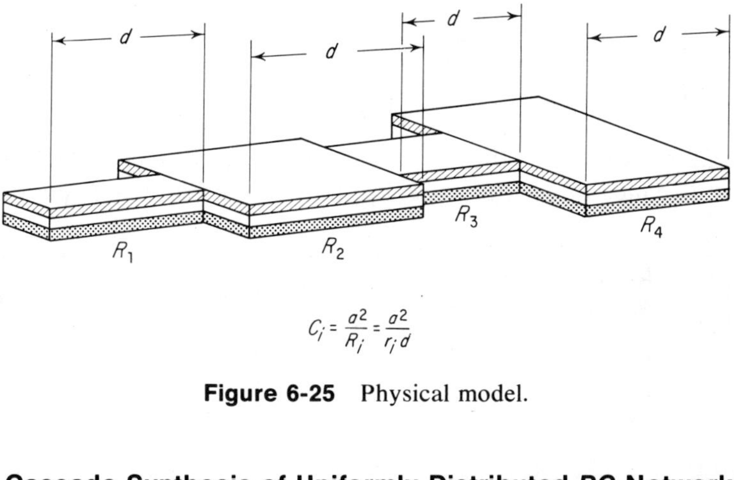

$$C_i = \frac{a^2}{R_i} = \frac{a^2}{r_i d}$$

Figure 6-25 Physical model.

6-6 Cascade Synthesis of Uniformly Distributed *RC* Networks

Consider the cascade configuration shown in Figure 6-26, in which each block represents a two-port uniformly distributed *RC* network. Each line is assumed to have the same electrical length but the individual resistance and capacitance may be different. In other words $\sqrt{r_0 c_0 d^2} = a$ is the same for each network. This restriction is implied by the transformation in Equation (6-20).

In a cascade connection the *ABCD* parameters are very useful, since the overall *ABCD* parameters of the system are obtained by simply multiplying the (*ABCD*) matrix of the cascaded stages. The

$ABCD$ parameters, as defined in Figure 1-2 and Equation (1-15), of a uniformly distributed RC two-port are given by

$$\begin{bmatrix} A_i & B_i \\ C_i & D_i \end{bmatrix} = \begin{bmatrix} \cosh a\sqrt{s} & \left(\sqrt{\frac{r_0}{c_0}}\right)_i \frac{\sinh a\sqrt{s}}{\sqrt{s}} \\ \left(\sqrt{\frac{c_0}{r_0}}\right)_i \sqrt{s}\sinh a\sqrt{s} & \cosh a\sqrt{s} \end{bmatrix} \tag{6-27}$$

$$= \cosh a\sqrt{s} \begin{bmatrix} 1 & \left(\sqrt{\frac{r_0}{c_0}}\right)_i \frac{1}{\sqrt{s}} \tanh a\sqrt{s} \\ \left(\sqrt{\frac{c_0}{r_0}}\right)_i \sqrt{s}\tanh a\sqrt{s} & 1 \end{bmatrix} \tag{6-28}$$

From Equation (6-28) and the frequency transformation, Equation (6-20), we obtain

$$\begin{bmatrix} A_i & B_i \\ C_i & D_i \end{bmatrix} = \frac{1}{\sqrt{1-\Lambda^2}} \begin{bmatrix} 1 & \left(\sqrt{\frac{r_0}{c_0}}\right)_i \frac{\Lambda}{\sqrt{s}} \\ \left(\sqrt{\frac{c_0}{r_0}}\right)_i \sqrt{s}\Lambda & 1 \end{bmatrix} \tag{6-29}$$

If a load Z_L is connected to the ith stage as shown in Figure 6-26, the input impedance of the ith stage, Z_{in_i} in terms of the $ABCD$ parameters

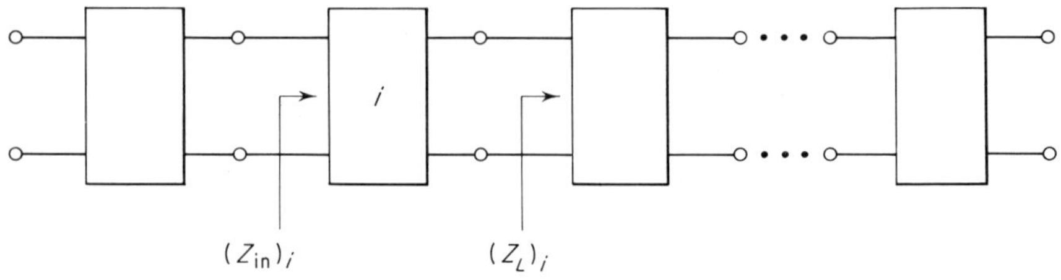

Figure 6-26

are given by

$$Z_{\text{in}_i} = \frac{A_i Z_{L_i} + B_i}{C_i Z_{L_i} + D_i} \tag{6-30}$$

Solving for Z_{L_i} in terms of the $A_iB_iC_iD_i$ parameters and Z_{in_i}, we obtain

$$Z_{L_i} = \frac{B_i - D_i Z_{\text{in}_i}}{C_i Z_{\text{in}_i} - A_i} \tag{6-31}$$

Substitution of the expressions for A_i, B_i, C_i, D_i from Equation (6-28) into

Equation (6-31) yields

$$Z_L(s) = \frac{\sqrt{\frac{r_0}{c_0}}\frac{1}{\sqrt{s}}\tanh a\sqrt{s} - Z_{\text{in}}(s)}{\sqrt{\frac{c_0}{r_0}}\sqrt{s}\tanh a\sqrt{s}\, Z_{\text{in}}(s) - 1} \tag{6-32}$$

(Subscript i which designates the ith stage is understood and omitted for simplicity.)

In the Λ plane, Equation (6-32) is

$$Z_L(\Lambda) = \sqrt{s}\, Z_L(s) = \frac{\sqrt{\frac{r_0}{c_0}}\Lambda - Z_{\text{in}}(\Lambda)}{\sqrt{\frac{c_0}{r_0}}\Lambda\, Z_{\text{in}}(\Lambda) - 1}$$

$$= \sqrt{\frac{r_0}{c_0}}\,\frac{Z_{\text{in}}(\Lambda) - \sqrt{\frac{r_0}{c_0}}\Lambda}{\sqrt{\frac{r_0}{c_0}} - \Lambda Z_{\text{in}}(\Lambda)} \tag{6-33}$$

Now Equation (6-33) is in a form that enables us to apply Richards' theorem.[5] Consider the following expression

$$F(p) = \frac{kZ(p) - pZ(k)}{kZ(k) - pZ(p)} \tag{6-34}$$

where p is a complex variable and k is a real non-negative constant. Richards' theorem states that, for Equation (6-34), $F(p)$ is p-r if $Z(p)$ is p-r and vice versa. Note that k is a positive real number. This theorem has also been utilized by Bott and Duffin in their transformerless driving-point synthesis of lumped networks. The proof of this theorem may be found in most texts on network synthesis,[9] and will not be repeated here.

A comparison of Equations (6-33) and (6-34) shows that if we identify $k \to 1$, $Z(k) \to \sqrt{r_0/c_0}$, $p \to \Lambda$ we can then at once apply Richards' theorem; thus $Z_L(\Lambda)$ is also a p-r function if $Z_{\text{in}}(\Lambda)$ is a p-r function. The significance of the theorem in the present discussion is that since $Z_L(\Lambda)$ is of lower degree than $Z_{\text{in}}(\Lambda)$, which is evident from Equation (6-33) or Equation (6-34) because a cancellation of factors occurs in the numerator and denominator, an RC line may always be extracted from the specified function. The resulting simpler driving-point immittance may always be realized as a cascade of a finite number of RC lines of different r_0 and c_0 but equal electrical length through a repetition of the process. Recall that synthesis is actually performed in the Λ

[9] For example, see Balabanian (Ref. 3), pp. 104–113.

plane with a finite number of critical frequencies in that plane. The necessary and sufficient condition for $Z_{\text{in}}(\Lambda)$ to be realizable as a network consisting of uniform RC lines of equal length is that $Z(\Lambda)$ is a reactance function. In other words, $Z_{\text{in}}(\Lambda)$ is of the same form as Z_{LC} in the s plane. Note further that since Z_L is an LC function in the Λ plane when $Z(k)|_{k=1}$ is extracted we still have an LC function in the Λ plane. The procedure is best illustrated through an example.

Example 7

Consider the driving-point function of Equation (6-26); that is,

$$Z(\Lambda) = \frac{\Lambda(\Lambda^2 + 4)}{(\Lambda^2 + 1)(\Lambda^2 + 9)} \tag{6-35}$$

It is desired to synthesize the network into a cascade configuration. Let the original specification require that $a = 1$ for simplicity (of course this is not necessary). If $a = 1$, then $C_i = 1/R_i$ for each section, where $C_i = c_i d$, $R_i = r_i d$. Then

$$Z \equiv Z_1 = Z_1(\Lambda) = \frac{\Lambda(\Lambda^2 + 4)}{(\Lambda^2 + 1)(\Lambda^2 + 9)}$$

$$Z_1(k) = Z_1(1) = R_1 = \frac{1(5)}{2(10)} = \frac{1}{4} = \left(\sqrt{\frac{r_0}{c_0}}\right)_1$$

From Equation (6-33),

$$Z_2(\Lambda) = R_1 \frac{Z_1(\Lambda) - R_1\Lambda}{R_1 - \Lambda Z_1(\Lambda)}$$

$$= \frac{1}{4}\,\frac{\dfrac{\Lambda(\Lambda^2 + 4)}{(\Lambda^2 + 1)(\Lambda^2 + 9)} - \dfrac{1}{4}\Lambda}{\dfrac{1}{4} - \dfrac{\Lambda^2(\Lambda^2 + 4)}{(\Lambda^2 + 1)(\Lambda^2 + 9)}}$$

$$= \frac{1}{4}\,\frac{\Lambda(\Lambda^2 + 7)\cancel{(\Lambda^2 - 1)}}{3(\Lambda^2 + 3)\cancel{(\Lambda^2 - 1)}}$$

Repeat the process:

$$Z_2(k) = Z_2(1) = \frac{1}{12}\,\frac{1(8)}{4} = \frac{1}{6} = \left(\sqrt{\frac{r_0}{c_0}}\right)_2 = R_2$$

$$Z_3(\Lambda) = \frac{1}{6}\,\frac{\dfrac{1}{12}\,\dfrac{\Lambda(\Lambda^2 + 7)}{(\Lambda^2 + 3)} - \dfrac{1}{6}\Lambda}{\dfrac{1}{6} - \Lambda\left[\dfrac{1}{12}\,\dfrac{\Lambda(\Lambda^2 + 7)}{(\Lambda^2 + 3)}\right]}$$

$$Z_3(\Lambda) = \frac{1}{6}\,\frac{\Lambda\cancel{(\Lambda^2 - 1)}}{(\Lambda^2 + 6)\cancel{(\Lambda^2 - 1)}}$$

Repeat another cycle:

$$Z_3(k) = Z_3(1) = \frac{1}{6}\,\frac{1}{7} = \frac{1}{42} = \left(\sqrt{\frac{r_0}{c_0}}\right)_3 = R_3$$

$$Z_4(\Lambda) = \frac{1}{42}\,\frac{\dfrac{1}{6}\dfrac{\Lambda}{\Lambda^2+6} - \dfrac{1}{42}\Lambda}{\dfrac{1}{42} - \Lambda\left[\dfrac{\Lambda}{6(\Lambda^2+6)}\right]}$$

$$Z_4(\Lambda) = \frac{1}{42}\,\frac{\Lambda(\cancel{\Lambda^2-1})}{6(\cancel{\Lambda^2-1})} = \frac{1}{252}\Lambda$$

The final step is recognized to be the driving-point impedance of a short-circuit uniform *RC* line in the Λ plane; see Equation (6-22). The network corresponding to the calculations of this example is shown in Figure 6-27.

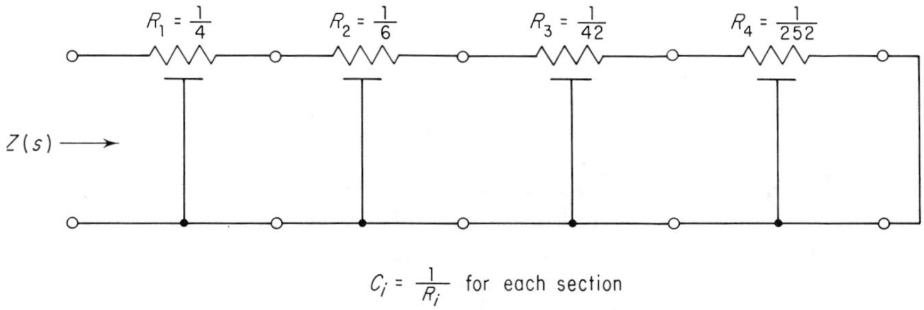

Figure 6-27

Note that in this case $a = \sqrt{r_0 c_0 d^2} = 1$; thus, if

$$R_1 = \left(\sqrt{\frac{r_0}{c_0}}\right)_1 = \frac{1}{4}$$

We have $r_0 d = R_1 = 1/4$ ohm and $c_0 d = 1/r_0 d = 4$ farads. The element values are not practical due to the normalization employed in the specified driving-point function.

Notice that in each step of the Richards' theorem a cancellation of poles and zeros in the Λ plane occur. This should serve as a check on the computation. As a final illustration, consider the following example.

Example 8

Let $$Y(s) = \sqrt{s}\left[\frac{\tanh a\sqrt{s}\,(\tanh^2 a\sqrt{s} + 9)}{(\tanh^2 a\sqrt{s} + 4)}\right]$$

Transforming the s plane into the Λ plane we have

$$Y(\Lambda) = \frac{Y(s)}{\sqrt{s}} = \frac{\Lambda(\Lambda^2+9)}{(\Lambda^2+4)}$$

We could proceed in terms of the impedance; however, this is not necessary, and instead we shall work directly in terms of the admittance function. Note that in this case a is not specified and our element values will be in terms of a, where $a = \sqrt{r_0 c_0 d^2}$.

We apply Richards' theorem, and find

$$Y_{i+1}(\Lambda) = \left(\sqrt{\frac{c_0}{r_0}}\right)_i \frac{Y_i(\Lambda) - \Lambda\left(\sqrt{\frac{c_0}{r_0}}\right)_i}{\left(\sqrt{\frac{c_0}{r_0}}\right)_i - \Lambda Y_i(\Lambda)}$$

Hence,

$$Y_1(\Lambda) \equiv Y(\Lambda) = \frac{\Lambda(\Lambda^2+9)}{(\Lambda^2+4)}$$

$$Y_1(1) = \frac{1(10)}{5} = 2 = \left(\sqrt{\frac{c_0}{r_0}}\right)_1$$

$$Y_2(\Lambda) = 2\frac{\dfrac{\Lambda(\Lambda^2+9)}{\Lambda^2+4} - \Lambda(2)}{2 - \Lambda^2\dfrac{(\Lambda^2+9)}{\Lambda^2+4}}$$

$$Y_2(\Lambda) = 2\frac{\Lambda\cancel{(\Lambda^2-1)}}{(\Lambda^2+8)\cancel{(\Lambda^2-1)}}$$

Applying the same procedure once more:

$$Y_2(1) = \frac{2(1)}{9} = \frac{2}{9} = \left(\sqrt{\frac{c_0}{r_0}}\right)_2$$

$$Y_3(\Lambda) = \frac{2}{9}\frac{\dfrac{2\Lambda}{\Lambda^2+8} - \Lambda\left(\dfrac{2}{9}\right)}{\dfrac{2}{9} - \dfrac{2\Lambda^2}{\Lambda^2+8}}$$

$$= \frac{2}{9}\frac{2\Lambda\cancel{(\Lambda^2-1)}}{16\cancel{(\Lambda^2-1)}} = \frac{1}{36}\Lambda$$

This is the final step and is recognized to be the input admittance of an open-circuited uniformly distributed RC two-port [see Figure 6-20(a)]. The network corresponding to this example is shown in Figure 6-28.

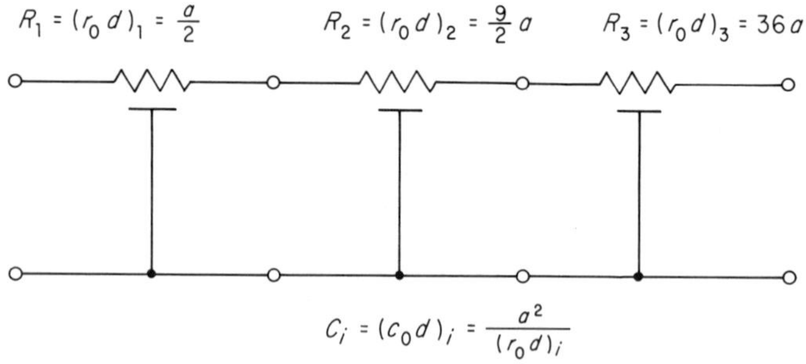

Figure 6-28

Note that the element values are in terms of the a, which need not be normalized. The physical embodiment of this realization is shown in Figure 6-29.

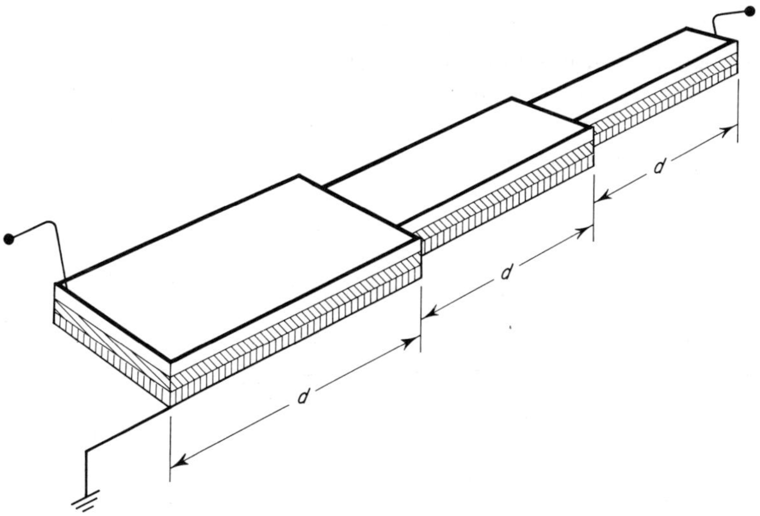

Figure 6-29

6-7 Driving-Point Synthesis of Distributed *RC* Networks Based on O'Shea's Transformation

Exact driving-point synthesis of uniformly distributed networks can also be achieved by a transformation proposed by O'Shea.[10] Driving-point synthesis based on this transformation usually results in a greater number of $\overline{RC}$ sections and the resulting networks may not be as convenient to fabricate as the networks realized in the previous sections. However, O'Shea's transformation does provide some flexibility in the realization. The similarity of the realization to that of lumped *RC* networks makes this transformation particularly attractive for adapting to the realization of active $\overline{RC}$ networks. Using it, the large body of active *RC* transfer function realizations can be adapted to active $\overline{RC}$ transfer realization. Some of this is discussed in Sections 6-9 and 6-10. But first let us examine the transformation, and the driving-point synthesis procedure that is based on it. The open-circuit impedance parameters of a uniform *RC* line are given by Equation (6-16), repeated here for convenience

$$[z_{ij}] = R \begin{bmatrix} \dfrac{\coth a\sqrt{s}}{a\sqrt{s}} & \dfrac{\operatorname{csch} a\sqrt{s}}{a\sqrt{s}} \\[2ex] \dfrac{\operatorname{csch} a\sqrt{s}}{a\sqrt{s}} & \dfrac{\coth a\sqrt{s}}{a\sqrt{s}} \end{bmatrix} \tag{6-36}$$

[10] R. P. O'Shea, *IEEE Trans. on Circuit Theory*, **CT-12** (1965), 546–554.

where $R = r_o d$ and $a = \sqrt{r_0 c_0 d^2} = \sqrt{RC}$ = a constant.

It is noted that if we multiply Equation (6-36) by $a\sqrt{s}\,\sinh a\sqrt{s}$ and then let $\cosh a\sqrt{s} \equiv P$, we get rational impedance parameters in the new P plane $(P = U + jW)$. The new impedance parameters in the P plane shall be designated as $z_{ij}{}^P$. Hence

$$[z_{ij}{}^P] = R\begin{bmatrix} \cosh a\sqrt{s} & 1 \\ 1 & \cosh a\sqrt{s} \end{bmatrix}_{\cosh a\sqrt{s}=P} = R\begin{bmatrix} P & 1 \\ 1 & P \end{bmatrix} \tag{6-37}$$

From Equation (6-37) we see that the impedance parameters are rational in P. Thus, any combinations of $\overline{URC}$ lines with a constant RC product will yield rational immittance parameters in the P plane. From a two-port representation of Equation (6-37), as shown in Figure 6-30, it can be

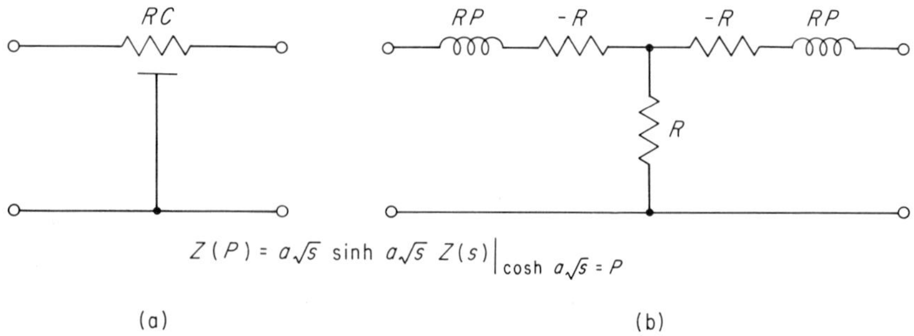

Figure 6-30 **(a)** $\overline{URC}$ in the *s plane*. **(b)** Network representation for Equation (6-37) in the P plane $(P = U + jV)$.

seen that the transformation is not p-r. However, this does not mean that we cannot realize $\overline{RC}$ networks. On the contrary, we shall show that by introducing this transformation we can always realize $\overline{RC}$ networks.

In fact, the necessary and sufficient conditions for $Z(P)$ to be a driving-point impedance function can be stated as shown in Table 6-5. The proof of the necessity follows readily[11] from a consideration of Figure 6-30(b) and is left as an exercise in Problem 6-18. The sufficiency is established in the synthesis procedure.

Synthesis procedure. From Table 6-5, it is seen that a physically realizable network comprised of $\overline{URC}$ networks with constant RC

[11] O'Shea (Ref. 10), p. 547.

Table 6-5 NECESSARY AND SUFFICIENT CONDITIONS FOR DRIVING-POINT IMPEDANCE $Z(P)$

(a) $Z(P)$ must be a real rational function of P.

(b) If $Z(P) = k\dfrac{\prod_{i=1}^{N+1}(P - z_i)}{\prod_{j=1}^{N}(P - p_j)}$ then $k > 0$.

(c) The poles and zeros of $Z(P)$ are simple, lie along the U axis, and interlace each other.

(d) The most negative and most positive critical points are zeros.

(e) All the finite poles and zeros are less than or equal to one in magnitude.

product can be expressed as

$$Z(P) = k\frac{(P - z_1)(P - z_2)\cdots(P - z_{N+1})}{(P - p_1)(P - p_2)\cdots(P - p_N)} \tag{6-38}$$

where $k \geqslant 0$ and

$$-1 \leqslant z_1 < p_1 < z_2 < p_2 \cdots < p_N < z_{N+1} \leqslant 1 \tag{6-39}$$

The procedure is to use a partial fraction expansion of $Z(P)/(P^2 - 1)$, as follows:

$$\frac{Z(P)}{P^2 - 1} = \frac{Z(P)}{(P-1)(P+1)} = \frac{k_1}{P-1} + \frac{k_2}{P+1} + \sum_{j=1}^{N}\frac{h_j}{P - p_j} \tag{6-40}$$

We shall show first that the constants $k_1, k_2, h_1, h_2, \ldots h_N$ are all nonnegative and second that the realization for each term of $Z(P)$ is always possible. Consider k_1;

$$k_1 = \frac{Z(P)}{2} = \frac{k}{2}\frac{(1 - z_1)(1 - z_2)\cdots(1 - z_{N+1})}{(1 - p_1)(1 - p_2)\cdots(1 - p_N)} \tag{6-41}$$

However,

$$\begin{aligned} z_i &\leqslant 1 \qquad i = 1, 2, \ldots, N+1 \\ p_i &< 1 \qquad i = 1, 2, \ldots, N \end{aligned} \tag{6-42}$$

Thus from the foregoing condition (see Table 6-5) we have $k_1 \geqslant 0$. Now consider h_j:

$$h_j = k\frac{(p_j - z_1)(p_j - z_2)\cdots(p_j - z_{j-1})(p_j - z_j)\cdots(p_j - z_{N+1})}{(p_j - 1)(p_j + 1)(p_j - p_1)(p_j - p_2)\cdots(p_j - p_{j-1})(p_j - p_{j+1})\cdots(p_j - p_N)} \tag{6-43}$$

Since the number of factors with negative signs in the numerator and denominator are equal, we have $h_j \geqslant 0$. The same argument applies to

k_2, hence $k_2 \geqslant 0$. Thus from Equation (6-40) we obtain

$$Z(P) = k_1(P+1) + k_2(P-1) + \sum_{j=1}^{N} \frac{h_j(P+1)(P-1)}{(P-p_j)} \tag{6-44}$$

where all the constants are shown to be non-negative.

It remains to be shown that each term of Equation (6-44) can be realized by $\overline{URC}$ structures. From Figure 6-19(a)

$$Z(s) = \frac{R}{2a\sqrt{s}} \coth \frac{a\sqrt{s}}{2} \tag{6-45}$$

Multiply Equation (6-45) by $a\sqrt{s} \sinh a\sqrt{s}$ to get $Z_T(s)$ and then let $\cosh a\sqrt{s} = P$:

$$Z_T(s) = \frac{R}{2a\sqrt{s}} \frac{\cosh \dfrac{a\sqrt{s}}{2}}{\sinh \dfrac{a\sqrt{s}}{2}} (a\sqrt{s} \sinh a\sqrt{s}) \tag{6-46}$$

But

$$\sinh a\sqrt{s} = 2 \sinh \frac{a}{2}\sqrt{s} \cosh \frac{a\sqrt{s}}{2} \tag{6-47}$$

From Equations (6-47) and (6-46), we obtain

$$Z_T(s) = \frac{R}{2}\, 2\cosh^2 \frac{a\sqrt{s}}{2} \tag{6-48}$$

But

$$2\cosh^2 \frac{a\sqrt{s}}{2} = \cosh a\sqrt{s} + 1 \tag{6-49}$$

Thus, from Equations (6-49) and (6-48), we obtain

$$Z_T(s) = \frac{R}{2} (\cosh a\sqrt{s} + 1) \tag{6-50}$$

Now let $\cosh a\sqrt{s} = P$ in Equation (6-50) to get

$$Z(P) = \frac{R}{2}(P+1) \tag{6-51}$$

Similarly, from Figure 6-19(b),

$$Z(s) = \frac{2R}{a\sqrt{s}} \tanh \frac{a\sqrt{s}}{2} \tag{6-52}$$

Using the transformation and substitution as before, we get

$$Z(P) = 2R(P - 1) \tag{6-53}$$

The realizations in the P domain for Equations (6-51) and (6-53) are shown in Figure 6-31(a) and (b) for convenience. Note that one could also obtain the foregoing results directly, from Figure 6-30(b) in the P domain.

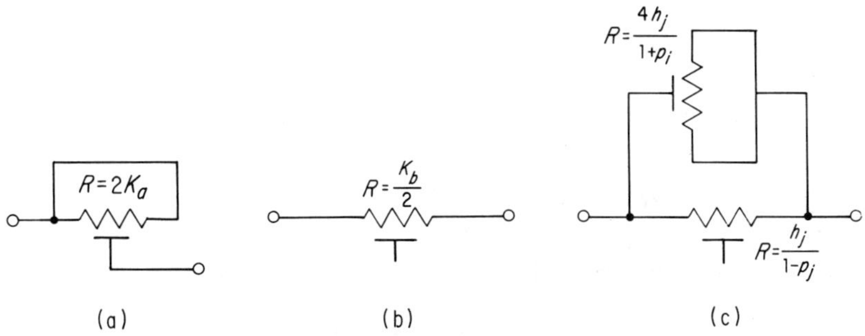

Figure 6-31 (a) $Z(P) = K_a(P+1)$. (b) $Z(P) = K_b(P-1)$. (c) $\dfrac{1}{Z(P)} = Y(P) = \dfrac{(1+p_j)/2h_j}{P+1} + \dfrac{(1-p_j)/2h_j}{P-1}$.

Figure 6-32 (a) $Y(P) = \dfrac{k_i}{P - P_i}$ for $P_i \geqslant 0$. (b) $Y(P) = \dfrac{k_i}{P - P_i}$ for $p_i \leqslant 0$.

Now consider the admittance of a typical term in the summation of Equation (6-44):

$$Y_j = \frac{1}{Z_j} = \frac{(P - p_j)}{h_j(P+1)(P-1)} = \frac{\dfrac{(1+p_j)}{2h_j}}{P+1} + \frac{\dfrac{(1-p_j)}{2h_j}}{P-1} \tag{6-54}$$

Since the poles are restricted by the condition

$$-1 < p_j < 1 \tag{6-55}$$

the numerators of the expansions in the right-hand side of Equation (6-54) are non-negative. Thus a realization for the typical term is shown in Figure 6-31(c), which is a parallel combination of Figure 6-31(a) and (b). We have thus established the sufficiency condition.

The realizations for the admittance functions $Y(P)$ are shown (Problem 6-31) in Figure 6-32.

Example 9

Let us consider an example, by realizing the specification in Equation (6-25); that is, with $a = 1$,

$$Z(s) = \frac{1}{\sqrt{s}} \frac{(\tanh \sqrt{s})(\tanh^2 \sqrt{s} + 4)}{(\tanh^2 \sqrt{s} + 1)(\tanh^2 \sqrt{s} + 9)} \tag{6-56}$$

Making the transformation in the P plane, we obtain

$$Z(P) = \frac{P(P^2 - 1)(5P^2 - 1)}{(2P^2 - 1)(10P^2 - 1)} \tag{6-57}$$

Now form $Z(P)/(P^2 - 1)$ and expand it in a partial fraction:

$$\frac{Z(P)}{P^2 - 1} = \frac{1}{4} \frac{P\left(P^2 - \frac{1}{5}\right)}{\left(P^2 - \frac{1}{2}\right)\left(P^2 - \frac{1}{10}\right)} = \frac{3/32}{P - \frac{1}{\sqrt{2}}} + \frac{3/32}{P + \frac{1}{\sqrt{2}}} + \frac{1/32}{P - \frac{1}{\sqrt{10}}} + \frac{1/32}{P + \frac{1}{\sqrt{10}}}$$

Multiply both sides by $(P^2 - 1)$ to obtain

$$Z(P) = \frac{(3/32)(P^2 - 1)}{P - \frac{1}{\sqrt{2}}} + \frac{(3/32)(P^2 - 1)}{P + \frac{1}{\sqrt{2}}} + \frac{(1/32)(P^2 - 1)}{P - \frac{1}{\sqrt{10}}} + \frac{(1/32)(P^2 - 1)}{P + \frac{1}{\sqrt{10}}} \tag{6-58}$$

Each term is realized as in Figure 6-32, and thus the RC network realization for Equation (6-56) is shown in Figure 6-33. Compare Figure

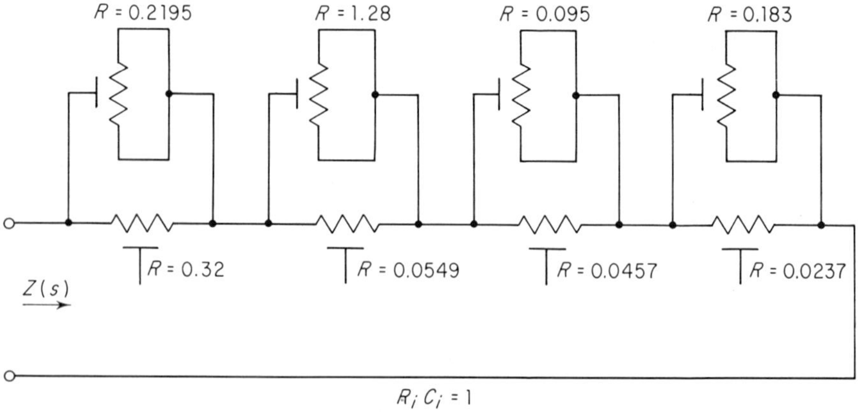

Figure 6-33

6-33 with 6-27, which represents another realization for Equation (6-56).

It should be noted that by a simple transformation one can obtain $Z(\Lambda)$ from $Z(P)$; hence, a specified $Z(P)$ can also be realized by the methods of Sections 6-5 and 6-6.

6-8 Transfer-Function Synthesis

The synthesis of transfer functions for lumped and/or distributed networks, when all the immittance parameters are specified, is a vast topic which cannot be adequately covered in one or two chapters. This topic, for lumped networks, is discussed in detail in network-synthesis texts,[12] and we shall not attempt to cover it here.

The advent of integrated circuits has stimulated considerable research in the area of active *RC* synthesis. Using this technology, a number of synthesis procedures have been reported for specific configurations. In particular, a large body of literature exists for the design of active *RC* filters.[13] Most of the methods use *RC* two-ports and transistors as the active devices. These active devices are used as amplifiers, operational amplifiers, gyrators, negative-impedance converters, and so forth.

For simplicity of synthesis (without going into two-port *RC* synthesis), we shall consider here only two specific useful active *RC* configurations and the synthesis procedures developed for them. Both of these synthesis procedures are quite general in the sense that complex transmission zeros are allowed anywhere in the *s* plane. The natural frequencies may be complex and/or real but are restricted in the left half plane for reasons of stability.

The transfer function synthesis procedures, as will be shown shortly, reduce to the synthesis of one-port *RC* and $\overline{RC}$ networks. Therefore, with the material developed so far, we are able to synthesize transfer functions. Although we consider mainly voltage ratio transfer functions, the synthesis can be adapted to other transfer functions such as transimmitance functions.

The two synthesis procedures to be discussed in the next two sections use the active devices as a negative-impedance converter and practical amplifiers, respectively.

Negative-impedance converter. An ideal negative-impedance converter (abbreviated as NIC) is an active two-port whose input impedance

---

[12] E. Guilemin, *Passive Network Synthesis* (New York, Wiley, 1958).

[13] M. S. Ghausi, *Principles and Design of Linear Active Circuits* (New York, McGraw-Hill, 1965), Chap. 17; K. L. Su, *Active Network Synthesis* (New York, McGraw-Hill, 1965).

is the negative of the load impedance.[14] It has the following idealized h parameters (see Table 1-1 for the definitions)

$$h_{11} = h_{22} = 0 \tag{6-59a}$$

$$h_{21} = h_{12} = \pm 1 \tag{6-59b}$$

With $h_{21} = h_{12} = +1$ the device is called a current-inversion negative-impedance converter or I-NIC, while with $h_{12} = h_{21} = -1$ the device is called a voltage-inversion negative-impedance converter or V-NIC for short.

Consider the NIC network shown schematically in Figure 6-34.

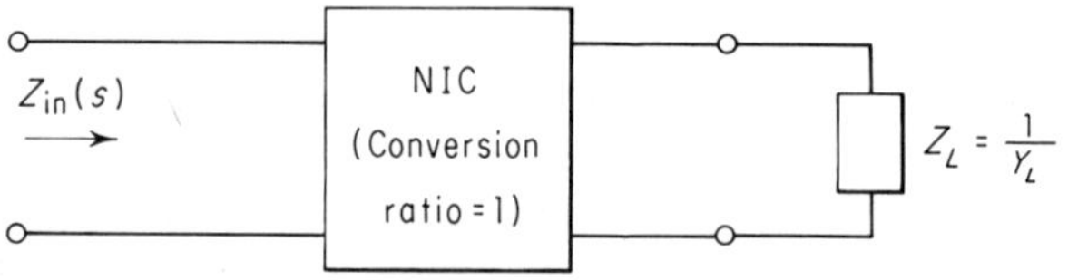

Figure 6-34 Negative-impedance converter.

The input impedance of the network is

$$Z_{\text{in}} = h_{11} - \frac{h_{12}h_{21}}{h_{22} + Y_L} \tag{6-60}$$

From Equations (6-60) and (6-59),

$$Z_{\text{in}} = -\frac{1}{Y_L} = -Z_L \tag{6-61}$$

This property of the network makes it very attractive for synthesis procedures. It should be noted that the NIC is a potentially unstable device and improper passive terminations can cause instability.

6-9 Transfer-Function Synthesis Using NIC and One-Port $\overline{RC}$ Networks

In order to understand and appreciate the synthesis procedure we shall first consider briefly a configuration with lumped RC one-ports and an NIC network.

Lumped active-RC case. Consider the configuration proposed by Yanagisawa,[15] as shown in Figure 6-35. Analysis of the network yields the following voltage transfer function:

---

[14] A. I. Larky, *IRE Trans. Circuit Theory*, **CT-4** (1957), 124–131; see also Ghausi (Ref. 13), pp. 526–529.

[15] T. Yanagisawa, *IRE Trans. Circuit Theory*, **CT-4** (1957), 140–143.

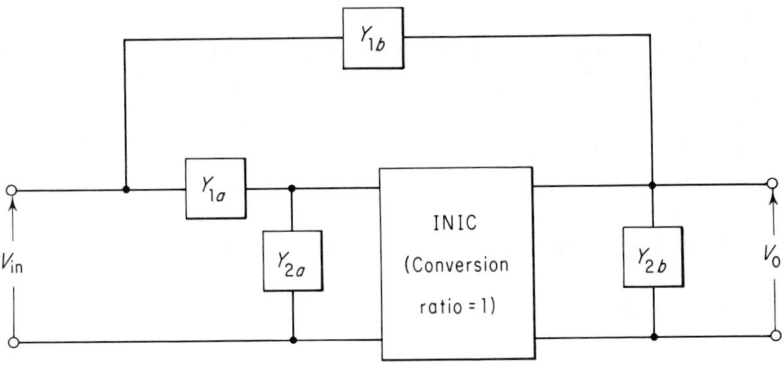

Figure 6-35 NIC-*RC* configuration (Yanagisawa).

$$A_v = \left.\frac{V_0}{V_{in}}\right|_{I_2=0} = \frac{Y_{1b} - Y_{1a}}{(Y_{1b} - Y_{1a}) + (Y_{2b} - Y_{2a})} \tag{6-62}$$

The transfer function specified for a lumped network may be described in the following form:

$$A_V = \frac{N(s)}{D(s)} = \frac{n_0 + n_1 s + n_2 s^2 + \cdots + n_N s^N}{d_0 + d_1 s + d_2 s^2 + \cdots + d_M s^M} \tag{6-63}$$

In other words, $N(s)$ and $D(s)$ are the specified polynomials with real and/or complex roots.

The synthesis procedure is described as follows: Choose a polynomial with distinct negative real roots and of degree at least $D - 1$, where D is the degree of the numerator or denominator, whichever is larger. Let

$$Q(s) = \prod_{i}^{D-1} (s + \sigma_i) \qquad \sigma_i > 0 \tag{6-64}$$

Divide the numerator and the denominator of Equation (6-63) by Equation (6-64), as follows:

$$A_V = \frac{N(s)}{D(s)} = \frac{N(s)}{N(s) + [D(s) - N(s)]} = \frac{\dfrac{N(s)}{Q(s)}}{\dfrac{N(s)}{Q(s)} + \dfrac{D(s) - N(s)}{Q(s)}} \tag{6-65}$$

Comparison of Equations (6-65) and (6-62) suggests the following identifications:

$$Y_{1b} - Y_{1a} = \frac{N(s)}{Q(s)} = k_\infty s + k_0 + \sum_{i=1}^{D-1} \frac{k_i s}{(s + \sigma_i)} \tag{6-66}$$

$$Y_{2b} - Y_{2a} = \frac{D(s) - N(s)}{Q(s)} = h_\infty s + h_0 + \sum_{i=1}^{D-1} \frac{h_i s}{(s + \sigma_i)} \tag{6-67}$$

In Equation (6-66) and (6-67) the various residues will be real and either positive or negative depending on the coefficients of $N(s)$ and $D(s)$ and the choice of zeros of $Q(s)$. The terms with only positive values of k_i and h_i are associated with Y_{1b} and Y_{2b}, respectively, whereas those with negative value are associated with Y_{1a} and Y_{2a}. Thus, the individual one-port realizations are obtained directly in Foster form (see Figure 6-9).

The following example illustrates the synthesis procedure.

Example 10

Realize the open-circuit voltage ratio

$$A_V = \frac{(s+1)(s-1)}{s^2+s+1} \tag{6-68}$$

Choose

$$Q(s) = (s+1)$$

$$\frac{N(s)}{Q(s)} = \frac{\cancel{(s+1)}(s-1)}{\cancel{(s+1)}} = s - 1 = Y_{1b} - Y_{1a}$$

Hence, $$Y_{1b} = s \qquad Y_{1a} = 1$$

Also, $$\frac{D(s) - N(s)}{Q(s)} = \frac{s+2}{s+1} = 2 - \frac{s}{s+1} = Y_{2b} - Y_{2a}$$

Hence, $$Y_{2b} = 2 \qquad Y_{2a} = \frac{s}{s+1}$$

The network realization for Equation (6-68) is shown in Figure 6-36.

Note that in this synthesis procedure any load can be specified merely by adding the load to Y_{2b} and Y_{2a} without changing the results.

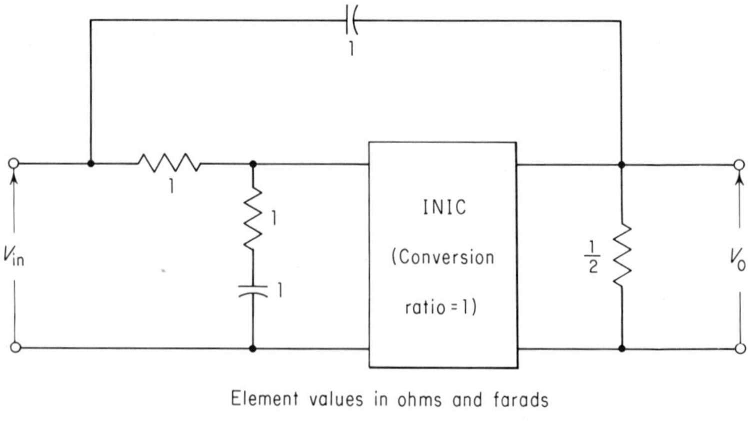

Element values in ohms and farads

Figure 6-36

For example, if a capacitive load of 1 farad is specified with Equation (6-62), we merely add s to Y_{2b} and Y_{2a}; the realization is shown in Figure 6-37. Again the reader is cautioned that the NIC is a potentially unstable device and improper terminations will cause instability.

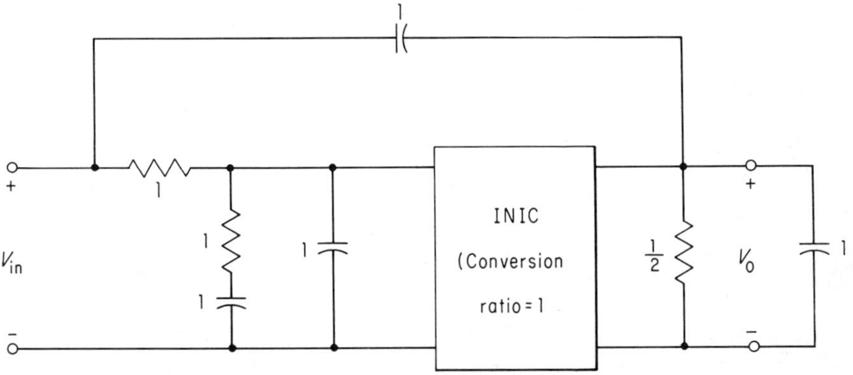

Element values in ohms and farads

Figure 6-37

Extension to a distributed *RC* network. If we wish to extend the above method to a distributed RC network, one approach is to design in the P plane and use the method of Section 6-7. We assume that the designer knows what he wants with this specification. In other words, the specification is to be in the transformed P plane. The superscript P shall be used for the admittances in the P plane. Let

$$A(P) = \frac{N(P)}{D(P)} = \frac{N_0 + N_1P + N_2P^2 + \cdots + N_nP^n}{D_0 + D_1P + D_2P^2 + \cdots + D_dP^d} \tag{6-69}$$

Note that the poles and zeros can lie anywhere in the P plane and the synthesis procedure is thus quite general. For stability reasons, the poles of $A(P)$ must be restricted. The stability criterion for poles in the P plane can be established by considering the locus of $P = \cosh a\sqrt{s}$. The mapping of the portion of $j\omega$-axis for $-20 \leqslant \omega \leqslant 20$ into the P plane is shown in Figure 6-38.[16] For a stable system the P-plane poles must lie in the enclosed region. The ideal NIC has no frequency dependence. The frequency range, over which the NIC conversion ratio is unity, is assumed to be well beyond the distributed RC cutoffs, and it is not affected by the transformation.

---

[16] $s_n = \frac{1}{RC}\{ln|P_k + \sqrt{P_k^2 - 1}| + j\, arg\, [P_k + \sqrt{P_k^2 - 1} + j^{n\pi}]\}^2 \; n = 0, \pm 1, \pm 2, \ldots$

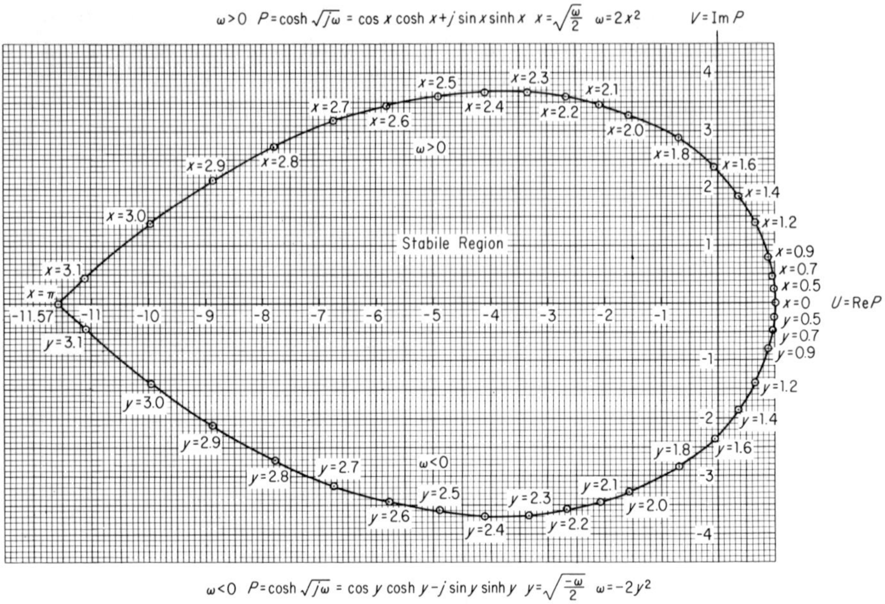

Figure 6-38 Stability region in the P plane.

The synthesis procedure is substantially the same as in the lumped RC case except that it is in the P, rather than s, plane. One important difference in the procedure is that the polynomial $Q(P)$ that we choose must be of a degree at least one larger than the numerator or denominator (whichever is larger) and have distinct roots real in the P plane ($P = U + jV$) and in the range

$$-1 \leqslant P \leqslant 1 \tag{6-70}$$

The synthesis procedure is best illustrated by an example.

Let us realize the following specification with $\overline{URC}$ networks all having $RC = 1$.

$$A_V(P) = \frac{(P-1)(P+2)}{P^2+P+1} \tag{6-71}$$

Choose $$Q(P) = P(P-1)(P+1)$$

We arbitrarily pick the roots of P at 0 and ± 1 to illustrate the procedure. The degrees of freedom in the choice of roots can be used to obtain a realization that provides the best compromise between minimum difference of resistance values and minimum sensitivity of A_V due to the changes of poles in the P plane. This problem is not easy to solve. A rule of thumb is to space the roots of $Q(P)$ evenly along the U axis, taking care not to place any factors too close to ± 1 or too close to zero (except for zero itself).[17]

For the foregoing choice of $Q(P)$ we have

$$Y_{1b}^P - Y_{1a}^P = \frac{N(P)}{Q(P)} = \frac{\cancel{(P-1)}(P+2)}{P\cancel{(P-1)}(P+1)} = \frac{2}{P} - \frac{1}{P+1}$$

Hence,
$$Y_{1b}^P = \frac{2}{P} \qquad Y_{1a}^P = \frac{1}{P+1}$$

Also,

$$Y_{2b}^P - Y_{2a}^P = \frac{D(P) - N(P)}{Q(P)} = \frac{3}{P(P-1)(P+1)} = \frac{-3}{P} + \frac{3/2}{(P+1)} + \frac{3/2}{(P-1)}$$

Hence,
$$Y_{2b} = \frac{3/2}{P+1} + \frac{3/2}{P-1} \qquad Y_{2a} = \frac{3}{P}$$

The distributed RC network realization for Equation (6-71) is shown in Figure 6-39.

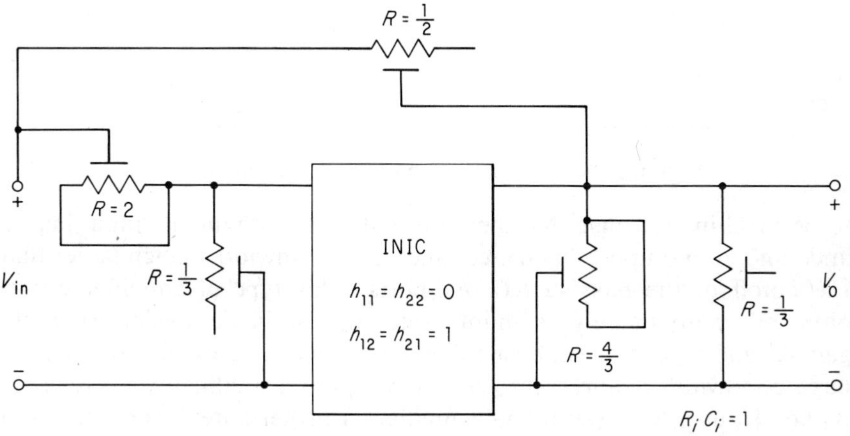

Figure 6-39 NIC-RC configuration.

Note that in this procedure lumped and/or distributed terminations can be specified, and this specification is included in the final step by adding the specified admittance to Y_{2b}^P and Y_{2a}^P. The stability of the overall network, however, must be insured.

[17] For example, in this case, the choice of

$$Q(P) = P(P - 0.55)(P + 0.66)$$

yields a much smaller sensitivity of poles and zeros of $A_V(P)$.

6-10 Transfer-Function Synthesis Using Two Grounded Voltage Amplifiers and One-Port $\overline{RC}$ Networks

In order to illustrate the following synthesis procedure, we review again the synthesis method in the familiar s-plane domain for lumped RC networks and then extend it to distributed RC networks.

Lumped active RC case. Consider the configuration shown in Figure 6-40.[18] The voltage amplifiers are assumed, for the time being,

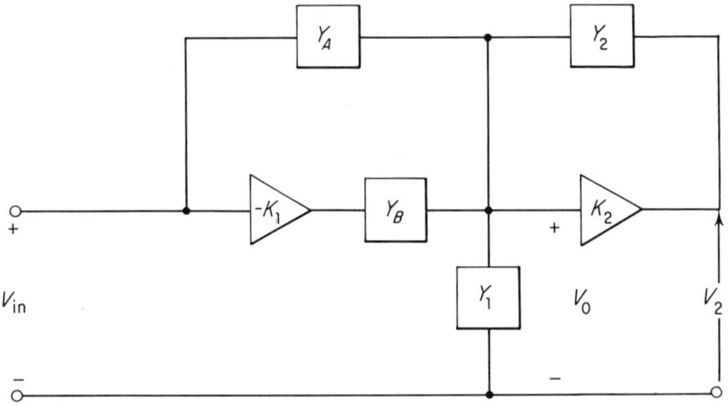

Figure 6-40 Grounded-amplifier RC configuration.

to be ideal in the sense that they are unilateral with infinite input impedance and zero output impedance, and have bandwidths much larger than the cutoff of the passive RC one-ports. This type of amplifier can be obtained approximately as an integrated operational amplifier. Since the gain K_1 and K_2 can be set by local feedback to be of the order of unity, the large bandwidth requirement presents no practical difficulty for realizing K_1 and K_2 using the operational amplifiers. Furthermore, by proper design of the one-ports, the finite nonzero immittance of the amplifier can often be incorporated in the synthesis.

The transfer function of the network with the foregoing assumptions, as obtained by a straightforward analysis, (Problem 6-30) is

$$A_v = \frac{V_0}{V_{in}} = \frac{Y_A - K_1 Y_B}{Y_A + Y_B + Y_1 - (K_2 - 1)Y_2} \tag{6-72}$$

With no loss of generality we can choose K_1 and $(K_2 - 1)$ in Equation (6-72) to be both unity; hence, Equation (6-72) becomes

---

[18] R. J. A. Paul, *Proc. IEE* (British), 113 (January 1966), 83–88, Also S. K. Mitra, *Proc. first Ann. Princeton Conf. Information Sci. Systems,* 1967.

$$\frac{V_0}{V_{\text{in}}} = \frac{Y_A - Y_B}{Y_A + Y_B + Y_1 - Y_2} \tag{6-73}$$

Note that if the output is taken after the amplifier K_2, $V_2 = K_2 V_0$. This choice is useful for cascading.
The synthesis procedure for Equation (6-73) is quite similar to the procedure presented in Section 6-9.

The transfer function specified for the lumped network may be in the form

$$A_V = \frac{V_0}{V_{\text{in}}} = \frac{N(s)}{D(s)} = \frac{n_0 + n_1 s + n_2 s^2 + \cdots n_N s^N}{d_0 + d_1 s + d_2 s^2 + \cdots d_M s^M} \tag{6-74}$$

Choose a polynomial $Q(s)$ with negative real roots of a degree at least $D - 1$, where D is the degree of the numerator or denominator, whichever is larger. For example, $D = \text{Max.}\ [N, M]$. The freedom in the choice of Q can be used to accommodate practical amplifiers in that its immittances can be included with those of the passive one-ports. Let

$$Q(s) = \prod_{i}^{D-1} (s + \sigma_i) \qquad \sigma_i > 0 \tag{6-75}$$

We divide the numerator and denominator of Equation (6-74) by Equation (6-75) to get

$$A_V = \frac{N(s)}{D(s)} = \frac{N(s)/Q(s)}{D(s)/Q(s)} \tag{6-76}$$

Comparison of Equations (6-76) and (6-73) suggests the following identifications:

$$Y_A - Y_B = \frac{N(s)}{Q(s)} = k_\infty s + k_0 + \sum_{i=1}^{D-1} \frac{k_i s}{(s + \sigma_i)} \tag{6-77}$$

$$Y_A + Y_B + Y_1 - Y_2 = \frac{D(s)}{Q(s)} = h_\infty s + h_0 + \sum_{i=1}^{D-1} \frac{h_i s}{(s + \sigma_i)} = Y^a - Y^b \tag{6-78}$$

In Equations (6-77) and (6-78) the various residues will be real and either positive or negative depending on the coefficients of $N(s)$ and $D(s)$ and the choice of roots for $Q(s)$. The terms having positive values in Equation (6-77) are associated with Y_A and those having negative values are associated with Y_B.

In Equation (6-78) there is considerable degree of freedom in the identification. However, a completely general identification is to associate all the positive residue terms with Y_1 and then obtain Y_2 from Equation (6-78). In other words, from Equation (6-78) we set

$$Y_1 = Y^a$$

then

$$Y_2 = Y^b + Y_A + Y_B$$

Hence, all the driving-point admittances are guaranteed to be *RC* admittance functions.

The termination, if specified, may be associated with Y_1, since adding G_1 to Y_1 $(=Y^a)$ and Y^b does not affect Equation (6-78). By adding a conductance in this manner one could also realize a specified $Y_{21} = I_0/V_{\text{in}}$, where $I_0 = G_1 V_0$, by this configuration. Let us illustrate the procedure by designing an active *RC* tuned filter.

Example 11

Realize the voltage ratio

$$A_V = \frac{s}{s^2 + 0.2s + 1} \tag{6-79}$$

Choose

$$Q(s) = s + 1$$

$$\frac{N(s)}{Q(s)} = \frac{s}{s+1} = Y_A - Y_B$$

Hence,

$$Y_A = \frac{s}{s+1} \qquad Y_B = 0$$

Also,

$$\frac{D(s)}{Q(s)} = \frac{s^2 + 0.2s + 1}{s+1} = s + 1 - \frac{1.8s}{s+1} = Y_A + Y_B + Y_1 - Y_2$$

Since Y_A and Y_B are already determined, the following identification can be made:

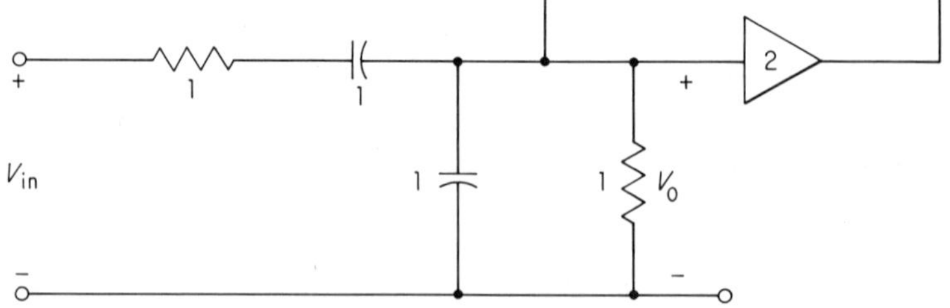

Element values in ohms and farads

Figure 6-41

$$Y_1 = s + 1 \qquad Y_2 = \frac{2.8s}{s+1}$$

The network realization for Equation (6-79) is shown in Figure 6-41. Note that in this case the network may be designed without the amplifier K_1 since $Y_B = 0$.

Extension to distributed *RC* networks. By now the reader can anticipate the extension of this method, for the idealized case, in the transformed P plane. The method follows closely the one described in the previous section for the distributed one-ports and NIC configuration. We choose $Q(P)$ as discussed in Section 6-9 and then follow the synthesis procedure as discussed in this section in the P plane.

Example 12

Let us realize the voltage transfer function specified in the transform domain of Section 6-9 (with $RC = 1$); that is,

$$\frac{V_2(P)}{V_{\text{in}}(P)} = \frac{(P-1)(P+2)}{2(P^2+P+1)} \tag{6-80}$$

Note that for $K_2 = 2$, $V_2 = 2V_0$ and $A_v(P) = \frac{1}{2}\left(\frac{V_2}{V_{\text{in}}}\right)$

Choose

$$Q(P) = P(P-1)(P+1)$$

$$\frac{N(P)}{Q(P)} = \frac{\cancel{(P-1)}(P+2)}{P\cancel{(P-1)}(P+1)} = \frac{2}{P} - \frac{1}{P+1} = Y_A^P(P) - Y_A^P(P)$$

Hence,

$$Y_A^P(P) = \frac{2}{P} \qquad Y_B^P(P) = \frac{1}{P+1}$$

Also,

$$\frac{D(P)}{Q(P)} = \frac{P^2+P+1}{P(P-1)(P+1)} = \frac{-1}{P} + \frac{3/2}{P-1} + \frac{1/2}{P+1}$$

Thus,

$$\frac{1/2}{P+1} + \frac{3/2}{P-1} - \frac{1}{P} = Y_A^P + Y_B^P + Y_1^P - Y_2^P$$

But we have already determined Y_A^P and Y_B^P, hence the following identifications can be made

$$Y_2^P(P) = \frac{3}{P} + \frac{1/2}{P+1} \qquad Y_1^P = \frac{3/2}{P-1}$$

(Note that the term ½$(P+1)$ is subtracted from both $Y_1{}^P$ and $Y_2{}^P$ for simplicity in the realization.) The distributed RC network realization for Equation (6-80) is shown in Figure 6-42.

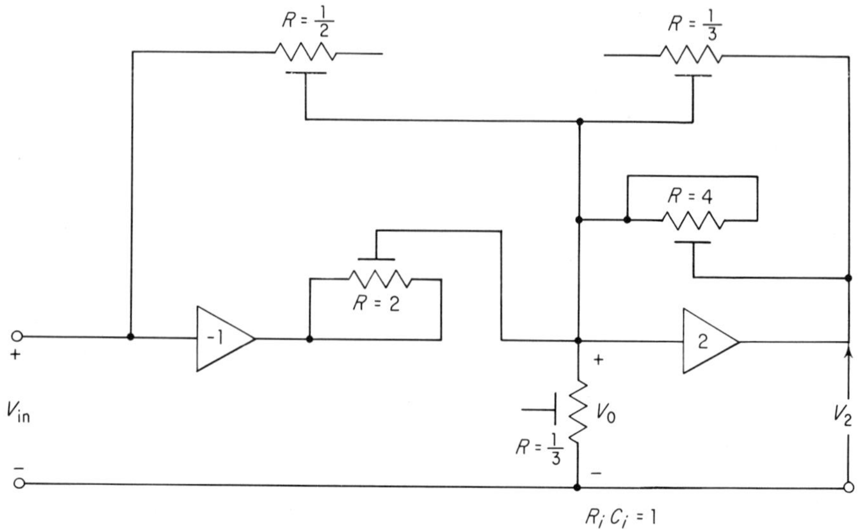

Figure 6-42

So far we have considered the realization of transfer voltage ratio. If the network function desired is specified as the transfer current ratio $I_0/I_{in}(s)$, we can use a circuit similar to that of Figure 6-40 by interchanging the amplifier and its associated one-port *RC* admittances as shown in Figure 6-43. Analysis of the circuit in Figure 6-43, assuming again ideal voltage-controlled voltage sources as was done in the previous case, yields the current ratio function in the form of

$$A_I = \frac{I_0}{I_{in}} = \frac{K_2(Y_3 - K_1Y_4)}{Y_1 - (K_2 - 1)Y_2} \tag{6-81}$$

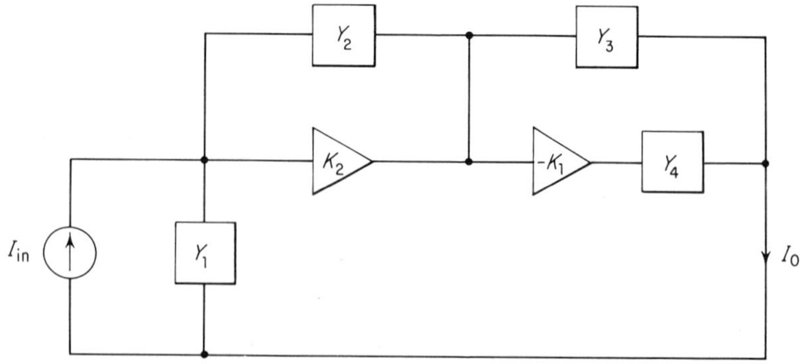

Figure 6-43 Grounded-amplifier *AC* configuration for current ratio realization.

Again with no loss of generality we can set K_1 and $(K_2 - 1)$ to be equal to unity. Hence, Equation (6-81) reduces to

$$\frac{I_0}{I_{in}} = \frac{2(Y_3 - Y_4)}{Y_1 - Y_2} \tag{6-82}$$

The synthesis procedure for Equation (6-82) is quite similar to that for (6-62) or (6-73) and will therefore not be pursued any further. Note that if we choose $K_1 = K_2 = K$, the two amplifiers in Figure 6-43 can be replaced by a single differential output voltage amplifier.

6-11 Critique and the Approximation Problem

In this section we briefly re-examine the synthesis procedures for distributed networks. As shown in the previous sections, frequency transformations have been introduced that changed the expressions from the s plane to the Λ plane or the P plane. The transformations that are not one-to-one enabled us to reduce the transcendental functions to algebraic functions. We then applied the lumped synthesis techniques to obtain network realizations. In order to perform a distributed synthesis we required the specifications in the transformed plane Λ or P.

Unfortunately, one seldom meets specifications of this type. Very often the specifications may be in a graphical form or in the s plane, with which we should have considerable familiarity. When the specification is in a graphical form, such as in the time domain, the problem is by no means simple, even for time-invariant lumped networks. Fortunately, a great deal of information is available to solve the approximation problem for the time-invariant lumped networks in the frequency domain.

For distributed networks, the problem is more difficult and relatively unexplored. Consider the transformation from the s to the Λ plane; that is,

$$Z(\Lambda) = \sqrt{s}\, Z(s)\Big|_{\tanh a\sqrt{s} = \Lambda} \tag{6-83}$$

Thus, it is clear that if the specification is in a graphical form in the frequency domain, an analytic expression most suitable for the distributed RC impedance function is of the form

$$Z\Big|_{RC} = \frac{1}{\sqrt{s}} \frac{N(\epsilon^{b\sqrt{s}})}{D(\epsilon^{b\sqrt{s}})} \tag{6-84}$$

where b is a constant $(b = 2a)$, N and D are rational polynomials in $\epsilon^{b\sqrt{s}}$. The rational function $Z(\Lambda)$ is then obtained by the direct substitution of Equation (6-83); in other words,

$$\Lambda = \tanh a\sqrt{s} = \frac{\epsilon^{2a\sqrt{s}} - 1}{\epsilon^{2a\sqrt{s}} + 1} \tag{6-85}$$

We solve for $\epsilon^{2a\sqrt{s}}$ in terms of Λ, to obtain

$$\epsilon^{2a\sqrt{s}} \equiv \epsilon^{b\sqrt{s}} = \frac{1+\Lambda}{1-\Lambda} \tag{6-86}$$

Thus a rational function of $\epsilon^{b\sqrt{s}}$ leads to a rational function of Λ and the synthesis is then carried according to the procedures discussed in Sections 6-5 and 6-6.

Next, consider the transformation from the s into the P plane; that is,

$$Z(P) = a\sqrt{s}\sinh a\sqrt{s}\, Z(s)\Big|_{\cosh a\sqrt{s}=P} \tag{6-87}$$

In this case the graphical specifications may be approximated by

$$Z\Big|_{\overline{RC}} = \frac{1}{(a\sqrt{s}\sinh a\sqrt{s})}\left[\frac{N(\cosh a\sqrt{s})}{D(\cosh a\sqrt{s})}\right] \tag{6-88}$$

where N and D are rational functions of $\cosh a\sqrt{s}$ only. In other words, the specification is interpreted in the P plane and the synthesis is performed as in Sections 6-8 and 6-10. Approximation to the graphical form directly in the P plane is also not an easy task and relatively little has been done in this area. Distributed network synthesis can gain some strength if effective approximation schemes are developed to obtain the network function directly in the transformed plane. Synthesis by active-$\overline{RC}$ to realize magnitude specifications in the s-domain can be achieved approximately. The use of computers to obtain design charts seems to be particularly good in offering possibilities. For example, design curves could be prepared which would enable one to obtain the pole-zero locations in the P-plane corresponding to the pole-zero location in the s-plane. Another approach which has been offered is to work entirely in the s-plane using practical active circuits containing lumped and distributed RC elements. Design charts for a few specific circuits are prepared[19] for this purpose, wherefrom the element values of the lumped RC, distributed RC, and the amplifier gain can be read for specified pole-zero locations in the s-plane. The zeros are limited to the $j\omega$-axis and negative σ-axis. This method has been shown to yield very simple and practical integrated circuits.

In the cascade synthesis it is understood that each line section has an equipotential line at the borders connecting two sections of different widths; Figure 6-44. An additional fabrication step is required here. If there is no equipotential line in the borders, significant differences between calculated and experimental results could occur because of

[19] W. Kerwin, Doctoral *Dissertation Technical Report,* **6560–14**, Stanford University, August 1967.

boundary effects. This error will be especially great for large width ratios of adjoining lines. This topic will be discussed in the next chapter.

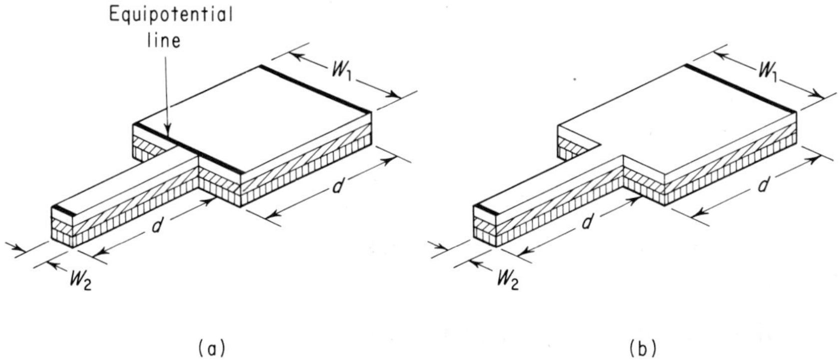

Figure 6-44 **(a)** Equipotential line fabricated at the border. **(b)** No equipotential line at the border.

In some cases of cascade synthesis, the resulting overall length of the network may be sufficiently large to be objectionable. However, there are fabrication techniques that can circumvent this problem.[20]

Furthermore, in integrated circuit technology it is often desirable, for size reasons, for the overall network not to have components that differ from each other materially in width ratios. Thus, if there are degrees of freedom available, such as in transfer function synthesis, the designer must use this size-ratio factor in optimization techniques. Hence if the width ratios are about equal, the fabrication step does not require this precaution and the resulting error may be tolerable.

PROBLEMS

6-1 Synthesize the following two-element networks in the four canonical forms:

a. $Z(s) = \dfrac{s(s^2+2)(s^2+4)}{(s^2+1)(s^2+3)}$

b. $Z(s) = \dfrac{(s+1)(s+2)(s+3)}{(s+1.5)(s+2.5)}$

c. $Z(s) = \dfrac{s^3+13s^2+38s+20}{2s(s^2+7s+10)}$

[20] L. Holland, *Thin Film Microelectronics* (New York, Wiley, 1966).

6-2 Synthesize the following admittance function:

$$Y(s) = \frac{s^4 + 3s^3 + 3s^2 + 3s + 1}{(s + 1)(s^2 + 1)}$$

6-3 Assume a biquadratic immittance function given by

$$W(s) = K\frac{s^2 + a_1 s + a_0}{s^2 + b_1 s + b_0}$$

where K, a_1, a_0, b_1, and b_0 are real and positive. What are the conditions imposed on the coefficients in order for $W(s)$ to be a p-r function? A reactance function? An RC impedance function? An RL impedance function?

6-4 Given the following impedance function:

$$Z(s) = \frac{2s^3 + s^2 + 2s + 1}{s^3 + 3s^2 + 2s + 1}$$

Is the function p-r? If so, show a network realization.

6-5 Prove the properties listed in Table 6-4.

6-6 The input admittance of a uniform lossless line with short-circuited load is given by

$$Y\Big|_{\overline{LC}} = (y_{11})_{LC} = \sqrt{\frac{c}{l}}\coth sd\sqrt{lc}$$

Develop a ladder synthesis, showing the element values of the first three sections.

6-7 The input admittance of a uniform RC network with short-circuited termination is given by

$$Y\Big|_{\overline{RC}} = (y_{11})_{\overline{RC}} = \sqrt{\frac{cs}{r}}\coth d\sqrt{scr}$$

Develop a ladder synthesis, showing the element values of the first three sections.

6-8 Derive the one-port impedances given by Equations (6-45) and (6-52).

6-9 Given

$$Z(s) = \frac{1}{\sqrt{s}}\,\frac{(\tanh^2 a\sqrt{s} + 1)(\tanh^2 a\sqrt{s} + 4)}{\tanh a\sqrt{s}\,(\tanh^2 a\sqrt{s} + 2)}$$

Synthesize the distributed RC network in the Cauer forms. Show the realized network.

6-10 Solve Problem 6-9 but in a cascade synthesis.

6-11 Solve Problem 6-9 by the method of Section 6-7.

6-12 Given

$$Y(\Lambda) = \frac{(\Lambda^2+1)(\Lambda^2+9)}{\Lambda(\Lambda^2+4)(\Lambda^2+16)}$$

Show a cascade realization.

6-13 Solve Problem 6-12 by the method of Section 6-5.

6-14 Solve Problem 6-12 by the method of Section 6-7.

6-15 Realize the following impedance function by the method of Section 6-7:

$$Z(s) = \frac{\tanh\sqrt{9s}}{\sqrt{s}} + \frac{4}{\sqrt{s}\tanh\sqrt{9s}} + \frac{2\tanh\sqrt{9s}}{\sqrt{s}\,(\tanh^2\sqrt{9s}+4)}$$

6-16 Repeat Problem 6-15 using the snythesis method of Section 6-5.

6-17 Repeat Problem 6-15 using the method of Section 6-6.

6-18 Prove the necessary conditions in Table 6-5.

6-19 Determine the s-plane pole locations for the following P-plane locations:

a. $P = -5$
b. $P = -15$
Which pole represents an unstable system?

6-20 **a.** Realize the following open-circuit voltage ratio transfer function using an NIC and one-port RC networks:

$$T_V(s) = \frac{1}{s^2+\sqrt{2}+1}$$

b. Realize (a) but with a specified load termination of 1 ohm.

6-21 Realize the following transadmittance function using an NIC and one-port RC networks:

$$Y_{21} = \frac{I_0(s)}{V_{in}(s)} = \frac{(s-1)}{s^2+s+1}$$

where I_0 represents the current through a 2-ohm load resistance.

6-22 Realize the following voltage-ratio functions by an NIC and $\overline{RC}$ one-ports:

a. $A_V(P) = \dfrac{P}{P^2 + \sqrt{2}P + 1}$

b. $A_V(P) = \dfrac{P^2 + P + 1}{P^2 + 4P + 8}$

6-23 Realize the following voltage ratio transfer functions by using amplifiers and one-port RC networks:

a. $A_V(s) = \dfrac{1}{s^3 + 2s^2 + 2s + 1}$

b. $A_V(s) = \dfrac{s + 1}{s^2 + \sqrt{3}\, s + 1}$

6-24 Realize the following voltage-ratio functions by using amplifiers and $\overline{RC}$ one-ports:

a. $A_V(P) = \dfrac{3}{P + 2}$

b. $A_V(P) = \dfrac{1}{P^2 + \sqrt{2}P + 1}$

c. $A_V(P) = \dfrac{P}{P^2 + 4P + 8}$

6-25 Realize the following current-ratio functions by using amplifiers and RC one-ports:

a. $A_I(s) = \dfrac{s + 1}{s^2 + \sqrt{3}s + 1}$

b. $A_I(s) = \dfrac{s}{s^2 + 0.1s + 1}$

6-26 Realize the following current-ratio functions by using amplifiers and $\overline{RC}$ one-ports:

a. $A_I(P) = \dfrac{0.5}{P - 0.5}$

b. $A_I(P) = \dfrac{1}{P^2 + \sqrt{2}P + 1}$

6-27 Realize the following current-ratio function by using a single amplifier having a differential output and show your circuit.

$$A_I(s) = \frac{s}{s^2 + 0.1s + 1}$$

6-28 Realize Problem 6-22(a) as $Y_{21}(P) = I_0/V_{\text{in}}$.

6-29 Realize Problem 6-24(a) as $Y_{21}(P) = I_0/V_{\text{in}}$.

6-30 **a.** Derive Equation (6-62).
b. Derive Equation (6-72).

6-31 Verify the realizations shown in Figure 6-32 for the admittance functions $Y(P)$.

6-32 For the active RC network shown in Problem 5-5:

a. Show that $A_V(P)$ is of the form

$$A_V(P) = \frac{K}{P + B}$$

Determine K and B in terms of A if $RC = 1$.

b. For what values of A does the circuit become unstable? (Hint: Use Figure 6-38.)

c. For $B = 1.995$, the magnitude response as a function of ω corresponds to that of a two-pole Butterworth filter. What should the amplifier gain be for this case? (Compare your results with those of Problem 5-5.)

CHAPTER

7

Miscellaneous Topics

7-1 Introduction

In the preceding chapters we developed a general approach to the description of single-layer two-port nonuniform distributed-parameter networks with emphasis on pole-zero locations in the complex-frequency plane. So far, we have not mentioned the physical realization of tapered networks. In this chapter we show the construction and realization of an $\overline{RC}$ network with a given electrical taper.

It is shown in Section 7-2 that electrical taper and geometric shape are generally different. For instance, an exponential electrically tapered $\overline{RC}$ network does not have an exponential geometric shape. A construction procedure is developed in Section 7-3 for finding the geometric shape corresponding to a given electrical taper.

So far, we have also considered only $\overline{RC}$ networks composed of a single-sheet resistance and a dielectric layer. More complex $\overline{RC}$ networks, the so-called multilayer networks, may also be encountered. For the sake of completeness, we have devoted Section 7-4 to a brief discussion of a multilayer uniform $\overline{RC}$ network.

In the final section an approximate method of realizing lumped network transfer functions by means of distributed $\overline{RC}$ sections is treated. The approach involves the specification of the degree of separation required between dominant and nondominant groups of poles and zeros to maintain a good approximation within a given error bound. A passive low-pass structure and an active bandpass structure are considered. The sensitivity of the center frequency and the bandwidth of the bandpass structure to parameter variations is discussed briefly.

7-2 Boundary Effects in Distributed *RC* Structures

Up to this point, we have concerned ourselves with the network properties of distributed circuits with one-dimensional variation in per-unit-length series impedance and shunt conductance. We have placed particular emphasis on the analysis and synthesis of distributed *RC* networks since these structures have applications in microelectronics. However, we have tacitly assumed the possibility of one-dimensional network variation and it is appropriate at this point to take a closer look at the tapered or shaped *RC* network.

Consider the pair of uniform *RC* network sections shown in Figure 7-1. These networks are typical of the configurations that are obtained

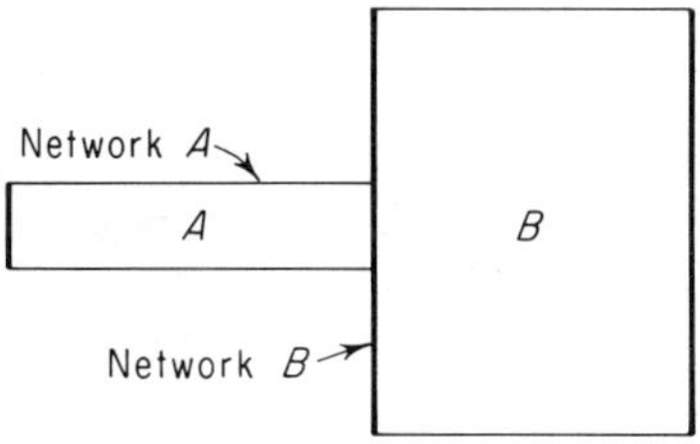

Figure 7-1 Top view of cascaded $\overline{URC}$ networks.

using the synthesis procedures of Section 6-6. The synthesis procedures of Section 6-6 are dependent on the abrupt transition in resistance and capacitance per unit length at the junction of $\overline{URC}$ networks *A* and *B*. To determine whether an abrupt transition occurs, refer to Figure 7-2, in which the equipotential lines and current-flow lines are shown. Figure 7-2(a) has an equipotential strip placed at the juncture of the two $\overline{URC}$ networks. Because of this conducting strip, the equipotentials and current-flow lines are undistorted and an abrupt transition in per-unit-length resistance and capacitance takes place. Thus, the networks connected as in Figure 7-2(a) satisfy the synthesis requirements of Section 6-6.

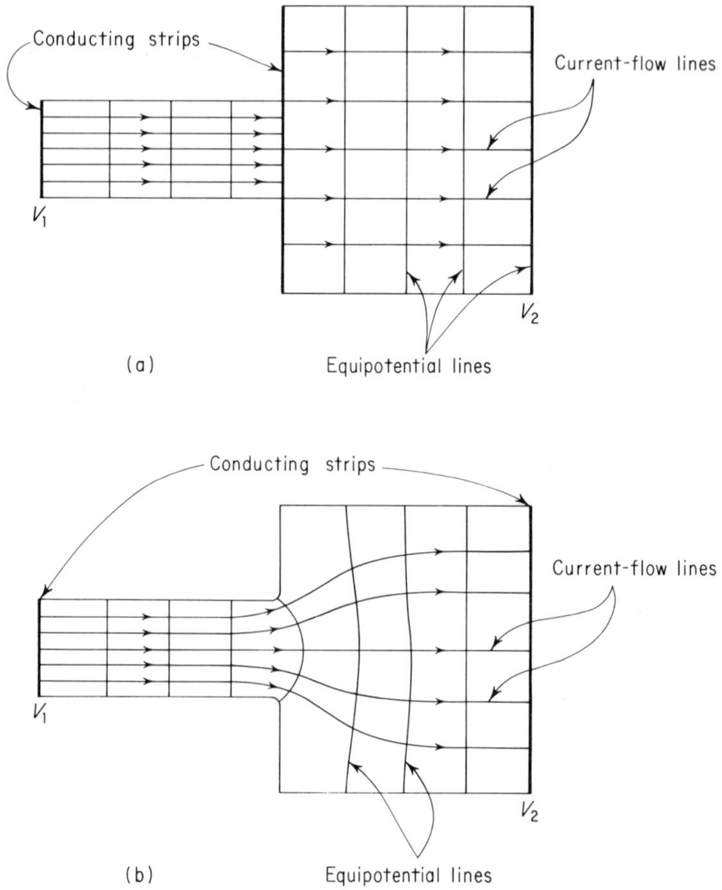

Figure 7-2 **(a)** $\overline{URC}$ networks joined by an equipotential strip. **(b)** $\overline{URC}$ networks with no conducting boundary.

Next, we refer to the networks connected as shown in Figure 7-2(b). Here, no conducting strip appears at the juncture of the two $\overline{URC}$ networks. As a consequence, the equipotential lines and current-flow lines are distorted in the neighborhood of the junction. Hence, there is a gradual transition from the per-unit-length resistance and capacitance of network A to network B. The abrupt transition is lost and this type of interconnection does not satisfy the synthesis procedure of Section 6-6. The difference (in the 3-dB point of the frequency response of the two cases, for example) can be quite appreciable.

Upon referring to the equipotentials and current-flow lines, it is obvious that the network of Figure 7-2(a) has a one-dimensional variation in r and c, but the network of Figure 7-2(b) does not. We therefore draw the conclusion that the electrical taper or shape need not necessarily be identical with the geometric shape of the network.

We shall now proceed to develop the relationships for one-dimensional resistance and capacitance variations for networks made of thin sheets of resistive and dielectric material.

A thin film or semiconductor distributed-parameter *RC* network is shown in Figure 7-3. It is flat, or planar. The sheets are homogeneous

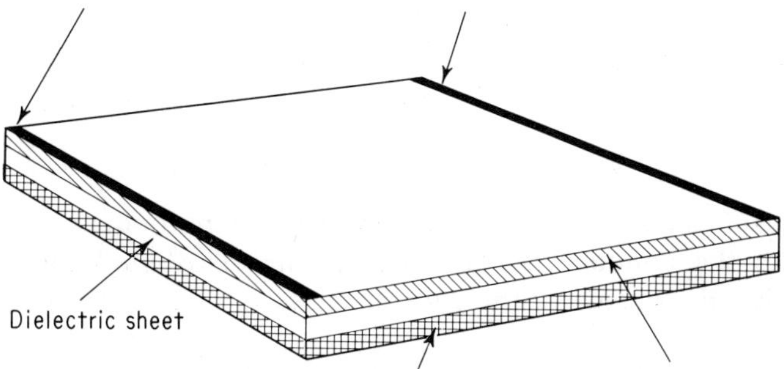

Figure 7-3 Thin film or semiconductor $\overline{RC}$ structure.

and of constant thickness. Resistance and capacitance per unit length are functions of network width and current flow is essentially two-dimensional. Further, typical dimensions and values of resistance and capacitance are such that inductive effects are negligible. Also, the equipotential lines and current-flow lines are essentially two-dimensional in character.

Under these conditions and assumptions, we can describe the behavior of the two-dimensional distributed *RC* network by considering an incremental square section of the network, as shown in Figure 7-4.

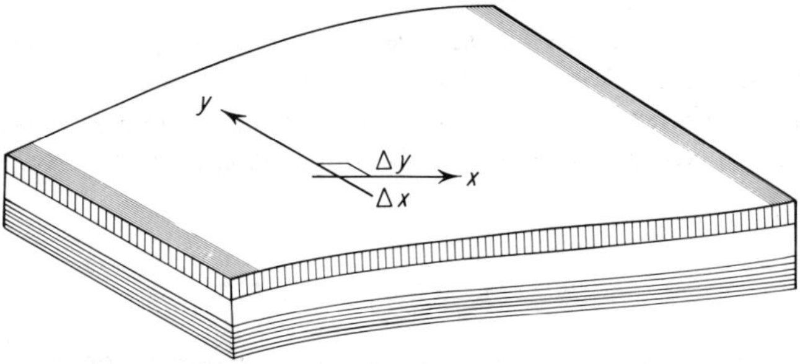

Figure 7-4 A tapered $\overline{RC}$ network.

The relationship between the electric-field vector $\mathbf{E}(t, x, y)$ and the current-density vector $\mathbf{J}(t, x, y)$ in the resistive layer is given by

$$\mathbf{E}(t, x, y) = r(x, y)\mathbf{J}(t, x, y) \tag{7-1}$$

where $r(x, y)$ is the resistance per square of the resistive layer, x and y are the position coordinates, and t is time. Note that $\mathbf{J}(t, x, y)$ has the dimensions of amperes per meter. Since the induction effects are assumed to be negligible, the field in the x-y plane is

$$\mathbf{E} = -\nabla v \tag{7-2}$$

and Equation (7-1) may be rewritten in terms of the potential $v(t, x, y)$ between a point in the resistive sheet and the conductive sheet as

$$\nabla \mathbf{v}(t, x, y) = -r(t, x, y)\mathbf{J}(t, x, y) \tag{7-3}$$

The displacement current from the incremental square of resistive material to the conducting substrate via the distributed capacitance is equal to the divergence of the current density. The relationship is

$$\nabla \cdot \mathbf{J}(t, x, y) = -c(x, y)\,\frac{\partial \mathbf{v}(t, x, y)}{\partial t} \tag{7-4}$$

where $c(x, y)$ is the capacitance per unit area. Equations (7-3) and (7-4) are the "telegrapher's equations" in vector form for the two-dimensional network.

From Equation (7-3), we note that the current density vector $\mathbf{J}$ is given by

$$\mathbf{J}(t, x, y) = -\frac{\nabla \mathbf{v}(t, x, y)}{r(x, y)} \tag{7-5}$$

Taking the divergence of $\mathbf{J}$ and relating it to the capacitance gives the two-dimensional analog of the Sturm equation, as follows:

$$\nabla \cdot \left[\frac{\nabla \mathbf{v}(t, x, y)}{r(x, y)}\right] = c(x, y)\,\frac{\partial v(t, x, y)}{\partial t} \tag{7-6}$$

Note that $r(x, y)$ is the resistance per square and $c(x, y)$ is the capacitance per unit area. For homogeneous resistive and dielectric sheets of constant thickness, $r(x, y) = r =$ a constant, and $c(x, y) = c =$ a constant. We have the simpler vector differential equation for this case; that is,

$$\nabla^2 \mathbf{v}(t, x, y) = rc\frac{\partial \mathbf{v}(t, x, y)}{\partial t} \tag{7-7}$$

where rc is the product of the per-square resistance and per-unit-area capacitance.

In transform notation, assuming an initially relaxed network, we have

$$\nabla^2 V(s, x, y) = s\tau V(s, x, y) \tag{7-8}$$

where s is the Laplace complex frequency variable and $\tau = rc$, the natural time constant of the network. It is noted that Equation (7-8) is a type of vector differential equation known as a diffusion equation; it is also classified as a Helmholtz equation. Solutions of this equation are found in the study of heat flow, of semiconductor theory, of acoustics, and of chemical processes—to name but a few fields of related interest. The methods of solution of Equation (7-8) are of interest to us since these methods provide insight into the relationship between electrical and geometric taper or shape.

Let us begin our solution of Equation (7-8) by examining the uniformly distributed *RC* network, as shown in Figure 7-5. Conducting surfaces

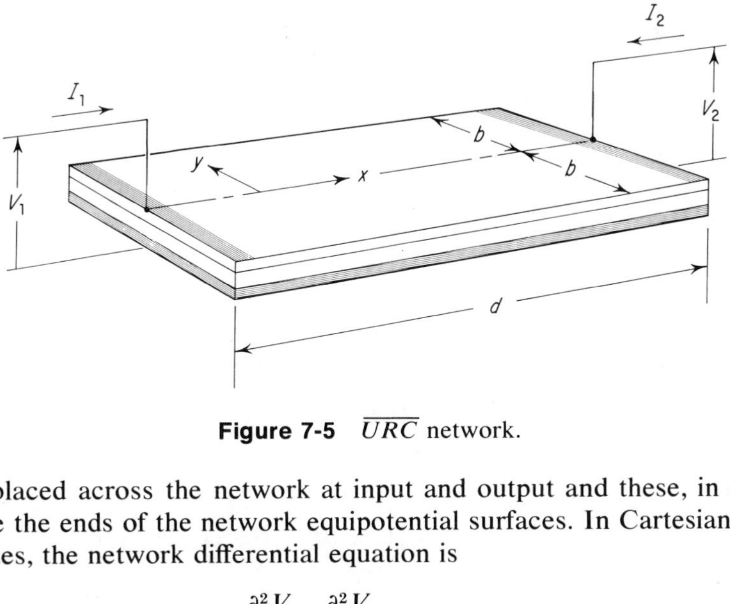

Figure 7-5 $\overline{URC}$ network.

are placed across the network at input and output and these, in effect, make the ends of the network equipotential surfaces. In Cartesian coordinates, the network differential equation is

$$\frac{\partial^2 V}{\partial x^2} + \frac{\partial^2 V}{\partial y^2} - s\tau V = 0 \tag{7-9}$$

A standard means for solving Equation (7-9) is to employ the method of *separation of variables*, in which $V(s, x, y)$ is assumed to be formed by the product of a function of s, x, and a function of s, y; that is, we assume that $V(s, x, y)$ can be written as

$$V(s, x, y) = X(s, x) \cdot Y(s, y) \tag{7-10}$$

Using this method, we have, upon substitution into Equation (7-9) and clearing fractions,

$$\frac{1}{X}\frac{\partial^2 X}{\partial x^2}+\frac{1}{Y}\frac{\partial^2 Y}{\partial y^2}-s\tau=0 \tag{7-11}$$

Note that this equation is the sum of functions of x alone and y alone. Hence, it can be separated into two ordinary differential equations

$$\frac{d^2 Y}{dy^2}+a^2 Y=0 \tag{7-12a}$$

$$\frac{d^2 X}{dx^2}-(a^2+s\tau)X=0 \tag{7-12b}$$

where a is the separation constant, which takes on values determined by the network boundary conditions. Equation (7-12a) has as a solution

$$Y=A\cos ay+B\sin ay \tag{7-13a}$$

Equation (7-12b) has as a solution

$$X=C\cosh \gamma x+D\sinh \gamma x \tag{7-13b}$$

where $\gamma=\sqrt{a^2+s\tau}$.

From the symmetry of the network, $B=0$; the complete solution is

$$V(x,y)=\sum_{i=1}^{\infty}\cos a_i y\,[C_i\cosh \gamma_i x+D_i\sinh \gamma_i x] \tag{7-14}$$

where a_i, C_i, D_i, and γ_i are found by imposing the boundary conditions

$$\begin{aligned} V&=V_1 && \text{at } x=0\\ V&=V_2 && \text{at } x=d\\ \frac{\partial V}{\partial y}&=0 && \text{at } x=0 \text{ and } x=d \end{aligned} \tag{7-15}$$

Now

$$\frac{\partial V}{\partial y}=\sum_{i=1}^{\infty}-a_i\sin a_i y\,[C_i\cosh \gamma_i x+D_i\sinh \gamma_i x] \tag{7-16}$$

and at $x=0$, $x=d$, $\partial V/\partial y$ can be zero for all y only if $a_i=0$. Thus, only one value of a_i exists, which is a_1, and this value is equal to zero. Hence, there is only one term in the summation for V [Equation (7-14)]. Thus, from the boundary conditions $\partial V/\partial y=0$ at $x=0$, $x=d$, we have

$$V(x,y)=C\cosh \gamma x+D\sinh \gamma x \tag{7-17}$$

At $x=0$ we also have

$$V_1=C \tag{7-18a}$$

and at $x=d$ we have

$$V_2=C\cosh \gamma d+D\sinh \gamma d \tag{7-18b}$$

The currents at ports 1 and 2 are found from the integral of the current density along the equipotentials at ports 1 and 2; that is,

$$I_1 = I(0) = \int_{-b}^{b} J_x(0, y)\, dy \tag{7-19a}$$

and

$$I_2 = -I(d) = -\int_{-b}^{b} J_x(d, y)\, dy \tag{7-19b}$$

From Equation (7-5) and (7-17),

$$-J_x = \frac{\nabla V}{r} = \frac{\gamma C \sinh \gamma x + \gamma D \cosh \gamma x}{r} \tag{7-20a}$$

from which we find that

$$-J_x(0, y) = \frac{\gamma D}{r} \tag{7-20b}$$

and

$$-J_x(d, y) = \frac{\gamma C \sinh \gamma d + \gamma D \cosh \gamma d}{r} \tag{7-20c}$$

Substitution of Equation (7-20) into (7-19), and performing the required integration, gives I_1 and I_2 as

$$-I_1 = \frac{2bD\gamma}{r} \tag{7-21a}$$

and

$$I_2 = \left[\frac{2bC\gamma}{r} \sinh \gamma d + \frac{2bD\gamma}{r} \cosh \gamma d\right] \tag{7-21b}$$

Using Equations (7-18) and (7-21), and eliminating the constants C and D, we can write the chain parameter or $ABCD$ matrix relation between input and output ports as

$$\begin{bmatrix} V_2 \\ I_2 \end{bmatrix} = \begin{bmatrix} \cosh \gamma d & \dfrac{r \sinh \gamma d}{2b\gamma} \\ \dfrac{2b\gamma}{r} \sinh \gamma d & \cosh \gamma d \end{bmatrix} \begin{bmatrix} V_1 \\ -I_1 \end{bmatrix} \tag{7-22a}$$

or in the impedance or Z-matrix form as

$$\begin{bmatrix} V_1 \\ V_2 \end{bmatrix} = \frac{r}{2b\gamma} \begin{bmatrix} \coth \gamma d & \operatorname{csch} \gamma d \\ \operatorname{csch} \gamma d & \coth \gamma d \end{bmatrix} \begin{bmatrix} I_1 \\ I_2 \end{bmatrix} \tag{7-22b}$$

where $2b$ is the network width and $\gamma = \sqrt{s\tau}$.

The equipotential and current-flow lines may be determined from the solution of the voltage equation with V_2 set equal to zero. Then, from Equations (7-17) and (7-18),

$$D = -V_1 \frac{\cosh \gamma d}{\sinh \gamma d} \tag{7-23}$$

To determine the equipotential lines, let us evaluate the potential at zero frequency—that is, at $s=0$. Since $\gamma=0$, we find V by passing to the limit. Thus,

$$V(x,y)=\lim_{\gamma\to 0} V_1\left[\cosh \gamma x-\cosh \gamma d\,\frac{\sinh \gamma x}{\sinh \gamma d}\right]=V_1\left(1-\frac{x}{d}\right) \tag{7-24}$$

and V is seen to be a linear function of x.

The electric-field vector $\mathbf{E}$ is found from Equation (7-24) as

$$\mathbf{E}=-\nabla V=\mathbf{i}\,\frac{V_1}{d}=\mathbf{i}E_x \tag{7-25}$$

The electric-field intensity is constant, and from Equation (7-1), the current-density vector is

$$\mathbf{J}=\mathbf{i}J_x=\mathbf{i}\,\frac{V_1}{rd} \tag{7-26}$$

Hence, the current density is constant in the x direction for $s=0$ and does not change in the y direction for $|y|\leqslant b$. Further, we note from Equations (7-24) and (7-26) that the potential V and current density J are functions of x only and hence we have an RC network with one-dimensional flow.

We illustrate the equipotential lines and flow lines in Figure 7-6. The equipotentials are equally spaced along the x axis and the current-

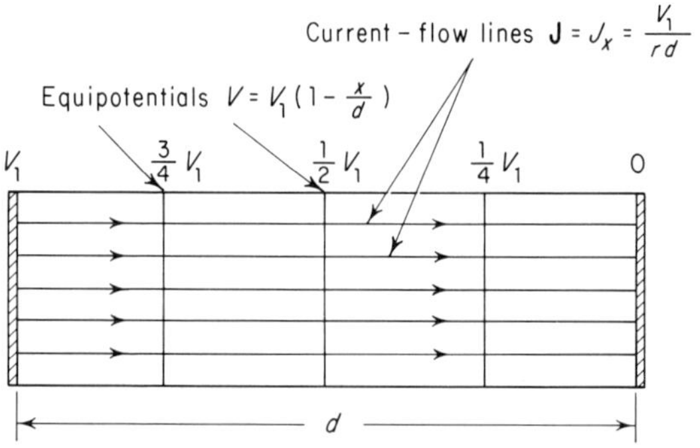

Figure 7-6 Equipotential lines and current-flow lines for $\overline{URC}$ network $(s=0)$.

flow lines are equally spaced and parallel to the x axis, as shown in Figure 7-6. In this case the electrical and geometrical shapes are the same.

The potential equation (7-8) was solved for the $\overline{URC}$ network by the method of separation of variables. In certain cases, if the coordinate system chosen matches the physical boundaries of the distributed circuit, then the solution may be obtained by separation of variables. Unfortunately, only four such coordinate systems exist for planar two-dimensional networks. These are the rectangular, polar, parabolic, and elliptic coordinate systems.[1] For distributed networks of other shapes, the variables cannot be separated and hence one-dimensional flow is not possible. However, in some cases one-dimensional flow can be approximated to an acceptable degree of accuracy.

We shall now consider the problem of approximating a given electrical taper by means of thin sheets of resistive and dielectric material cut to a geometrical pattern. To start, we must determine the flow lines and equipotentials and vary the width in a prescribed fashion.

The coordinate systems in which one-dimensional variation in planar RC networks can be achieved exactly are shown in Figure 7-7. One-dimensional RC networks may be realized by setting the network boundaries along the coordinate lines in the various systems. For instance, the $\overline{URC}$ and linear taper RC networks are realized using the coordinates of Figure 7-7(a) and (c), respectively.

Let us catalog some of these networks. Figure 7-7(a) represents the $\overline{URC}$ network. In this case the geometric and electric shapes are the same. The remaining coordinate systems have not been treated so far. First, we will determine the characteristics of the polar coordinate system of Figure 7-7(c). Here, we choose equipotential lines as circles, and current-flow lines as radii. By symmetry, equal angles subtend equal amounts of current, and the equipotentials and flow lines for polar-coordinate geometries are as shown in Figure 7-8.

Denoting port 1 as $x = 0$, and port 2 as $x = d$, with the coordinate system center at $x = -x_0$ we compute the network width W as

$$W = \frac{\theta x_0}{2\pi}\left(1 + \frac{x}{x_0}\right) = W_0\left(1 + \frac{x}{x_0}\right) \tag{7-27}$$

where $W_0 = \theta x_0/2\pi$ is the network width at $x = 0$, and θ is the total angle subtended by the network. Since capacitance per unit length (length is measured radially) is proportional to width, and resistance per unit length is inversely proportional to width, we have

$$c(x) = c_0\left(1 + \frac{x}{x_0}\right) \tag{7-28a}$$

$$r(x) = \frac{r_0}{1 + x/x_0} \tag{7-28b}$$

where c_0 and r_0 are per-unit-length capacitance and resistance at $x = 0$. Note that width is measured along an equipotential, in this case an arc.

[1] See P. M. Morse and H. Feshbach, *Methods of Theoretical Physics* (New York, McGraw-Hill, 1953), pp. 498–503. Also, P. Moon and D. Spencer, *Field Theory for Engineers* (Princeton, N. J., Van Nostrand, 1961), Chap. 12.

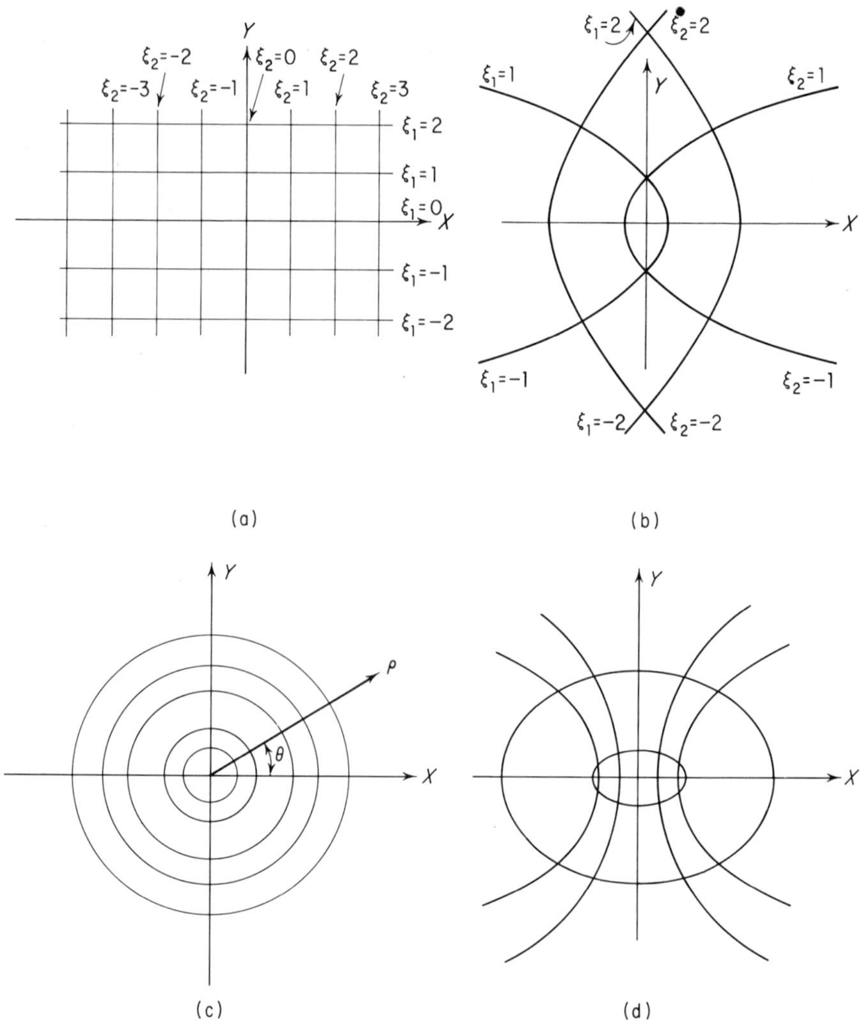

Figure 7-7 (**a**) Rectangular coordinates. (**b**) Parabolic coordinates. (**c**) Polar coordinates. (**d**) Elliptic coordinates.

Note that Equation (7-28) represents a linear variation of $r(x)$ and $c(x)$. Hence, the *polar coordinate geometry* represents the *linear electrical taper.*

Now, let us compute the voltage at various points in the network. To do this, put voltage V_0 at port 1 and zero voltage at port 2. The potential equation is

$$\frac{dV}{dx} = -ir(x) = \frac{-ir_0}{1+\dfrac{x}{x_0}} \tag{7-29}$$

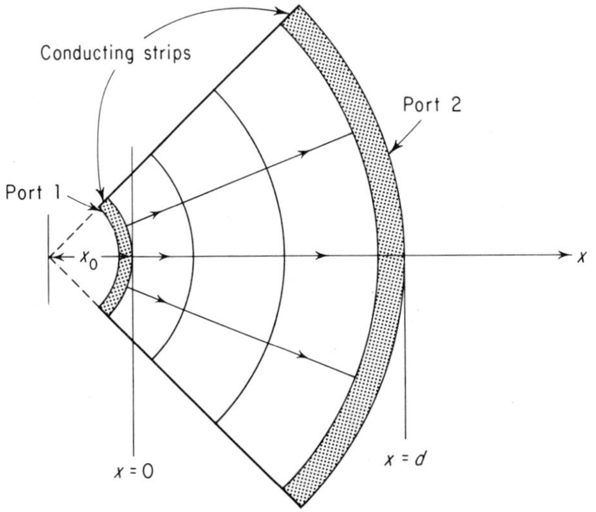

Figure 7-8 Polar coordinate $\overline{RC}$ network corresponding to linear electrical taper.

with the solution

$$V = V_0 - ir_0x_0 \ln\left(1 + \frac{x}{x_0}\right) \tag{7-30}$$

The total network resistance R is found from

$$R = \int_0^d r(x)\, dx = r_0x_0 \ln\left(1 + \frac{d}{x_0}\right) \tag{7-31}$$

Now, $i = V/R$; hence, from Equations (7-30) and (7-31),

$$V(x) = V_0\left[1 - \frac{\ln\,(1 + x/x_0)}{\ln\,(1 + d/x_0)}\right] \tag{7-32}$$

From Equation (7-32), we note that $V(x) = V_0$ at $x = 0$, and $V(x) = 0$ at $x = d$. Further, equal potential drops do not occur for equal increments of network length. The potential is $V/2$ where

$$2 \ln\left(1 + \frac{x}{x_0}\right) = \ln\left(1 + \frac{d}{x_0}\right) \tag{7-33a}$$

or where

$$\frac{x}{x_0} = \left(1 + \frac{d}{x_0}\right)^{1/2} - 1 \tag{7-33b}$$

Let us now consider the parabolic coordinate system shown in Figure 7-9. Here the coordinates are P and Q. The lines of constant P satisfy the equation

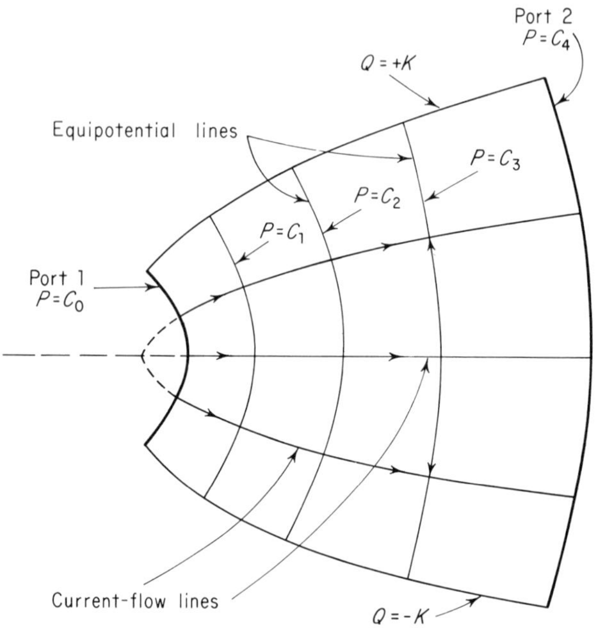

Figure 7-9 Parabolic geometry $\overline{RC}$ network (approximates square root electrical taper).

$$P = \pm \left[(x^2 + y^2)^{1/2} + x \right]^{1/2} \tag{7-34a}$$

while the lines of constant Q satisfy the equation

$$Q = \pm \left[(x^2 + y^2)^{1/2} - x \right]^{1/2} \tag{7-34b}$$

We have chosen the line $P = C_0$ as the input port 1, and $P = C_4$ as port 2. Hence, lines of constant P represent equipotentials. Since Q is orthogonal to P, lines of constant Q are current-flow lines, and the network boundary is $Q = \pm K$.

The voltage solutions to Equation (7-8) in separated variables for the parabolic coordinate system are $F(P)$ and $G(Q)$, as given by the product

$$V = F(P)G(Q) \tag{7-35a}$$

Further, F and G satisfy the Weber equations[2]

$$\frac{d^2F}{dP^2} + (K^2 - s\tau P^2)F = 0 \tag{7-35b}$$

[2] Morse and Feshbach (Ref. 1), pp. 501–502.

$$\frac{d^2G}{dQ^2} - (K^2 + s\tau Q^2)G = 0 \qquad \textbf{(7-35c)}$$

where K^2 is the separation constant similar to the separation constant a^2 in the Cartesian-coordinate case [see Equation (7-12)]. Note that the taper function associated with $r(x)$ and $c(x)$ no longer appears explicitly in Equation (7-35). We therefore use a different approach to determine $r(x)$ and $c(x)$. For small taper ratios in any planar orthogonal coordinate system, $r(x)c(x)$ is approximately constant. If the taper ratio is large, the taper functions for $r(x)$ and $c(x)$ can differ substantially.

To determine $r(x)$ and $c(x)$, we must find the network width measured along equipotentials—that is, along curves of constant P. From Equation (7-34), in (x, y) coordinates,

$$x = \tfrac{1}{2}(P^2 - Q^2) \qquad y = PQ \qquad \textbf{(7-36a)}$$

For $P =$ a constant D, we have

$$x = \tfrac{1}{2}(D^2 - Q^2) \qquad \frac{y}{D} = Q \qquad \textbf{(7-36b)}$$

Hence, on curves of constant P, the relationship

$$x = \frac{1}{2}\left(D^2 - \frac{y^2}{D^2}\right) \qquad \textbf{(7-37)}$$

holds, and we can solve for network width by integrating; that is,

$$W = \text{are length} = \int_{-DK}^{DK}\left[1 + \left(\frac{dx}{dy}\right)^2\right]^{1/2} dy \qquad \textbf{(7-38)}$$

where $y = DQ$, and the network bounds are $-K \leqslant Q \leqslant K$. Hence, from Equation (7-37),

$$\frac{dx}{dy} = -\frac{y}{D^2} \qquad \textbf{(7-39)}$$

and, from Equation (7-38),

$$W = \int_{-DK}^{DK}\left(1 + \frac{y^2}{D^4}\right)^{1/2} dy$$

$$= DK\left(1 + \frac{K^2}{D^2}\right)^{1/2} + \frac{D^2}{2}\ln\left[\frac{\left(1 + \frac{K^2}{D^2}\right)^{1/2} + \frac{K}{D}}{\left(1 + \frac{K^2}{D^2}\right)^{1/2} - \frac{K}{D}}\right] \qquad \textbf{(7-40)}$$

On the boundaries, $x = \tfrac{1}{2}(D^2 - K^2)$ and we have

$$W(x) = K[1 + (2x + k^2)^{1/2}] + \frac{(2x + k^2)}{2}\ln\left[\frac{K + (2x + 2k^2)^{1/2}}{K - (2x + 2k^2)^{1/2}}\right]$$

In the limit, for large x and small K, the parabolic geometry has

$$W(x) \to K\sqrt{2x} \tag{7-42}$$

and hence represents approximately a square-root electrical taper. Note that a large value of x and small K represents a small-taper-ratio case.

The elliptic-coordinate system is not analyzed here. However, it degenerates to a polar-coordinate geometry for large x, giving a close approximation to a linear taper.

Let us now treat a network obtained by a conformal transformation of the rectangular-coordinate system. Note that conformal transformation is not an exact method for $\overline{RC}$ networks since it is exact only for Laplace's equation—that is, static flow. However, the approximation is good for small taper ratios, in which case the product $r(x)c(x)$ is approximately constant. Using the transformation, $w = 1/z$, where $z = x + jy$, we get the coordinate geometry shown in Figure 7-10. If we choose circles of constant K for our network boundaries, our equipotentials become circles of constant D, as shown. The equipotential

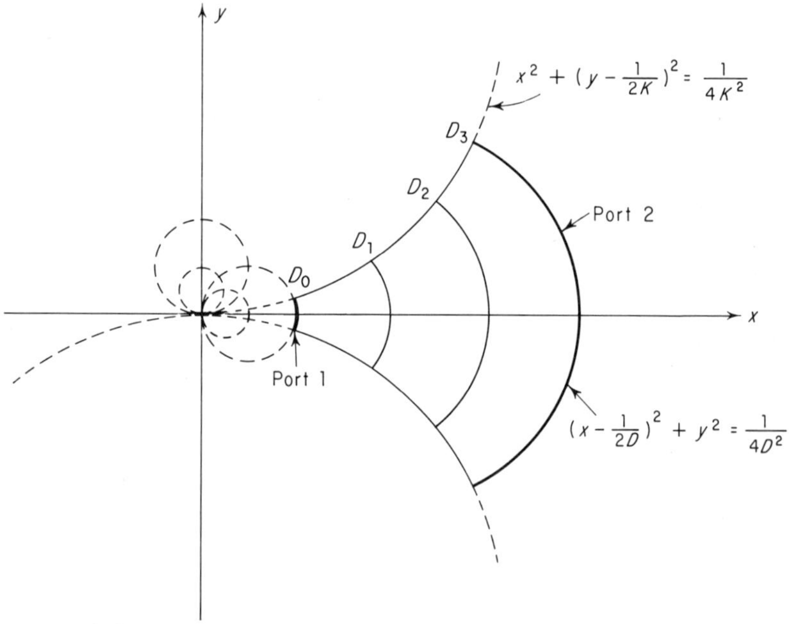

Figure 7-10 $\overline{RC}$ network from conformal transformation of $\overline{URC}$ using $w = 1/z$, $z = x + jy$ (approximates square electrical taper).

lines intersect the network borders at

$$x = y\frac{D}{K} \tag{7-43}$$

Also, along the x axis, we have

$$D = \frac{1}{x} \tag{7-44}$$

Using Equation (7-43), the network width is found from the integral

$$\begin{aligned} W &= 2\int_0^{K/D^2}\left[1+\left(\frac{D}{K}\right)^2\right]^{1/2} dy \\ &= 2\frac{K}{D^2}\left[1+\left(\frac{D}{K}\right)^2\right]^{1/2} \end{aligned} \tag{7-45}$$

Now, from Equation (7-44), the network width in terms of x is

$$W = 2Kx^2\left[1+\left(\frac{1}{Kx}\right)^2\right]^{1/2} \tag{7-46}$$

For large K and large x, the width varies approximately as the square of x. Hence, the transformation $w = 1/z$ provides a means for obtaining a geometric shape that approximates a square electrical taper.

7-3 Approximation of Electrical Taper by a Geometric Shape

We have seen that only the uniform and linear electrical tapers can be realized exactly by planar RC networks made up of homogeneous resistive and dielectric sheets. We shall now develop a graphical construction procedure by which we can determine the geometrical shape that gives a good approximation to a desired electrical taper. The construction technique is based on the use of curvilinear squares[3] to synthesize a planar RC network with the proper shape to give one-dimensional flow and approximate the desired electrical taper.

A curvilinear square is a right-angled figure, usually with four sides, that a process of regular subdivision ultimately will reduce to a collection of actual squares. Some properties of curvilinear squares are illustrated in Figure 7-11. In Figure 7-11(a), we see a rectangular figure subdivided

---

[3] See Moon and Spencer (Ref. 1), p. 15.

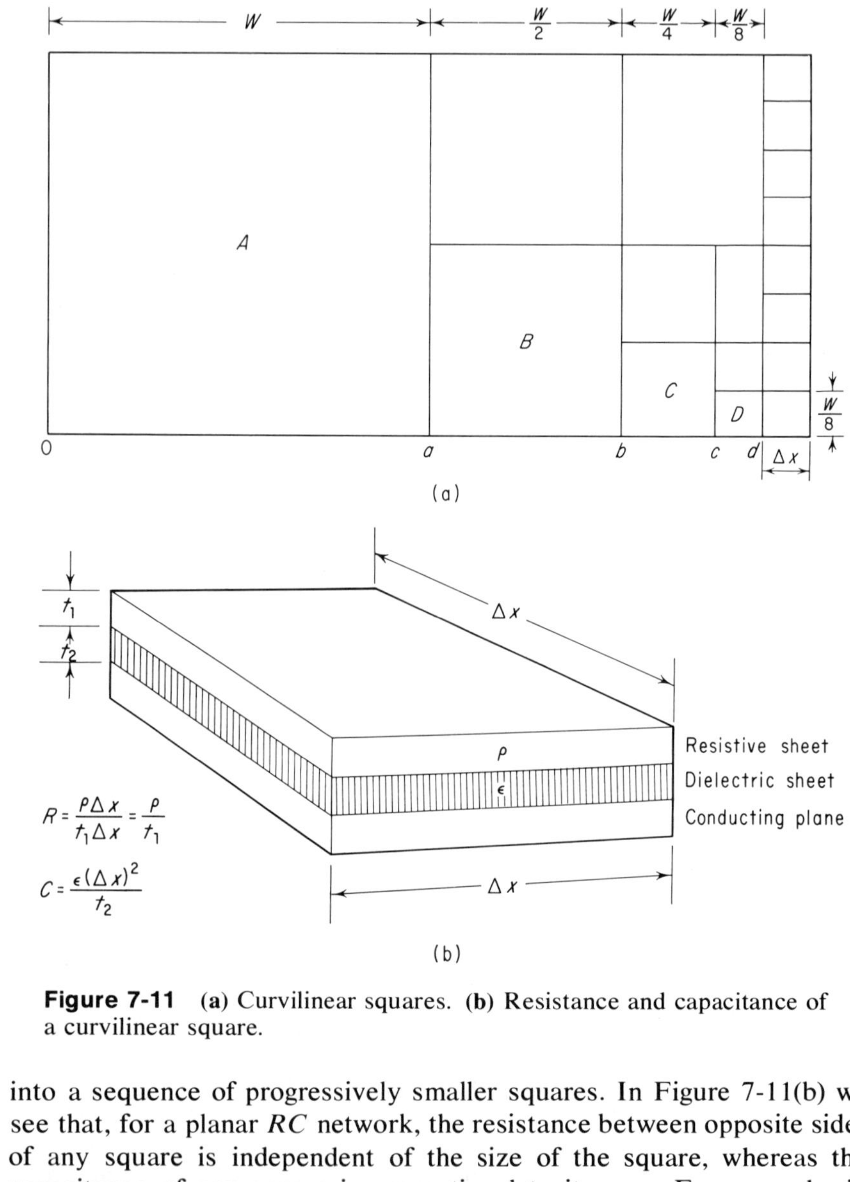

Figure 7-11 **(a)** Curvilinear squares. **(b)** Resistance and capacitance of a curvilinear square.

into a sequence of progressively smaller squares. In Figure 7-11(b) we see that, for a planar *RC* network, the resistance between opposite sides of any square is independent of the size of the square, whereas the capacitance of any square is proportional to its area. For example, in Figure 7-11(a), squares *A*, *B*, *C*, and *D* have the same resistance, whereas the capacitance of square *B* is one fourth the capacitance of square *A*.

Let us now suppose that we have mapped the flow lines and equipotentials of a planar *RC* network in curvilinear squares, as shown in Figure 7-11(a). We can then find the resistance and capacitance per unit length simply by counting squares. For example, in the length Δx shown in Figure 7-11(a), the network width is eight curvilinear squares. Since the resistive elements are in parallel, the resistance per unit length is $R/8W$, while the capacitance per unit length is $8WC$, where W is the network width and Δx, the unit length, is $W/8$.

A graphical technique for obtaining field patterns in curvilinear square form when the flow lines are known has been developed by Moore.[4] In Figure 7-12, *abcd* is assumed to be a true curvilinear square. When a

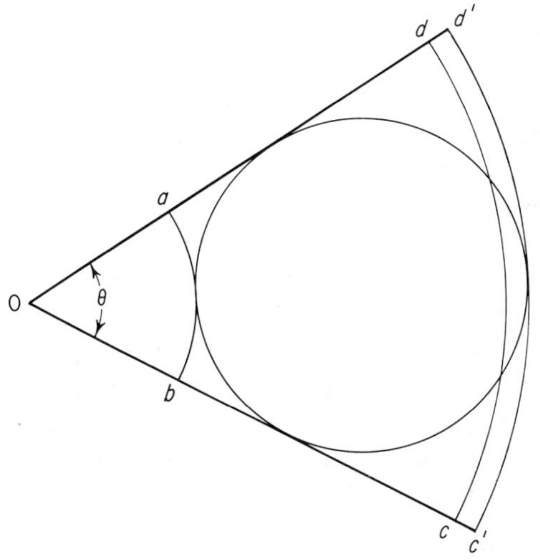

Figure 7-12 True and approximate curvilinear squares.

circle is fitted tangent to three sides (*ab*, *ad*, *bc*) and a fourth tangent to the circle ($c'd'$) drawn, then the new figure $abc'd'$ is approximately a curvilinear square. Moore has tabulated the error in the approximation as a function of the angle θ, as given in Table 7-1.

Table 7-1 THE EXCESS IN $abc'd'$

θ, DEGREES	EXCESS AS A PERCENTAGE OF *abcd*	EXCESS AS A PERCENTAGE OF CIRCLE DIAMETER
10	0.15	0.16
20	0.52	0.60
30	1.16	1.48
40	2.10	2.84
50	3.33	4.82
60	4.91	7.52

[4] A. D. Moore, *Trans. AIEE,* **71** (1952), pt. I, 1–6. See also J. D. Kraus, *Electromagnetics* (New York, McGraw-Hill, 1963), pp. 567–573.

For example, for an angle of 60 degrees, the resistance of ab to $c'd'$ is 1.0491 times the resistance of the true curvilinear square ab to cd, and the distance ac' to the equipotential line $c'd'$ is 7.52 percent greater than it should be for a true curvilinear square. However, for angles of 20 degrees and less, these errors are negligibly small, 0.52 and 0.60 percent, respectively, and the circle method provides an accurate and simple way of constructing curvilinear squares. (See Problem 7-8.)

In addition, from Figure 7-11, we see that the resistance and capacitance per unit length will be inversely proportional to each other only if the curvilinear squares have the same dimensions across the width of the network. This is equivalent to saying that the distance between equipotentials must be constant over the network length for the product $r(x)c(x) = \tau(x)$ to be a constant. Now, let us describe a construction technique that produces orthogonal flow lines and equipotential lines. Those regions obtained in the construction where distances between equipotentials remain constant over the network width can be used to synthesize planar RC networks with a specified electrical taper.

We construct an electrical taper, $p(x)$, where $p(x)$ is width measured along an equipotential from centerline to border. Interior flow lines are constructed separately. For four interior flow lines, $p_1(x) = p(x)$, $p_{3/4}(x) = (3/4)p(x)$, $p_{1/2}(x) = (1/2)p(x)$, and so on. As shown in Figure 7-13(a), the construction procedure is as follows:

1. Calculate $p_1(x_1)$ at $x = x_1$.
2. Calculate $p_1'(x_1)$ at $x = x_1$.
3. Calculate $\theta_1 = \tan^{-1} p_1'(x_1)$ at $x = x_1$.

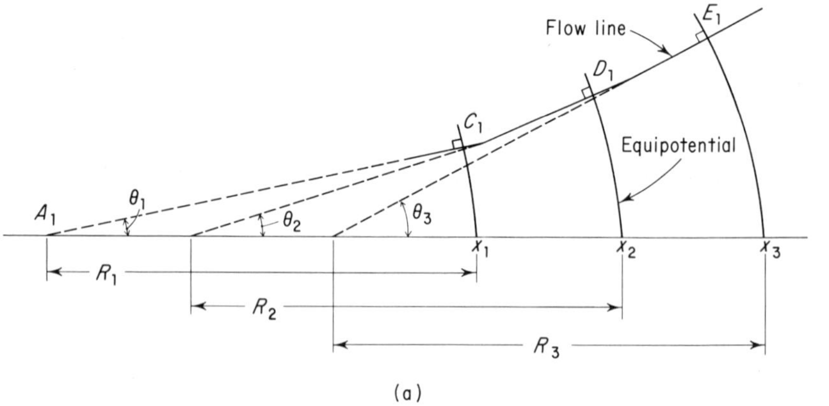

Figure 7-13 (a) Figure illustrating construction procedure to obtain geometric shape for a given electrical taper.

Flow line	$X_1 = 3$	$X_2 = 4$	$X_3 = 5$
$p_1(x)$	$R_1 = 2.59$, $\theta_1 = 14.88°$	$R_1 = 2.62$, $\theta_1 = 21.6°$	$R_1 = 2.77$, $\theta_1 = 30.55°$
$p_{3/4}(x)$	$R_{3/4} = 2.53$, $\theta_{3/4} = 11.28°$	$R_{3/4} = 2.57$, $\theta_{3/4} = 16.52°$	$R_{3/4} = 2.66$, $\theta_{3/4} = 23.90°$
$p_{1/2}(x)$	$R_{1/2} = 2.51$, $\theta_{1/2} = 7.56°$	$R_{1/2} = 2.53$, $\theta_{1/2} = 11.21°$	$R_{1/2} = 2.57$, $\theta_{1/2} = 16.49°$
$p_{1/4}(x)$	$R_{1/4} = 2.50$, $\theta_{1/4} = 3.81°$	$R_{1/4} = 2.50$, $\theta_{1/4} = 5.68°$	$R_{1/4} = 2.51$, $\theta_{1/4} = 8.40°$

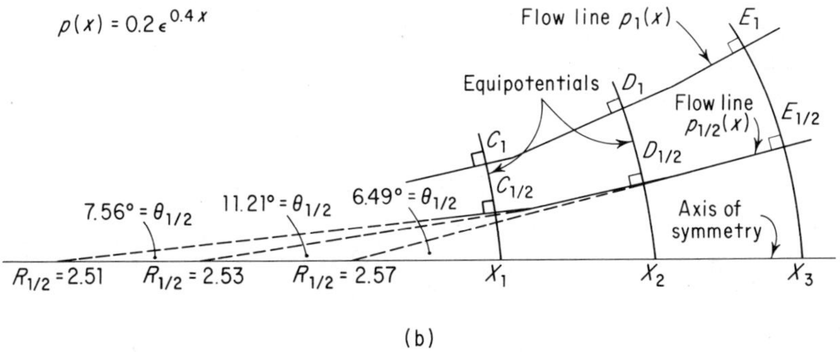

Figure 7-13 (b) Construction detail for an exponential electrical taper.

4. Calculate $R_1 = p_1(x_1)/\theta_1$ at $x = x_1$, that is, $p_1(x_1) = R_1\theta_1$.
5. Lay off R_1 from x_1 to locate point A_1, that is, $A_1 = x_1 - R_1$.
6. At point A_1, lay off line A_1C_1 with angle θ_1 to the x axis.
7. From point A_1, draw an arc of radius R_1 from x_1 to intersect A_1C_1. This locates point C_1.
8. Repeat steps 1 through 7 to locate point D_1 and E_1 corresponding to $x = x_2$ and $x = x_3$.
9. Join points C_1, D_1 and E_1 to form a portion of a flow line.
10. Arcs x_1C_1 and x_2D_1 and x_3E_1 represent equipotentials.
11. Repeat steps 1 through 10 for flow line $p_{1/2}(x)$.
12. Repeat the process for as many flow lines as desired.

The construction technique for obtaining intermediate flow lines is shown in Figure 7-13(b), where the electrical taper function is

$$p(x) = 0.2\epsilon^{0.4x} = p_1(x)$$

The details of calculation and construction for $p_{1/2}(x)$ is shown in Fig. 7-13(b) and the Table accompanying it.

In Figure 7-14 exponential, square, and square-root electrical tapers are developed using the construction technique just described. The lower portions of each figure show the flow lines obtained by the construction. The upper portions of the figures show curvilinear squares fitted to the flow lines. Those regions in which the distance between equipotentials

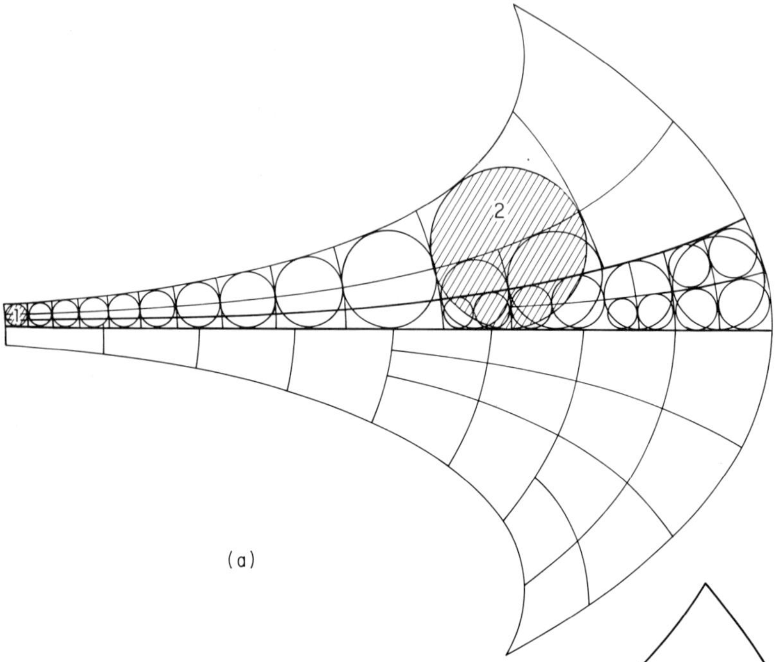

(a)

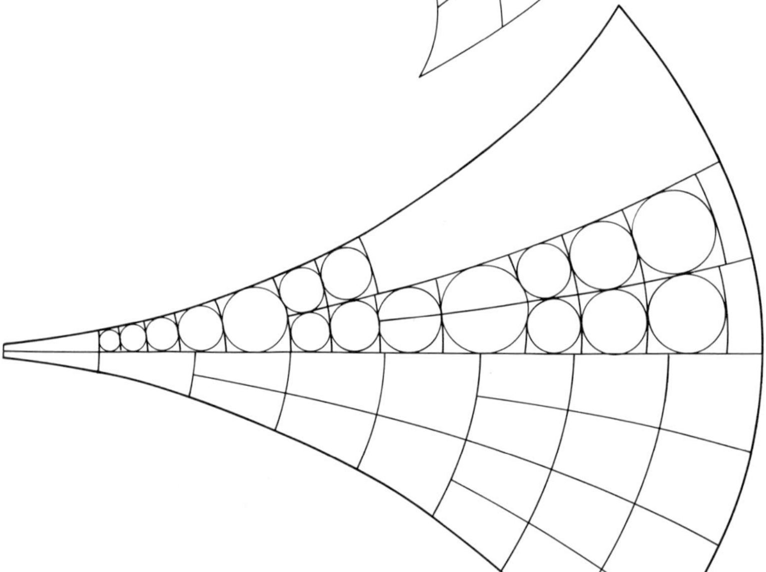

(b)

remains constant are regions of one-dimensional flow and are the regions in which the construction technique realizes the specified electrical taper.

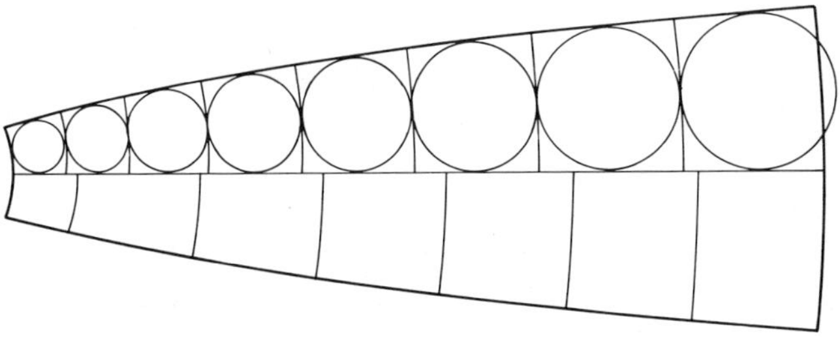

(c)

Figure 7-14 (a) Geometric shape for an exponential electrical taper. (b) Geometric shape for a square electrical taper. (c) Geometric shape for a square-root electrical taper.

Note that the method of curvilinear squares shows the two-dimensional flow lines and equipotentials at zero frequency for planar homogeneous material. That is, it is a graphical means of solving Laplace's equation $\nabla^2 V = 0$. The method described above establishes the flow lines at zero frequency. The flow lines and equipotential lines will stay approximately the same for other than zero-frequency excitation provided the network geometric shape is restricted so that the resistance and capacitance per unit length are approximately constant across the width of the network. In other words, in Figure 7-14(a), the area marked by the bold-faced outline provides a more accurate approximation to the exponential electrical taper for the same taper ratio than does the complete figure. Note also that the resistance of curvilinear squares (1) and (2) in Figure 7-14(a) are the same, whereas the capacitances are proportional to the area. Since large-area sections represent only a small fraction of the total number of squares, the error due to variation of the flow lines in the larger squares is small.

7-4 Multilayer Distributed *RC* Networks

Multilayer structures offer potential advantages in integrated circuits. A multilayer distributed *RC* structure is shown in Figure 7-15 along with its circuit representation. This network is also sometimes referred to as the double Kelvin line. Note that the structure shown is a four-port network, and hence its analysis is more involved than the single-layer two-port distributed networks considered so far. The incremental model

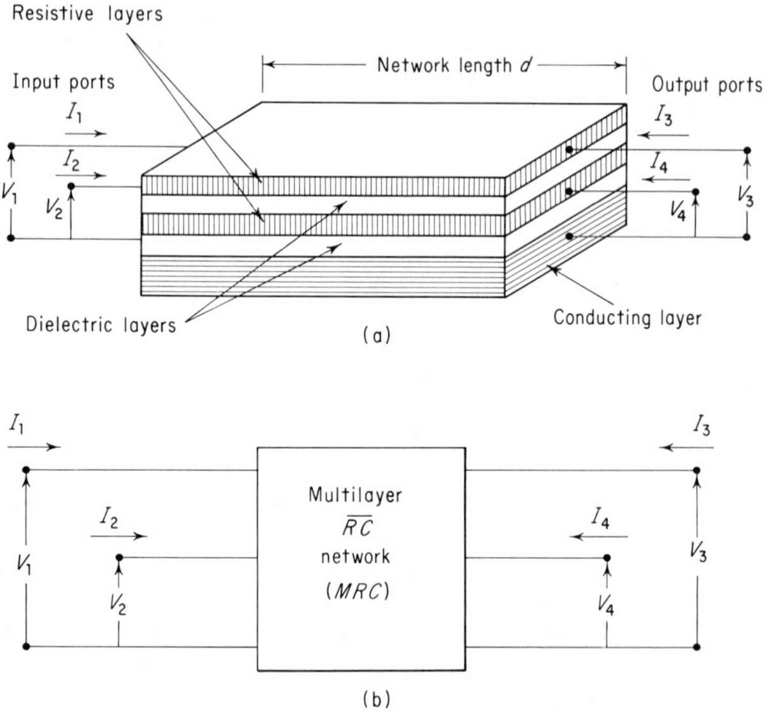

Figure 7-15 **(a)** Multilayer $\overline{RC}$ structure. **(b)** Four-port schematic representation.

for the multilayer network is shown in Figure 7-16. In terms of the four-port quantities, we define $V_1 = \mathscr{L}[e_1(0) + e_2(0)] = E_1(0) + E_2(0)$, $V_2 = \mathscr{L}[e_2(0)]$, $V_3 = \mathscr{L}[e_1(d) + e_2(d)]$, and $V_4 = \mathscr{L}[e_2(d)]$; also, $I_1 = \mathscr{L}[i_1(0)]$, $I_2 = \mathscr{L}[i_2(0)]$, $I_3 = \mathscr{L}[-i_1(d)]$ and $I_4 = \mathscr{L}[-i_2(d)]$, where $\mathscr{L}$ is the Laplace transform. To obtain the solution of the four-port relationships, we first solve for E_1, E_2, I_1, and I_2; we then combine the resulting equations to find I_1, I_2, I_3, I_4, V_1, V_2, V_3, and V_4.

First, let us find the differential equations describing the general multilayer distributed RC network ($\overline{GMRC}$) with parameters $r_1(x)$, $r_2(x)$, $c_1(x)$, and $c_2(x)$. Assuming that the network is initially relaxed, we have, in transform notation,

$$E_1(s, x) = E_1(s, x + \Delta x) + I_1(s, x) r_1(x)\ \Delta x - I_2(s, x) r_2(x)\ \Delta x \qquad \textbf{(7-47)}$$

and in the limit, as $\Delta x \to 0$,

$$\frac{dE_1(s, x)}{dx} = -r_1(x) I_1(s, x) + r_2(x) I_2(s, x) \qquad \textbf{(7-48a)}$$

In a similar fashion, we obtain the relations for the remaining variables; thus,

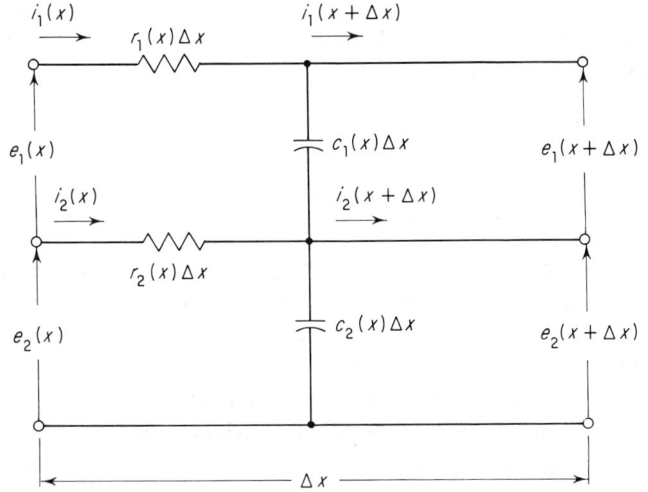

Figure 7-16 Incremental model for $\overline{MRC}$.

$$\frac{dE_2(s,x)}{dx} = -r_2(x)I_2(s,x) \tag{7-48b}$$

$$\frac{dI_1(s,x)}{dx} = -sc_1(x)E_1(s,x) \tag{7-48c}$$

$$\frac{dI_2(s,x)}{dx} = sc_1(x)E_1(s,x) - sc_2(x)E_2(s,x) \tag{7-48d}$$

where E_1, E_2, I_1, and I_2 are the Laplace transforms of the voltages and currents, respectively, and $r_1(x)$, $r_2(x)$, $c_1(x)$, and $c_2(x)$ are the per-unit-length resistance and capacitance of the network layers.

A number of methods are available for the solution of the network equations (7-48). In the general case, with tapered r_1, r_2, c_1, and c_2, closed-form solutions do not exist. Hence, the study of the general solution of tapered $\overline{GMRC}$ structures lies in the realm of numerical methods of solution of systems of differential equations and is beyond the scope of this book. However, the study of the uniform (nontapered) multilayer circuit is not so complex and is treated here. For the uniform multilayer distributed RC network ($\overline{UMRC}$), the voltage and current relations can be written in matrix form as

$$\frac{d}{dx}\begin{bmatrix} E_1 \\ E_2 \\ I_1 \\ I_2 \end{bmatrix} = \begin{bmatrix} 0 & 0 & -r_1 & +r_2 \\ 0 & 0 & 0 & -r_2 \\ -sc_1 & 0 & 0 & 0 \\ +sc_1 & -sc_2 & 0 & 0 \end{bmatrix} \begin{bmatrix} E_1 \\ E_2 \\ I_1 \\ I_2 \end{bmatrix} \tag{7-49}$$

where r_1, r_2, c_1, and c_2 are constants. The system of equations given by Equation (7-49) is homogeneous and linear, and the solutions are known to be of the form $E = a\epsilon^{\lambda x}$, $I = b\epsilon^{\lambda x}$. Substitution of these into Equation (7-49) and canceling the common factor $\epsilon^{\lambda x}$ gives the relationship in determinant form as

$$\begin{bmatrix} \lambda a_1 \\ \lambda a_2 \\ \lambda b_1 \\ \lambda b_2 \end{bmatrix} = \begin{bmatrix} 0 & 0 & -r_1 & +r_2 \\ 0 & 0 & 0 & -r_2 \\ -sc_1 & 0 & 0 & 0 \\ +sc_1 & -sc_2 & 0 & 0 \end{bmatrix} \begin{bmatrix} a_1 \\ a_2 \\ b_1 \\ b_2 \end{bmatrix} \tag{7-50}$$

Nontrivial solutions of Equation (7-50) are those for which $a_i \neq 0$, $b_i \neq 0$. They are obtainable by setting the determinant of the coefficients of a and b equal to zero. This determinant is called the characteristic equation of the system of linear differential equations. The roots, the values of λ for which the determinant vanishes, are called the characteristic roots. For the $\overline{UMRC}$, the characteristic equation, found by rearranging Equation (7-50), is

$$\begin{bmatrix} -\lambda & 0 & -r_1 & r_2 \\ 0 & -\lambda & 0 & -r_2 \\ -sc_1 & 0 & -\lambda & 0 \\ sc_1 & -sc_2 & 0 & -\lambda \end{bmatrix} = 0 \tag{7-51}$$

The characteristic roots λ_i are found by expanding this determinant. Straightforward expansion yields the characteristic equation

$$\lambda^4 - \lambda^2 s[r_1c_1 + r_2(c_1 + c_2)] + s^2 r_1 r_2 c_1 c_2 = 0 \tag{7-52a}$$

with characteristic roots given by

$$\lambda^2 = \frac{s[r_1c_1 + r_2(c_1 + c_2)]}{2}\left[1 \pm \left\{1 - \frac{4r_1r_2c_1c_2}{[r_1c_1 + r_2(c_1 + c_2)]^2}\right\}^{1/2}\right] \tag{7-52b}$$

On taking the root, we obtain two pairs of solutions

$$\lambda_{1,2} = \pm\alpha \qquad \lambda_{3,4} = \pm\beta \tag{7-53}$$

where α and β are used for brevity to represent the roots.

Example 1

When $r_1 = r_2 = r$ and $c_1 = c_2 = c$,

$$\lambda^2 = s\,\frac{3rc}{2}\left[1 \pm \left(1 - \frac{4r^2c^2}{9r^2c^2}\right)^{1/2}\right] \tag{7-54}$$

$$\lambda^2 = s\,\frac{3rc}{2}\left[1 \pm \frac{\sqrt{5}}{3}\right]$$

$$= 0.382\,src \quad \text{or} \quad 2.62\,src$$

and $$\alpha = \pm\sqrt{0.382\,src} = \pm 0.618\sqrt{src}$$
$$\beta = \pm\sqrt{2.62\,src} = \pm 1.62\sqrt{src}$$

Note that the characteristic roots for the $\overline{UMRC}$ involve $\sqrt{src}$, just as does the simpler single-layer $\overline{URC}$ network. Since the network is passive RC, we expect the natural frequencies to be on the negative real axis.

Before pursuing further the solution of the network equations, let us determine whether λ can be a complex number. Upon expansion of the terms inside the radical in Equation (7-54) we find the expression

$$\left\{1 - \frac{4r_1r_2c_1c_2}{[r_1c_1 + r_2(c_1 + c_2)]^2}\right\} = \frac{(r_1c_1)^2 + (r_2c_2)^2 + \cdots - 2r_1r_2c_1c_2}{\text{DENOMINATOR}} > 0 \tag{7-55}$$

The numerator of Equation (7-55) is a larger positive number than $(r_1c_1 - r_2c_2)^2$, and since the square of a real number is never negative, the term inside the radical of Equation (7-52b) is positive. Hence, the radical is itself a real number. From this, we infer that λ^2 is always a positive real number and that the characteristic roots α and β are always real for the $\overline{UMRC}$ network.

The general solution for the $\overline{UMRC}$ network voltages and currents in the traveling-wave sense is given by the exponential relations

$$E_1 = A_1\epsilon^{\alpha x} + B_1\epsilon^{-\alpha x} + C_1\epsilon^{\beta x} + D_1\epsilon^{-\beta x} \tag{7-56a}$$

$$E_2 = A_2\epsilon^{\alpha x} + B_2\epsilon^{-\alpha x} + C_2\epsilon^{\beta x} + D_2\epsilon^{-\beta x} \tag{7-56b}$$

$$I_1 = A_3\epsilon^{\alpha x} + B_3\epsilon^{-\alpha x} + C_3\epsilon^{\beta x} + D_3\epsilon^{-\beta x} \tag{7-56c}$$

$$I_2 = A_4\epsilon^{\alpha x} + B_4\epsilon^{-\alpha x} + C_4\epsilon^{\beta x} + D_4\epsilon^{-\beta x} \tag{7-56d}$$

where the coefficients A_i, B_i, C_i, and D_i are evaluated by specifying boundary conditions on the network voltages and currents at $x = 0$ and $x = d$. The procedure is tedious using Equation (7-56) since sixteen constants are involved. However, only four of these constants are independent. A better method of proceeding is to express the variables in Equation (7-56) in standing-wave notation as hyperbolic forms and find the relationship between them and the remaining variables using Equation (7-48). An example will illustrate this point.

Example 2

Find V_3/V_1 for an $\overline{UMRC}$ network with r_1, r_2, c_1, and c_2, and length d. The boundary conditions are

$$E_1(0) + E_2(0) = V_1$$
$$I_1(d) = I_2(0) = I_2(d) = 0$$

From Figure 7-15(b), $V_1 = E_1(0) + E_2(0)$ and $V_3 = E_1(d) + E_2(d)$. Thus, to find V_3/V_1, we must evaluate $E_1(x)$ and $E_2(x)$ at $x=0$ and at $x=d$. This may be done by using Equations (7-56) and (7-48) and evaluating sixteen unknowns. Alternatively, we may write $E_2(x)$ in hyperbolic form and use Equation (7-48) to find the coefficients of the other network variables. We pursue this course, and write

$$E_2(x) = A \cosh \alpha x + B \sinh \alpha x + C \cosh \beta x + D \sinh \beta x \tag{7-57a}$$

which is equivalent to Equation (7-56b). From Equation (7-48b),

$$I_2(x) = -\frac{\alpha}{r_2}[A \sinh \alpha x + B \cosh \alpha x] - \frac{\beta}{r_2}[C \sinh \beta x + D \cosh \beta x] \tag{7-57b}$$

From Equation (7-48d),

$$E_1(x) = [\phi - 1][A \cosh \alpha x + B \sinh \alpha x] + [\psi - 1][C \cosh \beta x + D \sinh \beta x] \tag{7-57c}$$

and from Equation (7-48c),

$$I_1(x) = -\frac{\alpha}{r_1}\phi[A \sinh \alpha x + B \cosh \alpha x] - \frac{\beta\psi}{r_1}[C \sinh \beta x + D \cosh \beta x] \tag{7-57d}$$

where

$$\phi = \left[1 + \frac{c_2}{c_1} - \frac{\alpha^2}{sc_1r_2}\right]$$

and

$$\psi = \left[1 + \frac{c_2}{c_1} - \frac{\beta^2}{sc_1r_2}\right]$$

Using the specified boundary conditions, we find

$$A = \frac{V_1\beta \cosh \alpha d \sinh \beta d}{\phi} \tag{7-58a}$$

$$B = \frac{-V_1\alpha \sinh \beta d \sinh \beta d}{\phi} \tag{7-58b}$$

$$C = \frac{-V_1\alpha \sinh \beta d \sinh \alpha d}{\phi} \tag{7-58c}$$

$$D = \frac{V_1\alpha \sinh \beta d \sinh \alpha d}{\phi} \tag{7-58d}$$

From Equations (7-57) and (7-58), and knowing that $V(x) = E_1(x) + E_2(x)$, we get

$$V(x) = V_1 \frac{\beta\phi \sinh \beta d \cosh (d-x)\alpha - \alpha\psi \sinh \alpha d \cosh (d-x)\beta}{\phi} \tag{7-59}$$

from which V_3/V_1 is calculated as $V(d)/V(0)$. Thus,

$$\frac{V_3}{V_1} = \frac{\beta\phi \sinh \beta d - \alpha\psi \sinh \alpha d}{\beta\phi \sinh \beta d \cosh \alpha d - \alpha\psi \sinh \alpha d \cosh \beta d} \tag{7-60}$$

and a general solution for the open-circuit voltage transfer function has been found.

The solution given by Equation (7-60) has been discussed in detail by Googe and Su.[5] Using the simplifying notation

$$u = \sqrt{s r_1 c_1 d^2} \qquad \tau = \frac{1}{2}\left[1 + \frac{r_2}{r_1} + \frac{r_2 c_2}{r_1 c_1}\right] \tag{7-61a}$$

$$A = \sqrt{\tau + \sqrt{\tau^2 - \frac{r_2 c_2}{r_1 c_1}}} \qquad B = \sqrt{\tau - \sqrt{\tau^2 - \frac{r_2 c_2}{r_1 c_1}}} \tag{7-61b}$$

from which $\alpha d = uA$ and $\beta d = uB$, Googe and Su write the open-circuit voltage transfer function $[T(u) = V_3/V_1]$ expressed in Equation (7-60), as

$$T(u) = \frac{A(A^2 - 1)\sinh Au - B(B^2 - 1)\sinh Bu}{A(A^2 - 1)\sinh Au \cosh Bu - B(B^2 - 1)\sinh Bu \cosh Au} \tag{7-62}$$

From a study of Equation (7-62), as r_2/r_1 and c_2/c_1 are varied, Figure 7-17 results. When the resistance ratio is large $(r_2/r_1 >> 1)$ the $\overline{UMRC}$ network behaves like a $\overline{URC}$ network, as shown by region a of Figure 7-17.

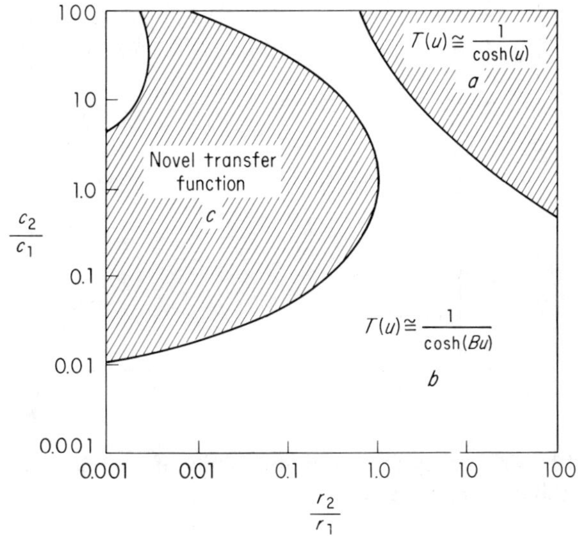

Figure 7-17 Transfer function behavior of $\overline{UMRC}$ networks. (After Googe and Su.)

A region of values of r_2/r_1 and c_2/c_1 for which the open-circuit transfer function exhibits notch-filter characteristics is shown as region c. This corresponds to the region in which Equation (7-62) has complex conjugate zeros. The zeros of the voltage transfer function are the roots of

[5] J. M. Googe and K. L. Su, *IEEE Trans. Circuit Theory*, **CT-11** (1964), 372–377.

$$\sinh Au - K \sinh Bu = 0 \tag{7-63}$$

where
$$K = \frac{B(1 - B^2)}{A(A^2 - 1)} > 0$$

Complex conjugate zeros occur for $K > 1$. A plot of the transfer functions for various ratios of r_2/r_1 and c_2/c_1 for $K = 23.12$ is shown in Figure 7-18. Note that the depth of the nulls is greatest at the highest frequency.

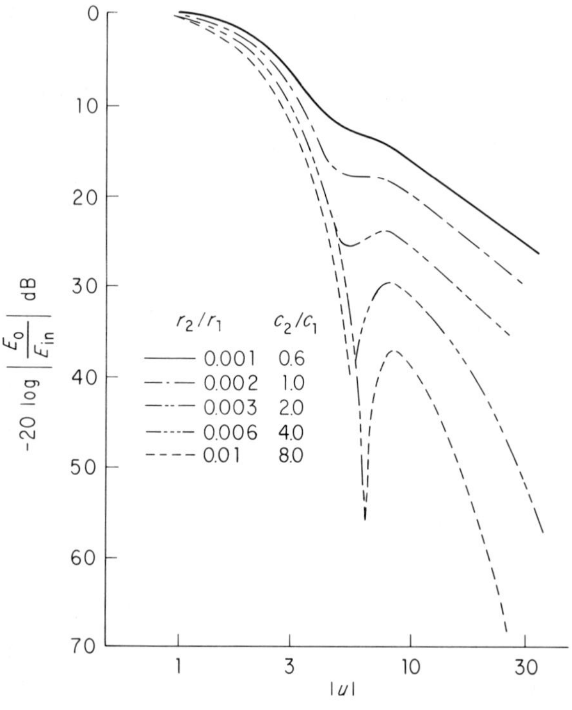

Figure 7-18 Frequency response of a family of $\overline{UMRC}$ networks having $K = 23.12$ (after Googe and Su).

This completes our brief treatment of multilayered $\overline{RC}$ networks. Those interested in further pursuit of this subject are referred to the work done by Bertnolli[6] for a discussion of the general tapered multi-layered structure.

[6] E. C. Bertnolli, Doctoral Dissertation, Spec. Rep. 57, Kansas Engineering Experiment Station, Manhattan, Kans., September 1965.

7-5 Design Considerations for $\overline{RC}$ Networks

In this section, factors of importance in the design of low-pass and bandpass network functions using $\overline{RC}$ two-ports are discussed. As shown in the previous chapters, networks made up of $\overline{RC}$ elements have an infinite number of poles and zeros. This prevents the exact realization of lumped network functions using $\overline{RC}$ elements. However, good approximations to lumped network functions can be achieved using $\overline{RC}$ elements when a group of poles and zeros of the $\overline{RC}$ network are located much closer to the origin than are the remaining poles and zeros. This group was referred to earlier as the dominant group of poles and zeros. The remaining poles and zeros, which are infinite in number, were referred to as the nondominant group. When the dominant and nondominant situation exists, the distributed RC network behaves, in the frequency range of interest, much like a lumped RC network with the poles and zeros of the dominant group. The degree of separation of the dominant and nondominant groups of poles and zeros determines the region over which a lumped network function can be realized approximately by distributed RC network elements.

Using this as a basis for design, a low-pass and a bandpass function are considered in this section. It should be pointed out that there are no unique methods of solution to the design problem using this approach. This is so because there is a large variety of $\overline{RC}$ network combinations that give equally satisfactory approximate solutions. Because the uniform $\overline{RC}$ network has the simplest $\overline{RC}$ two-port parameters, it is a good starting point for a design.

Low-pass network. First we consider an example of the design of a low-pass transfer function using distributed RC elements. Let us take the simple lumped low-pass transfer function

$$T_V(s) = \frac{V_2}{V_1} = \frac{K_0}{1 + \dfrac{s}{p_0}} \tag{7-64}$$

where K_0 is the scale factor and p_0 is the pole of the network function. Now, let us realize approximately the transfer function, Equation (7-64), using $\overline{URC}$ network elements. For the $\overline{URC}$ realization, the transfer function is written in the form

$$T_V(s) = \frac{K_0}{1 + \dfrac{s}{p_0}} N_\epsilon(s) \tag{7-65}$$

where K_0 is the scale factor, p_0 is the dominant pole of the $\overline{URC}$ network and $N_\epsilon(s)$ is a factor that contains all the nondominant poles and zeros of the transfer function. Thus, $N_\epsilon(s)$ is a measure of the error in the approximation. Let us place restrictions on the amplitude and phase of $N_\epsilon(j\omega)$.

It is desired to realize the transfer function, Equation (7-65), within a magnitude error of 1 dB and a phase error of 10 degrees from zero frequency to a frequency ten times the -3-dB frequency p_0. Writing $N_\epsilon(s)$ in terms of its magnitude and phase, these requirements are

$$0.89 \leqslant |N(j\omega)| \leqslant 1.12$$

$$\arg N_\epsilon(j\omega) \leqslant 0.175 \text{ radian}$$

$$\omega \leqslant 10\, p_0 \tag{7-66}$$

It is noted that (7-66) cannot be evaluated until an expression for $N_\epsilon(s)$ is obtained. This implies that a network configuration must be chosen and the error estimated as the first step in the realization of the transfer function. From the error estimate, the required separation of dominant and nondominant poles and zeros is determined and related to the network parameters.

To illustrate the design procedure, let us choose a $\overline{URC}$-$\overline{URC}$ network whose transfer function resembles the desired function. Since Equation (7-64) contains only a single pole, let us use a $\overline{URC}$-$\overline{URC}$ network which is known to have an all-pole transfer function; see Figure 7-19. This network was discussed in Section 5-4. Its transfer function, with $d_1 = 2d_2$, is

$$T_V = \frac{1}{\cosh 2\theta_2 + K_1 (\cosh 2\theta_2 - 1)} \tag{7-67}$$

where $\theta_2 = (sT_2)^{1/2}$, $T_2 = r_{02}c_{02}d_2^{\,2}$, and $K_1 = 2W_2/W_1$. The poles of Equation (7-67) lie at

$$p_m = \frac{-1}{4T}\left[PV\left\{\cos^{-1}\frac{K_1}{1+K_1}\right\} \pm 2m\pi\right]^2 \tag{7-68}$$

where PV stands for *principal value*. Aside from p_0, the dominant pole, the remaining poles are grouped in pairs about

$$p_{n_{1,2}} = -\frac{(n\pi)^2}{T_2}$$

For large K_1, $\cos^{-1} K_1/(1 + K_1) << 1$ and these nondominant poles are very nearly second order. Thus, we can write $N_\epsilon(s)$ as

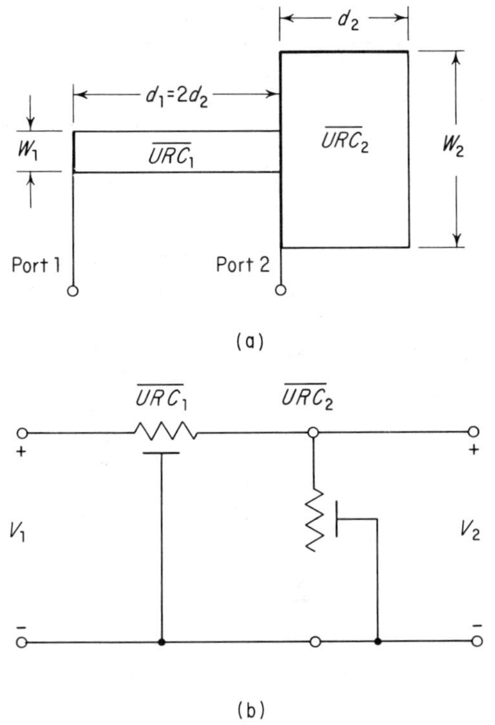

Figure 7-19 (a) $\overline{URC}$-$\overline{URC}$ network. (b) Schematic representation of $\overline{URC}$-$\overline{URC}$ network.

$$N_\epsilon(s) \approx \prod_{n=1}^{\infty} \left[\frac{1}{1 + \dfrac{sT_2}{(n\pi)^2}} \right]^2 \tag{7-69}$$

and find the error magnitude function as

$$|N_\epsilon(j\omega)|^2 \approx \prod_{n=1}^{\infty} \left[\frac{1}{1 + \dfrac{(\omega T_2)^2}{(n\pi)^4}} \right]^2 \tag{7-70}$$

which has the approximate value, obtained by expanding Equation (7-70) in an infinite series, and inverting and truncating at the second term,

$$|N_\epsilon(j\omega)|^2 \approx 1 - \frac{(\omega T_2)^2}{45} \tag{7-71}$$

Now, from Equation (7-66), $(\omega T_2)^2/45 < 0.12$, and $\omega < 10p_0$. Hence, from the restrictions on the magnitude function

$$|p_0| < \frac{1}{T_2}\left(\frac{0.12 \times 45}{100}\right)^{1/2} < \frac{0.232}{T_2} \tag{7-72}$$

Also, from Equation (7-68), the first nondominant pole pair is grouped about $p_1 = -\pi^2/T_2$. Hence, Equation (7-72) can also be written as

$$|p_0| < \frac{0.232}{\pi^2}|p_1| < \frac{|p_1|}{43} \tag{7-73}$$

Thus, for the magnitude function to be good within 1 dB up to $\omega = 10p_0$, the first nondominant pole must be 43 times farther removed from the origin than p_0.

Now let us consider the phase function, which from Eq. (7-69) is

$$\arg N_\epsilon(j\omega) \approx -2\sum_{n=1}^{\infty} \text{arc tan}\, \frac{\omega T_2}{(n\pi)^2} \tag{7-74a}$$

For $\omega < (n\pi)^2/T_2$, as required by Equation (7-71), we can replace the arc tangent by its angle in Equation (7-74a), and since

$$\sum_{n=1}^{\infty} \frac{1}{n^2} = \frac{\pi^2}{6}$$

we find that

$$\arg N_\epsilon(j\omega) \approx -\frac{\omega T_2}{3} = -\frac{\omega\pi^2}{3p_1} \tag{7-74b}$$

From the phase angle restriction of Equation (7-66), with $\omega_0 = 10p_0$, we find that

$$0.175 \approx \frac{10\pi^2 p_0}{3p_1} \tag{7-75a}$$

or

$$p_0 \approx \frac{3 \times 0.175 p_1}{10\pi^2} = \frac{p_1}{188} \tag{7-75b}$$

Hence, comparing Equations (7-73) and (7-75b), we see that the restriction on phase is more severe than the restriction on magnitude and that $p_0 \leqslant p_1/188$. Now, from Equation (7-68), we solve for K_1; thus,

$$\cos^{-1}\frac{K_1}{1+K_1} \leqslant \frac{2\pi}{\sqrt{188}} \leqslant 0.459 \tag{7-76a}$$

which gives

$$K_1 = 2\frac{W_2}{W_1} = \frac{\cos 0.495}{1 - \cos 0.495} = 8.5 \tag{7-76b}$$

Thus, using two $\overline{URC}$ networks, as shown in Figure 7-19a, with $W_2/W_1 = 4.25$, we have realized the lumped RC network transfer function

$$T_V \approx \frac{1}{1 + j\dfrac{\omega}{p_0}} \tag{7-77}$$

within a magnitude error of 1 dB and a phase error of 10 degrees up to $\omega = 10p_0$.

If the network is loaded in a resistive load Y_L, it tends to reduce the separation of the dominant and nondominant poles, and either a larger value of K_1 must be used to meet the requirements on magnitude and phase or a different configuration may be chosen.

If only magnitude approximation is of interest and active element is allowed with the distributed network the design is more flexible. (See Figure P5-5.)

Bandpass network. An important class of distributed $\overline{RC}$ circuit configurations is the bandpass network. One method of obtaining bandpass characteristic is to use a distributed $\overline{RC}$ null network in conjunction with an active network. A typical circuit configuration is shown in Figure 7-20.

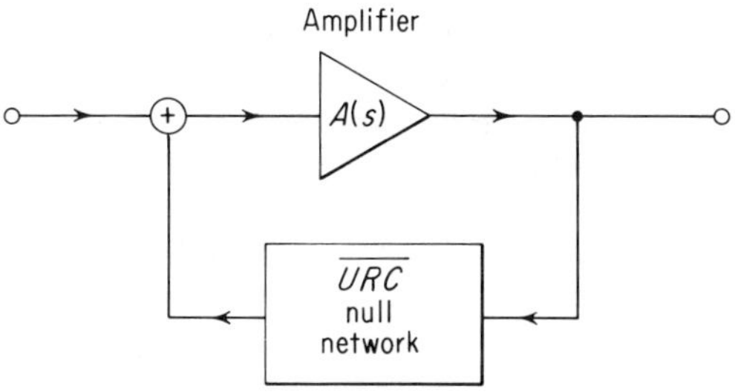

Figure 7-20 Block diagram of bandpass configuration.

Let us assume an ideal amplifier with very high gain and negligible input and output immittances. The bandpass characteristic then is determined solely by the characteristics of the feedback network. This idealization is useful in establishing an initial design. (Later, we will determine in a qualitative fashion the network performance when the amplifier is not assumed to be an ideal device.)

Consider the schematic representation of the bandpass network shown in Figure 7-21. In this representation the amplifier is assumed to have an input admittance Y_i, a negligible output impedance, and a gain $A(s)$. For the circuit shown using basic-set notation for the parameters of the null network for generality, the voltage transfer function of the circuit is

$$G(s) = \frac{V_2}{V_1} = \frac{A(s)}{1 - \dfrac{A(s)[1 + (sC/g)V_{\text{II}}]}{V'_{\text{II}} + [V_{\text{II}}(sC/g) + (Y_i/g)]}} \tag{7-78}$$

where g is $y_{11}(0)$ of the $\overline{RC}$ network, $Y_i = 1/R_i$, $A(s)$ is the gain of the

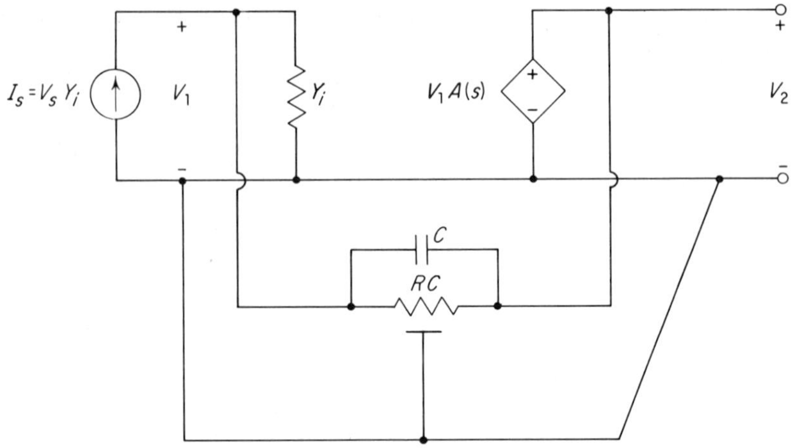

Figure 7-21 Schematic of bandpass configuration.

amplifier.

When the amplifier low-frequency gain is very large ($A_0 \to \infty$, such as in an operational amplifier) and the input admittance is assumed zero, Equation (7-78) reduces to

$$G_1(s) \approx \frac{V'_{\text{II}} + sCV_{\text{II}}/g}{1 + sCV_{\text{II}}/g} \tag{7-79}$$

The s-plane zeros of $G_1(s)$ are the roots of

$$V'_{\text{II}} + sCV_{\text{II}}/g = 0 \tag{7-80}$$

The locations of the zeros of Equation (7-80) were found in Chapter 5 for the $\overline{URC}$ network and were shown to lie on the negative real axis. The same statements can be made for the arbitrarily tapered $\overline{RC}$ two-port.

Consider now the poles of $G_1(s)$. From Equation (7-79), these are the s-plane zeros of

$$1 + sCV_{\text{II}}/g = 0 \tag{7-81}$$

These were determined in Chapter 5 for the $\overline{URC}$ network bridged by a capacitor. For other types of $\overline{RC}$ networks, where V_{II} is not available in closed form, it is possible to determine the imaginary-axis crossover of the principal loci of Equation (7-81) using the methods of Chapter 5. The imaginary-axis crossover is the null frequency of the bridged $\overline{RC}$ network and corresponds to the poles of $G_1(s)$. As such, the imaginary-axis crossovers of the principal loci of Equation (7-81) represent the center-frequency of the bandpass network described in Equation (7-79).

With V_{II} written in equivalent dominant-root and excess-phase approximation form (see Section 3-8), Equation (7-81) is

$$1 + Ks\left(1 + \frac{s}{Z_1}\right) \exp \frac{ms}{Z_1} = 0 \tag{7-82}$$

where $K = CV_{\text{II}}(0)/g$, $g = 1/r_0 d$, and Z_1 and m are the equivalent dominant-zero and excess-phase factor of V_{II}. To find the null frequency of the bridged $\overline{RC}$ network, it is necessary to find the value of ω for which

$$\arg j\omega\left(1 + \frac{j\omega}{Z_1}\right) \exp \frac{j\omega m}{Z_1} = \pi \tag{7-83}$$

Using Newton's method of approximation (see Appendix E), with

$$f(\omega) = \tan^{-1} \frac{\omega}{Z_1} + \frac{\omega m}{Z_1} - \frac{\pi}{2} \tag{7-84}$$

and

$$f'(\omega) = \frac{1}{Z_1}\left[\frac{1}{1 + (\omega/Z_1)} + m\right] \tag{7-85}$$

we find the intercept by iterating

$$\omega_{i+1} = \omega_i - \frac{f(\omega_i)}{f'(\omega_i)} \tag{7-86}$$

where ω_i is the ith approximation to the null frequency of the bridged $\overline{RC}$ network. Using the initial try $\omega_1 = Z_1$, Equation (7-86) gives

$$\omega_1 = Z_1\left[\frac{1.285}{0.5 + m}\right] \tag{7-87}$$

which provides a good design estimate of the imaginary-axis crossover of the principal locus. Hence, Equation (7-87) is a good estimate of the center frequency of the bandpass network.

Take, for example, the class of tapered $\overline{RC}$ networks for which $2y' = 4k^2 - y^2$. This class includes the uniform, exponential, hyperbolic, trigonometric, and square tapers. For this class of networks

$$V_{\text{II}} = \frac{\sinh \theta}{\theta} \tag{7-88}$$

where $\theta = \sqrt{sT + (kd)^2}$ and $T = r_0 c_0 d^2$. The equivalent dominant zero Z_1 and the excess-phase factor m for this class of networks is shown in Figure 7-22. These quantities are shown plotted as a function of kd, which is a measure of the amount of taper of the networks. It is noted from Figure 7-22 that Z_1 and m change by a moderate amount as kd varies from zero to three.

Using Z_1 and m for the tapered networks in Equation (7-87) makes it possible to determine the null frequency of the bridged $\overline{RC}$ networks. The results for the $\overline{ERC}$ and square tapers are shown in Figure 7-23, where the null frequency is plotted as a function of the taper ratio

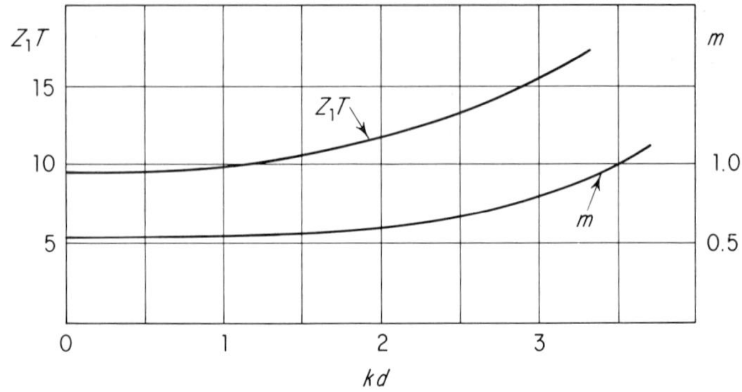

Figure 7-22 Effective dominant zero, Z_1, and excess-phase factor, m, for sinh θ/θ.

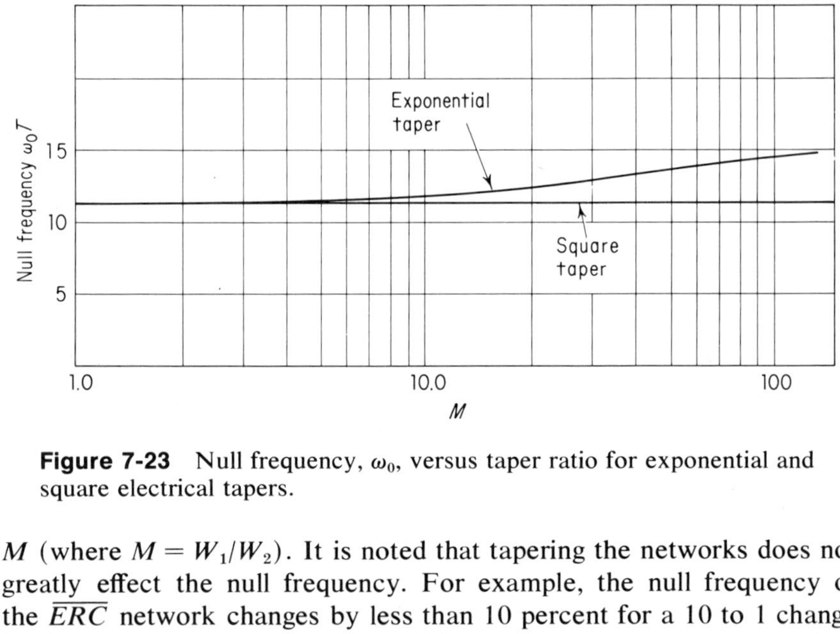

Figure 7-23 Null frequency, ω_0, versus taper ratio for exponential and square electrical tapers.

M (where $M = W_1/W_2$). It is noted that tapering the networks does not greatly effect the null frequency. For example, the null frequency of the $\overline{ERC}$ network changes by less than 10 percent for a 10 to 1 change in the taper ratio, whereas the null frequency of the square taper does not change at all. The principal effect of tapering is to change the quantity $V_{II}(0)$, and hence the value of K required for a null on the imaginary axis [see Equation (7-82)].

Based on the information given in Figure 7-23, it is seen that the tapering has only a slight effect on the center frequency of the bandpass network. For this reason, the $\overline{URC}$ is a good choice for an initial design, because of all the possible choices of tapered networks, the equations that describe the $\overline{URC}$ network are the simplest to handle.

In the design of bandpass structures, it is desirable to be able to specify the element values from a knowledge of the center frequency and the bandwidth. Consider now the configuration of Figure 7-21 with $A(s)$ a constant quantity A_0 in the frequency range of interest. For the initial step in the design, take the amplifier input admittance Y_i as zero and let the $\overline{RC}$ null network be a bridged $\overline{URC}$ network. Using Equation (7-79), we can construct a root-locus diagram of the poles of $G_1(s)$ as the value of A_0 is changed from zero to infinity. (It is assumed that A_0 is a negative number.) In this case, the loci of the poles of $G_1(s)$ start at the roots of

$$F_1(s) = V'_{\text{II}} + \frac{V_{\text{II}} sC}{g} = \cosh \theta + K\theta \sinh \theta = 0 \tag{7-89}$$

and terminate on the roots of

$$F_2(s) = 1 + \frac{V_{\text{II}} sC}{g} = 1 + K\theta \sinh \theta = 0 \tag{7-90}$$

as A_0 goes from zero to infinity. The bridging capacitance C is chosen so that the roots of Equation (7-90) lie on the imaginary axis. For the bridged $\overline{URC}$ network,

$$\frac{C}{c_0 d} = K = 0.0561 \tag{7-91}$$

and the center frequency of the bandpass configuration, for large A_0, lies very close to the null frequency of the bridged URC network; that is,

$$\omega_0 T = 11.19 \tag{7-92}$$

where ω_0 is the center frequency and $T = r_0 c_0 d^2$.

Using the value of $K = 0.0561$, the points of departure and arrival of the loci of the poles of $G(s)$ are found by numerical solution of Equations (7-89) and (7-90). The first few solutions of these equations are listed in Table 7-2.

Table 7-2 DEPARTURE AND ARRIVAL OF LOCI OF POLES OF $G(s)$ FOR $K = 0.0561$ AND $Y_i = 0$

DEPARTURE OF LOCI ZEROS OF $F_1(s)$	ARRIVAL OF LOCI ZEROS OF $F_2(s)$
$s_1 = -\dfrac{2.22}{T}$	$s_{1,2} = \pm j\dfrac{11.19}{T}$
$s_2 = -\dfrac{19.9}{T}$	

The breakaway points for the loci are at the solutions of $F_1F_2' - F_2F_1' = 0$. For the case in point, the first breakaway point occurs at $s_{b_1} = -8.19/T$.

The angle of arrival of the loci is found next. For the structure in question, $Y_i = 0$ and the angle of arrival is given by

$$\phi_a = \arg\left[\frac{-F_1(s_j)}{F_2'(s_j)}\right] = \arg\left[\frac{\cosh\theta_j + K\theta_j \sinh\theta_j}{(\theta_j\cosh\theta_j + \sinh\theta_j)2\theta_j}\right] \qquad \textbf{(7-93)}$$

where $\theta_j = \sqrt{j\omega_0 T} = 3.35\underline{/45^\circ}$ for the first locus. From Equation (7-93), the angle of arrival of the first locus is 196.8 degrees. A sketch of the loci for this case is shown in Figure 7-24. As shown in the diagram, the

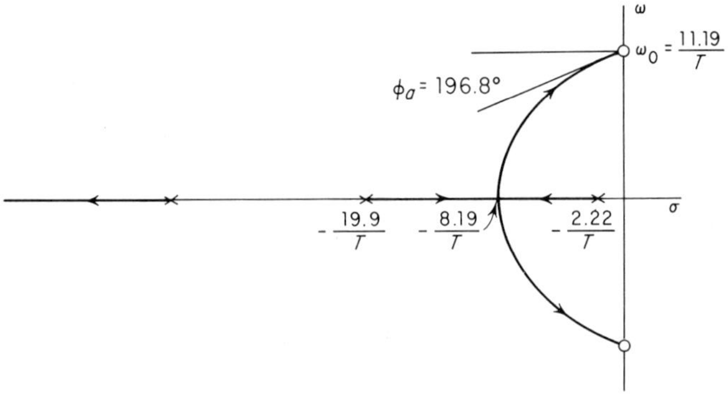

Figure 7-24 Loci of the dominant poles of $G(s)$, $K = 0.0561$, $Y_i = 0$.

poles of $G(s)$ approach the imaginary axis at an angle less than 90 degrees. Thus, it can be seen that the center frequency of the bandpass configuration changes with the gain of the system. Further, since the bandwidth is proportional to the distance of the pole from the imaginary axis, the root-locus diagram shows clearly that the bandwidth and center frequency of the bandpass configuration are related. In some applications this design would not be considered satisfactory.

It is noted that the angle of arrival of the dominant locus can be altered by moving the poles to the left on the locus diagram. This tends to reduce the angle of arrival. An ideal situation, which gives no change in the center frequency as the gain changes, occurs when the angle of arrival is 180 degrees. In this case the loci intersect the imaginary axis at right angles and the bandwidth and the center frequency are essentially independent of each other. Hence, for the narrow-band case, changes in amplifier gain do not affect the center frequency.

The angle of arrival can be altered by proper selection of Y_i, the input admittance of the amplifier. Up to this point, Y_i has been assumed to be zero; for $Y_i \neq 0$,

$$F_1(s) = \left[\cosh\theta + K\theta\sinh\theta + \frac{Y_i}{g}\frac{\sinh\theta}{\theta}\right] \quad \textbf{(7-94)}$$

but $F_2(s)$ is unchanged. The added term in $F_1(s)$, Equation (7-94), moves the zeros of $F_1(s)$ to the left along the negative real axis and thus reduces the angle of arrival. Application of numerical techniques shows that the angle of arrival is 180 degrees when $Y_i = 1.88\ g$, where $g - 1/r_0 d$. With this value of Y_i, the first few roots of Equation (7-94) are found. They are $s_1 = 4.8/T$ and $s_2 = -23.2/T$. The new breakaway point for the first locus is found approximately as $s_{b_1} = -10/T$.

The root locus for the bandpass configuration with $K = 0.0561$ and $Y_i/g = 1.88$ is shown in Figure 7-25.

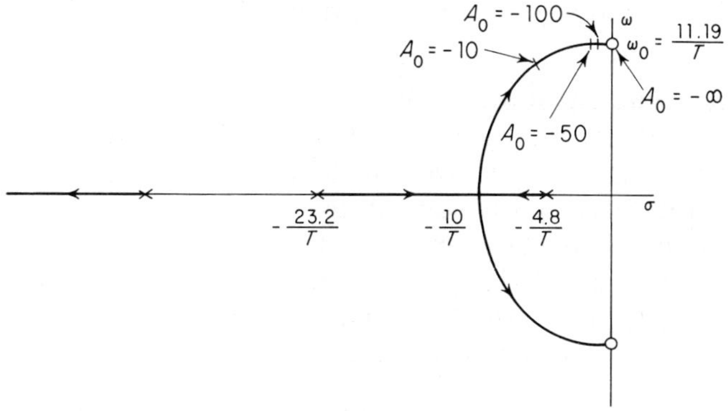

Figure 7-25 Loci of the dominant poles of $G(s)$, $K = 0.0561$, $Y_i = 1.88g$.

Behavior of the loci of the poles of $G(s)$ near the imaginary axis can be determined using the Taylor expansion of $R(s)$ discussed in Chapter 5. Thus, near ω_0(where $\omega_0 = s_j$), we find

$$s = \left[-\frac{F_1(s_j)}{F_1'(s_j) - A_0 F_2'(s_j)}\right] + s_j \quad \textbf{(7-95)}$$

where $s_j = j(11.19/T) = j\omega_0$. The numerical values of the quantities in Equation (7-95) are

$$F_1'(s_j) = \frac{8.23}{T}\ \underline{/126^\circ}$$

$$F_1(s_j) = 1.24\underline{/87^\circ}$$

$$F_2(s_j) = 0.182\underline{/126^\circ}$$

Using these values in Equation (7-95), and letting A_0 range from -10 to -100, we can construct a table that shows the behavior of the dominant pole of $G(s)$ near the imaginary axis; see Table 7-3.

Table 7-3 BEHAVIOR OF DOMINANT POLE OF $G(s)$ FOR $K = 0.0561$, $Y_i/g = 1.88$

A_0	s	ω_{cf}	$\omega_{3\text{dB}}$
-10	$-\frac{2.76}{T} + j\frac{10.41}{T}$	$\frac{10.41}{T}$	$\frac{5.52}{T}$
-50	$-\frac{0.81}{T} + j\frac{11.11}{T}$	$\frac{11.11}{T}$	$\frac{1.62}{T}$
-100	$\frac{0.429}{T} + j\frac{11.18}{T}$	$\frac{11.18}{T}$	$\frac{0.958}{T}$

For larger values of A_0, the real part of s near s_j is very nearly equal to $45.2/A_0T$, which is twice the bandwidth of the system.

Sensitivity considerations. In any bandpass design, it is desirable to know the sensitivity of the center frequency and the bandwidth to changes in circuit parameters. In the case of $\overline{RC}$ bandpass design, the sensitivity of center frequency and bandwidth to changes in the nominal value of amplifier gain A_0 and to changes in the nominal value of the bridging capacitance C are of principal interest. First, consider the sensitivity of the center frequency and bandwidth to changes in A_0.

The sensitivity functions are defined as

$$S_{A_0}^{\omega_{\text{cf}}} = \frac{\Delta\omega_{\text{cf}}/\omega_{\text{cf}}}{\Delta A_0/A_0} \tag{7-96}$$

and

$$S_{A_0}^{\omega_{3\,\text{dB}}} = \frac{\Delta\omega_{3\,\text{dB}}/\omega_{3\,\text{dB}}}{\Delta A_0/A_0} \tag{7-97}$$

where ω_{cf} and $\omega_{3\,\text{dB}}$ are the center frequency and bandwidth, respectively, of the $\overline{RC}$ bandpass network.

For a given A_0, ω_{cf} and $\omega_{3\,\text{dB}}$ may be found either by direct solution of Equation (7-78) for the real and imaginary parts of the dominant poles of $G(s)$, or from the Taylor expansion of points on the loci of the poles of $G(s)$ about ω_0 given in Equation (7-95). The latter procedure, which is the simpler to implement, is used here. From Equation (7-95),

$$\omega_{\text{cf}} \approx \omega_0 + \text{Im}\left[\frac{-F_1(j\omega_0)}{F_1'(j\omega_0) - A_0F_2'(j\omega_0)}\right] \tag{7-98}$$

and

$$\omega_{3\,\text{dB}} \approx 2\ \text{Re}\left[\frac{-F_1(j\omega_0)}{F_1'(j\omega_0) - A_0F_2'(j\omega_0)}\right] \tag{7-99}$$

where ω_0 is the point of arrival of the dominant locus of the poles of $G(s)$ on the imaginary axis.

A measure of the sensitivity of ω_{cf} and $\omega_{3\,dB}$ in the $\overline{RC}$ bandpass design may be obtained by computing the change in ω_{cf} and $\omega_{3\,dB}$ for small changes in A_0. Using the values of A_0 listed in Table 7-2, the changes in ω_{cf} and $\omega_{3\,dB}$ have been calculated for a 10 percent change in A_0 using Equations (7-98) and (7-99). These numerical values have been used in Equations (7-96) and (7-97) to estimate the sensitivity. The results are listed in Table 7-4.

Table 7-4 SENSITIVITY OF ω_{cf} AND $\omega_{3\,dB}$ FOR $K = 0.0561$, $Y_i = 1.88g$

A_0	$S_{A_0}^{\omega_{cf}}$	$S_{A_0}^{\omega_{3\,dB}}$
−10	0.0865	0.616
−50	0.0268	0.779
−100	0.001	0.885

It is noted that the sensitivity of ω_{cf} to changes in A_0 is very small and decreases considerably as A_0 becomes very large. The sensitivity of $\omega_{3\,dB}$ is higher and approaches the value of 0.904 asymptotically as A_0 approaches infinity.

The calculation of the sensitivity functions for changes in the bridging capacitance is much more difficult than the calculation of the sensitivity function for A_0. A change in the bridging capacitance C changes K in Equation (7-89), and hence changes the position of the points of arrival of the dominant loci of $G(s)$, as well as the points of arrival of all the non-dominant loci. The points of arrival are not explicit functions of C, but must be found by solution of a transcendental equation.

After we have obtained the new points of arrival by numerical techniques, Equation (7-95) can be used to determine the new positions on the loci of the poles of $G(s)$ for a specific value of A_0 when C is changed. The results are listed in Table 7-5.

Table 7-5 SENSITIVITY OF ω_{cf} AND $\omega_{3\,dB}$ TO CHANGES IN C (+9.6% CHANGE IN C USED FOR CALCULATIONS)

A_0	$S_{A_0}^{\omega_{cf}}$	$S_{A_0}^{\omega_{3\,db}}$
−10	−0.19	−0.6
−50	−0.45	−0.15
−100	−0.594	+1.88

It is noted that the sensitivity of ω_{cf} to changes in C is moderate, and is less for small values of A_0 than for large values. The sensitivity of bandwidth to changes in C reverses sign as A_0 is varied from −100 to −50. This implies that the sensitivity of bandwidth to the bridging capacitance can be made zero by proper selection of the nominal value of amplifier gain. The value of A_0 for zero sensitivity of bandwidth to changes in bridging capacitance may be found by numerical methods. However, since it in turn depends on the percent change in C, this is not treated here.

In summary, the design procedures outlined in this section can be extended to more complex network configurations. For example, the root-locus procedure can be used to determine the effects on the $\overline{RC}$ bandpass network of amplifier output impedance and of amplifier gain when it is a function of the complex-frequency variable s.

As demonstrated in the design procedure, a step-by-step approach to the final design, using the root locus, and starting with simple initial configurations, gives insight into the effects of changes in parameter values in the network performance. This insight enables the design engineer to choose parameter values with some knowledge of the effects on the performance and to converge on a final design.

PROBLEMS

7-1 A linear-taper distributed RC network is realized using a circular geometry. Using polar coordinates, ρ and θ, determine the following for the linear $\overline{RC}$ network shown.

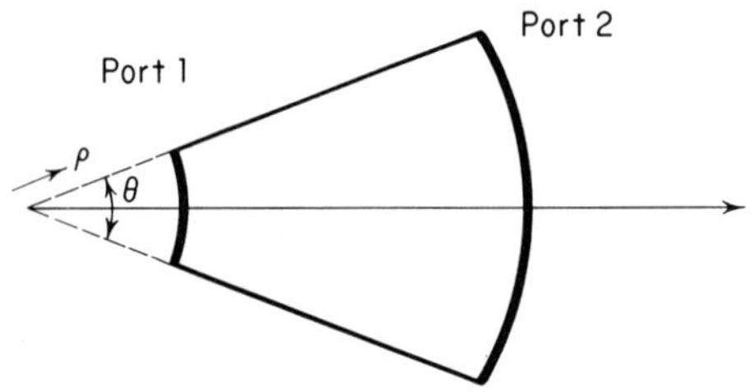

Figure P7-1

a. Determine the equations for the equipotentials in terms of ρ and θ with potential V at Port 1 and zero potential at Port 2. Let the frequency of excitation be zero (dc).
b. Draw the network equipotentials at $V/4$, $V/2$, $3V/4$.
c. Find the one-dimensional relationships between current and voltage.
d. Using the method of separation of variables and the appropriate boundary conditions, find the $ABCD$ parameters of the network.
e. From the results of (d), find the Z-matrix parameters of the network.

7-2 Use the method of curvilinear squares to construct an RC network with a square taper. Let $W(x) = W_0(1 + x^2)$, where W_0 is a unit distance.

a. Compute the approximate taper of the network by determining the area between equipotentials divided by the increment along the x axis to find the approximate width of the network.
b. Plot the width as a function of x and compare with the desired function $W(x) = W_0(1 + x^2)$.
c. Repeat for the range $1 < x < 6$. What difficulties arise in the construction?

7-3 For the $\overline{UMRC}$ network with $I_1(d) = I_2(0) = I_2(d) = 0$ (see the example), and with $r_2/r_1 = 0.01$ and $c_2/c_1 = 10$.
a. Find the first and second pairs of zeros of transmission of $T(s) = V_3/V_1$.
b. Repeat, with $r_2/r_1 = 0.001$, $c_2/c_1 = 1$.

7-4 Compute the open-circuit impedance parameters (z parameters) for the $\overline{UMRC}$ network.

7-5 **a.** Show that, for the given multilayer network, with variable r_1, r_2, c_1, and c_2, that the voltage e_a satisfies the differential equation

$$D\left\{\frac{1}{r_b}\left(D\left[\frac{1}{sc_a}D\left(\frac{1}{r_a}De_a\right)\right]\right)\right\} - D\left[\frac{1}{er_b}De_a\right] - \left(1 + \frac{c_b}{c_a}\right)D\left(\frac{1}{r_a}De_a\right) + sc_b e_a = 0$$

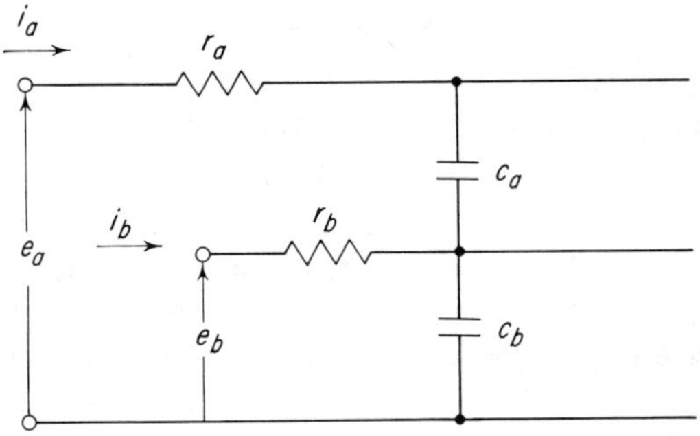

$$\frac{dE_a}{dx} = -r_a I_a \qquad \frac{dE_b}{dx} = -r_b I_b$$

$$\frac{dI_a}{dx} = -sC_a E_a + sC_a E_b \qquad \frac{dI_b}{dx} = sC_a E_a - s(C_a + C_b)E_b$$

Where E_a is the transform of e_a, I_a is the transform of i_a, and so forth

Figure P7-5 $\overline{MRC}$ network model.

b. Let $r_1 = r_a\epsilon^{2kx}$, $c_1 = c_a\epsilon^{-2kx}$, $r_2 = r_b\epsilon^{2kx}$, $c_2 = c_b\epsilon^{-2kx}$. Find the differential equation for e_a, and find the open-circuit impedance matrix (z matrix).

7-6 If a load admittance G_L is connected across the output of Figure 7-19, show that

a. The voltage transfer function is given by

$$T_V(s) = \frac{1}{\cosh 2\theta_2 + K_1\,(\cosh 2\theta_2 - 1) + \dfrac{K_2 \sinh \theta_2}{\theta_2}}$$

where $K_2 = r_{01} d_1 G_L$.

b. For $K_1 = 16$ and $K_2 = 0.1$ show that the dominant pole p_0 is located at the normalized value of 0.0132, and the first nondominant pole p_1 at the normalized value of 3.60. (The normalization factor is the same as in the example of the text.)

c. Compare the error in phase and magnitude of this example with the single-pole response of Equation (7-64) at $\omega = 0.1\ p_0$.

7-7 For the circuit of Figure 7-22, assume that the null network is $\overline{URC}$, with $T = r_0 c_0 d^2$. If the amplifier is a practical operational amplifier with the equivalent circuit shown here, determine the center frequency and the 3-dB bandwidth of the circuit if the source and load impedances are 100 ohms.

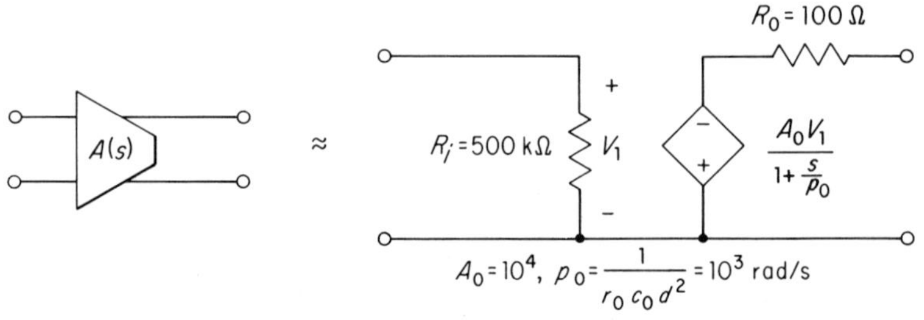

Figure P7-7 Operational amplifier equivalent circuit.

7-8 For Table 7-1 and Figure 7-12, which show the error in the approximation as a function of the angle θ,

a. Show that the excess between the circle diameter and the true curvilinear square Δ is given by

$$\frac{\Delta = 0d' - 0d}{\text{CIRCLE DIAMETER}} = \epsilon^{\theta/2}\left[\cosh - \frac{\theta}{2}\frac{\sinh \theta/2}{\sinh \theta/2}\right]$$

Hint: For circular geometry, as in Figure 7-12, the distance $0d = 0a\epsilon^{\theta/2}$.

b. For $\theta = 60°$ show that $\Delta/ad' = 7.52$ percent.

APPENDIX

A

Analogous Physical Systems

Many physical systems are described by sets of partial differential equations similar to those that relate the current and voltage on a distributed-parameter electrical network. These analogs are useful to know because they give insight into the properties and applications of other types of distributed structures. For example, the natural frequencies of a vibrating string that is constrained at both ends are analogous to the natural frequencies of a lossless transmission line.

In this appendix, we shall show a few analogs of distributed-parameter electrical networks with a view toward gaining an intuitive feel for the behavior of other distributed systems.

Consider the problem of one-dimensional heat flow in a solid. Radiation and convection effects are neglected. Referring to Figure A-1, we have the Fourier equation for heat conduction[1]

$$q(t, x) = -k \frac{\partial \tau}{\partial x}(t, x) \tag{A-1}$$

where q_x is the heat flow per unit area (joules/meter^2-second)
k is the conductivity in watts per degree Centigrade
τ is the temperature in degrees Centigrade

Rearranging Equation (A-1) and using transform notation, we obtain the first equation of heat flow

[1] See J. Fourier, *Analytic Theory of Heat* (New York, Dover reprint, 1955), Chap. 1.

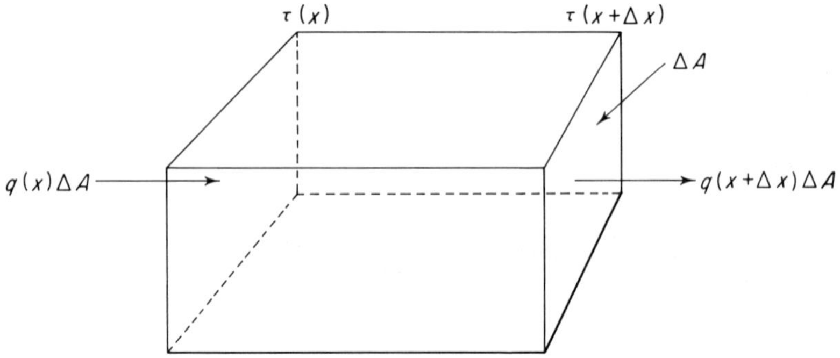

Figure A-1 Incremental volume for heat conduction.

$$\frac{\partial T}{\partial x}(s, x) = -\frac{1}{k} Q(s, x) \tag{A-2}$$

where T and Q are the Laplace transforms of τ and q, respectively. In this form T is analogous to voltage, Q to current, and $1/k$ to resistance when compared with the first Telegrapher equation for the $\overline{RC}$ network.

The second equation for one-dimensional heat flow is found by considering the time rate of change of heat flow from the infinitesimal volume. The governing equation is

$$\Delta q\,(t, x) = [q(t, x + \Delta x) - q(t, x)]$$

$$= -S\rho\, \Delta x \frac{\partial \tau}{\partial t}(t, x) \tag{A-3a}$$

where S is the specific heat per unit mass of material and ρ is the density in kilograms per cubic meter. Passing to the limit and using transform notation, we have the second equation for thermal conduction

$$\frac{\partial Q}{\partial x}(s, x) = -sS\rho T(s, x) \tag{A-3b}$$

From Equations (A-2) and (A-3), it is seen that the thermal analog is representative of the $\overline{RC}$ network, and T and Q are analogs of voltage and current, respectively.

By differentiating Equations (A-2) and (A-3), we obtain the equation pair

$$\frac{d^2T(s, x)}{dx^2} = \frac{S\rho}{k} sT(s, x) \tag{A-4a}$$

and

$$\frac{d^2Q(s, x)}{dx^2} = \frac{S\rho}{k} sQ(s, x) \tag{A-4b}$$

with solutions

$$T(s,x) = A_1 \cosh x\sqrt{\frac{S\rho}{k}s} + A_2 \sinh x\sqrt{\frac{S\rho}{k}s} \qquad \text{(A-5a)}$$

$$Q(s,x) = B_1 \cosh x\sqrt{\frac{S\rho}{k}s} + B_2 \sinh x\sqrt{\frac{S\rho}{k}s} \qquad \text{(A-5b)}$$

Upon insertion of boundary conditions such as $T = 0$ or $Q = 0$ at end points, thermal impedances may be defined for the problem at hand.

Many other analogs exist for distributed-parameter electrical systems. A short list of these is given in Table A-1. Note that the $\overline{LC}$

Table A-1 PHYSICAL ANALOGS

TYPE OF SYSTEM	FIRST EQUATION	SECOND EQUATION
General transmission line	$\frac{dV}{dx} = -(r+sl)I$	$\frac{dI}{dx} = -(g+sc)V$
V = voltage, I = current, $(r+sl)$ = series impedance per unit length, $(g+sc)$ = shunt admittance per unit length		
Vibrating string	$\frac{dU}{dx} = \frac{1}{T}sF$	$\frac{dF}{dx} = msU$
U = velocity, F = force, T = tension, m = mass per unit length		
Acoustic in gas	$\frac{dU}{dx} = -\frac{1}{\gamma P_a}sP$	$\frac{dP}{dx} = -\rho sU$
U = velocity, P = pressure, γ = ratio of specific heats at constant pressure and constant volume, P_a = ambient pressure, ρ = density		
Thermal conduction	$\frac{dT}{dx} = -\frac{1}{k}Q$	$\frac{dQ}{dx} = s\rho ST$
T = temperature, Q = quantity of heat, k = conductivity, ρ = density, S = specific heat		
Diffusion	$\frac{dC}{dx} = \frac{-1}{D}M$	$\frac{dM}{dx} = -sC$
C = concentration, M = mass, D = diffusion constant		

solutions apply for the vibrating-string equations and the acoustic equations in gas, whereas the $\overline{RC}$ solutions apply for the thermal conduction and the diffusion equation.

A great many other physical systems analogous to distributed-parameter networks exist. The interested reader is referred to the literature[2] for additional examples.

As a final example of analogous systems, we present the analogs between the uniform and exponentially distributed $\overline{RC}$ network and the diffusion and drift transistors[3] as given in Table A-2.

[2] R. K. Moore, *Traveling Wave Engineering* (New York, McGraw-Hill, 1960).

[3] M. S. Ghausi, *Principles and Design of Linear Active Circuits* (New York, McGraw-Hill, 1965).

Table A-2 COMPARISON OF THE $\overline{URC}$ AND $\overline{ERC}$ STRUCTURES AND THE DIFFUSION AND GRADED-BASE TRANSISTORS

$\overline{URC}$ NETWORK	$\overline{ERC}$ NETWORK	DIFFUSION TRANSISTOR	GRADED-BASE TRANSISTOR
$y_{11} = \frac{g\theta}{d} \coth \theta$	$y_{11} = \frac{g\theta}{d} \coth \theta - gk$	$y_{11} = g_e'\theta \coth \theta$	$y_{11} = g_e' \frac{\sinh \eta}{\eta} (\theta \coth \theta + \eta)$
$T_{vo}(s) = \frac{1}{\cosh \theta}$	$T_{vo}(s) = \frac{\epsilon^{kd}}{\cosh \theta + \frac{kd \sinh \theta}{\theta}}$	$T_{vo}(s) = \frac{1}{\cosh \theta}$	$T_{vo}(s) = \frac{\epsilon^{\eta}}{\cosh \theta + \frac{\eta \sinh \theta}{\theta}}$
$g = \frac{1}{r_0}$	$g = \frac{1}{r_0}$	$g_e' = I_e \left(\frac{q}{kT}\right)$	$g_e' = I_e \left(\frac{q}{kT}\right)$
$\theta = d\sqrt{s\tau_0}$	$\theta = d\sqrt{k^2 + s\tau_0}$	$\theta = \frac{W}{L}\sqrt{1 + s\tau}$	$\theta = \frac{W}{L}\sqrt{(1 + s\tau) + \eta^2}$
$\tau_0 = r_0 c_0$	$\tau_0 = r_0 c_0$	W = base width	W = base width
d = length	d = length	L = diffusion length	L = diffusion length
	k = taper factor	τ = minority-carrier lifetime	τ = minority-carrier lifetime
			η = gradient constant in the base

Note that for $\eta = 0$, the equations for the graded-base transistor are identical with those of the diffusion transistor, and that for $k = 0$, the $\overline{ERC}$ network reduces to the $\overline{URC}$ network.

APPENDIX

B

Factor Theorem of Weierstrass

The factor theorem of Weierstrass is a formal mathematical statement that, under certain conditions, analytic functions can be expressed in factored form. It can be regarded as an extension of the concept of factorization from algebraic functions to transcendental functions. Viewed in this light, the factor theorem justifies the expansion of distributed network functions in product form and hence permits the use of pole-zero techniques in the study of distributed network functions.

The factor theorem applies to both finite- and infinite-product expansions, but the finite-product expansion is trivial and is not treated here. The factor theorem for infinite products[1] may be stated as follows:

Let $f(s)$ be analytic for all s [that is, $f(s)$ is an entire function] and suppose that it has simple zeros at $\lambda_1, \lambda_2, \lambda_3, \ldots$, where

$$0 < |\lambda_1| < |\lambda_2| < |\lambda_3| < \cdots \quad \text{and} \quad \lim_{n \to \infty} |\lambda_n| = \infty$$

Then $f(s)$ can be expressed as an infinite product of the form

$$f(s) = f(0) \exp \frac{f'(0)\, s}{f(0)} \prod_{k=1}^{\infty} \left\{ \left(1 - \frac{s}{\lambda_k}\right) \epsilon^{s/\lambda_k} \right\} \tag{B-1}$$

A generalization of this theorem states that if $f(s)$ has zeros at $\lambda_k \neq 0$, for $k = 1, 2, 3, \cdots$, of respective multiplicities or orders μ_k, and if for some integer N,

---

[1] See M. Spiegel, *Complex Variables* (New York, Schaum, 1964), p. 267.

$$\sum_{k=1}^{\infty} 1/\lambda_k{}^N$$

is absolutely convergent, then

$$f(s) = f(0)\epsilon^{G(s)} \prod_{k=1}^{\infty} \left[\left(1 - \frac{s}{\lambda_k}\right) \exp\left(\frac{s}{\lambda_k} + \frac{1}{2}\frac{s^2}{\lambda_k{}^2} + \cdots + \frac{1}{N-1}\frac{s^{N-1}}{\lambda_k{}^{N-1}}\right)\right]^{u_k} \quad \textbf{(B-2)}$$

where $G(s)$ is an entire function. The result is also true if some of the λ_k's are poles, in which case their multiplicities are negative.

Distributed network functions can be expressed as basic-set solutions of the Sturm equation and, in general, fulfill the conditions for product expansion of the type given by Equation (B-1). For example, take the uniform *RC* distributed network function

$$V_I(\theta) = \cosh\theta \quad \textbf{(B-3)}$$

where $\theta = d\sqrt{sr_0c_0}$. This function has simple zeros at

$$\theta_n = \pm j\,\frac{(2n-1)\pi}{2} \qquad n = 1, 2, 3, \ldots \quad \textbf{(B-4)}$$

and $$0 < |\theta_1| < |\theta_2| < \cdots \quad \text{and} \quad \lim_{n\to\infty} |\theta_n| = \infty$$

Thus, the conditions for using Equation (B-1) are met. Also, $V_{\mathrm{I}}(0) = 1$ and $V_{\mathrm{I}}'(0) = 0$. Thus, the infinite-product expansion of $V_{\mathrm{I}}(\theta)$, using Equation (B-1), is

$$V_{\mathrm{I}}(\theta) = \prod_{n=1}^{\infty}\left(1 + j\frac{2\theta}{2n-1}\right)\exp\left(-j\,\frac{2\theta}{2n-1}\right)\left(1 - j\,\frac{2\theta}{2n-1}\right)\exp\left(j\,\frac{2\theta}{2n-1}\right) \quad \textbf{(B-5)}$$

We note that there are two complex conjugate factors for each value of n in Equation (B-5). When these are multiplied together, we obtain the more compact expression

$$V_{\mathrm{I}}(\theta) = \cosh\theta = \prod_{n=1}^{\infty}\left[1 + \frac{4\theta^2}{(2n-1)^2\pi^2}\right] \quad \textbf{(B-6)}$$

For a uniformly distributed *RC* network, $\theta = d\sqrt{sr_0c_0}$; thus, substitution in Equation (B-6) gives

$$V_{\mathrm{I}}(s, d) = \prod_{n=1}^{\infty}\left[1 + \frac{4d^2r_0c_0s}{(2n-1)^2\pi^2}\right] \quad \textbf{(B-7)}$$

When the distributed network function $f(s)$ that we wish to write in product form has simple complex conjugate roots λ_n and λ_n^* satisfying the conditions

$$0 < |\lambda_1| < |\lambda_2| < \cdots \quad \text{and} \quad \lim_{n\to\infty} |\lambda_n| = \infty$$

then Equation (B-1) becomes

$$f(s) = f(0) \exp \frac{f'(0)}{f(0)} \prod_{n=1}^{\infty} \left(1 + \frac{s^2}{|\lambda_n{}^2|}\right) \tag{B-8}$$

As demonstrated in the example above, Equation (B-8) can be used directly.

The case of multiple-order roots described in Equation (B-2) is more difficult to handle than the case of simple roots because the exponential multiplying function, $\epsilon^{G(s)}$, must be determined. However, cases of multiple-order roots are not frequently encountered in the study of distributed networks of the type described in this book, except as breakaway points in the application of the root locus. Here, second-order roots are encountered, but the product expansion of the function at the breakaway points is rarely required.

Nonetheless, let us demonstrate the application of Equation (B-2) for a function with second-order zeros. Consider

$$f(\theta) = \frac{1 - \cosh \theta}{\theta^2} \tag{B-9}$$

which has complex conjugate second-order zeros at θ_n and θ_n^*, where

$$\theta_n = j2n\pi \qquad n = 1, 2, 3, \ldots \tag{B-10}$$

The infinite series S, where

$$S = \sum_{n=1}^{\infty} \left(\frac{1}{j2n\pi}\right)^N \tag{B-11}$$

is absolutely convergent for $N = 2$. Hence one of the exponential multipliers in Equation (B-2) is simply $\epsilon^{-j\theta/2n\pi}$. Further, since the roots appear in complex conjugate pairs, Equation (B-2) can be written as

$$f(\theta) = f(0)\epsilon^{G(\theta)} \prod_{n=1}^{\infty} \left(1 + \frac{\theta^2}{|\theta_n{}^2|}\right) \tag{B-12}$$

Also,

$$f(0) = \lim_{\theta\to 0} \frac{1 - \cosh \theta}{\theta^2} = \frac{1}{2}$$

and Equation (B-12) can be rewritten as

$$f(\theta) = \frac{1}{2} \epsilon^{G(\theta)} \prod_{n=1}^{\infty} \left(1 + \frac{\theta^2}{4n^2\pi^2}\right)^2 \tag{B-13}$$

where $G(\theta)$ is still to be determined.

For the particular example chosen, we note that $1 - \cosh\theta = -2\sinh^2\theta/2$. The product expansion of $\sinh\theta/2$ is

$$\sinh\frac{\theta}{2} = \frac{\theta}{2} \prod_{n=1}^{\infty} \left(1 + \frac{\theta^2}{4n^2\pi^2}\right) \tag{B-14}$$

The product expansion of $\sinh^2\theta/2$ is simply the square of Equation (B-14), or

$$\sinh^2\frac{\theta}{2} = \frac{\theta^2}{4} \prod_{n=1}^{\infty} \left(1 + \frac{\theta^2}{4n^2\pi^2}\right)^2 \tag{B-15}$$

and hence

$$2\sinh^2\frac{\theta}{2} = \frac{\theta^2}{2} \prod_{n=1}^{\infty} \left(1 + \frac{\theta^2}{4n^2\pi^2}\right)^2 \tag{B-16}$$

Noting the identity

$$2\sinh^2\frac{\theta}{2} = -(1 - \cosh\theta)$$

and comparing Equations (B-13) and (B-16), we find $G(\theta) = 0$ and hence

$$f(\theta) = \frac{1}{2} \prod_{n=1}^{\infty} \left(1 + \frac{\theta^2}{4n^2\pi^2}\right)^2 \tag{B-17}$$

For cases in which a simple identity is not available, the function $G(\theta)$ is more difficult to evaluate. Such cases rarely arise in the study of distributed networks and are not treated here. The interested reader is referred to the literature[2] for treatment of these special cases.

[2] See for example, K. Knopp, *Theory of Functions* (New York, Dover, 1947), Vol. II.

APPENDIX

C

Some Useful Infinite-Product Expansions

An infinite-product expansion is a means of writing transcendental functions in terms of their roots. Consider the transcendental function $P(s)$, which may be written as

$$P(s) = \left(1 + \frac{s}{\sigma_1}\right)\left(1 + \frac{s}{\sigma_2}\right) \cdots \left(1 + \frac{s}{\sigma_n}\right) \cdots \tag{C-1}$$

The σ_i are the negatives of the roots of $P(s)$. Equation (C-1) is usually written in the following convenient form:

$$P(s) = \prod_{n=1}^{\infty} \left(1 + \frac{s}{\sigma_n}\right) \tag{C-2}$$

Using this notation, a short table of infinite-product forms for common transcendental functions is given.[1]

$$\sin \theta = \theta \prod_{n=1}^{\infty} \left(1 - \frac{\theta^2}{n^2\pi^2}\right) \tag{C-3}$$

$$\sinh \theta = \theta \prod_{n=1}^{\infty} \left(1 + \frac{\theta^2}{n^2\pi^2}\right) \tag{C-4}$$

$$\cos \theta = \prod_{n=1}^{\infty} \left[1 - \frac{4\theta^2}{(2n-1)^2\pi^2}\right] \tag{C-5}$$

---

[1] See, for example, G. Chrystal, *Textbook of Algebra* (New York, Chelsea reprint, 1964), Vol. 2, pp. 348, 359.

$$\cosh\theta = \prod_{n=1}^{\infty}\left[1 + \frac{4\theta^2}{(2n-1)^2\pi^2}\right] \tag{C-6}$$

$$\frac{\sin(\theta+\phi)}{\sin\theta} = \frac{\theta+\phi}{\theta}\,\frac{\prod_{n=1}^{\infty}\left(1 - \frac{(\theta+\phi)^2}{n^2\pi^2}\right)}{\prod_{n=1}^{\infty}\left(1 - \frac{\theta^2}{n^2\pi^2}\right)} \qquad \theta \neq n\pi \tag{C-7}$$

$$\cos\phi + \sin\phi\cot\theta = \left(1 + \frac{\phi}{\theta}\right)\prod_{n=1}^{\infty}\left(1 - \frac{2\theta\phi + \phi^2}{n^2\pi^2 - \theta^2}\right) \qquad \theta \neq n\pi \tag{C-8}$$

$$\cos\phi - \sin\phi\tan\theta = \prod_{n=1}^{\infty}\left[1 - \frac{4(2\theta\phi + \phi^2)}{(2n-1)^2\pi^2 - \theta^2}\right] \qquad \theta \neq \frac{(2n-1)\pi}{2} \tag{C-9}$$

$$1 + \csc\theta\sin\phi = \left(1 + \frac{\phi}{\theta}\right)\prod_{n=1}^{\infty}\left[1 - \frac{(-1)^n 2\theta\phi + \phi^2}{n^2\pi^2 - \theta^2}\right] \tag{C-10}$$

$$\frac{\epsilon^{b+x} + \epsilon^{c+x}}{\epsilon^b + \epsilon^c} = \prod_{n=1}^{\infty}\left[1 + \frac{4(b-c)x + 4x^2}{(2n-1)^2\pi^2 + (b-c)^2}\right] \tag{C-11}$$

$$\frac{\epsilon^{b+x} - \epsilon^{c-x}}{\epsilon^b - \epsilon^c} = \left(1 + \frac{2x}{b-c}\right)\prod_{n=1}^{\infty}\left[1 + \frac{4(b-c)x + 4x^2}{(2n)^2\pi^2 + (b-c)^2}\right] \tag{C-12}$$

$$\frac{\cosh y + \cosh c}{1 + \cosh c} = \prod_{n=1}^{\infty}\left[1 + \frac{\pm 2cy + y^2}{(2n-1)^2\pi^2 + c^2}\right] \tag{C-13}$$
[2]

$$\frac{\cosh y - \cosh c}{1 - \cosh c} = \left(1 - \frac{y^2}{c^2}\right)\prod_{n=1}^{\infty}\left[1 - \frac{\pm 2cy + y^2}{(2n)^2\pi^2 + c^2}\right] \tag{C-14}$$

$$\frac{\sinh y + \sinh c}{\sinh c} = \left(1 + \frac{y}{c}\right)\prod_{n=1}^{\infty}\left[1 + \frac{(-1)^n 2cy + y^2}{n^2\pi^2 + c^2}\right] \tag{C-15}$$

$$\frac{\sinh y - \sinh c}{\sinh c} = -\left(1 - \frac{y}{c}\right)\prod_{n=1}^{\infty}\left[1 + \frac{(-1)^{n-1} 2cy + y^2}{n^2\pi^2 + c^2}\right] \tag{C-16}$$

$$\frac{\cos\phi + \cos\theta}{1 + \cos\theta} = \prod_{n=1}^{\infty}\left\{1 - \frac{\phi^2}{[(2n-1)\pi \pm \theta]^2}\right\} \tag{C-17}$$

$$\cos\phi + \tan\theta/2\,\sin\phi = \prod_{n=1}^{\infty}\left\{\left[1 + \frac{2\phi}{(2n-1)\pi - \theta}\right]\left[1 - \frac{2\phi}{(2n-1)\pi + \theta}\right]\right\} \tag{C-18}$$

$$\frac{\cos(\theta - \phi)}{\cos\theta} = \prod_{n=1}^{\infty}\left\{\left[1 + \frac{2\phi}{(2n-1)\pi - 2\theta}\right]\left[1 - \frac{2\phi}{(2n-1)\pi + 2\theta}\right]\right\} \tag{C-19}$$

---

[2] The ± signs inside the brackets mean that the terms with + and − sign must both be included in the product, for example,

$$\prod_{n=1}^{\infty}\left[1 - \frac{\pm 2cy + y^2}{(2n)^2\pi^2 + c^2}\right] = \prod_{n=1}^{\infty}\left[1 - \frac{2cy + y^2}{(2n)^2\pi^2 + c^2}\right]\left[1 - \frac{-2cy + y^2}{(2n)^2\pi^2 + c^2}\right]$$

$$\frac{\sin(\theta-\phi)}{\sin\theta}=\left(1-\frac{\theta}{\phi}\right)\prod_{n=1}^{\infty}\left[\left(1+\frac{\phi}{2n\pi-\theta}\right)\left(1-\frac{\phi}{2n\pi+\theta}\right)\right] \tag{C-20}$$

$$\cosh 2v-\cos 2\mu=2(\mu^2+v^2)\prod_{n=1}^{\infty}\left[\frac{(n\pi\pm\mu)^2+v^2}{n^2\pi^2}\right] \tag{C-21}$$

$$\cosh 2v+\cos 2\mu=2\prod_{n=1}^{\infty}\left\{\frac{[(2n-1)\pi\pm 2\mu]^2+4v^2}{(2n-1)^2\pi^2}\right\} \tag{C-22}$$

$$\cosh 2\mu-\cos 2\mu=4\mu^2\prod_{n=1}^{\infty}\left(1+\frac{4\mu^4}{n^4\pi^4}\right) \tag{C-23}$$

$$\cosh 2\mu+\cos 2\mu=2\prod_{n=1}^{\infty}\left[1+\frac{2^4\mu^4}{(2n-1)^4\pi^4}\right] \tag{C-24}$$

APPENDIX

D

Summation of Infinite Series

To obtain numerical values for two-port parameters of distributed networks and to obtain dominant-pole and excess-phase approximations, it is sometimes necessary to sum infinite series. The series in question are generally of the form

$$S = \left(\frac{4}{\pi^2}\right)^k \sum_{n=1}^{\infty} \left[\frac{1}{(2n-1)^2 + \eta}\right] \tag{D-1}$$

where S is the sum, n and k are integers, and η is parameter dependent on the type of distributed network.

There are many ways to obtain the sum S. In the majority of cases it is an irrational number. The number of significant figures required for S is determined by the nature of the problem. For many engineering works, three-figure accuracy is often sufficient.

For example, the transcendental irrational number π often appears in engineering problems. One way to obtain a numerical value for π is to use the identity

$$\frac{\pi}{4} = \tan^{-1} 1 \tag{D-2}$$

and evaluate the sum of the series

$$\tan^{-1} x = x - \frac{x^3}{3} + \frac{x^5}{5} - \frac{x^7}{7} + \cdots \tag{D-3}$$

with x set equal to 1. Since Equation (D-3) is an alternating series, the error after summing a finite number of terms is bounded by the magnitude of the first term omitted. If N terms are added, the approximate value of π, from Equations (D-2) and (D-3), is

$$\pi \approx 4 \sum_{n=1}^{N} \frac{(-1)^{n+1}}{2n-1} \tag{D-4}$$

with an error of

$$|e| \leqq \frac{4}{2N+1} \tag{D-5}$$

Thus, to find π to three decimal places, using Equation (D-4),

$$|e| \leqq 0.0005 = \frac{4}{2N+1} \tag{D-6}$$

and, solving for N, we get

$$N = \frac{1}{2}\left(\frac{4}{0.0005} - 1\right) = 4000 \tag{D-7}$$

to the nearest integral value.

Clearly, it is impractical to use the direct summation of the terms in Equation (D-4) to evaluate π to a large number of decimal places.

As another example of the limits of the direct method of summation, consider the infinite series

$$\frac{\pi^2}{8} - \frac{\pi u}{4} = \sum_{n=1}^{\infty} \frac{\cos\,(2n-1)u}{(2n-1)^2} \tag{D-8}$$

With $u = 0$, we obtain the infinite series

$$\pi^2 = 8 \sum_{n=1}^{\infty} \frac{1}{(2n-1)^2} \tag{D-9}$$

Since Equation (D-9) is not an alternating series, we have to use a different method from that just described to determine the error due to truncation after N terms. A useful method of finding the truncation error is the following. Replace n in Equation (D-9) by x; then, let

$$f(x) = \frac{1}{(2x-1)^2} \tag{D-10}$$

We shall show that

$$\int_1^{\infty} f(x)\,dx < \sum_{n=1}^{\infty} f(x) < f(1) + \int_1^{\infty} f(x)\,dx \tag{D-11}$$

as can be seen by referring to Figure D-1.

In Figure D-1(a) are shown a sequence of rectangles of unit width

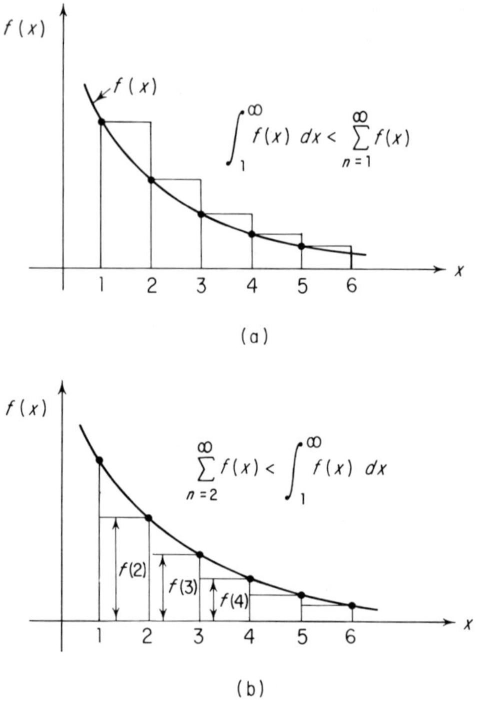

Figure D-1

whose height is bounded by $f(x)$ on the left-hand side. Thus, the area of the rectangles is

$$\sum_{n=1}^{\infty} f(x)$$

and the area under the curve $f(x)$ is

$$\int_1^\infty f(x)\, dx$$

As shown in Figure D-1(a),

$$\int_1^\infty f(x)\, dx < \sum_{n=1}^{\infty} f(x)$$

Figure D-1(b) shows a sequence of rectangles of unit width whose height is bounded by $f(x)$ on the right-hand side. The area of these rectangles is

$$\sum_{n=2}^{\infty} f(x)$$

which is less than the area under the curve $f(x)$, given by

$$\int_1^\infty f(x)\ dx$$

Thus,

$$\sum_{n=2}^{\infty} f(x) < \int_1^\infty f(x)\ dx$$

The inequality holds when $f(1)$ is added to both terms, so that

$$\sum_{n=1}^{\infty} f(x) < f(1) + \int_1^\infty f(x)\ dx$$

The inequality also holds for the case when the starting point for the summation is a number other than 1, say N. Thus, the infinite series

$$S = \sum_{n=1}^{\infty} f(x)$$

can be rewritten as

$$S = \sum_{n=1}^{N-1} f(x) + R_N \tag{D-12}$$

where R_N is the remainder. Also,

$$R_N = \sum_{n=N}^{\infty} f(x) \tag{D-13}$$

and it is bounded between

$$\int_N^\infty f(x)\ dx < R_N < f(N) + \int_N^\infty f(x)\ dx \tag{D-14}$$

From Equations (D-12) and (D-14), the sum of the infinite series can be written approximately as

$$S \approx \sum_{n=1}^{N-1} f(x) + \int_N^\infty f(x)\ dx \tag{D-15}$$

with an error e, due to truncation, that lies between the bounds

$$0 < e < f(N) \tag{D-16}$$

Using Equation (D-15), we can solve Equation (D-9) for π^2 to any desired number of decimal places. For example, if it is desired to obtain π^2 accurate in the third decimal place, then

$$8e < 0.0005 \tag{D-17}$$

or $e < 0.0000625$. From Equations (D-9) and (D-16),

$$e < \frac{1}{(2N-1)^2} \tag{D-18}$$

and hence the number of terms required in the summation is

$$N = \frac{1}{2}\left[\left(\frac{1}{e}\right)^{1/2} + 1\right] \tag{D-19}$$

$$= \frac{1}{2}\left[\left(\frac{10^4}{0.625}\right)^{1/2} + 1\right] = 63$$

As in the first example, the direct summation technique is clearly not practical when a sum is required to a large number of decimal places. A better technique for obtaining the value of an infinite summation is the Euler-Maclaurin expansion.[1]

With the infinite series written in the form

$$S = \sum_{n=1}^{\infty} f(x) \tag{D-20}$$

the approximate value of the sum given by the Euler-Maclaurin expansion is

$$\begin{aligned} S \approx {} & \sum_{n=1}^{N-1} f(x) + \int_N^{\infty} f(x)\, dx \\ & + \frac{1}{2}\left[f(\infty) + f(N)\right] + \frac{1}{12}\left[f'(\infty) - f'(N)\right] \\ & - \frac{1}{720}\left[f'''(\infty) - f'''(N)\right] + \frac{1}{30{,}240}\left[f^{(5)}(\infty) - f^{(5)}(N)\right] \\ & - \frac{1}{1{,}209{,}600}\left[f^{(7)}(\infty) - f^{(7)}(N)\right] + \cdots \end{aligned} \tag{D-21}$$

Comparison of Equations (D-15) and (D-21) shows that the first two terms are identical. However, Equation (D-15) stops after two terms; the extra terms in Equation (D-21) serve to reduce the error in the truncated sum.

To illustrate, let us calculate the value of π^2 using Equation (D-21),

$$f(x) = \frac{1}{(2x-1)^2}; \quad \int_N^{\infty} \frac{dx}{(2x-1)^2} = \frac{1}{2(2x-1)}\Bigg|_N^{\infty} = \frac{1}{2(2N-1)}$$

$$f'(x) = \frac{-2(2)}{(2x-1)^3} = \frac{-4}{(2x-1)^3}; \quad f''(x) = \frac{-3(-2)(2)}{(2x-1)^4} = \frac{12}{(2x-1)^4}$$

[1] See R. G. Stanton, *Numerical Methods for Science and Engineering* (Englewood Cliffs, N. J., Prentice-Hall, 1961), pp. 128–133. See also Whittaker and Watson, *A Course of Modern Analysis* (New York, Cambridge), Chap. 7, Sec. 7–21.

$$f'''(x) = \frac{-4(12)(2)}{(2x-1)^5} = \frac{-96}{(2x-1)^5}; \quad f^{(4)}(x) = \frac{-96(-5)(2)}{(2x-1)^6} = \frac{960}{(2x-1)^6}$$

$$f^{(5)}(x) = \frac{-6(960)(2)}{(2x-1)^7} = \frac{-11{,}520}{(2x-1)^7}$$

and

$$S \approx \sum_{n=1}^{N-1} \frac{1}{(2n-1)^2} + \frac{1}{2(2N-1)} + \frac{1}{2}\frac{1}{(2N-1)^2} + \frac{1}{3}\frac{1}{(2N-1)^3} - \frac{96}{720}\frac{1}{(2N-1)^5} + \frac{11{,}520}{30.240}\frac{7}{(2N-1)^7} - \cdots \tag{D-22}$$

For $N = 6$,

$$S_6 \approx 1.00000 + 0.11111 + 0.04000 + 0.02041 + 0.01235 + 0.04545 + 0.00413 + 0.00025 = 1.23370 \tag{D-23}$$

and $$\pi^2 = 8 \cdot S = 9.86960$$

To determine the accuracy of S, let $N = 7$, and recompute, and compare results.

$$S_7 \approx 1.00000 + 0.11111 + 0.04000 + 0.02041 + 0.01235 + 0.00826 + 0.003846 + 0.00296 + 0.00015 = 1.23370$$

Since S_6 and S_7 are identical, the sum is good to four decimals (round-off errors in the terms cause uncertainty of ± 0.00005 in the sum S_7) and $\pi^2 = 9.8696$ to four decimals.

As demonstrated in the preceding example, the Euler-Maclaurin expansion provides efficient means of obtaining the sums of infinite series. A short listing of sums based on the Euler-Maclaurin expansion is given in Table D-1.

Table D-1 EULER-MACLAURIN SUMMATIONS

(1) $$\sum_{n=a}^{\infty} \frac{1}{(2n-1)^2+\eta^2} = \sum_{n=a}^{N=1} \frac{1}{(2n-1)^2+\eta^2} + \frac{1}{2\eta}\left(\frac{\pi}{2} - \tan^{-1}\frac{2N-1}{\eta}\right) + \frac{1}{2}\left[\frac{1}{(2N-1)^2+\eta^2}\right] + \frac{1}{3}\frac{2N-1}{[(2N-1)^2+\eta^2]^2} - \cdots$$

good to four decimals for $N > 6$, $\eta^2 > 0$

(2) $$\sum_{n=a}^{\infty} \frac{1}{(2n-1)^2} = \sum_{n=a}^{N-1} \frac{1}{(2n-1)^2} + \frac{1}{2}\frac{1}{(2N-1)} + \frac{1}{2}\frac{1}{(2N-1)^2} + \frac{1}{3}\frac{1}{(2N-1)^3} - \cdots$$

good to four decimals for $N > 6$

(Table D-1 cont. on page 300)

Table D-1 *cont.* EULER-MACLAURIN SUMMATIONS

(3) $$\sum_{n=a}^{\infty}\left[\frac{1}{(2n-1)^2+\eta^2}\right]^2=\sum_{n=a}^{N-1}\left[\frac{1}{(2n-1)^2+\eta^2}\right]^2+\frac{1}{4\eta^3}\left[\frac{\pi}{2}-\tan^{-1}\frac{2N-1}{\eta}-\frac{(2N-1)\eta}{(2N-1)^2+\eta^2}\right]+\frac{1}{2}\frac{1}{[(2N-1)^2+\eta^2]^2}+\frac{2}{3}\frac{2N-1}{[(2N-1)^2+\eta^2]^3}-\cdots$$

good to four decimals for $N > 4$, $\eta^2 > 0$

(4) $$\sum_{n=a}^{\infty}\frac{1}{(2n-1)^4}=\sum_{n=a}^{N-1}\frac{1}{(2n-1)^4}+\frac{1}{6}\frac{1}{(2N-1)^3}+\frac{1}{2}\frac{1}{(2N-1)^4}+\frac{2}{3}\frac{1}{(2N-1)^5}-\cdots$$

good to four decimals for $N > 4$

(5) $$\sum_{n=a}^{\infty}\frac{1}{n^2+\eta^2}=\sum_{n=a}^{N-1}\frac{1}{n^2+\eta^2}+\frac{1}{\eta}\left[\frac{\pi}{2}-\tan^{-1}\frac{N}{\eta}\right]+\frac{1}{2}\frac{1}{(N^2+\eta^2)}+\frac{1}{6}\frac{N}{(N^2+\eta^2)^2}-\cdots$$

good to four decimals for $N > 6$, $\eta^2 \geqslant 0$

(6) $$\sum_{n=a}^{\infty}\left[\frac{1}{n^2+\eta^2}\right]^2=\sum_{n=a}^{N-1}\left[\frac{1}{n^2+\eta^2}\right]^2+\frac{1}{2\eta^3}\left[\frac{\pi}{2}-\tan^{-1}\frac{N}{\eta}-\frac{\eta N}{N^2+\eta^2}\right]+\frac{1}{2}\left[\frac{1}{N^2+\eta^2}\right]^2+\frac{N}{3(N^2+\eta^2)^3}-\cdots$$

good to four decimals for $N > 4$, $\eta^2 \geqslant 0$

Sums of Series in Closed Forms

Some infinite summations may be expressed in closed form, for example[2]:

(a) $$\sum_{n=1}^{\infty}\frac{1}{n^2+x^2}=\frac{\pi}{2x}\frac{\cosh \pi x}{\sinh \pi x}-\frac{1}{2x^2}$$

(b) $$\sum_{n=1}^{\infty}(-1)^n\frac{1}{n^2+x^2}=\frac{\pi}{x}\frac{1}{\epsilon^{\pi x}-\epsilon^{-\pi x}}-\frac{1}{2x^2}=\frac{\pi}{2x}\frac{2}{\epsilon^{\pi x}-\epsilon^{-\pi x}}-\frac{1}{2x^2}$$

[2] L. B. Jolley, *Summation of Series*, 2d rev. ed. (New York; Dover, 1961), Formulas 124, 125.

$$= \frac{\pi}{2x} \frac{1}{\sinh \pi x} - \frac{1}{2x^2}$$

Subtracting (b) from (a), we get

$$\frac{1}{n^2 + x^2} + \sum_{n=1}^{\infty} (-1)^{n+1} \frac{1}{n^2 + x^2} = 2\left[\frac{1}{1^2 + x^2} + \frac{1}{3^2 + x^2} + \frac{1}{5^2 + x^2} + \cdots\right]$$

$$= 2 \sum_{n=1}^{\infty} \frac{1}{(2n-1)^2 + x^2}$$

$$= \frac{\pi}{2x}\left[\frac{\cosh \pi x - 1}{\sinh \pi x}\right]$$

Also,

$$\cosh \pi x - 1 = 2 \sinh^2 \frac{\pi x}{2}$$

(c) $$\sum_{n=1}^{\infty} \frac{1}{(2n-1)^2 + x^2} = \frac{\pi}{2x} \frac{\sinh^2 \pi x/2}{\sinh \pi x} = \frac{\pi}{4x} \tanh \frac{\pi x}{2}$$

Differentiating with respect to x and combining terms,

$$\frac{d}{dx}\left[\sum_{n=1}^{\infty} \frac{1}{(2n-1)^2 + x^2}\right] = \frac{d}{dx}\left[\frac{\pi}{4x} \tanh \frac{\pi x}{2}\right] = \sum_{n=1}^{\infty} \frac{-2x}{[(2n-1)^2 + x^2]^2}$$

$$= \frac{\pi}{4x} \operatorname{sech}^2 \frac{\pi x}{2} \cdot \frac{\pi}{2} - \frac{\pi}{4x^2} \tanh \frac{\pi x}{2}$$

By cross-multiplication,

(d) $$\sum_{n=1}^{\infty}\left[\frac{1}{(2n-1)^2 + x^2}\right]^2 = \frac{1}{2x}\left(\frac{\pi}{4x^2} \tanh \frac{\pi x}{2} - \frac{\pi^2}{8x} \operatorname{sech}^2 \frac{\pi x}{2}\right)$$

$$= \frac{\pi}{8x^3}\left(\tanh \frac{\pi x}{2} - \frac{\pi x}{2} \operatorname{sech}^2 \frac{\pi x}{2}\right)$$

APPENDIX

E

Finding the Roots of Transcendental Equations

Two general methods of finding the roots of transcendental functions are described. Both methods are applicable to algebraic functions as well. The first method described is the method of iteration (method of successive approximation). In this method, a sequence of educated guesses at the solution is made. The method is most useful when the sequence converges rapidly. The second procedure described is the Newton-Raphson method. It is also an iterative scheme, but is somewhat more complex to apply than the first method. However, it converges more rapidly.

It should be pointed out that the roots of transcendental equations are usually irrational numbers—which can never be found exactly, no matter how many decimal places are carried along. Therefore, one should decide beforehand the degree of accuracy that one requires and terminate the computations when the desired accuracy is achieved. For example, the transcendental number π is commonly used to three places—that is, $\pi = 3.14$—in slide-rule computations and the customary rational approximation is $\pi = 22/7 = 3.142$. Rarely is π used to more than six places, that is, $\pi = 3.14159$ with the rational approximation $\pi = 355/113 = 3.14159$.

Iterative Method of Solution

The method of iteration can be applied to the solution of an algebraic or transcendental equation of the form

$$x = f(x) \tag{E-1}$$

where $f(x)$ is a function which changes slowly in the region of the root, x_0. Before discussing the conditions for convergence, the iterative process is described.

From Equation (E-1), an estimate of the solution is made; that is, we estimate the root as x_1. When $f(x)$ varies slowly near the root, then $f(x_1) \approx f(x_0)$ and a second approximation to the root x_2 can be found. Thus,

$$x_2 = f(x_1) \tag{E-2}$$

gives a better approximation to the root. The iteration procedure is continued with $x_3 = f(x_2)$, $x_4 = f(x_3)$, . . . $x_{n+1} = f(x_n)$ until the root is found to the desired accuracy.

Now let us investigate the requirements for convergence of the iteration process. Consider the error in the result at each step in the iteration. If the magnitude of the error decreases with each step, the process converges, while if the error increases with each step the process diverges. Thus,

$$e_n = x_0 - x_n \tag{E-3}$$

where e_n is the error in the nth approximate solution. By definition, $x_0 = f(x_0)$; also, $x_2 = f(x_1)$, and hence

$$x_0 - x_2 = f(x_0) - f(x_1) \tag{E-4}$$

Multiplying the right-hand side of Equation (E-4) by unity—that is, by $(x_0 - x_1)/(x_0 - x_1)$—we obtain the relation

$$x_0 - x_2 = \left[\frac{f(x_0) - f(x_1)}{x_0 - x_1}\right] (x_0 - x_1) \tag{E-5}$$

which can also be written as

$$e_2 = \left[\frac{f(x_0) - f(x_1)}{x_0 - x_1}\right] e_1 \tag{E-6}$$

where e_1 and e_2 are the errors after the first and second steps. Now, since $f(x)$ is continuous and differentiable for distributed networks (as proved by the Picard-Carson method, described in Chapter 2), the law of the mean[1] holds, and

$$\frac{f(x_0) - f(x_1)}{x_0 - x_1} = f'(\tilde{x}) \tag{E-7}$$

where $\tilde{x}$ lies between x_0 and x_1, and $f'(\tilde{x})$ is the derivative of $f(x)$ with respect to x. Hence,

---

[1] W. F. Kaplan, *Advanced Calculus* (Reading, Mass., Addison-Wesley, 1952).

$$|e_2| = |f'(\tilde{x})|\,|e_1| \tag{E-8}$$

and after the nth step, the error is

$$|e_{n+1}| \simeq |f'(\tilde{x})|\,|e_n| \tag{E-9}$$

In practice, $\tilde{x}$ is set equal to x_n. This is related to the initial error by

$$|e_{n+1}| \simeq |f'(\tilde{x})|^n |e_1| \tag{E-10}$$

From Equation (E-10), we see that the iteration method converges to the true solution provided that $|f'(\tilde{x})| < 1$ or what is equivalent, if $|f'(x_0| < 1$. For example, if $|f'(x_0)| = 0.1$, the error is reduced by a factor of 10 at each step, giving one more decimal place of accuracy for each iteration. The iteration method is illustrated in the following examples. First we treat an algebraic function, then we give examples of transcendental functions.

Example for an algebraic function. Given $x^3 + 10x + 1 = 0$, the function is known to have at least one negative real root by Descarte's rule of signs. To put it in a form suitable for iteration [that is, $x = f(x)$], rewrite the equation as $x = -0.1(x^3 + 1)$. Estimate the position of x_0 by tabulating the function, or by graphing it as shown in Figure E-1. From the

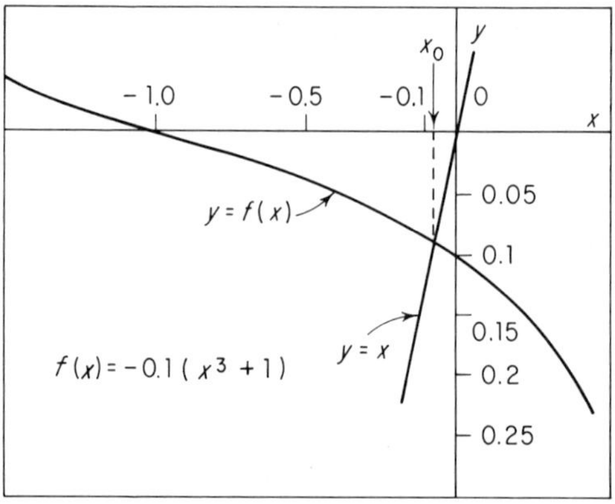

Figure E-1 Root of $x^3 + 10x + 1 = 0$.

graph, $-0.1 > x_0 > 0$. Also, $f'(x) = -0.3x^2$, and $0 < |f'(x_0)| < 0.003$. Hence, the iteration method converges very rapidly and the error is reduced by a factor of 0.003 at each step. The iteration steps are given in Table E-1.

Table E-1 REAL ROOT OF $x^3 + 10x + 1 = 0$, WHERE $x_{n+1} = f(x_n)$

1.	Choose x_1:	$x_1 = -0.1$
2.	Find x_2:	$x_2 = -0.1(0.999) = -0.0999$
3.	Find x_3:	$x_3 = -0.1(0.99900297) = -0.099900297$

The remaining error in the real root is in the eighth decimal place of x_3.

Example for a real transcendental function. Given $x - \epsilon^{-x} = 0$, find the root. For the iterative procedure, rewrite the function as $x = \epsilon^{-x}$. As shown in Figure E-2, the value of the root lies between the bounds

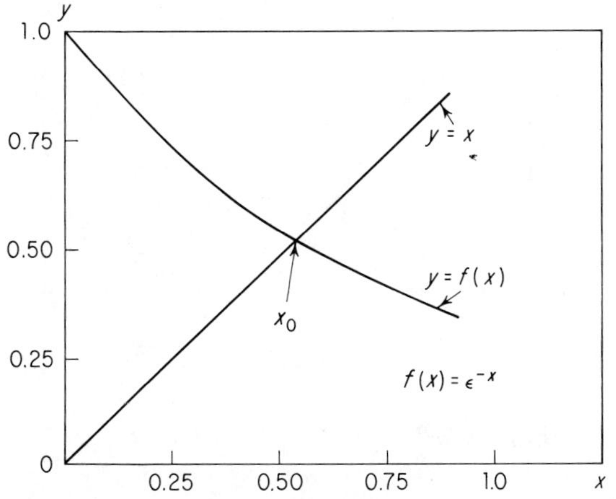

Figure E-2 Root of $x - \epsilon^{-x} = 0$.

$0.5 < x_0 < 0.75$. Further, $f'(x) = -\epsilon^{-x}$ and $f'(\tilde{x})$ lies between the bounds $-0.606 > f'(\tilde{x}) > -0.472$. The iteration converges, and the error is reduced approximately by a factor of two at each step. The iteration to four places proceeds as follows

1. Choose x_1: $x_1 = 0.5$
2. Find x_2: $x_2 = \epsilon^{-0.5} = 0.6065$
3. Find x_3: $x_3 = \epsilon^{-0.6065} = 0.5455$
4. Find x_4: $x_4 = \epsilon^{-0.5455} = 0.5734$
5. Find x_5: $x_5 = \epsilon^{-0.5734} = 0.5636$
6. Find x_6: $x_6 = \epsilon^{-0.5636} = 0.5691$
7. Find x_7: $x_7 = \epsilon^{-0.5691} = 0.5658$
8. Find x_8: $x_8 = \epsilon^{-0.5658} = 0.5670$
9. Find x_9: $x_9 = \epsilon^{-0.5670} = 0.5666$

10. Find x_{10}: $x_{10} = \epsilon^{-0.5666} = 0.5667$
11. Find x_{11}: $x_{11} = \epsilon^{-0.5667} = 0.5667$
Since $x_{10} = x_{11}$, $x_0 = 0.5667$ to four places.

Newton-Raphson Method

In the Newton-Raphson method, the roots of $f(x) = 0$ are found as follows. A graph of $f(x)$ is shown in Figure E-3, with a root of $f(x)$ at x_0. Point x_1 is near enough to x_0 that the tangent to $f(x)$ at x_1 cuts the

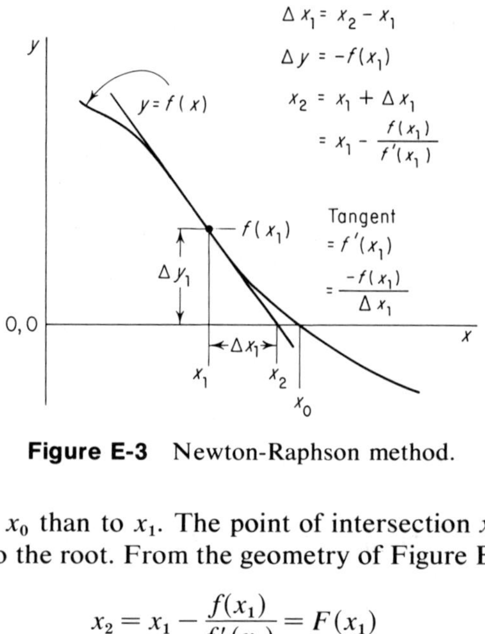

Figure E-3 Newton-Raphson method.

x axis nearer to x_0 than to x_1. The point of intersection x_2 is the second approximation to the root. From the geometry of Figure E-3, we find that

$$x_2 = x_1 - \frac{f(x_1)}{f'(x_1)} = F(x_1) \tag{E-11}$$

and, by successive applications of the method,

$$x_{n+1} = x_n - \frac{f(x_n)}{f'(x_n)} = F(x_n) \tag{E-12}$$

To determine convergence, we regard Equation (E-12) as an iterative step in the solution of

$$x = F(x) \tag{E-13a}$$

and hence seek the solution of

$$F(x) = x - \frac{f(x)}{f'(x)} \tag{E-13b}$$

Now

$$F'(x) = 1 \frac{[f'(x)]^2 - f(x)f''(x)}{[f'(x)]^2}$$
$$= \frac{f(x)f''(x)}{f'(x)^2} \qquad \textbf{(E-13c)}$$

From similarity to Equation (E-1), the condition for convergence is $|F'(x_0)| < 1$, or

$$\left| \frac{f(x_0)f''(x_0)}{[f'(x_0)]^2} \right| < 1 \qquad \textbf{(E-14)}$$

When $f'(x_0)$ is zero—that is, if $f(x)$ has a multiple root at x_0—then the procedure must be modified.[2]

To estimate the rate of convergence, we find the error after one step, which is

$$e_2 = x_0 - x_2 = F(x_0) - F(x_1) \qquad \textbf{(E-15)}$$

and $F(x_n)$ is given by Equation (E-12). To evaluate e_1, expand $F(x_1)$ in a Taylor series about x_0. This gives

$$F(x_1) = F(x_0) + (x_1 - x_0)F'(x_0) + (x_1 - x_0)^2 \frac{F''(x_0)}{2!} + \cdots \qquad \textbf{(E-16)}$$

Now $F(x_0) = x_0$, and $F'(x_0) = 0$ from Equation (E-13). Hence,

$$|e_2| \simeq \left| (x_1 - x_0)^2 \frac{F'(x_0)}{2} \right|$$
$$= \left| e_1^2 \frac{f''(x_0)}{2f'(x_0)} \right| \qquad \textbf{(E-17)}$$

Note that e_2 is proportional to e_1^2. This means that the Newton-Raphson method converges rapidly in the neighborhood of a root. For example, if $e_1 = 0.01$, then e_2 is proportional to 0.0001. The Newton-Raphson method is called a "second-order" method because of the rate of convergence. In using it, a rule of thumb has it that the number of decimals of accuracy approximately doubles with each step, provided one is close to a root with the first approximation. Let us illustrate the Newton-Raphson method with two examples.

Examples for real and complex functions. Find the root nearest the origin of

---

[2] See R. G. Stanton, *Numerical Methods for Science and Engineering* (Englewood Cliffs, N. J., Prentice-Hall, 1961), Chap. 4.

$$f(x) = \cos x + \frac{2 \sin x}{x}$$

From Figure E-4, we see that the first root lies in the range $\pi/2 < x_0 < 3\pi/4$. We choose our first approximation at the midpoint of this span at $x_1 = 5\pi/8$. Using the Newton-Raphson method, we obtain

$$x_{n+1} = x_n - \frac{f(x_n)}{f'(x_n)}$$
$$= x_n \left[1 - \frac{x_n \cos x_n + 2 \sin x_n}{2x_n \cos x_n - (2 + x_n^2) \sin x_n}\right]$$

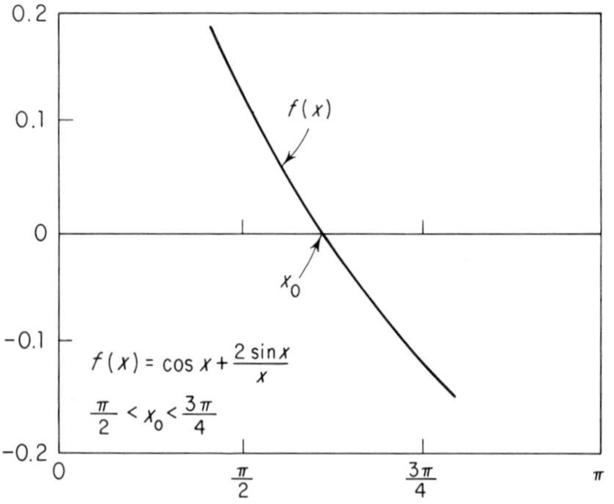

Figure E-4 Plot of $f(x) = \cos x + (2 \sin x/x)$ near first root, x_0.

and hence

$$x_2 = \frac{5\pi}{8}\left[1 - \frac{(0.750 + 1.85)}{-(1.50 + 5.43)}\right]$$
$$= 1.965[1.1586] = 2.277$$

Use $x_2 = 2.28$; then

$$x_3 = 2.28\left[1 - \frac{(-1.481 + 1.518)}{-(2.962 + 5.46)}\right]$$
$$= 2.28[1.0044] = 2.290$$

The correct answer to four places is 2.289.

The Newton-Raphson method may also be applied to the solution of equations with complex roots. One method of solution involves separation of the equation into real and imaginary parts. Then a common solution is found by application of the Newton-Raphson method to the pair of equations. A second method involves application of the Newton-Raphson procedure directly to the complex function.

The first Newton-Raphson procedure for complex roots requires splitting the function $f(z)$ into its real and imaginary parts. The derivation of the procedure for finding the roots then follows. In this case, we have

$$f(z) = U(z) + jV(z) \tag{E-18}$$

and

$$f'(z) = \frac{\partial U}{\partial x} + j\frac{\partial V}{\partial x} = \frac{\partial V}{\partial y} - j\frac{\partial U}{\partial y} \tag{E-19}$$

where $z = x + jy$. By using the Newton-Raphson procedure, we obtain

$$z_2 = z_1 - \frac{f(z_1)}{f'(z_1)} \tag{E-20}$$

and straightforward substitution yields the equations for the real and imaginary portions of the root $z_0 = x_0 + jy_0$. These are

$$x_2 = x_1 - \frac{U\dfrac{\partial U}{\partial x} + V\dfrac{\partial V}{\partial x}}{\left(\dfrac{\partial U}{\partial x}\right)^2 + \left(\dfrac{\partial V}{\partial x}\right)^2} \tag{E-21a}$$

$$y_2 = y_1 - \frac{V\dfrac{\partial U}{\partial x} - U\dfrac{\partial V}{\partial x}}{\left(\dfrac{\partial U}{\partial x}\right)^2 + \left(\dfrac{\partial V}{\partial x}\right)^2} \tag{E-21b}$$

The method is applicable when $f'(z_0) \neq 0$.

For example, take the algebraic expression

$$f(z) = z^3 + 2z^2 + 2z + 1$$

Then

$$U = x^3 - 3xy^2 + 2x^2 - 2y^2 + 2x + 1$$

and

$$V = 3x^2y - y^3 + 4xy + 2y$$

Also,

$$\frac{\partial U}{\partial x} = 3x^2 - 3y^2 + 4x + 2$$

and

$$\frac{\partial V}{\partial x} = 6xy + 4y$$

We start with $x_1 = 0$ and $y_1 = 1$, and obtain x_2 and y_2.

After several applications of the Newton-Raphson procedure, we find that $x_n = -0.5$ and $y_n = 0.9$. Then $U_n = -0.030$, $V_n = -0.054$, $U_n' = -1.68$, $V_n' = 0.90$, and

$$x_{n+1} = -0.5 - \frac{(-0.030)(-1.68) + (-0.054)(0.90)}{(-1.68)^2 + (0.90)^2}$$

$$= -0.50 + 0.0005 = -0.4995$$

$$y_{n+1} = 0.90 - \frac{(-0.054)(-1.68) - (-0.030)(0.90)}{(-1.68)^2 + (0.90)^2}$$

$$= 0.90 - 0.0324 = -0.8676$$

From the relationships between the coefficients and the sum of the roots, we find the three roots of the equation as

$$z = -0.4995 \pm j0.8676$$

$$z = -0.9990$$

The true solutions are $-0.5 \pm j0.866$ and -1.

Example for a complex transcendental function. Given

$$f(\theta) = 1 + K\theta \sinh \theta$$

find the zeros of $f(\theta)$ for $\theta = \sqrt{j\omega}$. Here, we have an equation for which the imaginary axis zeros in the frequency domain are required. These occur where $\arg(\theta \sinh \theta) = (2n-1)\pi$. Now for $\theta = \sqrt{j\omega}$, we can write $\theta = u + ju$, where substitution gives $\omega = 2u^2$. Then, expansion of $\theta \sinh \theta$ gives

$$\arg(\theta \sinh \theta) = \tan^{-1}\left(\frac{\sinh u \cos u + \cosh u \sin u}{\sinh u \cos u - \cosh u \sin u}\right) \tag{E-22}$$

Also,

$$\tan(2n-1)\pi = \frac{0}{-1}$$

and when the numerator in Equation (E-22) is zero, that is, where

$$\sinh u \cos u + \cosh u \sin u = 0 \tag{E-23}$$

then $\sinh u \cos u = -\cosh u \sin u$, and the denominator of Equation (E-22) is given by

$$\sinh u \cos u - \cosh u \sin u = -2 \cosh u \sin u \tag{E-24}$$

Therefore, since $\cosh u \geqslant 1$ for all u, the solutions of Equation (E-22) exist only where $\sin u > 0$—that is, for $2n\pi < u < (2n+1)\pi$, as shown by Equation (E-24). Further, from Equation (E-23), solutions exist only when $\cos u < 1$—that is, for

$$\left(2n + \frac{1}{2}\right)\pi < u < \left(2n + \frac{3}{2}\right)\pi$$

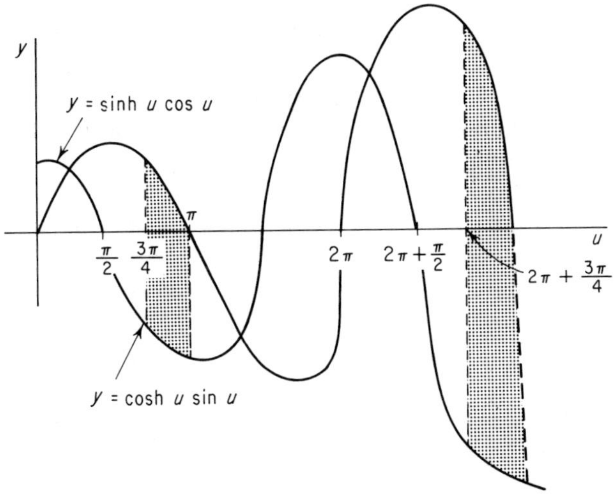

Figure E-5 Allowable regions for roots of arg $(\theta \sinh \theta) = n\pi$ $(\theta = \sqrt{j\omega}$, $\omega = 2u^2)$.

Also, $\sinh u \approx \cosh u$ for $u > 2$, and thus solutions exist in the neighborhoods of the points where $\cos u = -\sin u$—that is, in the vicinity of $u = (2n\pi + 3/4\pi)$. This is illustrated in Figure E-5.

Therefore, for our initial approximation in the Newton-Raphson procedure, we use $u_1 = (2n + 3/4)\pi$. The steps are as follows. From Equation (E-22), we seek the roots of

$$f(u) = \sinh u \cos u + \cosh u \sin u \tag{E-25}$$

in the vicinity of $u = (2n + 3/4)\pi$. Also,

$$f'(u) = 2 \cosh u \cos u \tag{E-26}$$

from which, after substitution and clearing terms, we have

$$\begin{aligned} u_2 &= u_1 - \frac{f(u_1)}{f'(u_1)} \qquad \text{(E-27)} \\ &= (2n + 3/4)\pi - (1/2)\ [\tanh (2n + 3/4)\pi + \tan (2n + 3/4)\pi] \end{aligned}$$

Now $\tan (2n + 3/4)\pi = -1.00000$, and $\tanh 3\pi/4 = 0.98233$, giving a correction term of $0.01767/2 = 0.0083$ for the first root $(n = 1)$. For the next root, $\tanh (2 + 3/4)\pi = 0.99999993$, giving a correction term of 0.00000003. Hence, for n greater than 1, the solutions

$$u \approx (2n + 3/4)\pi \tag{E-28}$$

are correct to seven decimal places. Hence, the imaginary axis zeros are

$$\omega = 2u^2 = (8n + 3)^2 \frac{\pi^2}{8} \tag{E-29}$$

to a minimum seven decimal places for $n \geqslant 2$.

It should be mentioned that the Newton-Raphson method is often used in electronic computing techniques.

Bibliography

Abraham, R. P., "Transistor behavior at high frequencies," *IRE Trans. Electron Devices,* vol. ED-7, no. 1, pp. 59–69, 1960.

Afansas'yev, K. L., and V. B. Golovchenko, "Theoretical investigation of the parameters of thin-film RC circuits," *Telecommun. Radio Eng.*, vol. 20, pt. 2, pp. 113–118, Feb, 1965.

Ansell, H. G., "Networks of transmission lines and lumped reactances," *IEEE Trans. Circuit Theory,* vol. CT-11, pp. 214–223, 1964.

Arnold, J. W., and P. F. Bechberger, "Sinusoidal currents in linearly tapered loaded transmission lines," *Proc. IRE,* vol. 19, pp. 304–310, 1931.

– – –, and R. C. Taylor, "Linearly tapered loaded transmission lines," *Proc. IRE,* vol. 20, pp. 1811–1817, 1932.

Ballantine, S., "Nonuniform lumped electric lines," *J. Franklin Inst.* vol. 203, pp. 561–582, 1927.

Barker, D. G., "Synthesis of active filters employing distributed-parameter networks," *IEEE Internat'l Conv. Record,* vol. 13, pt. 7, pp. 119–126, 1965.

Bassett, P. E., "Analysis and synthesis of networks of multiple layer, arbitrarily tapered distributed-parameter RC lines," Doctoral dissertation, University of Pittsburgh, 1966.

Berg, E. J., "Heaviside's operators in engineering and physics," *J. Franklin Inst.,* vol. 198, pp. 647–702, 1924.

Berger, H., "Generalized nonuniform transmission lines," *IEEE Trans. Circuit Theory*, vol. CT-13, no. 1, pp. 92–93, 1966.

Bertnolli, E. C., "Exact and numerical analysis of distributed parameter *RC* networks," *Doctoral Dissertation Special Report 57*, Manhattan, Kansas, September, 1965.

Bertnolli, E. C., "Analysis of the *n*-wire exponential line," *Proc. IEEE*, vol. 55, p. 1225, 1967.

Bevensee, R. M., "RLC log-periodic transmission lines," *Symp. Proc. Polytech. Inst. (Brooklyn)*, vol. XVI, pp. 137–148, 1966.

Bhattacharyya, B. B., and M. N. S. Swamy, "Dual distributions of solvable nonuniform lines," *Proc. IEEE,* vol. 54, pp. 1979–1980, 1966.

– – –, and – – –, "Interrelationships among the chain parameters of a nonuniform transmission line," *Proc. IEEE,* vol. 55, pp. 1763–1764, 1967.

Bogachev, V. M., "Synthesis of equivalent circuits of a junction transistor with distributed parameters," *Radio Eng. Electron. Phys.*, vol. 10, pp. 1627–1631, 1965.

Bolinder, E. F., "Fourier transforms and tapered transmission lines," *Proc. IRE,* vol. 44, p. 557, 1956.

– – –, "Fourier transforms in the theory of inhomogeneous transmission lines," *Trans. Roy. Inst. Technol. (Stockholm),* NR 48, 1951.

– – –, "Fourier transforms in the theory of inhomogeneous transmission lines," *Proc. IRE,* vol. 38, p. 1354, 1950.

Bourquin, J. J., and T. N. Trick, "Stability of distributed RC networks," *Proc. 10th Midwest Symp. Circuit Theory,* Purdue University, Lafayette, Ind., 1967.

Burrows, C. R., "The exponential transmission line," *Bell System Tech. J.,* vol. 17, pp. 555–573, 1938.

Carlin, H. J., "Network synthesis with transmission line elements," Tech. Rept. RADC-TDR-64-505, Rome Air Development Center, Feb. 1965.

– – –, and G. I. Zysman, "Linear phase microwave networks," *Symp. Proc. Polytech. Inst. (Brooklyn),* vol. XVI, pp. 193–226, 1966.

Carson, J. R., "Propagation of periodic currents over nonuniform lines," *Electrician (London),* vol. 86, pp. 272–273, 1921.

– – –, "Theory of transient oscillations of electric networks and transmission systems," *Trans. AIEE,* vol. 38, pt. 1, pp. 345–427, 1919.

– – –, and R. S. Hoyt, "Propagation of periodic currents over a system of parallel wires," *Bell System Tech. J.,* vol. 6, pp. 495–545, 1927.

– – –, and O. J. Zobel, "Transient oscillations in electric wave filters," *Bell System Tech. J.,* vol. 2, pp. 1–52, 1923.

Castro, P. S., "Microsystem circuit analysis," *Elec. Eng.,* vol. 80, pp. 535–542, 1961.

———, "RC distributed-parameter networks with circular geometry," *Proc. Nat'l Electron. Conf.*, vol. 19, pp. 98–108, 1963.

Cath, P. G., "The synthesis of nonuniform transmission lines," *Tech. Rept. 116,* Department of Electrical Engineering, Cooley Electronics Laboratory, University of Michigan, Ann Arbor, 1961.

Chang, F. Y., and O. Wing, "Uniform multilayer RC distributed networks," *Proc. Allerton Conf.,* 1967.

Chen, W. I. H., and R. C. Levine, "Computer-designed transversal filters using thin-film RC dispersion," *Proc. 10th Midwest Symp. Circuit Theory,* Purdue University, Lafayette, Ind., 1967.

Chirlian, P. M., *Integrated and Active Network Analysis and Synthesis,* Englewood Cliffs, N. J.: Prentice Hall, 1967.

Cohn, S. B., "Dissipation loss in multiple-coupled-resonator filters," *Proc. IRE,* vol. 47, pp. 1342–1348, 1959.

———, "Parallel-coupled transmission-line-resonator filters," *IRE Trans. Microwave Theory and Techniques,* vol. MTT-6, pp. 223–231, 1958.

Collin, R. E., "The optimum tapered transmission line matching section," *Proc. IRE,* vol. 44, pp. 539–548, 1956.

Cristal, E. G., "A frequency transformation for commensurate transmission line networks," *IEEE Trans. Microwave Theory and Techniques*, vol. MTT-15, pp. 348–357, 1967.

Desoer, C. A., "A general formulation of the Nyquist criterion," *IEEE Trans. Circuit Theory*, vol. CT-12, pp. 230–234, 1965.

Dicker, D., "Analysis of distributed parameter-networks – a general method," *Proc. Allerton Conf.*, pp. 144–150, 1965. Also in *SIAM Journ. on App. Math.*, vol. 14, pp. 1446–1453, 1966.

Doetsch, G., *Guide to the Applications of Laplace Transforms*. Princeton, N. J.: Van Nostrand, 1961.

Dutta Roy, S. C., "Matrix parameters of nonuniform transmission lines," *IEEE Trans. Circuit Theory,* vol. CT-12, pp. 142–143, 1964.

———, "On three-terminal lumped and distributed RC null networks," *IEEE Trans. Circuit Theory,* vol. CT-11, pp. 98–103, 1964.

———, "Some exactly solvable nonuniform RC lines," *IEEE Trans. Circuit Theory,* vol. CT-12, pp. 141–142, 1964.

———, and B. A. Shenoi, "Distributed and lumped RC realization of a constant argument impedance," *J. Franklin Inst.,* vol. 282, pp. 318–329, 1966.

———, and ———, "Notch networks using distributed RC elements," *Proc. IEEE,* vol. 54, pp. 1220–1221, 1966.

Edison, W. A., "Tapered distributed RC lines for phase-shift oscillators," *Proc. IRE,* vol. 49, pp. 1021–1024, 1961.

Eichmann, G., and J. Swartz, "Hypergeometric and spheroidal wave nonuniform RC lines," *Proc. 10th Midwest Symp. Circuit Theory,* Purdue University, Lafayette, Ind., 1967.

Ekstrom, J. L., "The Z-matrix parameters of tapered transmission lines," *IRE Trans. Circuit Theory,* vol. CT-9, pp. 132–135, 1962.

Elmore, W. C., "The transient response of damped linear networks with particular regard to wide-band amplifiers," *J. Appl. Phys.,* vol. 19, pp. 55–63, 1948.

Feldstein, A. L., "Generalized matrix theory for nonuniform lines," *Radio Eng. Electron. Phys.,* vol. 5, pp. 12–34, June 1960.

———, "Inhomogeneous transmission lines as filters," *Nachrichtentechnik,* vol. 4, pp. 264–266, 1964.

Fu, Y., and J. S. Fu, "n-port rectangularly shaped distributed RC networks," *IEEE Trans. Circuit Theory,* vol. CT-13, pp. 222–226, 1966.

Fuller, W. D., and P. S. Castro, "A microsystems bandpass amplifier," *Proc. Nat'l Electron. Conf.,* vol. 16, pp. 139–151, 1960.

———, and W. W. Happ, "Design procedures for thin-film distributed parameter circuits," *Proc. Nat'l Electron. Conf.,* vol. 17, pp. 597–610, 1961.

Galitzkiy, V. V., "Analysis of multilayer nonuniform distributed RC structures," *Radio Engineering*, vol. 11, pp. 249–256, Feb. 1966.

Gay, M. J., "The design of feedback tuned amplifiers using distributed bridge T networks," *Microelectron. Reliability,* vol. 3, pp. 93–107, 1964.

Gent, A. W., and P. J. Wallis, "Impedance matching by tapered transmission lines," *J. IEE (London),* vol. 93, p. IIIA, pp. 559–563, 1946.

Ghausi, M. S., and G. J. Herskowitz, "The effect of shaping and loading on distributed RC networks," *J. Franklin Inst.,* vol. 278, pp. 108–128, 1964.

———, and ———, "The transient response of tapered distributed RC networks," *IEEE Trans. Circuit Theory,* vol. CT-10, pp. 443–445, 1963.

Googe, J. M., and K. L. Su, "The double Kelvin transmission line and some applications," *IEEE Trans. Circuit Theory,* vol. CT-11, pp. 372–377, 1964.

Goto, M., and M. Morisue, "The stability of a distributed circuit connected with a nonlinear resistance," *Elec. Commun. (Japan),* vol. 49, pp. 49–57, 1966.

Gruner, L., "The steady-state characteristics of nonuniform RC distributed networks and lossless lines," *IEEE Trans. Circuit Theory,* vol. CT-12, pp. 241–247, 1965.

Guckel, H., P. A. Brennan and I. Paloćz, "A parallel plate wave guide approach to microminatureized, planar transmission lines," *IEEE*

Trans. Microwave Theory and Techniques, vol. MTT-15, pp. 468–476, 1967.

Gurley, J. G., "Impedance matching by means of nonuniform transmission lines," *IRE Trans. Antennas and Propagation,* vol. AP-4, pp. 107–109, 1952.

Hager, C. K., "Distributed-parameter networks for circuit miniaturization," *Proc. Electron. Components Conf.,* pp. 195–203, 1959.

Happ, W., "Synthesis of distributed-parameter RC networks," *Proc. IRE,* vol. 50, pp. 483–484, 1962.

——— and P. S. Castro, "Distributed-parameter circuit design techniques," *Proc. Nat'l Electron. Conf.,* vol. 17, pp. 44–70, 1961.

——— and ———, "Distributed-parameter circuits and microsystems electronics," *Proc. Nat'l Electron. Conf.,* vol. 16, pp. 448–460, 1960.

———, ———, and W. D. Fuller, "Synthesis of solid-state distributed-parameter functions," *IRE Internat'l Conv. Record,* vol. 10, pt. 6, pp. 262–278, 1962.

——— and G. C. Riddle, "Limitations of thin-film circuits consisting of resistive and capacitive layers," *IRE Nat'l Conv. Record,* vol. 9, pp. 141–165, 1961.

Heaviside, O., "Contributions to the theory of the propagation of current in wire," *Electrical Papers,* vol. I, pp. 141–181, 1892.

Heizer, K. W., "Distributed RC networks with rational transfer functions," *IRE Trans. Circuit Theory,* vol. CT-9, pp. 356–362, 1962.

———, "Rational parameters with distributed networks," *IEEE Trans. Circuit Theory,* vol. CT-10, no. 4, pp. 531–32, 1963.

Hellstrom, M. J., "Symmetrical RC distributed networks," *Proc. IRE,* vol. 50, pp. 97–98, 1962.

———, "Equivalent distributed RC networks or transmission lines," *IRE Trans. Circuit Theory,* vol. CT-9, pp. 247–251, 1962.

Herskowitz, G., "The propagation of electric signals in multilayer semiconductor networks," *Tech. Rept. 400–58*, New York University, April 1962.

——— and R. Wyndrum, "Design of distributed RC feedback networks for bandpass amplifiers," *Semicond. Prod.,* vol. 7, pp. 13–19, 1964.

Holm, C., "Distributed resistor-capacitor networks for microminiaturization," *R.R.E. Tech. Note 654,* Worcester, England, April 1960.

Hyltin, T. M., "Microstrip transmission on semiconductor dielectrics," *IEEE Trans. Microwave Theory and Techniques*, vol. MTT-13, pp. 777–781, Nov. 1965.

Ilin, V. A., "Long Lines with parameters varying along the line," *Elektrichestvo,* pp. 54–59, February 1950.

Ikeno, N., "Design of Distributed Constant Networks," *Rept. PIBMRI-1003-62,* Polytechnic Institute of Brooklyn, October 1962.

Ingram, W. H., "Electrical oscillations in a nonuniform transmission line," *University of Wash. Publ. Math.*, vol. 2, pp. 17–38, December 1930.

Irvin, J. C., "Resistivity of bulk silicon and of diffused layer in silicon," *Bell System Tech. J.*, vol. 41, pp. 387–410, 1964.

Jacobs, I., "A generalization of the exponential transmission line," *Proc. IRE,* vol. 48, pp. 1489–1490, 1960.

———, "The nonuniform transmission line as a broadband termination," *Bell System Tech. J.*, vol. 37, pp. 913–924, July 1958.

Karnik, A. R., and G. H. Cohen, "Optimal design of distributed-parameter circuits," *Proc. 10th Midwest Symp. Circuit Theory,* Purdue University, Lafayette, Ind., 1967.

Kaufman, H., "Bibliography of nonuniform transmission lines," *IRE Trans-Antennas and Propagation,* vol. AP-3, pp. 218–220, October 1955.

Kaufman, W. M., "Theory of a monolithic null device and some novel circuit applications," *Proc. IRE*, vol. 48, pp. 1540–1545, 1960.

——— and S. J. Garret, "Tapered distributed filters," *IRE Trans. Circuit Theory,* vol. CT-9, no. 4, pp. 329–336, 1962.

Kay, I., "Input impedances for the nonuniform 2*n* wire transmission line," *Tech. Summary Rept. 252*, Mathematics Research Center, U.S. Army, University of Wisconsin, August 1961.

Kazansky, B. G., "Outline of a theory of nonuniform transmission lines," *Proc. IEE (London),* vol. 105, pt. C, pp. 126–138, 1958.

Kelly, J. J., "Analysis and design considerations for distributed RC networks with arbitrary taper," *Tech. Report 400–115,* New York University, August 1965.

———, "Analysis of drift transistor current gain with applications to distributed RC networks," *Tech. Rept. 400-98,* New York University, July 1964.

———, and M. S. Ghausi, "Network properties of distributed RC networks with arbitrary geometric shapes," *Tech. Rept. 400-107,* New York University, March 1965.

———, and ———, "On the effective dominant pole of the distributed RC network," *J. Franklin Inst.*, vol. 297, pp. 417–429, June 1965.

———, and ———, "Poles of the alpha of drift transistors," *IEEE Trans.* vol. CT-12, pp. 593–595, 1965.

———, and ———, "Steady-state and transient response of arbitrary tapered distributed RC networks with lumped load terminations," *Proc. Nat'l Electron. Conf.*, vol. 21, 1965.

———, and ———, "Tapered distributed RC networks with similar immittances," *IEEE Trans. Circuit Theory,* vol. CT-12, pp. 554–558, 1965.

———, ———, and J. H. Mulligan, "On the analysis of composite lumped distributed systems," *IEEE Internat'l Conv. Record,* vol. 14, pt. 7, pp. 308–318, 1966.

Kil'metov, R. S., and Ye. B. Mekhantsev, "Transfer characteristics of distributed uniform R-C NR structures," *Telecommun. Radio Eng.*, vol. 22, pp. 114–118, January, 1967.

Kim, M., and H. Erzberger, "On the design of optimum distributed parameter system with boundary control function," *IEEE Trans. Automatic Control*, vol. AC-12, pp. 22–29, 1967.

Kinariwala, B. K., "Theory of cascaded structures: lossless transmission lines," *Bell Sys. Tech. J.*, vol. 45, pp. 631–649, 1966.

———, "Theory of cascaded transmission lines," *Symp. Proc. Polytech. Inst. (Brooklyn),* vol. XVI, pp. 345–352, 1966.

———, and A. Gersho, "A stability criterion for nonuniformly sampled and distributed parameter systems," *Bell System Tech. J.,* vol. 45, pp. 1153–1155, 1966.

Klopfenstein, R. W., "A transmission line taper of improved design," *Proc. IRE,* vol. 44, pp. 31–35, 1956.

Kolesoz, L. N., Ye. B. Mekhantsev, R. S. Kil'metov, V. I. Shapovalov, and V. L. Zhuravskiy, "Calculation of the characteristics of distributed *R-C NR* structures with capacitance discontinuity typical of *p-n* junctions," *Radio Eng. Electron. Phys.,* vol. 11, pp. 1246–1250, 1966.

Kolker, R. A., "The amplitude response of a coupled transmission line, all-pass network having loss," *IEEE Trans. Microwave Theory and Techniques,* vol. MTT-15, pp. 468–476, 1967.

Kurilin, B. I., "Analytical calculation of the resonant frequencies of a line segment," *Telecommun. Radio Eng.*, vol. 20, pt. II, pp. 93–96, May 1965.

Kurss, H., "A transmission line formulation for semiconductors," *Rept. PIBMRI 885–60,* Polytech. Institute of Brooklyn, 1960.

———, and W. K. Kahn, "A system of nonuniform transmission lines," *Proc. IRE,* vol. 48, p. 250, 1960.

Levy, R., and I. Whiteley, "Synthesis of distributed elliptic-function filters from lumped-constant prototypes," *IEEE Trans. Microwave Theory and Techniques,* vol. MTT-14, pp. 506–517, 1966.

Lindgren, A. G., "Transfer characteristics of a class of distributed RC networks," *Proc. IEEE,* pp 625–626, 1965.

Lindholm, F. A., and W. W. Happ, "Transient analysis of thin-film structures," *Radio Electron. Engr.,* vol. 26, pp. 421–435, 1963.

Litvinenko, O. N., "Synthesis of inhomogeneous lines on the basis of input impedance specified in the form of a rational function of frequency," *Radio Eng. Electron. Phys.*, vol. 6, pp. 1624–1630, 1961.

Litvinenko, O. N., and V. I. Soshnikov, "Synthesis of heterogeneous lines by solution of the inverse Sturm-Liouville problem," *Telecommun. Radio Eng.*, pt. II, pp. 14–22, September 1962.

Lomonosov, V., "Long lines with parameters varying along the line," *Elektrichestvo*, pp. 26–27, March 1951.

Maleyev, V. Ya., "Synthesis of nonuniform lines by the method of continued fractions," *Radio Eng. Electron. Phys.*, vol. 7, pp. 1682–1695, October 1962.

Matsumoto, A., "Network synthesis with multiwire lines," *Tech. Rept. RADC-TDR 63–369*, Rome Air Development Center, August 1963.

Matthaei, G. L., "Design of wide-band band-pass microwave filters, on the insertion loss basis," *IEEE Trans. Microwave Theory and Techniques,* vol. MTT-8, pp. 580–593, 1960.

Milnor, J. W., "Tapered transmission lines," *Trans. AIEE,* vol. 64, pp. 345–346, 1945.

Miracle, C. L., "Approximate solutions of the telegrapher's equation by difference-equation methods," *J. Soc. Indust. Appl. Math.*, vol. 10, pp. 517–527, 1962.

Mulligan, J. H., Jr., "The effect of pole-zero locations on the transient response of linear dynamic systems," *Proc. IRE,* vol. 37, pp. 516–529, May 1949.

Neiman, M. S., "Nonuniform lines with distributed constants," *Izv. Elektropromyshlennosti Slabogo Toka,* pp. 14–25, 1938.

Newcomb, R. W., "Nonreciprocal transmission line n-port synthesis," *Proc. Inst. Radio Electron. Engr. (Australia),* vol. 26, pp. 135–142, April 1965.

Oehler, K. L., and W. C. Duesterhoeft, "A graphical design for exponentially tapered RC circuits," *IEEE Trans. Circuit Theory,* vol. CT-12, pp. 288–290, 1965.

O'Shea, R. P., "Synthesis using distributed RC networks," *IEEE Trans. Circuit Theory,* vol. CT-12, pp. 546–554, Dec. 1965; also in, *IEEE Internat'l Conv. Record,* vol. 13, pt. 7, pp. 18–29, 1965.

Ozaki, H., and J. Ishii, "Synthesis of a class of strip-line filters," *IRE Trans. Circuit Theory,* vol. CT-5, pp. 104–109, 1958.

———, and ———, "Synthesis of transmission-line networks and the design of UHF filters," *IRE Trans. Circuit Theory,* vol. CT-2, pp. 325–336, 1955.

Palocz, I., "The integral equation approach to currents and fields in plane parallel transmission lines," *J. Math. Mech.,* vol. 15, pp. 541–559, 1966.

Parkin, R. E., "Approximations to the equations describing distributed RC networks," *IEEE Trans. Circuit Theory,* vol. CT-12, pp. 598–601, 1965.

Pederson, D. O., and G. H. Wilson, "Dominant zero and excess phase of a Hurwitz polynomial," *IEEE Trans. Circuit Theory,* vol. CT-11, pp. 104–108, 1964.

Pierce, J. R., "Note on transmission line equations in terms of impedance," *Bell System Tech. J.,* vol. 22, pp. 263–265, 1943.

Pipes, L. A., "Computation of impedances of nonuniform lines by a direct method," *Trans. AIEE,* vol. 75, pt. I, pp. 551–554, 1956.

———, "Direct computation of transmission matrices of electrical transmission lines," *J. Franklin Inst.,* vol. 281, pp. 275–292, 387–405, 1966.

———, "Matrix theory of multiconductor transmission lines," *Phil. Mag.,* vol. 24, pp. 97–113, July 1937.

———, "Steady-state analysis of multiconductor transmission lines," *J. Appl. Phys.,* vol. 12, pp. 782–799, 1941.

Pritchard, R. L., "Frequency variations of current-amplification factor for junction transistors," *Proc. IRE,* vol. 40, pp. 1476–1481, 1952.

Protonotarios, E., and O. Wing, "Analysis and intrinsic properties of the general nonuniform transmission line," *IEEE Trans. Microwave Theory Techniques,* vol. MTT-15, pp. 142–150, 1967.

———, and ———, "Computation of the step response of a general nonuniform RC distributed network," *IEEE Trans. Circuit Theory,* vol. CT-14, pp. 219–221, 1967.

———, and ———, "Delay and rise time of arbitrarily tapered RC transmission lines," *IEEE Internat'l Conv. Record,* vol. 13, pt. 7, pp. 1–6, 1965.

———, and ———, "The distribution of zeros of ABCD parameters of arbitrary RC transmission lines," *Proc. Allerton Conf.,* pp. 162–171, 1965.

———, and ———, "Theory of nonuniform RC lines, Part I—Analytic properties and realizability conditions in the frequency domain, Part II—Analytic properties in the time domain," *IEEE Trans. Circuit Theory,* vol. CT-14, pp. 2–20, March 1967.

Prozorovskiy, V. Ye., and K. L. Afanas'yev, and O. N. Negodenko, "Design of thin-film two-terminal networks with distributed parameters," *Telecommun. Radio Eng.*, pt. II, vol. 21, pp. 104–117, February 1966.

Ramachandran, V., "Network representation of exponential transmission lines, *IRE Trans. Circuit Theory*, vol. CT-9, pp. 136–143, 1962.

Rao, T. N., C. V. Shaffer, and R. W. Newcomb, "Realizability conditions for distributed RC networks," *ERL Tech. Rept. 6558*–7, Stanford University, May 1965.

———, and R. W. Newcomb, "Synthesis of lumped-distributed RC

n-Ports," *IEEE Trans. Circuit Theory,* vol. CT-13, pp. 458–459, 1966.

Raout, C., "Propagation des courants sinusoidaux sur des lignes quelconques," *Rev. Gen. L'Elect.*, vol. 7, pp. 611–615, May 1920.

Riblet, H. J., "An explicit derivation of the relationships between the parameters of an interdigital structure and the equivalent transmission line cascade," *IEEE Trans. Microwave Theory and Techniques,* vol. MTT-15, pp. 161–166, 1967.

Rice, S. O., "Steady-state solutions of transmission line equations," *Bell System Tech. J.,* vol. 20, pp. 131–178, 1941.

Richards, P. I., "A special class of functions with positive real part in a half plane," *Duke Math. J.,* vol. 14, pp. 777–786, 1947.

– – –, "Resistor transmission line circuits," *Proc. IRE,* vol. 30, pp. 217–220, 1948.

Rohrer, R. A., "Synthesis of arbitrarily tapered lossy transmission lines," *Symp. Proc. Polytechnic Inst. (Brooklyn),* vol. XVI, pp. 115–136, 1966.

– – –, J. Resh, and R. Hoyt, "Distributed network synthesis for a class of integrated circuits," *IEEE Internat'l Conv. Record,* vol. 13, pt. 7, pp. 18–29, 1965.

Saito, M., "Synthesis of transmission line networks by multivariable techniques," *Symp. Proc. Polytech. Inst. (Brooklyn),* vol. XVI, pp. 353–392, 1966.

– – –, "The condition for unit network extraction in mixed lumped and distributed networks," *IEEE Trans. Circuit Theory,* vol. CT-13, pp. 218–220, 1966.

– – –, and K. Nagai, "Equivalent network of a four-conductor line section," *Rept Res. Inst. Elec. Commun. (Tohoku Univ.),* vol. 16, pp. 13–35, March 1965.

– – –, and – – –, "Necessary and sufficient conditions for wave admittance of multiline to be realizable," *Record Elec. Commun. Eng. Conversazione (Tohoku Univ.),* vol. 32, pp. 1–4, December 1963.

Samuelson, R. E., "Electrical transmission lines with nonuniform parameters," *Doctoral dissertation,* Northwestern University, 1949.

Scanlon, J. O., and J. D. Rhodes, "Cascade synthesis of distributed networks," *Symp. Proc. Polytech. Inst. (Brooklyn),* vol. XVI, pp. 227–256, 1966.

– – –, and – – –, "Realizability and synthesis of a restricted class of distributed RC networks," *IEEE Trans. Circuit Theory,* vol. CT-12, pp. 577–585, 1965.

Schatz, E. R., and E. M. Williams, "Pulse transients in exponential transmission lines," *Proc. IRE,* vol. 38, pp. 1208–1212, 1950.

Schwartz, R. F., "Transformations in the analysis of nonuniform transmission lines," *J. Franklin Inst.*, vol. 278, pp. 163–172, 1964.

Scott, H. J., "The hyperbolic transmission line as a matching section," *Proc. IRE,* vol. 41, pp. 1654–1657, 1953.

Seshagiri, N., "Least weighted-square methods for analysis and synthesis of transmission lines," *IEEE Trans. Microwave Theory and Techniques,* vol. MTT-15, pp. 494–503, 1967.

Shaffer, C. V., "Transformerless n-port symmetrical transmission-line synthesis," *ERL Tech. Rept. 6558-2,* Stanford University, August 1965.

Sharpe, C. B., "An alternate derivation of Orlov's synthesis formula for nonuniform lines," *IEE (London) Monograph 483E,* November 1961.

———, "The synthesis of infinite lines," *Quart. Appl. Math.,* vol. 21, pp. 105–120, 1963.

———, "Some properties of infinite lines," *Quart. Appl. Math.,* vol. 21, pp. 337–342, 1964.

Shenoi, B. A., "Frequency characteristics of a double-Kelvin transmission-line network," *Proc. Allerton Conf.,* pp. 151–161, 1965.

Sinden, F. W., "Topology of thin-film RC circuits," *Bell System Tech. J.,* pp. 1639–1662, 1966.

Smith, A., "Rejection filters with distributed R and C," *Proc. Electron. Components Conf.,* pp. 23–28, 1960.

Stadmore, H. A., "Analysis and synthesis of nonuniform transmission lines incorporating loss," *IEEE Trans. Circuit Theory,* vol. CT-12, pp. 285–288, 1965.

Stannard, G. E., "Calculation of power on a transmission line," *Proc. IEEE,* vol. 55, p. 132, 1967.

Starr, A. T., "The nonuniform transmission line," *Proc. IRE,* vol. 20, pp. 1052–1063, 1932.

———, "The taper-loaded submarine cable," *Phil. Mag.,* vol. 17, pp. 83–96, Jan. 1934.

Steenaart, W., "A contribution to the synthesis of distributed all-pass networks," *Symp. Proc. Polytech. Inst. (Brooklyn),* vol. XVI, 1966.

Stein, J., and B. Cheo, "Analysis of an active solid-state distributed structure," *Tech. Note. 400-23,* New York University, November 1965.

Stein, J. J., J. H. Mulligan, Jr., and S. S. Shamis, "Realization of real transmission zeros using uniform distributed RC networks with common ground connections," *IEEE Internat'l Conv. Record,* vol. 15, pt. 6, pp. 98–105, 1967.

———, ———, and ———, "Realization of transfer functions using uniform distributed RC networks with common ground connections,"

Symp. Proc. Polytec. Inst. (Brooklyn), vol. XVI, pp. 149–172, 1966.

Sternberg, R. L., and H. Kaufman, "Applications of the theory of systems of differential equations to multiple nonuniform transmission lines," *J. Math. Phys.,* vol. 31, pp. 244–252, January 1953.

Su, K. L., "RC Filters with staggered notch frequencies," *Proc. IEEE,* vol. 54, pp. 1199–1200, 1966.

– – –, "Selectivity of notch filters using nonuniform RC lines," *Electron. Letters,* vol. 1, pp. 204–206, 1965.

– – –, "The trigonometric transmission lines," *IEEE Internat'l Conv. Record,* vol. 11, pt. 2, pp. 43–55, 1963.

Suezaki, T., S. Mori, and M. Tsukada, "A self-oscillating system with distributed line," *Electron. Commun. (Japan),* vol. 49, pp. 49–57, 1966.

Sugai, I., "A generalized Hildebrand's method for nonuniform transmission lines," *Proc. IRE,* vol. 49, p. 1944, 1961.

– – –, "A new exact method of nonuniform transmission lines," *Proc. IRE,* vol. 49, pp. 627–628, 1961.

– – –, "D'Alembert's method for nonuniform transmission lines," *Proc. IRE,* vol. 49, pp. 823–824, 1961.

– – –, "Ricatti's and Bernoulli's equations for nonuniform transmission lines," *IRE Trans. Circuit Theory,* vol. CT-8, pp. 359–360, 1961.

– – –, "The solutions of nonuniform transmission line problems," *Proc. IRE,* vol. 48, pp. 1489–1490, 1960.

Swamy, M. N. S., and B. B. Bhattachavya, "Generalized nonuniform lines and their equivalent circuits," *Proc. 10th Midwest Symp. Circuit Theory,* Purdue University, Lafayette, Ind., 1967.

– – –, and – – –, "Hermite lines," *Proc. IEEE,* vol. 54, pp. 1577–1578, 1966.

Tachibana, A., "Synthesis of distributed RC 1-port networks," *J. Inst. Electron. Commun. (Japan),* vol. 46, pp. 55–59, May 1963.

Taub, J. J., and Sleven, R. L., "Design of band-stop filters in the presence of dissipation," *IEEE Trans. Microwave Theory and Techniques,* vol. MTT-13, pp. 589–616, 1965.

Thomas, D. E., and J. L. Moll, "Junction transistor short-circuit gain and phase determination," *Proc. IRE,* vol. 46, pp. 1174–1184, 1948.

Tsandoulas, G. N., "The linearly tapered transmission line as a matching section—high- and low-frequency behavior," *Proc. IEEE,* vol. 55, pp. 1658–1659, 1967.

Vandivort, C. A., and E. C. Bertnolli, "Determining the transfer matrices of tapered multiwire transmission lines," *Proc. 10th Midwest Symp. Circuit Theory*, Purdue University, Lafayette, Ind., 1967.

Vokov, V. M., and V. P. Popov, "Analysis of networks with distributed parameters," *Telecommun. Radio Eng.*, pt. I, vol. 20, pp. 55–59, September, 1966.

———, and ———, "Analysis of selective amplifiers based on RC microstructures with distributed parameters," *Telecommun. Radio Eng.*, pt. II, vol. 22, pp. 86–89, January, 1967.

Volpert, A. R., "Lines with nonuniformly distributed parameters," *Elektrosyvaz,* pp. 40–65, 1940.

Walker, L. R., and N. Wax, "Nonuniform transmission lines and reflection coefficients," *J. Appl. Phys.*, vol. 17, pp. 1043–1045, 1946.

Wang, P. K. C., *Control of Distributed Parameter Systems Advances in Control Systems,* New York: Academic Press, 1964.

Wenzel, R. J., "Exact design of TEM microwave networks using quarter-wave lines," *IEEE Trans. on Microwave Theory and Techniques,* vol. MTT-12, pp. 94–111, 1964.

Wheeler, H. A., "Transmission lines with exponential taper," *Proc. IRE,* vol. 27, pp. 65–71, 1939.

Wheeler, W. H., "Transmission-line properties of parallel strips separated by a dielectric sheet," *IEEE Trans. Microwave Theory and Techniques,* vol. MTT-13, pp. 172–185, 1965.

Wilcox, C. H., "Electric wave propagation on nonuniform coupled transmission lines," *SIAM Review,* vol. 6, pp. 148–165, 1964.

Williams, E. M., and E. R. Schatz, "Design of exponential line pulse transformers," *Proc. IRE,* vol. 39, pp. 84–86, 1951.

Willis, J., and N. K. Sinka, "Nonuniform transmission lines as impedance matching sections," *Proc. IRE,* vol. 43, p. 1975, 1955.

Wilson, A. N., Jr., "A stability theory for nonlinear distributed networks," *Proc. 10th Midwest Symp. Circuit Theory,* Purdue University, Lafayette, Ind., 1967.

Wilson, B., and R. Wilson, "Shaping of distributed RC networks," *Proc. IRE,* vol. 49, pp. 1330–1331, Aug. 1961.

Wohlers, M. R., "A realizability theory for smooth lossless transmission lines," *IEEE Trans. Circuit Theory,* vol. CT-13, pp. 356–364, 1966.

Woo, B. B., and J. M. Bartlemay, "Characteristics and applications of a tapered, thin-film distributed-parameter structure, *IEEE Internat'l* Conv. Record, vol. 11, pt. 2, pp. 56–75, 1963.

———, and R. G. Hove, "Synthesis of rational transfer functions with thin-film distributed-parameter RC active networks," *Proc. Nat'l Electron. Conf.*, vol. 21, pp. 241–246, 1965.

Wu, T. T., "The imperfectly conducting coaxial line," *Quart. Appl. Math.*, vol. 19, pp. 1–13, 1961.

Wyndrum, R. W., Jr., "Distributed RC Notch Networks," *Proc. IRE,* vol. 51, pp. 374–375, 1963.

———, "The exact synthesis of distributed RC networks," *Tech. Rept. 400-76,* New York University, May 1963.

Yammamoto, S., T. Azakami, and K. Itakura, "Coupled nonuniform transmission line and its applications," *IEEE Trans. Microwave Theory and Techniques,* vol. MTT-15, pp. 220–231, 1967.

Yanai, H., T. Sugano, H. Sasaki, and M. Yoshida, "Theory and characteristics of multilayer RC distributed-constant circuits," *Electron. Commun. (Japan),* vol. 46, pp. 50–58, March 1963.

Yang, R. F. H., "Parabolic transmission line," *Proc. IRE,* vol. 43, p. 1010, 1955.

Yeh, H. H., and J. T. Ton, "Optimum control of a class of distributed parameter systems," *IEEE Trans. Automatic Control,* vol. AC-12, pp. 29–37, 1967.

Youla, D. C., "Analysis and synthesis of arbitrarily terminated lossless nonuniform lines," *IEEE Trans. Circuit Theory,* vol. CT-11, pp. 363–372, 1964.

———, "Synthesis of n-ports containing lumped and distributed elements," *Symp. Proc. Polytech. Inst. (Brooklyn),* vol. XVI, 1966.

———, P. Tissi, and W. Kohler, "The synthesis of networks containing lumped and distributed elements—Parts I and II," *Tech. Rept. RADG-TR-66-489,* Polytechnic Institute of Brooklyn, 1966.

Young, L., "Group delay and dissipation loss in transmission-line filters," *IEEE Trans. Microwave Theory and Techniques,* vol. MTT-11, 1963.

Zhabotinskii, M. E., M. L. Levin, and S. M. Rytov, "The telegraph equation for generalized transmission lines with small losses," *J. Tech. Phys. (U.S.S.R.),* vol. 20, pp. 257–281, 1950.

Index

Index

ABCD parameters, 6
  table, 7
  $\mathcal{ABCD}$, 7
Abel's identity, 32
Accoustic analog, 285
Active distributed networks, transfer synthesis, 220, 226, 230, 237
  stability, 173, 179, 182
Admittance parameters, table, 7
  short circuit $\overline{URC}$, 9
    $\overline{ULC}$, 9
    $\overline{ERC}$, 142
  tapered networks, table, 119
  in terms of basic set, table, 36
Analogous systems, 283
Approximation, curvilinear square, 256
  dominant pole, 90
    table, 98
  eigenvalues, Collatz, 64
    Lagrange, 52
    Rayleigh, 59
    Richardson, 58
    Schwarz, 62–63
  excess phase, 90
    table, 98
  magnitude, *P*-domain, 231–232
    λ-domain, 231–232
    $\overline{RC}$, 231–232, 267
    RC lumped, 11

Bandpass network, 220–231, 271
Basic set, definition, 31
  table, 36
Bessel network, 30, 123
    (see also *Linear taper*)
Bode plot, 52, 178
Boundary conditions, 4
  basic set, 31
Boundary effects, 239
Bridged $\overline{RC}$ networks, 273
    (see also *Notch networks*)

Capacitance, 19
Cascade, $\overline{RC}$ two ports, 160, 239–240, 269
  synthesis, 208
  two ports, 7
Cauer forms, 189, 195, 198
Characteristic equation, 146, 156, 262
Characteristic impedance, 5
Commensurate electrical length, 201
Common base alpha, 86
  analog, 286
Common emitter beta, 108
Complex mapping, 224
  (stability), 179
Conformal transformation, 252
Construction of tapered networks, 256
Controlled source, 220, 223, 226, 228–229
Coordinate systems, 248
Curvilinear square, 256

Delay time, 50 percent definition, 78
  Elmore's definition, 80
Diffusion equation, 243
Displacement current, 242
Distortionless line, 23, 122
Distributed network with rational parameters, 136
Dominant locus, 276
Dominant pole, 91, 101
  table, 95
Double Kelvin line, 259

Electrical taper, 40
Elmore's definitions, 79
Enclosure theorem, 64
Entire function, 34
Equipotential lines, 240, 256
Equivalent dominant pole, 190
Equivalent tapered networks, 129
Error function, 86
Euler-Maclaurin summation, 299
Excess phase, table, 95
Exponential taper, 40, 46
  construction of geometric taper, 258
  poles-zeros, 103
  rise time and bandwidth, 106
  [*y*] parameters, 142
  [*z*] parameters, 142

Flow lines, 240, 256
Foster form, 187, 194
Four-port network, 259
Frequency response, dominant pole approximation, 91
  table, 95
Frobenius' method, 43

[g] parameters (see *Two-port parameters*)
Geometric shape, 253

[h] parameters (see *Two-port parameters*)
Helmholtz equation, 243
Hybrid parameters (see [g] *and* [h] *parameters*)
Hyperbolic taper, 121

Impulse response, 80
Integrated circuit, 17, 207, 219
Invariant, 118
Iteration, 96, 302
Iterative lumped structure, nonuniform, 111
  pole-zero, 15
  transient response, 75
  uniform, 10

Ladder structure, 189, 195, 198
Lagrange method, 52
Laplace transformation, 4
Laplace's equation, 243
Linear taper, 127, 249
  (see also *Bessel taper*)
Low-pass network, 70, 267

Mapping (see *Transformation*)
Maximum-minimum principle, 64
Meromorphic function, 34
Monotonic response, 80
Multilayer $\overline{RC}$, 259

Natural frequencies, 144
Negative impedance converter, 219
Newton-Raphson procedure, 309
Nondominant poles and zeros, 267
Nonseries parallel, 191
Nonuniform distributed network, 26
  solutions, basic set, 31
    change of variable, 117
    Collatz, 64
    Frobenius, 43
    Lagrange, 52
    Picard-Carson, 37
    Rayleigh, 59
    Richardson, 58
  two-port parameters, 30
Normal form, 117
Notch network, 164
Nyquist diagram, 177

One-dimensional flow, 248
One-port, properties, lumped LC, 187
    RC, RL, 193
  necessary and sufficient conditions, LC, 186
    RC, RL, 193
    $\overline{RC}$, 215
Open-circuit impedance parameters (see [z] *parameters*)

Partial fraction expansion, 187
Picard-Carson method, 37
Pole-zero locations, $\overline{ERC}$, 105
  $\overline{LC}$, 9
  $\overline{RC}$, 9
Positive real function, definition, 185
  properties, 185
Product expansion, 48, 291
  table, 292
Propagation function, 5

$\overline{RC}$ network fabrication, geometric taper, 258
  integrated circuits, 17
  Teledeltos paper, 19
Rayleigh principle, 59
Realizability, 185
Reciprocal network, 33, 69
Resistance, 19
Riccati equation, 22
Richard's theorem, 209
Richardson's extrapolation procedure, 58
Rise time, 10–90 percent definition, 78

Elmore's definition, 80
Root locus, 145
  construction rules, 149
  examples, 155–179

Schwarz procedure, 60
  numbers, 62
Self-adjoint, 29
Sensitivity, 278
Separation of variables, 243
Solution, closed form, 114
  series, powers of s, 40–41
    powers of x, 43
  transcendental equation, 302
Square taper, 127, 252
Stability, 172
  region in P-plane, 224
    in W-plane, 179
Standing-wave solution, 5
Static flow, 252
Step response, $\overline{ERC}$, 106
  $\overline{URC}$, 92
Sturm equation, 21, 29
Summation of series, 294
  closed form, 299
Synthesis, 184
  driving point, one port, LC, 186
    RC, 192
    RL, 198
    $\overline{RC}$, 202
  $\overline{RC}$ cascade, 207
  P-plane (O'Shea), 213
  transfer, 219
    amplifier, RC, 226
    amplifier, $\overline{RC}$, 228–229
    RC, NIC, 220
    $\overline{RC}$, NIC, 223

Taper function, 125, 133
Taper ratio, 126
Tapered networks, 115 (see also *Nonuniform networks*)
  closed forms, 114
  comparison of, 125
  equivalence, 129
  series solutions, 40–43
  similar immitances, 121
Telegrapher's equations, 5, 27, 138
Temple's inequality, 61
Thermal analog, 285 (Appendix A)
Transfer function synthesis, amplifier, 226, 230
  NIC, 219
Transformation, LC to RC, 17, 192
  s-plane to λ-plane, 201
  s-plane to Λ-plane, 203
  s-plane to P-plane, 214
Transient response, $\overline{RLCG}$, 71
  $\overline{RC}$, 73
  $\overline{ERC}$, 103
  dominant pole, 101
  Elmore's definition, 79
  relation to bandwidth, 89, 107
Transmission line, analog, 285
  model, 3
  nonuniform, 27
  uniform, 3
Transistor, diffusion, 107
  drift, 109, 286
Traveling-wave solution, 5
Trigonometric taper, 121
Two-port parameters, basic set, 36
  nonuniform distributed, 30
  table, 7
  tapered networks, 119

Undetermined coefficients, 43 (see *Frobenius' method*)
Uniformly distributed networks, $\overline{LC}$, 9
  $\overline{RC}$, 9
  $\overline{RLCG}$, 9
  synthesis, 184
Uniform multilayer $\overline{RC}$ network, 261
  transfer function, 265

Vibrating string (see *physical analogs*, 285)

Weber equation, 250
Weierstrass factor theorem, 287
Wronskian, 31

[z] parameters (see *Two-port parameters*)
Z transform analogy, 177